AN INTIMATE REBUKE

The Religious Cultures of African
and African Diaspora People

Series editors: JACOB K. OLUPONA, HARVARD UNIVERSITY,
DIANNE M. STEWART, EMORY UNIVERSITY, AND
TERRENCE L. JOHNSON, GEORGETOWN UNIVERSITY

The book series examines the religious, cultural, and political expressions of African, African American, and African Caribbean traditions. Through transnational, cross-cultural, and multidisciplinary approaches to the study of religion, the series investigates the epistemic boundaries of continental and diasporic religious practices and thought and explores the diverse and distinct ways African-derived religions inform culture and politics. The series aims to establish a forum for imagining the centrality of Black religions in the formation of the New World.

AN INTIMATE REBUKE

FEMALE GENITAL POWER IN RITUAL

AND POLITICS IN WEST AFRICA

Laura S. Grillo

•

Duke University Press   Durham and London   2018

© 2018 DUKE UNIVERSITY PRESS. All rights reserved
Printed in the United States of America on acid-free paper ∞
Designed by Courtney Leigh Baker
Typeset in Garamond Premier Pro by Westchester Publishing Services

Library of Congress Cataloging-in-Publication Data
Names: Grillo, Laura S., [date] author.
Title: An intimate rebuke : female genital power in ritual and politics
in West Africa / Laura S. Grillo.
Description: Durham : Duke University Press, 2018. | Series: The religious cultures
of African and African diaspora people | Includes bibliographical references and index.
Identifiers: LCCN 2018008228 (print) | LCCN 2018013660 (ebook)
ISBN 9781478002635 (ebook)
ISBN 9781478001201 (hardcover : alk. paper)
ISBN 9781478001553 (pbk. : alk. paper)
Subjects: LCSH: Côte d'Ivoire—Religion. | Older women—Religious life—Côte d'Ivoire. |
Older women—Political activity—Côte d'Ivoire. | Generative organs, Female—Symbolic
aspects—Côte d'Ivoire. | Generative organs, Female—Religious aspects. |
Generative organs, Female—Political aspects—Côte d'Ivoire.
Classification: LCC BL2470.C85 (ebook) | LCC BL2470.C85 G75 2018 (print) |
DDC 305.4096668—dc23
LC record available at https://lccn.loc.gov/2018008228

Cover art: Michael Richardson, *Oshun, Healer, Prosperity, River of Love.*
Watercolor. 2016. Courtesy of the artist.

To Angela Lanza Grillo,
for the gift of life

To Jacob K. Olupona,
for the gift of friendship

To Henry Pernet,
for the gift of love

WITH LOVE FOREVER

Contents

Acknowledgments ix   Introduction 1

Part I. Home and the Unhomely

THE FOUNDATIONAL NATURE OF
FEMALE GENITAL POWER 19

•

1 Genies, Witches, and Women: Locating Female Powers 21
2 Matrifocal Morality: FGP and the Foundation of "Home" 54
3 Gender and Resistance: The "Strategic Essentialism" of FGP 81

Part II. Worldliness

FGP IN THE MAKING OF ETHNICITY,
ALLIANCE, AND WAR IN CÔTE D'IVOIRE 117

•

4 Founding Knowledge/Binding Power: The Moral Foundations
   of Ethnicity and Alliance 121
5 Women at the Checkpoint: Challenging the Forces of Civil War 152

Part III. Timeliness

URGENT SITUATIONS AND
EMERGENT CRITIQUES 171

•

6 Violation and Deployment: FGP in Politics in Côte d'Ivoire 175
7 Memory, Memorialization, and Morality 198

Conclusion. An Intimate Rebuke:
A Local Critique in the Global Postcolony 228

Notes 239   References 255   Index 275

Acknowledgments

First I acknowledge with gratitude she who came first: my mother, Angela Lanza Grillo, who provides love and support, both material and moral. My sisters Janet and Carolyn are an inextricable part of that nucleus of matrilineal strength.

The seeds for this book were sown long ago in Côte d'Ivoire by the love of another family that embraced me and never ceased to extend to me their hearts, hospitality, and help each time I returned. They have been my generous hosts, companions, and guides. They introduced me to friends who in turn freely offered the concrete assistance that made it possible to conduct local research. To them, I offer my most sincere gratitude and affection: Irène Melei Mel, Eugénie Meliane Mel, Dr. Pierre Adou, Marie-Noëlle Adou, and their girls Emmera, Sarah, Anna, Victoria, and Eve-Andrée, Alysse Adou, Fred Vamy, and Philippe Leite. Friends in Abidjan, both old and newfound, went out of their way to help me with my investigations. I cherish the camaraderie that we forged through the remarkable adventures, trials, and secrets that we shared along the way: Prof. Dakouri Gadou, François Bindje, Cindy Assi, and Mireille Lofton.

Others in Abidjan whom I must acknowledge and thank for their assistance with my research: Genevieve Bro-Grébé, Victorine Dongo, and Mme Yésone, Proviseur of the Lycée Moderne Nangui Abrogoua, and the students there.

I humbly thank the elders and ritual specialists of the Adioukrou village of Orbaff who were so generous with their knowledge and time: Djedjeroh Edouard, Sangroh Esaïe, Essoh Nomel Salomon, Yedoh Edouard, Sess Egue Mel Michel, Meless Akpa Esaie, Mansso Lorgng Yed, Akpro Bedi Mathieu, Owel Assra Antoine, Meledje Djedjero Theodore, Gbétou Yao Emmanuel, Kakré Marcel, Low Agnime Emilienne, Djedjero Nan Lili, and Akpa Akpess Paul. I am especially indebted to my host and interpreter, Jonas Amary Ly, his lovely wife, Marie-France, and their family.

In the Adioukrou village Yassap, Chef de Terre Meledge Djedjress Philippe, and Latte Mel Paul generously shared their deep knowledge and patiently gave of their time to interviews. I thank them as well as Akpa Alexi and Mme Margeritte Akpa, who offered warm hospitality as well as important introductions to village notables. I am especially grateful to my amiable hostess, Alice Nomel, who extended friendship as well as shelter.

In the Abidji village of Sahuyé I was the happy beneficiary of the patient and attentive assistance of Chief Tanau Laugau Julien, Chef de Terre Gnangra N'Guessan Bertin, and the elders and ritual specialists of Dipri: Djidja Adangba Marcel, Yao Tanoh Daniel, Lasme Tomah, Abo Brou Andre, Yede Okon Richard, Kassi Aby Simeon, and Koffi Akissi, as well as Tanoh Marie-Claire and Kamenan Adjoba. I owe particular thanks to my host, Koffi Begré, and the extended family of N'Dia Begré Bernard N'Guessan, whose hospitality extends back thirty years, to the time of my first study of Dipri. In the nearby village of Sokokro I was warmly welcomed and indulged by You Yvonne and Ako N'Drin Marcel; thank you.

Many of my colleagues in the American Academy of Religion (AAR) showed interest and appreciation for this study at various stages of its presentation at its meetings. I am particularly beholden to my friend and fellow Ivoirianist Joseph Hellweg, who as a guest editor of a feature of *Cultural Anthropology* elicited my earliest publication on "female genital power" (FGP), a reflection piece on the Ivoirian political crisis. Also thanks to him, I presented portions of this work at the 2017 conference of the Mande Studies Association (MANSA) at the University of Grand-Bassam in Côte d'Ivoire, where many new friends and colleagues offered validating examples of FGP elsewhere in the country as well as in Burkina Faso, Mali, Niger, and Togo. Special thanks for those go to Bintou Koné, Benjamin Lawrance, Moussa Moumouni, Ba Morou Ouattara, Serge Noël Ouedraogo, Kando Amédée Soumahoro, and Monica Blackmun Visonà.

I owe my deepest debt of gratitude to my colleague and great friend Jacob K. Olupona, whose faith in me was a powerful and steady beacon over the past four years. Without his encouragement and support this book would never have been written. It was thanks to his sponsorship that I was granted a Research Fellowship at Harvard Divinity School in 2013, which provided me the unique opportunity for consecrated time to devote to launching this book project. Since then he continually entrusted me with his patient confidence that I would succeed, a gift that cannot be matched with simple words of thanks. There is no better harbor than such a faithful friend.

During that Research Fellowship at Harvard I enjoyed stimulating exchanges at the Center for the Study of World Religion (CSWR), whose participants extended me warm collegiality and showed heartening interest in my project. I especially thank the Director, Francis X. Clooney, for welcoming me to the group. The goodwill and generosity of that fellowship was a reflection of his kind leadership.

I also want to gratefully acknowledge Sîan Hawthorne and Adriaan van Klinken, organizers of the 2012 conference on Catachresis at SOAS University of London, as well as its participants, particularly Morny Joy. That working conference provided inspiration for the methodological framework for the book. The paper that I delivered at SOAS and its subsequent publication in *Religion and Gender* gave this project critical impetus. Adriaan van Klinken has since championed the developing work, and his friendship has proved stalwart.

A presentation I made at another conference, a workshop on Religion and Global Civil Society organized by the Orfalea Center for Global Studies at the University of California Santa Barbara (UCSB) in 2012, also proved formative for this work. Happily, the many subsequent conversations about its development with the center's former Program Director, Victor Faessel, bloomed into an abiding friendship.

Teaching offers many rewards, but the most valuable is the enduring bond forged with students, fellow seekers of wonder. My former doctoral students' eager interest and engaging conversations elicited regular renewed commitment to seeing this project through to completion. Among those most faithful friends are Thea Bloom, Rebecca Diggs, Mary Diggin, Rebekah Lovejoy, Elizabeth Stewart, and Leslie Stoupas.

Other true friends who encouraged my work and, more importantly, lovingly stood with me during my woes are Karen Anderson, Teresa F. Blomquist, Carol A. Burnett, Fran Cho, Richard N. Chrisman, Hendrika de Vries, Rita Dragonette, Jennifer Kwong, Jan Rudestam, and Ann Taves. Each one has provided me with a very particular kind of sustaining hope over the years.

I am grateful to those at Duke University Press who immediately saw value and promise in this work and who brought it to print. First among these are the editors of this series on the Religious Cultures of African and African Diaspora People, Jacob K. Olupona, Dianne M. Stewart, and Terrence L. Johnson. From the outset Miriam Angress, Associate Editor, has been a remarkably responsive and encouraging companion in the journey to publication. I am also indebted to the two anonymous reviewers of the manuscript whose careful reading, insightful suggestions, and enthusiasm for the project were deeply rewarding.

Last but certainly not least among those deserving recognition is my husband, Henry Pernet, whose constant love has been my anchor. He faithfully supported every step of this project, even cheerfully braving the discomforts of the tropics to accompany me on my preliminary research trip back to Côte d'Ivoire. He regularly listened patiently as I unknotted puzzles aloud, he eagerly shared articles of interest, he read drafts of my work, and he made careful editorial corrections. Through all this and more, his joyful companionship and tender, steadfast love has given me true happiness.

There is no power greater than love.

INTRODUCTION

O, cock, stop this ostentation,
for we all came out of the egg-shell.
—ASANTE PROVERB, in Emmanuel Akyeampong and Pashington Obeng,
"Spirituality, Gender and Power in Asante History"

Ceremonial nakedness greatly increases
the magico-religious power of woman, and the chief
attribute of the Great Mother is her nakedness.
—MIRCEA ELIADE, "Masks: Mythical and Ritual Origins"

In the Abidji village of Sahuyé in southern Côte d'Ivoire in 2010, the carnivalesque ambiance of the evening had given way to a deep stillness. Even the electricity was cut, and all were thrust into the darkness of the moonless night. The hush prepared the village for "Dipri," the dangerous initiatory festival that was to take place the next day. In the small hours of the morning, my young companion shook me awake. "Auntie, Auntie, the old women, they're coming. Get up." I sat up on the mattress we shared in our shuttered and stifling room. In the distance a faint eerie knell, a shrill calling and a droning chant, and then a repeating thud like a heartbeat. "If you want to see them, Auntie, let's go." "No, no. That old woman made it clear I cannot join them. It is a sacred thing, a taboo to look upon them. It would be an offense." I knew the elderly women performing the rite were naked, they were crossing the village pounding the ground with pestles to curse the malevolent forces of witches who might threaten the initiates who were to be consecrated at the river the next morning, and to chase away death. They would make aspersions with water used to bathe their genitals and pour it at the village entrance to seal it. After that no one would be allowed to exit or enter until the next day's ceremonies were over. This was Egbiki, the secret, nocturnal ritual of female genital power. It was an act of spiritual warfare, a critical and dangerous enterprise that the women were undertaking on behalf of the whole village. I stood at the window with my recorder trying to capture the strange distant keening, their soft shuffle, and the thud. That sound was so chilling that even now, years later, I dread to listen to the recording.

Egbiki is not only an esoteric practice unique to this remote village or to the Abidji people who celebrate Dipri. For at least five centuries and throughout West Africa, women have made vivid appeal in ritual to a fundamental religious concept: that woman bears the innate spiritual power and embodies moral authority. The locus of this power is the female genitals. In times of social calamity female elders strip naked, wielding branches or old pestles, dance "lewdly," slapping their genitals and their breasts to curse the forces of evil. This constellation of paradigmatic gestures, enacted as a collective rebuke and a curse, constitutes the appeal to "Female Genital Power" (FGP).[1]

This power is *not* the reproductive capacity of women, nor does it allude to the office of motherhood, important as that status has been to women in African traditional societies. Rather, "the Mothers" are *postmenopausal* women who, having surpassed the defining stage of sexual reproduction, are ambiguously gendered. Like primordial beings, their incarnate power resides in that gender doubleness. As the living embodiment of the ancestors, the Mothers are guardians of the moral order and conduits of a spiritual power that is primary, paramount, and potent. The seat of their power is not only the womb, but also the vulva. Appealing to their sex as a living altar, the women ritually deploy their genital power to elicit the most perilous of curses as an act of "spiritual combat" against malevolent forces that threaten the community.

While the use of female genital power is a spiritual weapon, it is also invoked as a rebuke of immoral or injudicious governance and has therefore served as an equally potent deterrent to the pernicious use of political power. Women have regularly mobilized collectively, forming associations that sometimes even transcend ethnicity, to chastise the state and its military forces for reprehensible misuse of power and invoke FGP in public protests to assert their moral authority.

So critical is the conception of FGP as a guiding and sustaining force that this paradigmatic rite has been documented in material as varied as accounts of early Arab chroniclers, colonial administrative records and decrees, missionary tracts, travel diaries, ethnographic studies, and newspaper reports. In Côte d'Ivoire as early as 1894 the ethnographer Maurice Delafosse observed the Baoulé (Baule) women's ritual Adjanou (Adjanu), demonstrating obscene gestures to rebuke male transgressions of the moral order.[2] This same ritual figured prominently in the now celebrated nationalist uprisings of 1949, when a multiethnic coalition of 2,000 Ivoirian women marched to the colonial stronghold, Grand-Bassam, to take a stand against the French. Once gathered in front of the prison where nationalist leaders were being held, they deployed Adjanou. The descriptions of those women stripping naked, making lewd gestures and gyrations, chanting sexually explicit and aggressive lyrics, donning vines, and brandishing sticks clearly reiterate the critical features of traditional religious ritual, Egbiki. Transposed onto the political sphere, the secret, nocturnal spiritual rite becomes a shocking spectacle of protest against the contemporary state that has wielded its force without moral compass.

Aware of the ritual potency of their nudity and the conjuration of their sex, contemporary West African women still exploit this strong rhetorical form to resist social injustice, to condemn violations of human rights, and to demand accountability. During Côte d'Ivoire's recent civil war and its violent aftermath, Ivoirian women have repeatedly executed the rite of FGP to protest abuses on both sides of the political divide and to recollect the moral foundations of legitimate authority. But are their acts being properly recognized and their appeals understood beyond the immediate sphere of the local? Does the appeal to traditional religion and a mystical rite like Adjanou still have salience in today's increasingly globalized world?

The Problem with Tradition in the Modern Situation

The rapid pulse of technology, the massive migration and displacements of Africans on the continent, the increasing cultural homogenization of urban populations gravitating toward the European metropole, and the electric spread of geography-defying ideologies are all forces of globalization that overshadow and obscure distinct and idiosyncratic practices associated with the local. The study of particular indigenous traditions is being eclipsed by a shift of interest onto a fast-changing and interconnected world. More and more the focus is on bilocal studies, on migration and diaspora communities, on the new cosmopolitanism fostered by mass consumption of international commodities and rapid social media, or on the new virulent forms of Christianity and Islam seizing the African continent. It seems the local is no more.

One might imagine that this trend reflects the trajectory of the traditions themselves and the fate predicted for them at the turn of the last century—namely, that local practices and beliefs would be effaced by the encroachments of modernity, the advances of science, and the challenge and competing interests of the so-called world religions. But those predictions were based on the false idea of tradition as a set of customs and beliefs that are *timeless and unchanging*, belonging to *a closed society*, preserved from the taint of cultural encounter and exchange. By now it is well understood that such a conception of tradition as fixed, immune from history, and untouched by innovation was an invention by scholars of the last century with a decidedly Eurocentric perspective. Their depictions of traditional society as a fossilized version of Europe's historical past were based on Darwin's evolutionist biology, mistakenly applied to the social sciences. While they represented *remote* places and peoples in terms of distance in *time*, as nonmodern and without history, no such isolated and pristine communities ever existed. Distorting claims about traditional society were also the basis for the construction of the demeaning notion of "the primitive," which portrayed Africans in particular in sharp contrast to Westerners.[3] Such peoples purportedly *lacked reflexivity and therefore any true agency*, since the ability to act with intention depends on self-consciousness and the ability to distance oneself as an individual apart from the group or tribe. This was deemed beyond the capacity of peoples whose very identity presumably depended on the unquestioning acceptance and perpetuation of ancient ancestral ways.[4] More than a mere term, then, *tradition* is a construct heavily freighted by imperialism. The colonization of people in distant and exotic places was justified on the basis of the claim that they were "savages," as distinct from modern Europeans as were the original "primitives" of the human race (Chidester 2004, 84). Ultimately tradition came to signify all thought and practice that stands in contrast to modernity and to the defining institutions and ideals of the West, like individualism, secularism, development, and democracy.

Actually, the etymology of the word is from the Latin *traditio* ("handing over"), and in religious studies it simply refers to "the body of knowledge which has been preserved and transmitted, and whose original source is no longer accessible or verifiable [through written records or sacred texts]. It is both a means of engaging memory and the normative expression of ideals and solidarities" (Valliere 2005, 9267, 9280). Such knowledge, often embodied in ritual practice, can only be preserved and transmitted insofar as it is performed or rehearsed, an undertaking that implies commitment to its transmission, not only as a matter of historical record but especially as a vital means of orienting social life to what is held to be most deeply significant, and providing meaningful orientation as a result. Tradition as such endures, but the trend away from interest in it may have less to do with any actual obliteration of practices than with the fear of reproducing the epistemic violence of imperialism in a subtle new form. Postmodern critiques rightly shook the foundations of ethnography and forced a welcome shift in thinking "away from the traditional model of the study of 'peoples'" and reified treatments of traditional cultures that presented them as if they were not subject to the contingencies of real world events or capable of innovation (Marcus 1998, 20).

While we may be content to do away with the study of cultures as bounded wholes and closed systems, we can't do away with "the cultural, as a constitutive dimension" of meaningful life (Rabinow et al 2008, 106). How then can one make sense of those other meaningful cultural worlds without recapitulating the sins of the past?

The Problem with "the Local" in the Global Situation

Postcolonial theorists like Charles Piot (1999) have attempted to do so by "unsettl(ing) the orientalizing binarism—and conceit—that associates Europe with 'modernity' and Africa with 'tradition'" (2). In *Remotely Global: Village Modernity in West Africa*, Piot criticizes the use of the conventionalized categories that continue to inform scholarship about Africa but that "operate at some distance from *local conceptions*" and the actual realities on the ground and "fail to get at *local understandings* of social relations" (6–7, emphasis mine). Rather than eschewing terms like *tradition* or *local*, he makes an account of "apparently traditional features" in African society in a way that problematizes Eurocentric assumptions about them, disrupting facile distinctions between traditional and modern, local and global (2).

Reference to the local does not necessarily infer remote, circumscribed places or persons uninformed by outside contact. Nor are locals persons who have remained immobile and wedded to a definitive way of living that protects them from influence. To ascribe those notions to *the local* makes the term a counterpoint to *the global* in parallel to the way that *traditional* has been used to signify all that contrasts with *modernity*. That is, the local comes to designate a social space that is *fixed and unchanging*, while the domain of the global is associated with change and the dynamics of contemporary *transformation*: mobility and the rapid shifts in populations across the world, as well as communication and the rapid flows of ideas and information across world-space. Piot therefore recasts African *local* realities as instantiations of global dynamics, characterized by mobility and exchange.

Such a move corrects the distortions of early scholarship that depicted Africa as an isolated preserve in which circumscribed tribes are fixed in place. It underscores that Africans have always been full partners in shaping the world through migration and exchange of goods and ideas, a point that is especially poignant when considering the extent to which the world was reshaped by the forced extraction and dispersal of its population through slavery. However, globalization is more than migration or the impact of commodities, ideas, and practices across borders or cultural boundaries; certainly in this simple sense, Africa has always been involved in the globalizing project. Today reference to *the global* domain refers to more than the increase in mobility and the intensified flow of material, culture, or ideology. Globalization is moreover the consolidation of a dominant set of practices and ideologies. *Globalism* now implies the hegemony of the metropole, its culture, and its socioeconomic and political interests and advantages.

Although Africans also live with the fluidity and uncertainty that define the postmodern situation, that fact is not sufficient to identify even those most mobile and transient of African workers who regularly travel between villages and urban centers as *cosmopolitans* (Piot 1999, 132). A cosmopolitan is not only a person who moves rapidly and easily across boundaries and borders, but is most especially one who can enjoy the certainty that one will be at home anywhere in the world that reproduces the familiar patterns of the dominant metropole. Cosmopolitans move readily between metropoles that share a global frame of reference. By contrast, translocals are peoples who move or flee their native situation (such as migrant workers, refugees, evacuees, exiles), but who do not necessarily adopt the new, dominant worldview when they are displaced and dispersed (in the diaspora). Unlike the cosmopolitan who has no investment in any particular place as home, no commitment to carry familiar practices or defining values into the newly occupied spaces, and no aspiration to return to that geographic locus of identity, the translocal remains firmly rooted in the *habitus* of the culture of origin and brings a very particular epistemology and ontology into the new spatial context (P. Werbner, 1999; R. Grillo, 2007; L. Grillo 2010).

The local is a literal domain of *home*, grounded in place as well as conceptual reality. It refers to those contexts in which particular practices arose and were regularly practiced, giving charter to a common worldview as well as a social space as defined by the social imaginary. I therefore use *the local* to refer to those realities on the ground that are recognized by Africans themselves to be real and to have consequence in terms of their self-definitions and the orientation of their lives.

The local social imaginary is all that constitutes a sense of home. The local may extend beyond the circumscribed parameters of small communities, however. I intentionally use the term *local* to denote indigenous African values and practices, those that emerged in and are associated with the African context, even when that context is regional or continental in span. My intent is to differentiate those values and practices from supposedly global ones—which are, in fact, the consolidation of Western ideology that is circulated and adopted (or imposed) elsewhere.

Today, "the relentless drive of homogenizing and standardizing market forces to turn the whole world into a hi-tech consumerist landscape has irreversibly destabilized these familiar feelings of belonging" that constitute the "radiating warmth of 'home'" (Steger 2008, 196). The local phenomenon of FGP is an act of resistance to such external pressures to conform to Western hegemony. It recalls instead the fundaments of a uniquely African vision of the moral order and the society that arises from it. The ubiquity of the ritual phenomenon of FGP and the common moral precepts that it embodies undergird so much of West African culture as to represent a common epistemological grounding—a local, that is to say *particularly African*, way of understanding and organizing knowledge and meaning.

Writing New Histories and the Problem of Logocentrism

I join Piot and other postcolonial scholars who are "committed to writing histories that disrupt the conventional grand narratives . . . [or that] deny agency to subaltern groups" (Piot 1999, 6). Attempting to write a new critical history presents another problem, however. Language is itself a hallmark of colonial imperialism.

Most postcolonial theorists write from the privileged site of a neocolonial educational system, and the very use of European languages necessarily imports a Eurocentric analytical frame. From this situation, despite the laudable intention "to give voice and agency to the subaltern" (Piot 1999, 6), the subaltern—as Gayatri Spivak so famously argued—cannot and does not "speak" (Spivak 1988). Always incommensurate with the experience of the subaltern, representation of the "other" through words seems to be, at best, mimicry. It distorts the depiction of the other even as the text itself reproduces the hegemonic discourse of the foreign academic world. At worst, the attempt to have the subaltern speak through this discourse amounts to mere "ventriloquism," a projection of their voice through the scholar's own (Bewes 2006). The postcolonial project may well falter under such preoccupation with burdened terminology and the task of refiguring its own conceptual frameworks. Combined with that is a seeming need for self-denunciation, as if "by engaging in relentless self-examination [it] will be able to keep itself free from the hubris of modernity" (Benavides 1998, 200). Too great a concern over the avoidance of the fraught terms or antiquated constructs risks overshadowing the subject at hand and obscuring other media of expression in which the subaltern—one who is *not* identical to the colonial theorist—may in fact be "speaking" (Grillo 2015).

It is for this very reason that I turn my attention primarily to the ritual performances of FGP as a powerful form of self-representation in the actors' own local terms. The embodied performances of the Mothers simultaneously communicate vulnerability and lament, judgment and condemnation, yet do so without depending on language to bear their message (L. Grillo, 2013). The rebuke is accomplished without forcing anyone to narrate her trauma, without words that can be mistranslated or misconstrued, without negotiations that can be compromised. Those who deploy FGP are not speaking in the idiom of the (post)colonial world at all, but sidestep the problem of language altogether. Moreover, their ritual protest has a unique ability to stir public consciousness precisely because it is nondiscursive, making its case in the immediacy of the moment. The Mothers deploy traditional custom as a timely response to the contemporary situation and with a view to effecting change.

Genealogy and the Matri-Archive

The distinctive cultural element that extends beyond the limited scope of ethnicity is the still-vital construct that informs the episteme of West Africa: an understanding of the consonance between spiritual power and political authority, whose common source is woman. More precisely, it is female elders known as "the Mothers" who embody this power and who invoke it through the ritual appeal to FGP.

The aim of this study is not only to trace the conventional history of the institution of FGP in in West Africa but also to unearth the "genealogy" of matrifocality—to reveal the history that has no history, that has remained invisible because it has not been given value (Foucault 1977). The object of undertaking such a genealogical inquiry is to identify the source of that which endures in the local social imaginary even after the structural institutions that reflected those values have been dismantled and/or eclipsed. In this case, it is only in the vestiges, remnants, or refuse of history that we can locate evidence.[5] These archives of African history can be excavated in overlooked details of ethnography, unearthed through evidence and experience in the field, and extracted from oral histories.

Doing a genealogical history of FGP as a matri-archive posits no evolutionist trajectory. My premise is that Africa's societies and civilizations did indeed change, informed by their own intense heterogeneity, migratory dynamics, and cultural fluidity as much as by contact with the West or the modern world system. I certainly do not endorse the notion of a necessary and relentless progression from "the primitive" toward the development of a more sophisticated manifestation of a higher social order. In fact, the thrust of the argument of the book supports the opposite view: that the erosion of women's associations and women's rights has jeopardized the moral foundation of communal life.

It is certain that female genital power is grounded in religious and cultural constructs that are constitutive of certain ethnic identities. Even so, it is not primarily to this smaller notion of the local that I refer when I use this term. Rather, I suggest that the phenomenon of FGP—the unique conception of it and the ubiquitous appeal to it across a wide geographical expanse and for an extensive period of time—is uniquely African. The ritual rhetoric of FGP is one of the "sacred silent languages [that have operated as] the media through which the great global communities of the past were imagined" (Anderson 1991, 14). My objective is to reveal it to be the invisible (secret and hidden, but also overlooked and ignored) ingredient that lends to Africa a palpable yet ill-defined coherence and to show FGP to be the essential construct informing the African social landscape, responsible for forging much of the sub-Saharan region as a great global community.

Contemporary practices of FGP demonstrate just how adaptive and strategic this tradition continues to be, serving as a vital form of resistance to the postcolonial state and to the international pressures that increasingly inform civil unrest. The shocking spectacle of women's naked confrontation with politicians and armed troops is a formidable means to (re)awaken sensibility to the *local social imaginary*—that is, the "implicit background that makes possible communal practices and a widely shared sense of their legitimacy" (Steger 2008, 6). Its enduring eloquence shows that social imaginary to have considerable inventive ability and demonstrates that indigenous traditions can and still do have a bearing on the global situation.

An Intimate Rebuke

The repeated executions of FGP from the earliest chronicled incidents to present-day manifestations to which I call attention here therefore present a new kind of history, "intelligible only within a cultural tradition but, potentially, standing some critical distance part from it, . . . a startling reinterpretation, *an intimate rebuke*" (Lonsdale 2000, 14, emphasis mine). FGP is, indeed, "intimate" in its reference to the most private bodily parts. However, its intimacy is also cultural; those who are called the Mothers stand for the most intimate social unit, the mother-child bond, that is sacrosanct and the basis for the ethical relations on which West African society was founded. For those with deep inside knowledge of African tradition, the curse that is implied by their exhibition is a rebuke in the strongest of terms. In recent decades, the act is poignantly intimate also in that it no longer points to the injustices, indignities, and violations of foreign colonials, but is aimed at the forces of African society itself and their own postcolonial states. It especially condemns the most heinous violation of that sacred source, sexual violence.

Côte d'Ivoire is emerging from more than a decade of civil war and horrific violence. The repeated public enactments of FGP there present a striking, visible argument about political morality and stand as a warning of the calamitous result of ignoring religious values on which African society was founded. They show that the women's indigenous ritual is "far from unfathomable or irrelevant" (Lonsdale 2000, 15), but keenly applicable in the fractured and bloodied struggles being played out across Africa and the economic and social ruin that has been the result.

Emergent Constructs for an Urgent Situation: Unhomeliness, Worldliness, Timeliness

The situation in Côte d'Ivoire is emergent, in both the sense of calling for prompt, urgent attention and as something arising as a natural or logical consequence. What has given rise to the dire and crying situation of Ivoirian women is postcolonialism—that is to say, the aftermath of colonialism and the fractious enterprise of nation building. At the same time, and not unrelatedly, is the pressing need in the academy to find new concepts and methods that are better suited to interpret today's globalized world. Even the very terms *religion*, *gender*, and *postcolonialism* have been challenged as empty, invented, unstable, and misplaced (Bhabha 1994; Dubuisson 2003; Oyewùmí 1997a; Radhakrishnan 1993). Postmodernism ushered in a distrust of grand theories, challenged received ideologies, and disturbed conventional understandings of such basic notions and made us aware of the ways in which these constructs can themselves foster domination, exclusion, and violence. Their application to our increasingly complex world is questionable, making "examples of using the older concepts on contemporary material ... sound like they [are parodies]" (Rabinow and Marcus 2008, 43). Throughout this work I draw instead on emergent concepts that lend themselves better to what Edward Said called the "bristling paradox" (1989, 213) that characterizes the contemporary postcolonial situation: *unhomeliness, worldliness, and timeliness*. My adoption of these new constructs and my repeated use of them as themes offer an alternative theoretical scaffold on which to review the facts. They allow me to interrogate and shift the more familiar but troubling terms such as *tradition* or *the local* in light of the practice of FGP without jettisoning them altogether.

Nigerian scholar of African gender studies Oyèrónké Oyewùmí pointed out that "African experiences rarely inform theory in any field of study; at best such experiences are exceptionalized" (Oyewùmí 1997b, 18). In drawing on African historical and social reality to inform postcolonial thought, this study aims to make a corrective, even as it pushes beyond its typical impasses. By sustaining the tripartite focus on unhomeliness, worldliness, and timeliness simultaneously throughout this work, I wish to suggest that the appeal to female genital power is its own potent and "volatile mixture" of matters of vital concern in today's world: religion, gender, and postcolonial politics (Joy 2006). My intention is to use these new constructs to turn attention away from theorists' "obsessive focus" on postcolonialism as theory at the expense of postcolonialism-as-activism (Radhakrishnan 1993, 751), and, moreover, to highlight female genital power in West Africa as activism against postcolonialism.

UNHOMELINESS

The term *unhomely* speaks to the uncomfortable and uninviting reality of post-coloniality for the colonized and the colonizing subject alike. Postcolonial theorist Homi Bhabha adopts the term *unhomeliness* to signal "the estranging sense of the relocation of the home and the world" that is "a paradigmatic colonial and post-colonial condition" (Bhabha 1994, 13). To be "unhomed" implies not only displacement of the colonial but also an intrusion of global politics into the local, experienced as the disruptive imposition of political agenda on personal lives. In this new world order "nobody will feel fully at home" (Bewes 2006, 47).

"The unhomely" is the situation in Côte d'Ivoire, whose very name (Ivory Coast) suggests its legacy of colonial exploitation and commodification at its origin. It also signals the invention of this nation as an artificial entity. The extremely heterogeneous population grouped within its arbitrary borders was made more diverse in its postindependence heyday when those borders remained open to a swell of refugees fleeing surrounding impoverished and warring African states. It is no coincidence that a generation later the civil war was fueled by fractious discourses about "belonging" and "Ivoirianness" (*Ivoirité*). It is an unhomed country, peopled by the displaced—immigrant laborers contesting traditional land rights; "street urchins" born into the metropole, unmoored from any grounding in indigenous culture; women who are losing their rightful place in the visible structures of society and its invisible cultural underpinning that are the moral values they traditionally embody.

In the context of civil war, it is also no surprise that a traditional construct that speaks to the terrible destructive forces of evil prevails: witchcraft. By now it is a cliché that the postcolonial African state, visiting its unpredictable forces of evil on its suffering populace, is likened to a witch. The witch represents the opposite of "home." Witchcraft overturns all social conventions, disrupts the familiarity and safety of the immediate social circle, and operates by uncanny means. But uncanny powers are equally ascribed to those who fight fire with fire and deploy mystical resources on an invisible plane to effect good. This is the paradoxical unhomeliness that the Mothers possess. Because FGP effects the most potent curse, it also has an unsettling and alien nature. The rite bears the character of the unhomely, a quality Freud (2003 [1919]) associated with the uncanny. It is "the name for everything that ought to have remained . . . secret and hidden but has come to light" (Bhabha 1994, 14). Accordingly, when the secret ritual alluding to women's intimate parts is inverted and made a public spectacle, it is an expression of the unhomely par excellence. Introducing unhomeliness allows for a new consideration of the enduring conception of witchcraft in contemporary struggles for power and moral might. Such ideas are constitutive of local worlds. They define an "ontological-cultural epistemology that is coincidental with a certain practice of the world—a world moment, a world that understands its space as a place that is 'not at home'" (Long 2004, 90).

Finally, the construct of unhomeliness allows for a consideration of the progressive unhoming of women from their central place in originally matrifocal and matrilineal traditions that is at the heart of the unhomeliness of the postcolonial condition today. Female genital power as activism also resists the usurpation of women's place and power, challenges imported gender ideology, and provides a vehicle by which these African women reassert their own self-defined essentialism. The appeal of the Mothers to the female genitals as the seat and innate source of their spiritual power makes it clear that their femaleness is a condition of their agency. It is essential—both a necessary condition and defining attribute of the agents of FGP. But in West African cultures postmenopausal women, belonging to a distinct subset of womanhood, comprise a category of being that surpasses gender as it is construed in the West. The reiteration of FGP as public rebuke can therefore also be seen as a profound resistance to the unhomely imposition of gender and repressive gendered roles increasingly assigned to African women as colonial institutions—like patriarchal forms of naming and inheritance—that have been adopted into law.

WORLDLINESS

Edward Said invoked the ambiguous concept of worldliness as a particularly apt characterization of academic disciplines, like anthropology, that are "predicated on the fact of otherness and difference" but that today no longer begin with abstract projections about that "other"; instead the scholar is "remanded into the actual world," to the sites of a cultural situation where differences are realized (Said 1989, 212). Adopting a worldly approach means moving away from preoccupation with religion, gender, or postcolonialism as reified constructs from which to interpret cultural dynamics and turning instead to concrete instances governing reality on the ground.

African women's execution of FGP as political activism is itself a worldly enterprise. Its tactics are shrewd and strategic. It demonstrates worldliness, in the sense of being grounded in the affairs of "the secular world, as opposed to being 'otherworldly,' and also bears 'the quality of a practiced, slightly jaded *savoir faire*, worldly wise and street smart" (Said 1989, 212–13). The repeated deployment of FGP evinces both a sophisticated take on secular politics and a savvy use of civil disobedience to gain leverage on that worldly stage. Yet the Mothers' worldly engagement does not entirely dispense with the otherworldly concerns of moral authority and spiritual power. Women's spectacle creates a profoundly charged liminal situation, an "in-between" reality that challenges oppositional positions, offering an "interstitial intimacy" between the private and public, the past and present, the mythical and historical, the social and spiritual (Bhabha 1994, 19). More practical than the espousal of merely religious ideas and more profound than a merely political demonstration, FGP represents a conjuncture of both these domains. FGP is worldly too in that it has served as the moral foundation of social structure, the basis for social organization and alliance, and has provided the sanction of worldly rulership and the source of its legitimate authority.

TIMELINESS

One thinks of the timely as an intervention that occurs at a propitious moment, enhancing its efficacy. Timely acts are situated in particular historic instants, just as worldly ones are situated in particular places, and both involve reflexivity. Certainly, the women's ritual protests, as self-conscious acts of contestation, are necessarily timely, aiming to have consequences in the unfolding history in which they play an immediate part. Women's activism stands in contrast with the untimeliness of the scholarly production, which always happens "after the fact" (Geertz 1995) and which always "preserves a certain critical distance" (Rabinow and Marcus 2008, 58).[6]

The timeliness of female genital power in the context of politics can also be contrasted with the supposed time*less*ness of religious tradition and the presumed ahistoricity of myth and ritual. From this vantage point, tradition is easily dismissed, relegated to the profound time of mythic origins. Insofar as *tradition* refers to a timeless past, it is at best irrelevant in the face of globalizing forces; at worst, tradition serves as a conservative ideology that keeps the subaltern in a position of subservience to the interests of an elite. As Richards eloquently asserts, "Postcolonialism . . . *has little time* for the remembrance of *profound time*" (Richards 2007, 350, emphasis mine). I concur with Richards and other postcolonial theorists, like Gayatri Spivak, who forcefully assert that "nostalgia for lost origins" is an untimely preoccupation and detrimental to the critique of imperialism that our times demand (Spivak 1988, 291). However, I suggest that the rituals of FGP, by contrast, consciously affirm the relevance of history, including mythic history, to real politics. They are acts of re-collection in both senses of the word—remembrance and gathering. They engage collective memory, reminding those with eyes to see what women's presence and power have meant to African society, serving as a bridge between the distant past and the immediate moment. The Mothers' recollection of the repressed history of their status as bearers of moral authority doesn't romanticize or fetishize tradition but uses it as a point of interrogation of the present.

Organization of the Work

The book is divided into three parts, each giving prominent focus to one of these themes. Under the banner of one of these new constructs, each section considers the phenomenon of FGP from a new angle that aims to shed light on a uniquely African epistemology, one that offers a very different appraisal from that of the West about the foundation, nature, and way of transmitting knowledge. This approach suggests that the more common understanding of the problematic terms *religion, tradition, ethnicity, gender,* and *postcolonial politics* may be reconsidered in this light and even recovered as viable ways of speaking about their inextricably intertwined nature in the context of West Africa. The overarching structure of the book is also designed to suggest that such constructs, when considered as a synergistic whole in the form of FGP, offer a reappraisal of African history and the contemporary Ivoirian crisis.

Part I, "Home and the Unhomely: The Foundational Nature of Female Genital Power," situates the practice in the context of religious traditions in West Africa and shows it to function as a touchstone for the values that establish home.

Chapter 1, "Genies, Witches, and Women: Locating Female Powers," is based on my fieldwork investigations of Dipri and Egbiki, the local enactment of FGP as anti-witchcraft. The aim of this chapter is to situate the phenomenon of FGP in the intimate context of local spiritual practices where they are regularly rehearsed and where their acts have the deepest resonance. It draws on fieldwork spanning three decades and engages an intimate account and deep hermeneutical reading of the Abidji festival, its parallel celebration among the matrilineal Adioukrou, and women's rite that overarches both.

Chapter 2, "Matrifocal Morality: FGP and the Foundation of 'Home,'" aims to correct the predominant, persistent misconception about African women: that they have everywhere and always been the victims of cultural oppression and male dominance, subservient and in perpetual servitude, mute and without agency. While some have contended that "women's story is not the substance of great narratives" (Spivak 1988, 287), the history of Africa suggests that it is, in fact, a remarkable one, not an imagined female golden age or invented myth. It is the subject of griots' oral chronicles, of voyagers' ancient records, and colonial narratives alike. Therefore, without resorting to panegyric on the situation of women, this chapter establishes that the conception of FGP is a foundational moral force and shows that the tradition of appeal to it is both widespread and deeply rooted.

Scholars like Diop (1978) and Amadiume (1997) have argued that the origin of West African society rests on *matriarchy*, a structural organization of society. This chapter argues that, even along the coast of West Africa where matrilineal societies have long been in existence and still endure, it is not matriarchy that most profoundly marked the region's civilization as its founding order, but a less structural matter, a principle that I call "matrifocal morality."[7] While matriarchy or matriliny makes the line of descent from a particular woman a primary concern, matrifocality is not necessarily linked to the structural organization or the hierarchical offices within a given society. It is a values system that holds the female elders in esteem as the bearers of ultimate moral authority. On the basis of historical evidence and applying Foucault's genealogical method, the chapter presents matrifocal morality as an underlying principle common to West African society, the foundation of the unique "ontological-cultural epistemology" that lends an inchoate cultural coherence to the region (Long 2004, 90).[8]

Gender criticism has exposed the enduring tendency of Western thinkers to make universalizing assumptions and project homogeneity on all women and perhaps especially "Third World" women who are presumed to be unable to speak for themselves. Chapter 3, "Gender and Resistance: The 'Strategic Essentialism' of FGP," undertakes a historical and comparative review of various cases of African women's collective mobilizations and ritualized protests across West Africa in terms of three sorts of "gender troubles": (1) the troubles that African women *faced* as gender roles shifted; (2) the trouble that African women intentionally *created* to disrupt these "unhoming" forces with their ancient rite; and (3) the trouble that *Western interpreters* have shown when attempting to identify the phenomenon of FGP as a unique appraisal of gender and politics.[9]

While some scholars of gender in Africa eschew the very construct of gender as essentialist and an imposition of white Western feminist theory, I suggest that the postmenopausal women who voluntarily take up the duty to carry out the rite—whether in secreted ritual or as an act of public rebuke—self-consciously define themselves as belonging to a special subset of women. No longer defined by their reproductive function, they surpass the limits of spiritual power ascribed to either gender alone. In performing FGP these postmenopausal women become agents who engender power (pun intended) in a unique way and assert their prerogatives as the bearers of supreme moral authority.

This chapter argues that the performances of FGP are occasions in which African women elders assert their own self-defining essentialist identity as women of a particular kind. At the same time, the performances are themselves strategic efforts to resist the gender ideologies imported and imposed by colonialism and the Christian missions and defend the prerogatives and interests of African women that are being undermined. Therefore, theirs is a "*strategic* essentialism" (Joy 2006). African women's use of FGP embodies a unique appraisal of gender while engaging spiritual and moral matters under the most pressing political exigencies.

Part II, "Worldliness: FGP in the Making of Ethnicity, Alliance, and War in Côte d'Ivoire," argues that the principle that undergirds FGP is the founding knowledge and binding power on which West African civilizations were established. It shows how the matrifocal morality that the Mothers embody operated as the basis for the consolidation of ethnic groups and for alliances among them. The overarching argument here is that FGP, as a founding moral principle, helped establish alliances, allowing diverse peoples to meet in what was once the forest frontier to assimilate and form new identities and solidarities. However, I underscore that the principle of matrifocal morality and the practice of the appeal to FGP also ultimately supersede any particular ethnicity.

The ritual embodiment of moral authority stands as the ultimate sanction, both authorizing rulership and worldly powers and chastising their abuse. This worldly function of FGP has salience under the pressure of globalization and the recent civil war. Although the war is largely interpreted as an ethnic conflict, the women's collective manifestations reflect a solidarity that supersedes ethnic divisions. Moreover, their ritual condemnation of the violence represents a timely critique of the politics of the postcolonial state that has capitalized on such distinctions.

Chapter 4, "Founding Knowledge/Binding Power: The Moral Foundations of Ethnicity and Alliance," returns to the particular context of Côte d'Ivoire and a puzzlement surrounding Dipri and the Abidji women's rite called

"Egbiki." It investigates FGP as a common feature of social life that allowed the Abidji and Adioukrou peoples to share Dipri as a defining cult, despite the many structural differences between these two ethnic groups. A primary aim is to investigate the "*internal* vision of power" (Memel-Fotê 1980, 12) that enabled disparate peoples on the African forest frontier to consolidate as distinct sociopolitical entities and to establish critical alliances among them. These new polities do not necessarily fit the classic definition of *ethnic group*, in the sense of a group classed according to common racial order or bloodline. Other features also enable people to affiliate and consolidate as ethnicities, including language or common culture. I am proposing that in Côte d'Ivoire, a principle feature of such common culture was matrifocal morality.

While ethnicity has been vilified as the source of a backward-turning tribalism and violence responsible for Côte d'Ivoire's civil wars, this chapter returns to the original dynamics of ethnic politics to show FGP as the original means of establishing strategic peacetime alliances.

Chapter 5, "Women at the Checkpoint: Challenging the Forces of Civil War," introduces the dynamics of Côte d'Ivoire's decade-long strife and demonstrates that, although largely overlooked by journalists and scholars alike, the rhetorical work of the female elders deploying FGP has been as critical as other discursive tropes at play in the political arena. This chapter offers a rereading of the history of the Ivoirian civil war, which is generally cast as a result of ethnic infighting and divisions along religious lines. Given that the women's collective mobilizations appeal to overarching spiritual principles on which communal life depends and that are fundamental to interethnic alliances, their call for moral accountability surpasses the politics of ethnicity. Their activism therefore asserts a "portable identity" of a different kind (McGovern 2011). The Mothers' sanctions against the violent usurpation of power by youth are also shown to be surprisingly effective as a civilizing force. I argue that FGP is "part of the moral calculus of power," an indispensable ingredient of legitimate rulership that the state cannot afford to overlook (Lonsdale 1986, 141).

Part III, "Timeliness: Urgent Situations and Emergent Critiques," shifts attention from the *space* on which the battle is waged—land and bodies—to the *timeliness* of women's interventions as *emergency* measures today. It underscores that the women's engagement of FGP is not a nostalgic rehearsal of timeless tradition but a timely intervention that interrogates the present situation.

In the midst of the civil war and its protracted aftermath, Ivoirian women were often the targets of horrific sexual violence. Women's bodies became sites of the contest of power where society's unhomely dislocation was forcefully enacted. Rape and other sexual torture violently rend a woman's body and her body from herself, even as they rip the seams of society in civil war. These most intimate violations assault the very source of civilization by attacking the female foundations of social identity for matrilineal societies. Chapter 6, "Violation and Deployment: FGP in Politics in Côte d'Ivoire," documents not only women's victimization but also their strategic response to the contemporary crisis. Their collective mobilization offers a new *emergent* critique of the state accountability, especially in light of efforts toward truth and reconciliation. The Mothers have been forceful advocates for the indemnification of women victims of war, once again agitating for action through FGP.

Chapter 7, "Memory, Memorialization, and Morality," shows that, in contrast with state amnesia, its tendency to forget the wrongs of war and the culture of impunity for those in political power, the demonstrations of the Mothers actively recollect fundamental ethical mandates and stir civil society to demand accountability. The confrontation between the Mothers and the state is therefore a battle to control memory as much as direct morality.

The state attempts to co-opt collective memory and control a public account of history through the physical monuments it erects. Another way of domesticating history is by featuring certain traditions as a cultural heritage for which it purports to serve as protective guardian. Under its auspices, tradition is manipulated to serve as an emblem of the state. The Mothers' vivid performances are not so easily contained, controlled, or co-opted. The active engagement of FGP defies inscription and resists becoming monumentalized or memorialized. Instead, their embodied rebukes bring into focus the lost values of the fractured state.

The Conclusion, "An Intimate Rebuke: A Local Critique in the Global Postcolony," suggests that African women's mobilizations and their collective deployment of FGP in the political arena serve as a time-honored engagement of *civil society*, one that still has an effective reach in the globalizing world. While it is beyond the purview of this academic study to offer solutions to the profound problems challenging Ivoirian society, revealing the women's acts to be efforts to recollect the moral state may suggest possibilities for meaningful approaches to them. It presents the ritual of FGP as an eloquent commentary on power, offering a potentially rich new source of insight into the current plight of Africa.

Part I. Home and the Unhomely

THE FOUNDATIONAL NATURE
OF FEMALE GENITAL POWER

•

The "unhomely" is a paradigmatic colonial
and post-colonial condition.
—HOMI K. BHABHA, *The Location of Culture*

Home is the most intimate of domains. It is founded on affective bonds and the moral commitments to the immediate family that naturally arise from those bonds. Home defines the familiar; it is the locus of safety, the domain of custom, and the ground of identity. Home is therefore more than an inhabited territory; it is the social habitus itself. Home is the net of the social imaginary that catches and organizes experiences and casts them as significant events. Yet at the heart of home is the uncanny, which in West African cultures is referred to with discreet and disquieting reference to genies, witches, and the ambiguous powers of women. The Mothers therefore simultaneously stand for the essential bonds and values of home while paradoxically wielding the most dangerous and unhomely invisible force.

Their power is not primarily structural in nature, but effected as a fundamental moral value seamlessly woven into various patterns of social organization, from monarchies to secret societies. The moral mandates that Mothers embody and aggressively sanction through FGP especially informed the most prominent form of governance in the West African region, collective self-rule.

A consistent undercurrent in the dynamics of social organization throughout the region, matrifocal morality can therefore be understood to be the very foundation of home, the essential yet inchoate element that lends cultural coherence to the region, and the construct that best defines the local episteme.

This is not to say that FGP is a timeless tradition, rooted in a primordial past and remaining an ever-stagnant or unchanging practice. Tradition is always innovative and accommodating to history; the Mothers' vigorous interventions in worldly affairs, from precolonial alliances to anti-colonial nationalist efforts to current political crises, including the recent Ivoirian civil war, amply testify to its timeliness. Those women who appeal to FGP have acted as self-conscious, strategic players in efforts to resist the systematic unhoming of African society from foundational values.

I. GENIES, WITCHES, AND WOMEN

Locating Female Powers

When men are not present, women expose themselves.
—TSHI PROVERB, in J. G. Christaller, *Twi Mnebusem Mpensa-Ahansia Mmoano*

Disquieting References

It was over thirty years ago when I was living in Côte d'Ivoire, the young wife of an Ivoirian man, that I first saw *Dipri*, a spectacular traditional ritual shared by a subset of the Abidji and Adioukrou,[1] two neighboring ethnic groups in the southern lagoon region. Dipri is a calendrical celebration of the new harvest year and for that reason is simply referred to by the Adioukrou as "The Yam Festival." But it is also a rite of initiation, when the youth of the village are consecrated to the genie of the river and, as they are seized by its power, succumb one by one to a frenzied possession-trance. Therefore, the Adioukrou more properly call the festival *Kpol*, literally "possession-trance."[2] Even though the festival is over twenty-four hours long and requires spending at least one night in the village, Dipri always draws a crowd, for it is a sensational spectacle involving not only the chaotic display of the entranced but also their bloody self-stabbings and the seemingly miraculous instantaneous healings of their wounds by so-called witches.

My initial investigation of Dipri was stimulated by my need to understand the meaning and nature of African witchcraft, about which I regularly heard vague and disquieting references. The English term *witch* has decidedly negative connotations, typically referring to persons supposedly invested with supernatural powers and who use them to evil effect. In Africa the Western language terms have been unreflexively adopted, although indigenous conceptions of witchcraft are more equivocal; the spiritual power of witchcraft is an ambiguous force that can be channeled for evil or good. So even those who enjoy inordinate success are said to be witches.[3] This very ambiguity and the omnipresent reference to witches and witchcraft, whether in joking banter or in whispered gossip about unsettling and uncanny matters, made it seem to be the key to deeper cultural knowledge. At the time, my African husband self-consciously avoided overt discussion of these matters, protecting himself from being cast in terms of the exotic "other" under the distorted gaze of the West, even and perhaps especially the gaze of his white Western wife. I urged him to help me gain greater insight into what I perceived to be a fundamental cultural paradigm, persuading him that unless I could understand the constant refrain of witchcraft and unlock what were, for me, the closed doors of rumor, innuendo, and secrecy that loomed in everyday conversation, I could never feel at home there. "Okay," he finally conceded. "If you want to understand witchcraft, you'll have to see Dipri."

On the evening before Dipri, the village bustles with festive activity as guests arrive and are received, for anyone who is not a resident and who wishes to see the spectacle must spend the night in the home of a villager. In every courtyard meals are prepared, and before they are served libations are poured to honor the ancestors. At about ten o'clock in the evening all lights are extinguished and quiet is made to settle on the community in preparation for the solemnity of the occasion. A few voices are heard crying out "Bidyo-wo!, Bidyo-wo!" It's a funeral dirge for the ancestor, a reference to the mythic beginnings of the ritual, and the signal that the ceremonies are officially begun. All are shuttered away, warned that none must look upon the women elders who perform a nocturnal rite in the nude.

Early the next morning, young initiates are brought to the banks of the nearby river and are consecrated to the "genie," or divinity, who is said to reside in the waters and who protects the village inhabitants.[4] They smear their bodies with the white river clay, kaolin, a sign of purification. As they return to the village the initiates are surrounded by an entourage of youths from their quarter who accompany them, clapping and singing lively songs in praise of the genie and the genie's power, called *séké*. One by one, initiates are seized by séké and fall into the seeming chaos of possession-trance.

The trance is a fraught passage in which the initiates appear to struggle with an invisible adversary. Their eyes roll or stare in a wide unfocused gaze; they stumble aimlessly, pivoting and changing direction in an instant, and tear at their clothes and hair. They stumble against one another or fall and writhe on the ground. Some exhibit more bizarre behavior: one young man fell upon the egg that all initiates carry and licked the yoke from the ground. Others caught ground lizards (*agama agama*) with remarkable speed and bit and dangled them from their mouths. The force of séké supposedly builds in the abdomen and becomes "hard like an egg" until the mounting pressure irresistibly compels those seized by its power to release it with a blood-letting stab (Lafargue 1976, 234). Usually the wounds are minor, but as I witnessed, they are occasionally deep enough to reveal a protrusion of intestines. My journal entry from 1980 relates the arresting scene:

> Suddenly a wild-eyed initiate pushed past me, stopped, fixed his legs in a wide stance, extended his arm and in one mad gesture, rushed a dagger into his abdomen. Crimson blood spilled from the wound, and stained his white garments in brilliant contrast. He looked down, puzzled, and gripped at the gut-oozing gash. Then a "witch" stepped forward and broke an egg onto the gaping wound. He applied a thick white paste, made with the same river clay that had been smeared on the faces of the initiates. The cut immediately sealed into a puffy protrusion. The full force of the trance seemed to ease as well, and the boy wandered away in a daze.

The so-called witches are not only masters of the genie's healing gift but also command the extraordinary inborn ability to see into the spiritual realm. More properly called "people of sékè" or *sékèpuone* by the Abidji and "people of trance" or *okpolu* by the Adioukrou, they oversee the dangerous festivities and intervene to help the struggling initiates. During the frenzied course of the day they undertake a ludic contest among themselves. They are said to throw up invisible traps to ensnare the entranced initiates from other village quarters under the protection of their adversaries. They can be seen digging a small hole in the road or setting out some other innocuous obstacle like a planted palm branch or overturned mortar. When entranced initiates come upon the trap, they stop, blocked by the spell and the illusion of an insurmountable gulch or a pit of fire. When the sékèpuone sprinkle urine across the road it is said to appear as an impassable waterway. The *sékèpo* (singular) who accompanies the initiates from his quarter must either vanquish his challenger and destroy the trap or admit defeat and beg for the release of those who fell prey to the snare. In this way the witches playfully vie for dominance.

While such contests are invisible to most, the afternoon is dedicated to a public rivalry in which the sékèpuone display macabre feats of self-mutilation or ordeal without apparent pain or distress. In the Adioukrou village of Orbaff in 1980, for example, one of them playfully jumped in front of my camera and sewed his cheeks together. Another called me to join the ring of spectators gathered around him; there, in the middle of the road, the elder dropped his shorts and laid an egg. Later a local spectator pulled at my arm, saying, "Come, madam, come this way. You don't want to miss this. Here comes one of the 'strong' ones." A bare-chested man drew out a knife. In one quick gesture, he severed the front of his tongue. He held the bit of flesh in his outstretched hand for everyone to see. With the other hand, he held the point of his blade to the bloody stump in his mouth. Then, in one swoop, he replaced the pinkish muscle, twisted the blade, and reattached the member. He stuck out his tongue, perfect and unblemished, for the crowd to see.[5]

Whether these uncanny acts are agile tricks or real is not the issue here. Their spectacle is intended to make visible the claims about the invisible realm and to astonish spectators with their awesome power. The shocking acts of self-wounding are dangerous, not only because they defy nature but because the initiates and sékèpuone alike are vulnerable to other witches whose intentions are not so ludic. If allowed to have their way, those evil ones will make those wounds fatal. Therefore, according to the Abidji, Dipri cannot proceed without Egbiki, the preliminary secret and nocturnal rite of protection performed by elderly women.

Egbiki: Female Genital Power as Dipri's Authorizing Force

In the still hours between one and three o'clock in the morning, under the cover of darkness, women elders gather to perform the potent rite, Egbiki.[6] They cry out an invitation to all mature women to join them in their work and warn the population that their ceremony is beginning, since Egbiki is performed in the nude and males are prohibited from viewing the elders' nakedness. Should they look upon "the Mothers," especially in conscious defiance of the taboo, the result is said to be fatal: "[They] sound a cry 'Oooh!' to alert the population and surprise the witches who would have already undertaken their evil spells. Then one of them sings out: 'if there is a man in the road, he should leave. Misfortune for he who remains.' Then they invite other women from the quarter: 'The women who are sleeping must get up and come with us because we 'work' for the village'" (Lafargue 1976, 193–94).[7]

The naked elders cross the village, pounding the ground with old pestles, and chant to curse any witch who might seek to keep the initiates' wounds from healing. Their eerie incantations are made in Baoulé, the language of a neighboring ethnic group, considered to be spoken by the divinities that inhabit the region.[8] In 1980, sequestered behind shuttered windows with my husband, I could only imagine the secret rite as I listened to the women's chilling cries echo into the otherwise still, black night. Their full-throated rhythmic incantation was punctuated with a fearsome collective thud as their pestles hit the earth like a thunderbolt.

The chants announce that their pestles are striking the abdomens of those who intend harm: "May the ones who by Angrè (witchcraft) wish to keep the wounds . . . from closing. . . . *May this pestle strike their belly and make it swell so that they cannot get up from their beds*" (194). Their imprecations can be more menacing yet: "[Egbiki] must work: may whomever wishes to send evil die; may whomever wishes to kill by Angrè die" (93). The belly is thought to be the seat of *Angrè hun* (malevolent witchcraft). If Egbiki thus exposes malevolent witches, they are found the next day with painfully distended bellies and will die unless they are thrown into the river to deactivate their sorcery. This ritual provision for attenuating witchcraft underscores the positive and purificatory power of the female genie and her watery abode.

Most importantly, in Egbiki the women make appeal to the secret and sacred site of their power by bathing their genitals with water, which they then mix with urine and other secret ingredients to concoct a potion to magically entrap witches. They sprinkle it across the road to bar the way from these evil-doers. "They end by singing '*Munsuè na égé*' which means 'Evil, get behind!' (that is to say, [go] where there are no human beings)" (193–94). At the far end of the village, they throw their pestles into the bush beyond the limits of the village and, with aspersions of their potent mix, seal its borders. From this time on no one may enter or exit the village until the close of ceremonies. To violate the taboo would be to invite death, for death itself was ritually expelled and would surely follow anyone who leaves.

A senior officiant of the Adioukrou ceremonies in the village of Orbaff, Edouard Djedjroh, clearly asserted the importance of Egbiki at the time of Dipri. "The initiated cannot allow the festival to be compromised, to allow it to fail. So they take a precautionary measure. They call the women. It's women who do *Egbikng*. All the men go back home and hide their eyes. The women do it completely naked, so that all the evil spells retreat and they can conduct the festival under good conditions" (Djedjroh, Interview in Orbaff, April 2009).

"Subjugated Knowledges": Unhomely Powers and the Defense of Home

That Dipri depends on Egbiki as a prerequisite protective technique suggests that woman's spiritual power supersedes even the most impressive shows of male magical prowess and is Dipri's authorizing force. But on what grounds do the women claim such supremacy, and what is the nature of "genital power"? How can their violation of daytime decorum—nakedness, secrecy, spilling urine, and casting a deadly curse—effectively defend the values of home? Is Egbiki's appeal to female genital power a potent act of anti-witchcraft, or is the same unhomely power used toward different ends?

While a close reading of the details of the rituals is important to ground the phenomenon in its local milieu, a hermeneutic interpretation alone is insufficient for deciphering the strange and secret nature of female genital power.[9] Therefore, I propose to draw as well on the interpretive analytic that Foucault called "genealogy." Genealogy is not about tracing the origins of a people or documenting their overt institutional arrangements. Rather, it is the excavation of the "historical contents that have been buried and disguised in . . . formal systemization" (Foucault and Gordon 1980, 81). This approach aims at uncovering what Foucault calls "subjugated knowledges," principles and techniques that can be discerned in details that are usually glossed or dismissed as irrelevant but that play a role in configuring reality. "That which seemed the most hidden (because of its supposed importance) becomes not what it seemed. Its alleged hiddenness plays an essential role that is directly visible, once it is pointed out by the genealogist" (Dreyfus and Rabinow 1982, 107). Applying Foucault's critical analytic, genealogy, I aim to show that what is submerged beneath the visible, structural, and "surface practices" of Dipri is FGP, the most profound spiritual power on which all society depends.

The aim of this chapter is to situate the phenomenon of FGP in the intimate context of local religious practices and constructs, like witchcraft beliefs, where they are regularly rehearsed and where their acts have the deepest resonance, before entertaining instances in which the women elders perform them as acts of political rebuke. For as we shall see, FGP is also deployed to rebuke the evils of a country besieged by the violence of civil war and the encroaching forces of globalization threatening the values of home. Tracing this prototypical rite from the invisible religious realm to the public arena of politics will make clear that the women's performance of FGP is more solemn and profound than mere political protest. It is the activation of a curse that sanctions the violation of moral principles that have been foundational for African civilization.

The Myth of Bidyo: The Foundational Power of Female Blood

In some respects, Dipri is a public reenactment of the primordial founding of Abidji civilization. The myth of origins tells of a primordial sacrifice that enabled the ancestors to escape famine and establish the first yam harvest. According to the version first related to me, the chief of the clan, Bidyo, was confronted by a river genie (Abidji: *Eikpa*) named Kporu who promised to alleviate the people's suffering if Bidyo paid homage. Bidyo sacrificed his own child to the genie. Kporu then instructed that the body be cut into pieces and planted in the earth. From these burial mounds grew the first yams. In thanksgiving, the people prepared fufu (boiled and pounded yam mixed with palm oil), and the village celebrated the funeral rites of the sacrificed child, called "the one who gave us [food] to eat" (Lafargue 1976, 219).[10] The genie allowed the people to settle and served them as a protective spirit.

Through one of the first acts, Dipri recapitulates the covenant with the genie: the new yam is sprinkled with the blood of a chicken and offered to the genie at the river in sacrifice (100). Youth makes the rounds of the village chanting "Bidyo, Wo," a cry of mourning and anguish in memory of the primordial ancestor and his blood offering. Dipri is also a collective funeral that honors all the ancestors (*awenté*) (117). In the days preceding the festival offerings are made in private courtyards to the deceased lineage heads. However, Dipri marks the definitive end of the period of mourning for those who have died during that year (81), for once death is chased from the village it can no longer be acknowledged. To celebrate the new harvest and the renewal of life that mark the Abidji New Year, tradition maintains that all disputes are settled so that no resentments linger in the heart. This internal purification is matched by external acts: abstention from sexual relations and respect of dietary restrictions. No one may eat the new yam until it is consecrated at the end of the festival. Dipri is inaugurated in the darkest hour of the night with all lights extinguished, and the new day begins in peace.

Neither this version of the myth nor the associated ritual acts give much indication of the critical facts that underlie them: that female blood and the powerful female forces associated with the earth and earthly places, especially rivers, are the founding powers on which society depends and that establish the very grounds of home. Clues nevertheless exist, buried and disguised in details that are often concealed or disregarded.

When I first returned to the Abidji village of Sahuyé in May 2009, Chief Tanau Longau Julien formally received me. Wrapped in a traditional *pagne* cloth slung across his left shoulder, the chief regally occupied a high-backed chair that dominated the large open room where he conducted the business of daily adjudication. Hearing the purpose of my visit, Chief Longau immediately summoned the sékèpone to answer my questions. While we waited, I told him the version I knew of the myth of the ceremony's origin. The chief, a retired schoolteacher, seemed as uncomfortable as my first husband had been discussing sensitive matters in African traditions. "When we speak of cutting up yams, that is what we mean—the child. To give others food, he cut him up. In the old days they spoke [openly]. Those old men are no longer with us. When we tell it that way now it sounds a bit cruel." He asked me to await the arrival of others. Gnangra N'Guessan Bertin, the unassuming elder in shorts and open tennis shoes who took a seat with a shy smile, was introduced as the "Chef de Terre" (*Obu Nyane*), referred to in anglophone ethnography as "Earth Priest."[11] It is he who is responsible for overseeing Dipri as senior ritual officiant. One by one eight masters of the genie's power arrived in quick succession, making the rounds to shake hands as molded plastic chairs were hastily arranged to accommodate the expanding circle.[12] My question about the origin myth was put to them first, and the assembly conferred together with much commotion and gesticulation. Gnangra finally spoke: "What you said about the sacrifice, that's right, exactly," he said. "But Bidyo—his child was not a boy. *It was a girl, a daughter.* Every year at the festival, before the arrival of whites, a girl was sacrificed. Now we use a doe."[13] Kporu, the genie of the river, he told me, is also female. Gnangra went on to relate how the festival unfolds and, unprompted, underscored the inextricable association of Dipri with the women's rite. "On the day before, all quarrels in the village must be put to an end and we go from house to house to make sure everyone is reconciled. Then at one or two in the morning, we chase the evil spirits far off. *The women do it.* They strip naked. They carry wooden sticks and old pestles, they walk and sing asking that God watch over them and they curse the witches. They evoke all the powers that they can" (Interview, Sahuyé, May 2009).

Chief Tanau explained, "Woman is much respected. She is not in the habit of speaking out before men, but when it happens, it is an important affair. Woman annuls all that is bad." So while Dipri enacts the founding of the world through a covenant made with female blood, Egbiki exercises a practical and world-making power of its own, one that is not readily put on display but strategically deployed in secret to meet the pressing demands of the moment: to exorcise evil.

Another version of the myth was related to me by N'Guessan Edouard, a blind elder reputedly 103 years old and the senior member of Sahuyé's founding clan who had been a rival for the office of chef de terre.[14] As he recounted it he also related it to the preliminary women's rite:

> Long ago in the time of the ancestors, there was nothing to eat and they had to make sacrifice. There was a man who had a daughter. The girl's name was Bidjo. So they killed that child, cut the body up in little pieces, and made sacrifice by throwing the small pieces everywhere. When they went into the forest they found everything that we eat now. The anniversary of the day they killed the child, Bidjo, is Dipri.[15] On the day before the festival . . . at two or three o'clock in the morning, women go to chant and cry out. They chase away death and anything that might happen that is not good. They chase it away and send it out of the village. That way health is protected. Once daylight comes, they prepare food and the old

men pour libation. Then everyone goes into the road to have fun. (Interview in Sahuyé, May 2010)

"Fun," of course, meant the frenzied events of Dipri, from the chanting and drumming that accompanies the roving initiates throughout the course of the long day, to the wild chaos that erupts when one is seized by the possession-trance, to the terrible stabbings and ghastly manifestations of self-mutilation. While the old man's telling made it clear that Egbiki must precede the festival's dangerous and bloody undertaking, the myth itself remains mute on the subject of FGP.

The Myth of Kuao Dongro and the Gift of Sèkè

A second myth regarding the origins of Dipri is as critical as the first for understanding it as a recapitulation of the founding of Abidji society. This myth relates how the mystical powers of sèké were first acquired. However, it too appears to privilege male aggression and bloody warfare and offers no *immediate* clue about a possible association with female genital power.

According to Chef de Terre Gnangra, in the old days a hunter from Sahuyé named Kuao Dongro crossed paths with a genie of the forest.[16] The genie presented him with two leaves, each containing a magical power of a different kind. "The genie said, 'Here are the two leaves. You choose one [for yourself and the people of Sahuyé] and the other is for your brother and Gomon,' the village founded by the brother. 'If you choose this one you are courageous in war, and no one can vanquish you.' The second leaf provided miraculous healing of blood wounds, whether caused by accident [i.e., witchcraft] or war. 'If someone shoots you, it cannot kill you.' So, the hunter chose courage, while strength [the power to heal] went to the brother in Gomon" (Interview, Sahuyé, May 2009). Gnangra further explained that in the earliest days, only those from Gomon could "take up the knife," but through intermarriage, "the two groups mixed, so the people from Sahuyé can stab themselves as well."

When the blind elder N'Guessan related his version of this myth of Kuao Dungmbrou, he underscored that the gift chosen by Sahuyé made them indomitable warriors: "Even when you are fighting alone, you are not alone. There can be twenty of you—but the others don't see that there are only twenty. They see many more. And you can go into another village and fight, make war, and send [their attack] back to them. You come back [unharmed]."[17] The magical force of the genie casts an illusion on enemies in the same way that witches throw obstacles in the path of their adversaries during Dipri.

In the 1960s Fernand Lafargue, a French ethnographer who studied Abidji culture in depth, recorded yet another version that reinforces this protective aspect of the gift: "These [leaves] are not for Sahuyé alone. One is for your brothers from Gomon. . . . The one for Gomon allows anyone who is hurt by accident *to make his wound heal* with the aid of an egg. As for the other, it will render one powerful and allow him to dominate any evil-doers so *they can do no harm*" (Lafargue 1976, 146–47, emphasis mine). It further specifies that Kwao Dongbro was the first to prepare the healing balm by mixing the magic leaf with egg and kaolin clay taken from the sacred river, the same healing elements used today to seal the initiates' wounds (147). This balm is explicitly associated with the river, the source of the kaolin clay, and with the female powers that the genie of the waters bestows, as well as the egg, a symbol of the female matrix and generative power as well as a primordial source of nourishment. The leaves used during Dipri are vines, and other medicinal plants gathered at the marsh are considered female.

While these details suggestively link sékè's power to female elements, this version does not make clear how the brother from Sahuyé obtained the healing balm. Moreover, there is nothing in this myth, either, that indicates the requirement for Egbiki.

Acquiring Female Powers

Not only does Dipri have a double mythic origin, the two myths seem very much at odds. The myth of Bidyo appears to be a typical *horticultural* one about the establishment of a habitable world sustained by the yam harvest. By contrast, the story of the Genie's leaf and the gift of sèké has nothing to do with the yam or peaceful reconciliation; it is *a hunter's tale* that culminates with new possibilities for the aggressive and dangerous pursuit of war and spiritual combat. That second myth has little to do with founding an ordered world but rather accounts for the frenzied possession-trance and bloody manifestations that intrude into the solemn funerary rite and that otherwise appear incongruous with the pacific moment of New Year reconciliation.

One explanation for the simultaneous existence of two myths of origin is that Dipri is not one ritual but a synthesis of two very different traditions held on the same day. According to the renowned Ivoirian ethnographer Georges Niangoran-Bouah (1964), the festival represents the synchronic convergence of a *calendrical rite*, marking the yam harvest signaling the New Year, and an *initiatory ceremony*, the consecration to the genie of the river in the morning.[18] What is not evident from his hypothesis is why possession-trance and self-stabbing would figure in this cult to the *river* genie. Such manifestations are the gift of the *forest* genie and seemingly unrelated to the river. Also unexplained is how Dipri is "a New Year ceremony that *chases away death*" (Niangoran-Bouah 1964, 116), a feature that is associated neither with the new yam and the commemorative rite nor with initiation.[19]

The different myths and their overlapping references to different aspects of Dipri are indications of the strategic alliance forged between those Abidji and Adioukrou subgroups that cause only a subset of these ethnicities to celebrate the festival. Moreover, the double-origin myth provides evidence of the spiritual grounding of that interethnic alliance, a subject I will treat in Part II. For the present, what is most significant is that at the heart of both myths is a covenant initiated by a genie that enabled the people to lay the foundations of home: the settlement of the land and the capacity to defend it. Both indicate that salvific power lies in female sources. In the first instance, a female blood-sacrifice saves the people from famine.[20] In the second, the forest genie's gift explicitly forges a strategic alliance with Gomon; as we shall learn, it is Gomon that is most intimately connected to the *female river genie*, Kporu.[21] It is the alliance with this female source that is celebrated at the *initiatory ceremony* and her healing power that is actively manifest during the festival. However, the fiercest defenders of the land and village borders and the unrivaled combatants on the spiritual plane are the female elders. The ultimate prophylaxis and antidote against the witchcraft that threatens the village at Dipri are the invocation of FGP, through Egbiki, for it alone *chases away death*.

According to Lafargue, in the Abidji language *Dipri* means literally "to fall into the river" or "to wash oneself in the river," a reference to the initiates' consecration there (Rezo-Ivoire.net 2005). Among the Adioukrou who share in the ritual the festival is called *Kpol*, which literally means "trance." This name underscores that sékè is the principal focus of the day's spectacle. However, Yassap's chef de terre, Meledje Djedress Philippe, informed me that for those with deeper knowledge, the festival is known as *Erung Ok. Erung* means "river or stream," and *ok* means to "wash or bathe," a direct translation of Dipri, "to wash in the river." Both therefore refer to the secret rites that inaugurate the event, the consecration to the female river genie.

Symbolic elements employed in those rites of consecration to Kporu suggest a consonance between purification, initiation, and the natural processes of gestation and birth. For at least twenty-four hours prior to their descent to the river, all participants must abstain from sexual relations; at the river they are stripped naked, symbolically likened to the undifferentiated prenatal state. Some wear woven palm branches draped across their torso, braided into a long cord, and evocative of the umbilical cord.[22] At the riverbed initiates excavate white kaolin clay and anoint their faces and bodies. The smeared white substance represents the birth canal, drawing further symbolic correlation between the river as the spiritual source of power and woman as progenitor. Kaolin is fashioned into small mounds and brought back to the village to be used as an ingredient in the healing balm and other protective and magical ablutions made throughout the day.

At the water's edge the chef de terre sacrifices to the genie an egg, a hen, and a yam, associated with woman as matrix, *protector and source of all nourishment* (Meledje, Interview in Yassap, June 2010). The hen, of course, is a prolific progenitor and fierce protector of her young and so gives homage to the female genie as maternal source. The egg is the matrix itself. It is an emblem of wholeness, completeness, of cosmological order and self-sufficiency. The egg is an essential ingredient of the balm used during Dipri to close the initiates' wounds, further suggesting that this potent binding power has a female source. Also at the riverbank, medicinal leaves of various kinds are gathered as ingredients for the mysterious concoctions that calm sékè. The leaves are considered female. The yam is a common metaphor for the human body itself, in part because the huge tuber is harvested after a nine-month "gestation" and is grown in earth mounds that are likened to the protruding belly of a pregnant woman.[23]

The acknowledged association of these elements—egg, hen, and yam—with women's generative power lends probative weight to a reading of Dipri as a ritual of gender reversal that allows men to assume potent female power. One of the most potent (feared and revered) of female powers is the ability to shed blood without risking death. The immediate spectacle of Dipri appears to suppress women's full participation for men to usurp women's natural power. The violent abdominal stabs and the spectacle of male blood may be interpreted as the infliction of an imitative wound, substituting for the potent menstrual flow that does not kill but redoubles the life force that blood represents. With the overt spectacle of male blood and the domestication of its flow, the initiates of Dipri appropriate women's innate generative power and remake the social world.[24]

Dangers for Women, Dangers of Women

While both young men and women are consecrated to the genie of the river, and both enter trance, only male initiates stab themselves. The reason, ostensibly, is to protect the womb and preserve a woman's fertility and reproductive power.

This was the subject of much discussion in 2009 when I first returned to Orbaff, one of two Adioukrou villages that celebrate the festival. Two senior

Okpolu who met me at the chief's house were just returning from church and were still dressed in their Sunday best. Yedoh Edouard wore a bowler hat reserved for those who celebrated Ebeb, the festival that promotes the age groups that govern Adioukrou society. It indicated that he had ascended to the seniormost rank and was at least sixty-four years old. Djedjeroh Edouard, a man of about fifty, bore a scar over his right eye, a mark of his notorious Dipri feat (the removal of the eye from its socket). When I asked him why only young men performed the stab, Djedjeroh put it this way: "Woman is the procreative mother, and the genies know that. Women are vulnerable because when you stab with the knife, it touches the intestine and [the womb]. The genies saw that. So, when women try, the genies don't allow it . . . sometimes very powerful women will make the stab but from then on they will not bear children"[25] (Interview in Orbaff, May 2009).

I told Djedjeroh that I'd seen a young woman in a deep trance writhe on the ground and watched one of the powerful ones come and gently wipe her forehead with kaolin to draw her out of it. "Right," he said. "She is woman. In ceremonial matters, she is higher than others. She had drunk in too much of the thing [sékè]. Her situation is elevated, and therefore superior. In order for the spirit to leave her, she needed to be calmed."[26] Women's participation must be contained because women's power, being innately superior, cannot be further enhanced with sékè; "Those whose power must be attenuated are not admitted to ceremonies destined for its confirmation or augmentation" (Lafargue 1976, 164). In Yassap, the only other Adioukrou village that celebrates "Kpol," Chef de Terre Meledge Djedress Phillippe, a mild-mannered and obviously intelligent man in his forties, met with me on several occasions, eager to share his deep knowledge so it would be "documented for posterity." He clarified that women's sékè often exceeds that of men, but can have dangerous consequences: "[A woman] can be strong and not stab her belly and then have children, but once she does stab herself, once she spills blood, she won't have children. That is, she's made her sacrifice." It is not because her womb would be damaged, he explained, but because the genies take the life from her womb as a compensatory sacrifice. This is not a punishment meted out to a woman for her defiance, however, for in fact male initiates who spill their blood for the first time during the festival must make a blood sacrifice afterward to compensate for having been spared death. This is the purpose of the ceremony conducted one week following the festival: the sacrifice of a dog. The dog's slaughter substitutes for the initiate's own life.[27]

While the force of sékè and the stab are deemed too dangerous for women, women's own innate power presents a danger to the male participants in Dipri/

Kpol. As we shall see, the most dangerous of all are the female genitals, the locus of great magical force. Sékèpuone and Okpolu are especially prohibited from any contact with women's genitals and blood. For weeks, if not months, prior to Dipri, they remain celibate. Youths seeking initiation at the river must also abstain from sex. And no one, initiate or guest, is to have intercourse in the village once it is sealed.[28] According to Gnangra, Sahuyé's chef de terre, this is because "if you make love, in the morning when you stab, when you touch the wound it is as if you enter it. If you have made love, when the others go to the river, you must not go. It is forbidden" (Interview in Sahuyé, May 2009).

Other taboos, especially those relating to dietary restrictions, make symbolic association between the forbidden food and the dangerous impurity of women's menstrual blood. For example, red palm oil is not to be used on the day of Dipri, for its red and viscous quality suggests menses. Honey is also avoided, because "it is contaminated by menstrual blood upon which bees suck" (Lafargue 1976, 138). Honey then supposedly causes blood to flow and would be a hazard to healing.

Menstruating women are also prohibited from going to the stream or even attending the spectacle of Dipri, for contact with them would incur dangers for the initiates who wound themselves. In Orbaff one of the Okpolu made explicit the symbolic association between the female sex and the open, bleeding wound that does not heal.[29] "If one who has sexual relations comes among the Okpolu, when they try to heal [the initiates], they have problems. That's why it is forbidden. And if you are a woman and you have your period, it is not good for you to be there, otherwise to heal the wound is difficult" (Interview in Orbaff, June 17, 2010). Meledje Djedress Philippe reiterated that preparation for Kpol required careful avoidance of female blood: "When there are only a few weeks left [before Kpol], you must not even approach your wife. You must take your knife and wash it, and take your kaolin, your eggs, take all that away if your wife is having her period. You shouldn't see her until it's over. *You are going to shed blood and you must not see blood until you've done your work with a knife* (Yassap, June 26, 2010).[30]

Contact with women's blood is a powerful deterrent to healing, but so is the fecund sexual female herself. While I was in Yassap in 2010 a group of youths from the neighboring village Lopou attempted to seize control of land belonging to Yassap and considered sacred. The youths attacked a respected Okpolu. The machete wound proved fatal, despite the interventions of his fellows who are supposedly able to draw upon sékè even outside the context of Dipri. Meledje explained: "His wife touched him right away. When you are severely wounded in the bush, you know how women are . . . she had to touch him. She shouldn't have. *If she hadn't touched him, they wouldn't even have needed medical intervention.* He told her, he told her. . . . *Even if she wasn't having her period she shouldn't have touched him. . . . She was still bearing children.* That's not good, that's not good. The interventions couldn't work" (Yassap, June 26, 2010).

While women and their blood are dangerous during Dipri, their power dominates Dipri nonetheless. Youe Yvonne, an octogenarian living in Sokokro, an Abidji village just beyond Sahuyé, asserted, "Woman has even more sékè than man. They are stronger witches than the men. The power that women have surpasses that of man. *Therefore they don't have to manifest it.* The women who are behind [Dipri] are strong; they are great" (Interview, May 12, 2010). Although they appear to remain in the background, it is believed that these strong old women operate discreetly on the invisible plane.

According to the Adioukrou chef de terre, the paramount and most dangerous power that those elders control is their genital power. "Ehye! . . . Those strong women, they cough and you're dead. When you stab and the intestines come out, *the old women come and take out their thing there [genitals] and their buttocks and wipe it and you're done for.* Women are strong—oh! In this situation it is the woman who is strong" (Meledje, Interview, June 26, 2010).

If the women and their genital power represent a great threat, they also represent the strongest source of protection. Begré Koffi, Sahuyé's master of the great talking drum (*attungbanyé*) that opens the Dipri festivities, insisted that the "play" is dangerous because the threat of witches is real. Therefore, no male may participate or attempt the stab during Dipri unless he has obtained prior permission from his own mother, for her blessing provides the ultimate protection.

> Sékè is for everyone, but in principle it *is women who protect us. Women protect men.* If you want to go have fun, but your mother hasn't liberated you, you can't. If your mother is angry with you, it's very dangerous. . . . Before the festival, the day before, you go to your mother and you say, "I believe in you. Tell me if I did anything to hurt you." She will say to you, "there, you caught an animal, you didn't give it to me," or, "You insulted me." Then you ask forgiveness [for any slight or offense]. Now if she says [that you must make a compensatory offering of] one egg, two eggs, you give them to her. . . . Then your mother frees you. If you don't have your mother behind you, you yourself are in doubt. (Begré Koffi, Interview in Sahuyé, May 2010)

Some days later, during the Dipri festival in Sahuyé, I witnessed the consequences of the violation of this prohibition. A young man dressed only in white shorts, like the other initiates, was reluctantly led by the arms and made to kneel before an older woman. He was clearly distressed and remained before her with downcast eyes. "He must pray to his mother," someone leaned in to explain. "He has not asked permission, and now he must find out what he will have to pay to be released."

While Dipri *appears* to be a "gendered distribution of male authority and order, with men at the center and women at the margins" (Apter 2007, 122), on closer consideration, it is clear that woman's power is the real force that protects all enactments of the men's power and magical prowess. It attests to the natural preeminent power of women and, moreover, their innate genital power. This is why Egbiki is indispensable for the success of Dipri.

Interview with a Witch: The Ambiguity of Power

Sangroh Esaïe is renowned in Orbaff for his "special gift," the ability to remove his eyeball from its socket during the great afternoon demonstrations of Dipri.[31] At the conclusion of our initial interview, I asked if there was anything about which I hadn't asked that he might want to add. Sangroh said, "People have a tendency to say that *all* those who participate in the festival are witches (Adioukrou: *agnew*). This is not true. Not *everyone* who celebrates the festival is necessarily a witch. . . . [a witch has] second-sight, and it's a birthright. Don't neglect this point. It is not because one is initiated at the stream that one [has the power to] participate at this level" (Interview in Orbaff, May 3, 2009). A long discussion ensued in which he distinguished between the witch, as one who permanently possesses the power of witchcraft (*Agn*), and sékè, the power of the genie manifest in Dipri. According to Sangroh, sékè and witchcraft are complementary forces, and in some both are manifest simultaneously: "Those with double power are not only participants in the festival of yams but, *by birth, they are also witches.* . . . There are those who have both powers at the same time, the power to participate in the festival of yams, and who are also witches in the full sense of the word, but not the kind that will harm others" (Orbaff, May 3, 2009).

Another resident of Orbaff claiming to be a witch (Adioukrou: *agn*) with innate "double vision" reiterated the distinction. According to Djedjero Nan Lili, the innate power of "witches" (pl.: *agnew*) is stronger than the acquired powers of sékè because it is permanent. She said, "I can see witches (*agnew*) just like that. . . . I was born with the power of double vision; I didn't have to get initiated to have it. For others, sékè appears during Kpol, but afterwards it disappears. My power remains" (Interview, June 28, 2010). Those with such enduring powers belong to a society that oversees the festival. Female elder Low Agnime Emilienne revealed that the feats displayed at Dipri are planned among them: "There is a society. All those who have double vision, we gather. Everyone says how she is going to go about it. Each one demonstrates the power that is in her. There is a secret among us that we can't show others. *We bring out what we have in order to encompass the evil power, to block the others*" (Interview, June 28, 2010). Here she was alluding not only to vigilant protective oversight during the initiates' dangerous operations but also to Egbiki, the necessary antecedent to Dipri.

In his study of religion, magic, and witchcraft among the Abidji, Fernand Lafargue examined the respective natures of sékè and angrè and attempted to parse the complex relationship between them. Lafargue proposed that their distinction lies in their respective aims. "Sékè is not harmful, it doesn't seek to 'catch' a victim, to sicken or kill, whereas it is quite the opposite for angrè" (Lafargue 1976, 151). However, the truth is not quite so straightforward: "Not only is Sékè not evil-doing but it also can be beneficent and enable one for example to heal wounds. . . . Angrè, on the contrary, is very often evil-doing. *Yet one distinguishes the Angrèpuoné namu (good)* [those who possess and use Angrè for the good] *from Angrèpuoné hun (evil)* [those who use Angrè for evil] *whom they combat on their own terrain and with the same magical means*, situated at the same level" (151, emphasis mine). This attempt to clarify the distinction only serves to show the irreconcilable complexities of the subject, for the power of witchcraft proper is not of two kinds but is the very same magical means opposed only by intent.

Referring to the Alladian, a neighboring Ivoirian ethnic group with cultural and linguistic affinity to the Abidji and Adioukrou, the renowned French ethnographer Marc Augé underscored that while the nature of witchcraft was inscrutable, the indigenous terms that supposedly distinguish among powers were equally opaque. An example is sékè: "The power [of witchcraft called *awa*] is the very same as that of anti-witches. About the latter (*sékè* in Alladian and Ebrié) one identifies characteristics that are just as applicable to the power of aggression; *sékè* is sometimes stronger than *awa*, but *it is of the same nature*. At this point the theory becomes ambiguous and sometimes confusing: sékè is a power of legitimate defense, but it is of the same nature as *awa*; *it can at any time change purely and simply into awa*; in the extreme the anti-witch can very well be suspected of witchcraft" (Augé 1976, 130, emphasis mine).

The potential mutability of such spiritual forces is the reason that only those who have purified themselves may invoke them. Their hearts must be cleansed of any lingering resentment that might be secretly harbored against one's intimates, for power unleashed without self-conscious control and direction can take a dangerous toll. Here is a central tenet that links the purification rites that herald the New Year with those at the river performed at initiation. It is also a prerequisite for the dangerous evocation of FGP.

The elderly Koffi Akissi did not disguise the lethal threat of the Mothers' curse. She made clear that it is a spiritual weapon that targets evil and strikes with deadly force. After describing how they conduct the rite, she said, "Afterwards, if you try to do evil, it traps you, it reveals you [as a witch] and it kills you. But if you don't do evil anymore, it leaves you alone. But if you persist it kills you. Because it is a trap, it takes you and kills you" (Interview, Sahuyé, June 10, 2010). Therefore, those who perform Egbiki must "purify their hearts."

Whether there is a clear difference between the nature of sékè and other invisible spiritual powers identified as witchcraft remains a matter of debate. One thing that the participants of Dipri make clear is that nefarious acts of witchcraft are an omnipresent threat not only to the success of the Dipri's dangerous operations, but also to the community. The women's rite is a necessary protective measure against their malevolent designs. Yet the force that Egbiki elicits appears to be tantamount to witchcraft, for the woman's rite is an act of spiritual combat and can kill. Moreover, those who conduct Egbiki readily assert that they too are "witches." How does this square with popular folklore depictions of the witch as the epitome of evil and witchcraft as the "unhomely" art par excellence? And how can the performance of a curse with supposedly fatal repercussions be reconciled with religion? Drawing on the themes *intimacy*, *home*, and *unhomeliness*, I sketch out contentious issues surrounding witchcraft before returning to Egbiki.

Scholarship on witchcraft in Africa has a long pedigree, figuring prominently in anthropology from the earliest, now classic, studies (Evans-Pritchard 1935) to contemporary landmark works (Comaroff and Comaroff 1993; Geschiere 1997, 2013; Moore and Sanders 2004). The term *witch* in European languages is an "unhomely" one in the sense that it is imported and artificially applied to indigenous contexts, bearing with it the substantial cultural baggage of its European history. When colonialists introduced these words into the popular lexicon in the late nineteenth and early twentieth centuries, almost all foreign ideas and activities were deemed to be "rooted in ignorance and irrationality" (Geschiere 2013, xv). Even to this day "the very notion of witchcraft . . . has exoticizing implications" (xv). Until relatively recently "any religious activity by Africans that did not have some clear equivalent in the practice of contemporary European Christians risked being vaguely consigned to the category of 'witchcraft' . . . indigenous healers and specialists were described as 'witch-doctors' . . . without any deep consideration of the moral value attached to such practices" (Ellis 2007, 35). I suggest that the problem is not that witchcraft has become such an open category irrespective of moral intent. Rather, the problem is that the Western construct itself is so heavily weighted by the moral judgment that witchcraft is singularly negative.

Africans who accepted the use of these European terms with reference to indigenous practices may not have been initially aware that they were so negatively charged. Western language terminology entered common lexicon, although "local communities originally had a far more subtle language to describe the different meanings and conceptions of what today is often simply termed 'witchcraft'" (Ter Haar 2007, 15). Yet the mere replacement of the word with indigenous terminology in itself does little to avoid the mistaken conflation of African practices with European conceptions of the occult as the *antithesis of religion*. What is especially distorting in relation to those practices identified with witchcraft is the assumption of an "'unequivocal opposition between good and evil' where a more nuanced distinction taking into account a more fundamental ambiguity is required" (Geschiere 1997, 12–13, cited in Csordas 2013, 531). Given that in African ontologies, power is conceived as an ambiguous force, two paradoxically opposing conceptions of witchcraft are equally prevalent in the popular social imaginary.

Some African folklore about witches does depict them to be the epitome of evil, drawing on their supernatural powers to thwart the good. Their behavior perverts normal ethical standards and inverts the social order. Where normal society operates openly during the day, witches act in secret and at night. While human society supports life, seeks healing, and celebrates fertility, witches are considered to be the cause of misfortune, illness, and death. Witches are "soul eaters" who attack their victims in the spiritual realm, causing them to suffer in the actual material plane. They are said to feast on the souls of their victims as their actual bodies waste away until they die. When they do so, they are said to turn their backs to one another; it is a vivid image of the inversion of normal human communion and "the bonds of the shared pot."[32] Like their counterparts elsewhere in the world, African witches are believed to be able to transform themselves into birds and animals and to belong to associations that congregate periodically to celebrate their antisocial accomplishments. Moreover, witches violate the moral mandates of intimacy and trust, for their victims are members of the witch's own family, and especially the matrikin, the lineage that defines home.

People identified as witches are often those who display antisocial sentiments such as anger or jealousy, or whose behavior conveys that they are too self-sufficient: they are reclusive, arrogant, or ungenerous. From a sociopolitical perspective, the label is used as a means of keeping people in line, operating according to the moral mandates of society and therefore for the "good." Belief in witchcraft has therefore been understood as a critical moral paradigm in a small-scale and interdependent society that relies on harmonious relations. "Fear of witchcraft projects on a mystic plane the possible consequences of disrespect or lack of social conscience. There is a socially pragmatic basis for belief in witchcraft" (Thompson and Wight Art Gallery 1974, 199). Belief in witchcraft also provides an explanatory framework for misfortune. Projects that fail despite all efforts and precautions, as well as premature deaths (even those with overt causes) are explained as the result of supernatural intervention of these evildoers. Accordingly, in African metaphysics, witches, and not God or any demonic spirit, are responsible for evil. "The problem of evil" is constellated in the human sphere because human agents, witches, act on their own independent will.

For this very reason, it is believed that protective measures can and must be taken against witches to prevent the efficacy of their attacks. Those capable of countering these spiritual assaults include healers, diviners, and other ritual specialists. While academic literature on African religions tends to portray diviners as diagnosticians and healers who act to thwart and expose witches and to protect and redeem their clients, such an opposition between good and evil is simplistic and misleading. Diviners operate using the same spiritual means and occult powers and can even use them to attack and kill.[33] As a result, in common parlance the term *witch* is applied to any person perceived to have uncanny abilities, whether beneficent or pernicious. Witchcraft can therefore be understood in terms of moral choice.

Despite the essential ambiguity of the construct, most interpreters of African witchcraft still offer little more than brief acknowledgment that witchcraft has "a potential power for both good and evil" (Ter Haar 2007, 8). Little attention is devoted to the moral aspect of witchcraft as a practice with any socially constructive function. Recently Thomas J. Csordas proposed that the subject of witchcraft be taken up anew, suggesting that what is required now is "the analysis of '*local moral worlds*'" (Csordas 2013, 524, emphasis mine). Rather than universalizing "the moral," he favors situating moral activity contextually, within the social imaginary in which persons operate and as the actual struggle with the causes and effects of suffering. This places focus on "moral experience on an *intimate* level" (524, emphasis mine). "Intimacy" here refers to both the scale of the concern—the local and particular social world—and the very personal nature of the moral grappling.

The ritual of Egbiki embodies the distinctive way that the moral imagination is configured in local religious tradition to reassert the essential values of home. It exemplifies that local moral world in action. The evocation of female genital power makes a woman's most intimate body the site of moral reckoning. It is an *intimate* rebuke of evil, carried out in light of indigenous conceptions about how it is perpetrated and in the local idiom of collective moral sensibility.

Egbiki and the Mothers' Sex: Uncanny Intimacy

Dipri's manifestations publicly acknowledge that "certain disreputable truths" (Geshiere 2013, 23), like the existence and practice of witchcraft, are an undeniable, integral part of the fabric of that society. As we have seen, during Dipri, "witches," who are usually marginal persons treated with a caution, take center stage and are shown to be foundational to social structure. Dipri is the occasion when the unhomely—both that which is uncanny and that which is abhorrent—is shown to exist at the core of "home."

According to Sahuyé's chef de terre, "Dipri" is also the *name of the society* whose members are those with a higher degree of initiation into sékè. Unlike those who undergo the possession-trance and have access to sékè only on the day of Dipri, the sékèpuone permanently retain sékè's power. Moreover, they are endowed with second sight and use the power of witchcraft, *Angrè*, for the good. Deployed for positive ends, it is called *Angrè namu* (literally, "good witchcraft"). Their society gathers to prepare new initiates and plan strategies for their defense against witches of the evil kind. The Dipri society also evinces somewhat disturbing parallels to their adversaries in that the good *Angrèpuone namu* also require a sacrifice to enter into their ranks—namely, the initiate himself for which a dog stands as a substitute. The dog sacrifice discloses the unhomely (ghastly and pitiless) truth that the pact with the genie entailed the participant's very life. In exchange for having been spared, the initiate who has spilled his blood during Dipri must sacrifice a dog in his stead. The dog's throat is slit, and the blood is drunk from the dying beast in the manner that, folklore suggests, witches drink the blood of their human victims. The brutal ceremony embodies the tension between the intimate bond forged with the genie in the public festival and the private register of that entity's ambiguous nature and demands. The disreputable truth is that the genie, like the witch, is a liminal being with equivocal powers. Perhaps the most disquieting disreputable truth is that the Mothers, the most intimate source of being and the primary member of the most basic social unit, are also witches whose curse is the only power capable of disarming evil.

Because the threat of witchcraft is especially acute within the inner circle of the intimate social bond, African conceptions of witchcraft force one to acknowledge the deep tensions and ambiguity embedded in intimate relations (Geschiere 2013, 23). The trusted familial domain is the most dangerous because witchcraft is concealed and harbored there. Witchcraft accusations reveal the deep antisocial affect at play in the domestic sphere, which otherwise tends to be romanticized as a "haven of reciprocity" (xvii). The practice *of* witchcraft inverts the most fundamental principle of trust associated with the intimate domain of home; similarly, the discourse *about* witchcraft "brings out into the open what should remain private—the hidden tensions within the family or community, now exposed to the public gaze—and this is already *a step away from the vision of intimacy as a cozy protected sphere*" (24, emphasis mine). With this emphasis on concealment and exposure as a twinned threat, Peter Geschiere appears much indebted to Sigmund Freud.

In his eponymous classic essay on the uncanny, Freud calls magic the "*unhomely* art" and links witchcraft to the ambivalent nature of intimacy. Following the etymology of the German word *heimlich* (homely), Freud reveals that it also encompasses its opposite, *unheimlich*—that is to say, the "unhomely" or uncanny (Freud 2003 [1919], 4). For Freud, the intimacy of home is forged in candid, unrestrained behavior that is normally withheld from public view. So, intimacy and homeliness are created by openness and revelation even while, paradoxically, they are necessarily founded on privacy and concealment. But concealment also suggests that which is obscure and inaccessible and therefore dangerous. So when concealment is combined with things reminiscent of home, it produces the eerie feeling of unease, gloom, the ghastly associated with the uncanny. Quoting Schelling, Freud therefore defines the "'unhomely' [as] the name for *everything that ought to have remained . . . hidden and secret and has become visible*" (4). The ambivalent feeling produced may shed light on African conceptions of witchcraft as an intimate art, practiced in secret and targeting the family, characterized by bizarre inversions and bewitching strangeness.

In characteristic style, Freud ultimately ascribes the source of the uncanny to the repression of longing for that most *intimate* of relationships and primal impulses, the *mother* and the repressed infantile sexual desire.

> It often happens that male patients declare that they feel there is *something uncanny about the female genital organs*. This *unheimlich* place, however, is the entrance to the former *heim* [home] of all human beings, to the place where everyone dwelt once upon a time and in the beginning. . . . and whenever a man dreams of a place or a country and says to himself, still in the dream, "this place is unfamiliar to me, I have been there before," we may interpret *the place as being his mother's genitals or her body*. In this case, too, the *unheimlich is* what was once *heimisch*, homelike, familiar; the prefix "un" is the token of repression. (15, emphasis mine)

While too ready an imposition of Western constructs and especially Freudian interpretative associations onto African realities is problematic, the insight into the association of intimacy, home, and the uncanny does offer suggestive avenues for understanding a possible aspect of the African conception of the *female genitals as the site of uncanny powers, both awesome and frightening*.

The fact that those innately endowed with the terrible power to launch the most forceful curse are commonly addressed by the intimate title "the Mothers" makes the connection to Freud's insight unmistakable. The mother is the essential insider, the creator of the child and the primary mother-child bond that is the fundament of home—especially in the matrilineal societies that long predominated in West Africa. This intimate bond is so encompassing and so critical to personal well-being and even one's destiny that a curse by one's own mother is deemed to be instantly and irrevocably ruinous.[34] The close connection between intimacy, the unhomely, and the uncanny (witchcraft) serves to explain more fully why it is that the Mothers are deemed to be the most dangerous of beings.

In West African traditions women are commonly considered to be inherently endowed with an uncanny force, ambiguous in nature. Among the Yoruba of Nigeria, for example, it is thought that "if it is *according to their 'secret'* that women give birth, it is also with their 'secret' that they take life, by consuming the life essence of their kinsfolk. . . . witchcraft, like fertility, is endemic to Yoruba womanhood, *all women are potential witches*" (Apter 2007, 94, emphasis mine). The secret, however, is not her procreative capacity. The power innate in woman *manifests* in maternity, but is even greater on the invisible plane. Hers is a moral force that only a female elder, *beyond childbearing*, can assume. Simply put, "Women are thought to become even more powerful after menopause, when menstrual blood ceases to flow" (Drewal 1992, 179). Where menses are polluting and dangerous, female elders neutralize danger, even and especially the dangers of witchcraft. Djedjero Nane Lili therefore emphasized that "*only old women* perform Egbiki; those who are still menstruating are not involved" (Interview in Orbaff, June 2010).

The common epithet "the Mothers" does not refer to any actual maternity, nor is it a sentimental term of endearment relating to qualities of nurturance. Rather it is a respectful title honoring their innate force, both revered and feared. Among the Yoruba of Nigeria, for example, while it is understood that the Mothers are witches, one only reservedly applies that term (*aje*) to these elders to avoid offending them. The Yoruba masking festival *Gelede* is the means by which society honors and assuages them. Celebrated in playful pantomime, they are "seduced" so that they will channel their extraordinary *power (ase)* toward blessing (Drewal 1992, 179).

Considered to possess as commanding a force as the ancestors or even the secondary divinities, the Mothers' sacrality surpasses the capacity of one sex to contain it. After menopause the female body not only outgrows its reproductive function, it also takes on a double-sexed aspect. At this stage, for example, women commonly sprout chin hairs. Such a body thereby reveals its divine essence. For this reason, Gelede represents this with the mask of the bearded woman. The beard indicates the status, knowledge, and wisdom of an elder while referencing the Mothers' powerful gender-surpassing condition. In turn "a bearded woman [is considered to] possess extraordinary spiritual power" (Drewal and Drewal 1983, 71). Such a body becomes an aperture that discloses other dimensions of existence and possibilities for participating in the potentiality of another world. The praise names by which the Yoruba call the Mothers indicate their powers of transformation and the extent of their dominion: they are called "the 'owners of two bodies' (*abára méji*) and the 'owners of the world' (*oní l'oní aiyé*)" (11).

Women elders, freed from the social role ascribed to women in their reproductive years, are elevated to a status of being capable of overseeing the common good. Like the ancestors, the Mothers "have special responsibilities for establishing the moral order of society," for they are "freed of the human weaknesses and conditions of pettiness" associated with particular personalities of living persons and are capable of "behav[ing] without self interest" (Olupona 2001, 57). Their capacity is even greater, however, for they are their *living* embodiment of moral authority. Among the Yoruba, it is said that "the power of the mothers is equal or superior to that of the gods . . . the mothers own and control the gods" (Drewal and Drewal 1983, 8).

Thus the power of the Mothers resides in the capacity to *surpass* the biological function and social stage of maternity and to assume an equally consequential spiritual power, the secret and sacred locus of which is their sex. Therefore, there is a critical difference between "woman as mother" and "the Mothers" as women, whose genitals symbolically represent the essential values and social mandates upon which legitimate authority rests.

It was a man, one known as a great witch, who most forcefully articulated the status of the Mothers and the moral might of Egbiki to dispel evil; Koffi Begré of Sahuyé said, "The women do a rite but it is dangerous. Woman comes out when it is really serious because Woman holds power in her hands. . . . Women here are God. When God arrives, witches flee, because *Woman represents God. . . . So when they see the women naked and that thing [their genitalia], it is like seeing God*" (Interview in Sahuyé, May 22, 2010).

In ritual the body is the means by which complex psychological phenomena are revealed symbolically and through which both conceptions about the world spiritual principles are conveyed. In Africa, "power associated with sexuality and reproduction is especially strong, and potentially dangerous. Female genital power is especially potent" (Stevens 2006, 593). In many African traditions "the genitals are equated not only with fertility and reproduction, but also with insult, impotence, infertility, trickery, sorcery, and deception" (Blier 1995, 147). In the tradition of the Fon of Benin, for example, "the woman's genitals are 'more powerful than a *bo*,'" the power object used to intercede in the invisible realm to effect change on behalf of the owner (147). Among the Abidji the female genitals, as the locus of great power, even receive blood sacrifices, such as a chicken, as does the genie of the river. "This is why a woman can use them like a magical weapon . . . casting [a spell] with the curse: 'May my lopò catch you!'" (Lafargue 1976, 194). It concisely explains why FGP is the focal point of the nocturnal rite that protects the initiates of Dipri and the whole of the village.

In Sahuyé, Kamenan Adjoba forcefully underscored that the overriding spiritual power of women is innate and rooted in her genitals: "*The sex of the woman rules everything because it is woman who gives life to man. So it is that which rules everything*" (Interview, May 14, 2010). This is not only an assertion of the primacy of maternity, although the "firstness" of the life-giving female is one source of her claims to respect and certain prerogatives; the female genitals "rule" because they bear a preeminent and primordial power in their own right. As Djedjero Nan Lili said, "If it is woman who has the power, it is not by accident, because *God knows that it is by woman that the whole world came into being. She has power in her. Therefore she can push back evil*" (Interview in Orbaff, June 2010). That is to say, God conferred upon woman her natural generative capacity and maternity *as a consequence* of the fact that she has moral authority and not the reverse.

Another Yoruba case illustrates that the female genitalia are not only the source of fecundity and creation but also of spiritual might. The Yoruba Festival of Edì hails the goddess Mọrèmi as the only power capable of expelling evil from the community (Olupona 2011, 203). Her story is a classic tale of a heroic sacrifice that delivers the Yoruba of Ile-Ife from repeated incursions and enslavement by the neighboring Igbo. Mọrèmi used her beauty and seductive powers to wed the enemy king to discover the secret of his warriors' might and reveal their magic to her people. After their triumph, she fulfills a vow made to the divinity of the river in exchange for a benediction of her exploits. Mọrèmi sacrifices her only child. For both her captivating sexuality and the sacrifice of her offspring, she is hailed by her praise name (*oriki*) as "the courageous woman who used her vagina to conquer the Ìgbò," or she "who conquered rebellion and overcame intrigue with her vagina" (207–8) Mọrèmi is also hailed as "the Great Mother." The title is certainly not meant to extol her as a nurturer, for Mọrèmi's sacrifice of her own child is "an aberration from tradition" (209). Rather, it refers to the potency of what the Yoruba call "bottom power" (222), a reference to woman's innate and overriding spiritual power instantiated in her sexual organs and its capacity to overcome evil. In Edì, the chief priestess who represents Mọrèmi makes the incantation "We expel and cast out all evils," to which the audience responds, "Our Great Mother" (210). Significantly, in this ceremony "prayers and curses [are] freely mixed—prayers to expunge evil and curses to guard against agents of evil" (217), for it is with curses that the Mothers use their genitalia as a weapon.

Nudity has profound ritual significance. "As in many African societies, nakedness for the Fon and their neighbors has clear cut religious associations . . . individuals undergoing important religious ceremonies [go naked]" (Blier 1995, 169). Nudity is considered to reflect the full persona, including the incorporeal essence, and therefore is featured in oath taking to signify "righteousness of the heart" or to signify the good faith one makes in undertaking a solemn commitment (169). In Egbiki the curse, like an oath, requires such righteousness. The female elders must be spiritually prepared for the dangerous undertaking, purifying their hearts so that their performative utterances are properly directed and strike with their intended force.

Relating the details of the Egbiki rite in the Adioukrou village Yassap, the chef de terre emphasized that the mothers' capacity to dominate witches' evil designs relies on moral righteousness, and they wear their nakedness like armor: "We ask the women to do 'Egbikng' to block evil and it is simply *sent back to that sender. . . . So all of them strip naked* and walk with sticks of wood [pestles]. At the end of the village they spill urine and do what they need to do with their 'thing' [gesturing to the genital area], and then they come back. *One must not try to go look at that. No. It's our mothers who are naked and so they are trying to save things*" (Interview, Meledje Djedress Philippe, May 2010).

The nudity of the female elders looms all the more powerfully in the social imaginary for its invisibility. Among the Yoruba, "spectacle means both actual sights and mental images of ethereal entities," and therefore, what is intentionally withheld from sight in a ceremonial context is often that which has the greatest impact on ritual participants (Drewal and Drewal 1983, 78). Therefore, visible access to the representational depiction of the Great Mothers is purposefully restricted. Similarly, the occult nature of Egbiki reverberating in the dark is a kind of spectacle of power. The *taboo against the sight* of the naked Mothers and their denuded genitalia underscores the dangers of their occult powers instantiated in their very bodies. As one of the Okpolu of Orbaff put it, "Before chasing evil away, the women cry out to the people, 'Go inside, withdraw!' *No man must see those women naked.* And when they do that work, if you do see it, ah, that's a bad thing for you!" (Interview, July 2, 2010). When confronted in reality with the appearance of the elderly women and moreover with that "thing" that symbolizes the power these women wield, the full force of their power is produced in the imagination such that, as we shall see, even soldiers bearing arms flee.

The Performance of Paramount Power

While the Mothers' moral power is innate, the efficacy of Egbiki nevertheless relies on its actual performance, and its critical features are well known and regularly cited as key. Beyond the nudity of the female elders is a constellation of ritual components that constitute the technique of appealing to FGP: *urine* or other bodily effluvia as a means of setting a spiritual trap of evil; the invocation of *a curse* and the use of a *pestle* (branches or stick) to enforce it as a means of spiritual warfare.

Since the corporal language of the body is the prime idiom in ritual, natural bodily processes become the focus of critical cultural meaning. So too bodily effluvia are used as a primary symbolic medium. In Egbiki the women's urine emanating from their naked genitals is in effect an extension of this sacred locus and equally charged and potent. According to Nane Lili Djedjero of Orbaff, to prepare Egbiki the naked women take a recipient such as an old gourd, urinate in it, and keep it for three days. Then "they swear on it, [saying] 'if anyone wishes evil, may it fall on them.' They curse, curse, curse until [they reach] the other end of the village. Then they throw away the pot. They *expel evil* from the village" (Interview, June 28, 2010). The curse is thus sealed with the dispersal of urine.[35]

The women's sprinkling of urine and bathwater to entrap their antagonists mirrors the lighthearted contest of the male "witches" who urinate to set an invisible "trap" or obstacle to thwart their competitors. The magical creation of both the unbreachable village boundary and the impassable waterway shows that the flow emanating from the genitals assumes world-shaping capacity. The Mothers' ritual gesture is done in earnest, however, because the very success of Dipri, including the playful contest of powerful males, depends on their protection.

Describing her participation in Egbiki, Kamenan Adjoba detailed how the Mothers' genitals and the potent concoction associated with them are indissolubly linked with the power of the Earth through the pestle.

To do *Egbiki* women use old pestles and it traps witches. In the beginning we wash—that which you mentioned there [the genitals]—*we wash in front and we mix it with* hot pepper and salt. Then we go to speak [curse] saying, "*it is woman who has the power, it is woman who gives man life [gives birth] and woman who makes life.* So if you don't walk and if you are not born of woman, and if you don't eat hot pepper, and you want to go kill your neighbor, then that which we are doing is going to kill you." Then *we sprinkle the water everywhere.* We hit the ground with the pestle. *The earth represents woman and when we use the pestle, it is a way to curse. When we strike the ground we implore the earth.* That's why we use the pestle. (Sahuyé, May 14, 2010)

The pestle connects the women's bodies with the Earth, which in many African religions is itself a divinity, and more specifically a goddess.[36] The Earth Priest usually oversees rites connected to the land, its fertility, and harvest (as with Dipri's celebration of the yam). In Egbiki, however, the Mothers pound their pestles to "implore the Earth" to enforce their own sanction.

Through their imprecation, this primordial instrument of culture and social order is used in the "wrong way," no longer as household utensil but as an implement for "magic" and its dangerous aggressive force. When the pestle is thrown into the bush at the outskirts of the village (the place of excrement, garbage, and death), normal social order is symbolically negated, and the object is made an implement for that other side of life, the invisible underside that is celebrated in Dipri. From then until the close of Dipri, no woman is allowed to use a mortar and pestle. The social world is reversed; witches take center stage, and primordial chaos is unleashed within the confines of the sealed village. The pestle then reappears in the hands of young male initiates who use it to demonstrate sék's extraordinary force. I witnessed one, for example, pounding "medicines" in a mortar placed on the back of an elderly sékèpo stretched out on the ground.[37] Afterward the medicine was distributed to women who wanted a baby. So the pestle, usually exclusively reserved for the women's domain, is usurped by men in Dipri and is made an instrument of male fecundity and power. An intriguing parallel use of the pestle as a ritual implement invoking female spiritual power is found among the Luvale of Angola. There a diviner never buys his divinatory basket, *lipele*, but has a woman weave one and then ritually "steals" it from her. She must *"curse the thief, striking the ground [with a pestle] to enforce her imprecations"* (Silva 2011, 46, emphasis mine). Without her curse, the lipele is ineffective. Because in Luvale lore a woman wielding a wooden pestle made the first oracle, the pestle stands for woman's spiritual primacy, while the ritual theft recapitulates male usurpation of female power. In this the Luvale rite mirrors Dipri.

While Dipri makes visible the miraculous powers of sèké, what remains invisible yet implicit throughout are the forces of witchcraft, the ambiguous spiritual powers in which women are said to excel. The ability of the *old women* surpasses even the spectacular male prowess of sékèpuone. That paramount force is the innate genital power of the naked matriarchs.

In the days leading up to Dipri in Sahuyé, I made repeated inquiries about Egbiki to determine when it would be performed and whether I might be allowed to attend or participate. One of the first elders I approached, Tanoh Marie-Claire, first equivocated about the rite and then refused to confirm that it would take place at all: "There is a proverb: 'when you go to lay a trap, you lay a trap and you go off and the animal that comes, you trap it. Now if you wait for the animal to come and you have laid a trap, the animal will see you and run for its life'" (Interview, April 4, 2010). It was a charming rebuke. My insistent prying was giving away the chase.

Later I put the matter before Begré Koffi, a cousin of my former husband. He was surprisingly obliging: "We consider you family. Since you are from the family, you can do it. They will certainly accept you. Ah, certainly. *Woman is woman*" (Interview, April 5, 2010). He qualified this, however, in a way that I appreciated only later: "When they arrive in a place, they stop. There they are laying traps. The [witches] are going to struggle with the old women to take away the traps. *So you wait for them to finish that.* After they've done that, you can join them."

When I later approached a female elder reputed to perform the rite to ask permission to join the Egbiki performance, Kamenan Adjoba first denied that it would take place that year; then she suggested that they had done so already. Her equivocations signaled polite refusal. So I expressed regret that I had missed the event, saying that I would have liked to walk in solidarity with the other women, and joked, "Then you would have had a story to tell about the naked old white woman who did Egbiki." She laughed and then taking a more solemn tone, said, "Sincerely, what you ask, even if it were to happen tonight, we would not accept . . . when you look at that small, secret place of the woman, it's sacred. Really, it is and a thing of the genie. So even if we were going to do it, even if you are a woman, we would not allow it. What we do is dangerous. We can't take our gift and open it [to reveal its power] because it's like a chameleon. We don't know what it will look like later" (Sahuyé, May 22, 2010).

Egbiki unleashes a dangerous power akin to witchcraft, and its evocation is intended to turn witchcraft back on its sender. If one is not spiritually purified and prepared to exact the rite with moral rectitude, the curse can turn back on the performer herself. Like a chameleon, the power can change from anti-witchcraft to witchcraft. This was the danger to which Begré was alluding when he counseled me to wait until the trap had been laid before joining the women. As one of the elders in Orbaff had said earlier, "There is imminent danger for the women who do that work. They chase away evil spells and spirits and *they will leave with their curse*" (Orbaff, July 2, 2010). The spiritual weapon is an intimate one that cannot be divorced from the performer and will work against her if she harbors within her any taint of the evil that is its target.

Despite the risk, the trap was laid. Cindy, my young Abidji companion with whom I shared a mattress that night, shook me awake. "Auntie, Auntie. Wake up. It's Egbiki." We didn't go out to look upon the naked mothers, though. I dared not risk their menacing reproach. Woman is *not* Women; not every woman has the moral authority to take on evil, or is adequately prepared to walk with the Mothers.

In his 1976 treatise on the Abidji and specifically on Dipri, Fernand Lafargue detailed the women's rite as a singular type of conjuration of evil spells used by the good *Angrèpuoné* ("witches") to keep the evil ones from realizing their intended harm. However, he identified the Abidji name of the rite as "*sokroyibè*."

> It is a very secret rite to which men cannot participate under any circumstance. It is undertaken by village quarter and both quarters simultaneously, from top to bottom when the conjuration regards the entire village, as for example at a time of war or *on the night before Dipri.* . . . All post-pubescent women can participate in *sokoribé*,[38] *but it is above all married women and the old women who take part.* The ceremony always takes place in the middle of the night, between midnight and four in the morning. *A small group composed principally of old women, those who have the highest authority in sokroyibé,* gather, an old pestle in hand, at one end of their quarter at the end of the village and sound a cry "Oooh!" to alert the population and surprise the witches who would have already undertaken their evil spells. (Lafargue 1976, 193–94, emphasis mine)

Clearly, Lafargue was describing Egbiki. One of the greatest puzzlements and a knot in my fieldwork lay in the strange fact that no one in Sahuyé recognized the word *sokroyibè*. The Abidji shook their heads and said it must be an Adioukrou term. The Adioukrou knit their brows and claimed they'd never heard the word before. Could the French ethnographer whose exhaustive study is so carefully documented have gotten this one detail wrong? And if not, what might account for the disappearance of the term over the course of forty years?

The first possible explanation was offered by Akpa Akpess Paul, a retired schoolteacher whose life-long passion for documenting the history of the Adioukrou people began when his grandfather would patiently recount these details and Akpa would transcribe them in his school notebooks. With a collection of such books on his knee, he shared his knowledge with me. Toward the end of our almost three-hour interview, he spontaneously raised the subject of Egbiki and offered an etymology of the word: "When there is a threatening event, one that calls for curses, the Adioukrou calls Woman. . . . The night before Kpol [Dipri], the old women go out late at night when no one can see it . . . and chase away all that is accursed, all that is bad, from the village. Only the old women go out, not any who could still have sexual relations. *They don't speak of it to the young.* . . . As they chase death, they cry out '*Lou Igb.' Lou* means 'death'; *igb* means 'depart'" (Interview in Orbaff, July 1, 2010).

From this root the name of the ceremony eventually became known as *Igbikn*, meaning the one who makes [evil] depart or "one who bars the way to all that is accursed." Asked about the term *sokroyibè*, Akpa surmised that yibè, which ends with an aspirated sound (è), corresponds to *igb*, and was the original name of the rite. More likely is that *sokroyibè* was actually the *name of the society of women* authorized to perform the rite. A clue lies in Lafargue's description of the event, and in particular the assertion that "a small group *composed principally of old women, those who have the highest authority* in *sokroyibé*, gather" (Lafargue 1976, 193–94, emphasis mine). The proposition suggests that they held rank and therefore authority "*in sokroyibé*," as opposed to possessing the authority to *perform sokroyibé*.[39]

In actuality, the term is *Baoulé*. A study by French ethnopsychiatrist François Laplantine defines *sokroyibé* (with an accent *aigu*, marked from lower left to upper right) as "a rite used to fight witches during which the women of the village use their genitals which in Baoulé country are considered as a supremely powerful fetish" (Laplantine 2007, 161). He underscores that it is taboo for a man to view the rite (141). The Baoulé origin is a further indication of the strong Akan and matrifocal influence on Abidji culture and practice, especially relating to the spiritual and supranatural domain.

Ultimately, what Akpa thought might best account for the puzzling disappearance of the term *sokroyibè* was the simple fact that traditions were being lost to collective forgetting. What he lamented most was that the church demonizes these traditions, while relegating evil to a spiritual source beyond human intervention. So they were being increasingly neglected and were disappearing.

In the past the rite that the old women performed naked was always done, but people boycotted it because of the Church. The Church called it Satanic. Even Kpol, they say is Satanic. "Why spill blood? The blood that Jesus shed is enough," [they say]. While there is good and evil, they come from [human] actions, things that are truly praiseworthy and bad acts that are not desirable. What they did in the old days was good. Today, the rite that the old women performed naked, they neglect that, but these things are real. . . . We are losing a lot of things. (Orbaff, July 1, 2010)

His lament echoed that of Kamenan Adjoba, who had strutted back and forth in the courtyard at the end of our interview, bewailing the increasing neglect of Egbiki: "Last year there were only four of us who did it. Most of the others said, 'We go to church and we don't do that now.' But when the women do it, it is to protect everyone. It is dangerous. Why should four of us suffer to do it all? When we go to church they say we can't do it" (Sahuyé, May 14, 2010).

The progressive erosion of women's power such as the elimination of women's titles of rank and prestige by Christian missionaries and colonial administrators is well known and beyond the purview of the present discussion, except to acknowledge that African women did not accept this situation without protest.[40] Many of the documented cases of FGP are occasions of strong rebuke in the context of overt political manifestations. Ironically, in response to their forceful protests, women's societies and their collective mobilizations were in some cases outlawed and eliminated by force.

Nevertheless, Egbiki remains an independent rite, and its performers are not answerable to any higher authority or office. The Mothers mobilize themselves or are called upon to perform what they alone can achieve. As the elder in Orbaff, Djedjero Nane Lili, said, she and others take the initiative to undertake Egbiki "as soon as we see the evil. We cry out in the village and invoke the ceremony to push it back" (June 28, 2010). The village masters of the genie's power (the Okpolu) also emphasized that Egbiki is not a mere subset of Dipri but plays a critical role beyond the context of the festival: "In Orbaff, [Egbiki] is done, but it is *different from what the Okpolu do*. It has nothing to do with what [that]. It is a *supplementary precaution* that the women do the rite. It does not belong to Kpol [Dipri]. *They can also do it on other occasions. Whenever there is a real evil*, these women come out at midnight and they are naked and they do that work. They chase it away. *Women take the decision to do it*" (Interview in Orbaff, July 2, 2010).

Although they command the kind of knowledge and power that supersedes that of ritual specialists like the Earth Priest (chef de terre), these women occupy no public office. Their authoritative force is derived from the common local understandings of the world-making potential embodied in the altar of their sex. The predominance of FGP is attested to by the independence of the rite. The transformative capacity of FGP is deployed at the most critical moments of social crisis to meet the demands of a pressing situation and exercised as the most powerful technique to uproot evil. As Chef de Terre Gnangra N'Guessan Bertin stressed, Egbiki is an independent arm against all kinds of threats to the community as a whole:

> They can do it the night before Dipri but they can also do it at any other time. When there is a threat [such as] an epidemic, for example smallpox, [caused by] someone who sent a curse or used potions [cast a spell] to kill people. Then, in the night, when everyone is sleeping, the women strip themselves naked and they carry wooden sticks or old pestles and they walk in the road while singing and calling down on the witch all that they can evoke. . . . *It's not only on the day of the festival. It can happen on any day.* (Sahuyé, May 7, 2009)

To this the village chief added, "In the old days, when there was a military draft, and the colonials would come to the village to choose young men in good health, in the night the women would chant, do all that he said, so that the White man wouldn't take our children. They thought of it as slavery." Chief Tanau's allusion to the political potential of the rite is confirmed in historical record of women's mobilizations and resistance that is the subject of parts II and III.

As we shall see, FGP is still being evoked in the response to the catastrophe of civil war and its aftermath in Côte d'Ivoire. The elders call upon FGP to exercise their spiritual power as moral combat. Armed only with their nudity, the Mothers confront the military in full confidence that *"the last word belongs to women"* (Djedjroh, Orbaff, July 2, 2010).

2. MATRIFOCAL MORALITY

FGP and the Foundation of "Home"

> While men in principle hold political authority and power,
> women control the ritual power that makes political rule possible.
> —JACOB OBAFEMI KEHINDE OLUPQNA, "Women's Rituals,
> Kingship and Power among the Ondo-Yoruba of Nigeria"

> The King sucks the breast of the Queen Mother.
> —ASANTE PROVERB, in Beverly J. Stoeltje, "Asante Queen Mothers"

The conception of the innate power of woman and her sex is not an artifact of a particular culture; it is not unique to the Abidji or to the wider class of Akan ethnicities to which the Abidji belong, nor is it limited to the traditions of Côte d'Ivoire. Moreover, the understanding of primacy and the potent force of woman is not germane to the spiritual sphere of religion alone. So critical is the construct of female genital power as an emblem of moral authority that it has been a keystone of structural rulership and the underpinning of political and social organization in Africa for centuries.

A persistent and preponderant misconception about women in Africa is that everywhere they have been martyrs of traditional society. Through the deforming prism of missionaries, ethnologists, and administrators, colonial ideology reduced the image of women to a cliché, as "beings deprived of the most fundamental rights, living in absolute submission, veritable beasts of burden, at the limits of servitude" (Djibo 2001, 26). This bias has informed even contemporary scholarship, including, and perhaps especially, by early feminists who on the one hand mistakenly presupposed the homogeneity of women as a group on the basis of their oppressed status while on the other hand portrayed the average Third World woman as leading "an essentially truncated life" by comparison to those in the "liberated" West (Mohanty 2003, 22). With these underlying presuppositions comes the concomitant and equally mistaken presumption that the westernization of Africa brought with it women's emancipation and their greater valorization. In fact, "while the asymmetry of relations between males and females, with the dominance of the first over the second, was not totally unknown in [traditional African] societies in former time, it seems that they are accentuated today, tending to worsen under the effect of the forces of modernization" (Djibo 2001, 16).

Historical records dating back centuries show that throughout West Africa, and especially along the southern rainforest region from Senegal to Cameroon, where kinship systems are either matrilineal or traced through bilineal descent, female power is understood to be primary and paramount. It is *primary* because woman is the progenitor, and the mother-child bond, which constitutes the basis of the family unit, is the source of a fundamental morality on which all society depends. It is *paramount* because the Mothers are understood to be the living embodiment of the ancestors and, as such, are guardians of that moral order. This ancient ideology has not only informed the nature of rulership of the great African empires and kingdoms, but also prevailed as the basis for leadership among the more typical stateless societies of Africa, communities that resisted hierarchical forms of rulership. The fundamental moral principles on which the whole of social order rests were most forcefully sanctioned through the ritual appeal to female genital power.

Without resorting to panegyric on the situation of women or creating an apologia for an imagined female "golden age" or even an ancient matriarchy in Africa, this chapter aims to demonstrate that at the foundation of West African civilization is the widespread and deeply rooted conception that Woman is the innate bearer of spiritual power, the seat of moral authority, and the provenance of legitimacy for worldly rulership. On this basis I argue that the concept of matrifocal morality is the grounding construct and orienting ideology upon which civilization is founded and represents the values of home. It is most strongly articulated through the fierce ritual rhetoric of the rite of female genital power (FGP).

Kings and "Women-Kings": Spiritual Empowerment of Worldly Authority

As was long the case in Europe, kingship in Africa was considered to derive its power from a sacred source. From Mali to Nigeria, when a king took the throne he had to be ritually invested with female qualities. In "Initiation, Royalty and Femininity in Black Africa," Alfred Adler (2007) underscores that both the rituals of male initiation and the investiture of kings make strong symbolic associations between the male subjects and Woman, inculcating and making them embody female traits. Transcripts from the ancient kingdom of Ségou (present-day Mali) indicate that the griots and other notables who controlled the deep knowledge behind the esoteric ritual code were clear about the ideas and values behind such performative engendering practices. Court documents assert that "power is female: to obtain what he wants, the king must know how to humble himself . . . to act with femininity"; they also state that "in the beginning, woman was born to be king. Man is only wood, without offspring" (87). As a result, the kings were "doubled" with a parallel line of royalty, overseeing a complementary order of existence. The first was "masculine, indicated by material show of force, the other feminine, enigmatic, as efficacious as impotent, and . . . that would certainly be called 'magical'" (Bazin 1988, 379). In the nineteenth century in the state of Ségou, the male persons in this second category of kings were known as "women-kings." These Traoré king-priests were structurally identified as women and therefore considered the source of power of the royal clan.

Among the Traoré clan the women-kings did not control military arms, "a notion that Malians of today [still identify] with the modern state and with its administrative apparatus" (Adler 2007, 81). By contrast, they were considered able to prevent violent conflicts or even restore peace by the force of their word alone; they were "equally charged with performing the sacrificial rites of fecundity" (77). The woman-king's acquired symbolic sexual duality enabled him to assume the moral attributes required of his office. He would wear female attire and comport himself with the humility characteristic of ideal womanhood to embody plenitude and completeness. Adler suggests this practice amounts to hermaphrodism (85).[1] In extreme instances of intentional gender conflation, a future Traoré king of the Bambara would be secluded and actually castrated. "Castrating the king is a means of 'preparing' his body and making it susceptible for different appreciations: one can see in it not de-virilization, a half-change in sex, but the means of obtaining a state of maximum purity to increase his power" (425). This was thought to be the case of the famous fourteenth-century king of the ancient Mali empire, Mansa Musa.[2] "The term *masa* [or *mansa*], when employed absolutely, generally refers to the office of a sovereign, whereas *ma'samuso* means 'woman-kings'" (378). Thus this legendary ruler was literally a "woman king."

The premise that royal power is derived from the female and dependent on identification with the spiritual domain in which women excel is also asserted in myth. One account tells how the Traoré clan, associated with the Ségou royal lineage, gained its political power through the maternal line and its female divinity.

The Traoré had given one of their sisters to a "genie," *jine*, in exchange for which they received power. Actually, this legend is only one variation of a great West African myth tracing the origins and the end of the Wagadu Empire (the former Ghana). [In it] the serpent Bida, master of the subterranean waters and master of the gold on which the power of the empire rested, demanded the annual sacrifice of a young virgin in order to continue to dispense its acts of generosity. The first of these victims was a young girl of the Traoré clan, which obtained royalty in return. (Adler 2007, 85)

The parallel to the myth of the origin of Dipri is unmistakable. Even the name *Bida* evokes the name of the Abidji founding ancestor, Bidyo. Certainly, the subregion has a well-established history of migration and cultural diffusion, accounting for similar mythic themes.[3] The story is evidence of the widespread "orienting schemes, and systems of presumption" (Rabinow et al. 2008, 107) that I suggest are still determinative in West Africa, namely that home is founded on moral authority with a female source.

The Malian myth and ritual together demonstrate that alignment with female power was deemed necessary for the state to gain political legitimacy and to use its authority judiciously. The institution of the woman-king and the small network of those holding this title eventually became subsumed by male-dominated kingdoms. They eventually served the community in a more modest capacity as judges and peacemakers, an indication that the power that they maintained was grounded in *moral* authority.

This idea that female power is the critical underpinning of kingship endures and continues to authorize the kingship and invest it with sacrality. Among the Ondo-Yoruba of Nigeria, for example, the authority of the male Oba (king) is derived from his descent from the famed first ruler, the *female* woman-king, Pupupu. Pupupu is believed to have been the twin sister of Oduduwa, the legendary founder of the Yoruba, alternatively represented as the daughter of one of his twin offspring. "In the origin myth . . . she was accorded the rank of a Yoruba king" (Olupona 1991, 26). According to tradition, she ruled until great old age, when she installed her son as her substitute, inaugurating male rule. However, every succeeding king has derived authority from his mythic descent from Pupupu. From this, it is evident that "Ondo society lives with the paradox of a suppressed female ruler and political authority that has been replaced by female ritual power" (Olupona 1997, 318).

Yet even in the absence of a female in the overt position of political authority, women have safeguarded the preserve of female power through a parallel office, that of a ritual ruler who presided over the spiritual domain. "Since the change in chieftancy from female to male, women nevertheless have the right to have a woman leader, Lobun, also referred to as Oba Obinrin (woman king)" (Olupona 1991, 47). Her status in relationship to the king is "described as a mother-son relationship" (Lawuyi and Olupona 1987, 102). Certainly it is more than one of maternal nurture, for the spiritual authority of the Lobun is so great that "the office of Lobun is surrounded with mysteries and taboos" (Olupona 1991, 47). She is considered "ritually pure, dangerous and ambiguous" (Lawuyi and Olupona 1987, 102). The spiritual supremacy of the Lobun is clear in that she is the "ritual sponsor" of the king (102). Her major duty is to oversee the king's installation (Olupona 1991, 47). In fact, "without the Lobun no king can be enthroned" (37).[4] The political authority and power of a male king therefore cannot be considered absolute, for it is bound to "an equally significant ritual authority and power which women control" (Olupona 1997, 315–16). For this reason, Ondo-Yoruba "insist that the 'source of ultimate value' is portrayed as female" (316).

Significantly, "Yorùbá society authorizes males to take on appearances perceived and valued as female"; it was incumbent on the king and male sovereigns to "parade in procession wearing female clothing . . . [and] braid their hair in womanly plaits" (Olupona 2005, 75). In other words, the Ondo-Yoruba king was made to appear as a woman-king and signify that he had been invested with the fulsome moral qualities of gender-surpassing beings. Nevertheless, the king requires legitimation from the Mothers to succeed. Olupona details a moment during a ritual of sacred kingship that clearly shows their power is supreme and must therefore be assuaged: "*Yoruba women of age and experience are endowed with 'innate' power*, and they in turn [offer reassurance] . . . knowing that *the king needs their assurance of acceptance*. The *king needs their consent and goodwill* even before he enters his father's own house. . . . Yoruba women are 'openly loved, secretly feared'" (Olupona 2011, 136, emphasis mine). The Yoruba associate such esoteric and ambiguous spiritual knowledge, especially in the hands of women, with àjé. "This power, which Western cultures often describe as 'witchcraft,' in Yorùbá cosmology refers more specifically to the power of our mothers. The Yorùbá understand that women possess innate spiritual power *to control males, and indeed the universe*, used to their own advantage against the assumed supremacy of patriarchy. . . . [the Mothers draw on] a means of activism to counter male oppression" (Olupona 2005, 80, emphasis mine). While he does not name this form of activism, it suggests the ritual prescription that is FGP.

In the Oyo Yoruba tradition, in precolonial times, "the *aláàfin* (ruler) of Oyó traditionally had to kneel down for only one person— . . . the *iyámode*" a high official of the female sex. Her office was "to worship the spirits of the departed kings, calling out their *égúngúns* [ancestors]. . . . *The king looks upon her as his father*" (Oyewùmí 2005b, 105, emphasis mine). With this detail Oyèrónké Oyewùmí underscores that in ritual context a person with female anatomy can be given the designation and office of a male, demonstrating gender fluidity in Yoruba society. She goes on to discuss the posture of propitiation in this and other ritual contexts, offering another detail worth scrutiny. "The propitiations and thank-offerings to the lineage ancestors during the first two days of the Egúngún (annual festival of ancestor veneration) are named *ikúnlè*. . . . [This posture] was the preferred position of giving birth in traditional society and is central to the construction of motherhood. This position, *ikúnlè abiyanmo* (the kneeling of a mother in labor), is elaborated as the ultimate moment of human submission to the will of the divine" (105). It is also the very posture that Yoruba women of Ekiti assumed during a public protest in 2009, when the Mothers deployed FGP to rebuke government corruption and election fraud (Jeremy 2009). This direct and self-conscious association between the appeal to the female sex in the traditional religious context and its deployment in politics, even today, demonstrates just how fundamental is the principle to the whole of social life and just how deeply embedded it is in the West African social imaginary.

Queens and Queen Mothers: Female Moral Authority

Despite the supposed "cooling quality" of female spiritual power, detailed accounts by early Arab voyagers chronicle the exploits of remarkable queens and legendary female leaders from Senegal to Niger, some who ruled as "hotly" as their male counterparts. Among them is the celebrated sixteenth-century warrior Queen Amina of Zaria (contemporary Nigeria), whose military conquests over thirty years expanded Hausa territory (Djibo 2001, 38).[5] History bears account of more contemporary but equally powerful women rulers in West Africa, such as the heroic queen mother of the Asante Empire Yaa Akyaa, who took up arms to lead the final military stand against British colonial forces in Ghana in 1896 (Barnes 1997, 11). While these cases demonstrate that African women were indeed forceful rulers, the focus on the military strength and exploits of female political authorities betrays the preoccupations of chroniclers for whom the great states, their dynasties, and battles of conquest are the earmarks of history. Their accounts obscure a subtler conception of rulership in Africa in which secular might was always tempered and conditioned by spiritual and moral authority, the purview of women.

The office of queen mother, even more prevalent in West Africa, overtly links the structural authority of rulership to the spiritual and moral power embodied in women. The use of the English term *queen mother* to African female rulers seems to have been introduced by the British, but the office differs considerably from that of the English Queen Victoria from whom the term was evidently derived. Etymologies of titles in various indigenous languages indicate that such an authority is the "female chief, the female head or senior woman of a matrilineage" (Gilbert 1993, 5). In dual-sexed polities that maintain a system of complementary rulership by a male monarch and a queen mother, the appointment of *both* rulers is based on female kinship.[6] Therefore, even the male monarch represents the matriline (Stoeltje 1997, 53). As the head of the royal matrilineage from which a king must be a descendant, the queen mother may indeed emblematize "the procreative power of royal women, without whom the kingship would cease to exist" (Olupona 1997, 323). However, the power of the queen mother does not reside in her actual reproductive capacity, for even a barren woman could occupy the role. "Were she to be infertile, it . . . would not disqualify her from the position" (Gilbert 1993, 6). It may well be her duty to sustain the lineage system and the prestige of her matrilineage in rulership, but she does so through the selection of her coregent.

Indeed, the queen mother's most well-defined and politically significant role was her prerogative to nominate a candidate for this office from her matrikin. Selection had significant ramifications for the clan as well as for national politics. Various competing clans endeavored to form alliances of marriage to create dynastic houses of royal patrifiliation even within this system of matrilineal succession. "Competition for the golden stool [the royal seat of power] . . . was endemic because there were no fixed rules of succession. . . . Consequently the rotation of kingship . . . followed the vagaries of effective political power and manipulation" (Aidoo 1977, 15). The rotation of kingship through the various lines of descent and the vagaries in structural power reflect the abiding interests of maintaining a balance of visible and invisible power, structural and affective alliances, and matrilineal and patrilineal interests. The complexities involved in determining dynastic succession demonstrate an intricate braiding of matrilineality with patrifiliation, such that male and female interests are twinned and inextricably bound in rulership.

If the queen mother is often mistaken to be the representative of maternity itself, the office is just as frequently imagined to be an institutionalization of the supportive nurturer. The error may derive from the fact that the queen mother's male coregent is almost always her junior in age and that she serves as principal *advisor*. However, "the queen mother's position was *not merely an elevated domestic role*, arising out of the mother-son relationship, as has frequently been assumed by anthropologists" (33n5, italics mine). Rather, she served by virtue of the "*moral* quality of wisdom, knowledge, emotion, compassion, all that *pertains to her as a woman* and is not bestowed by male officials" (Gilbert 1993, 9, emphasis mine). That innate moral superiority gave her unique prerogatives; she was the only one permitted to criticize him publicly in the court. Should he fail her standards, "she had the right to initiate his deposition" (Aidoo 1977, 11). Her vigilant supervision over the king, her right to challenge his judgment, and her ultimate power to impeach him, especially on moral grounds, all demonstrate that what might appear to be a subordinate conciliating role was in actuality a significant office with real clout grounded in supreme values.

This is also demonstrated in the nature of the queen mother's essential duties. In precolonial Africa, her presence was required "whenever important matters of state were to be decided. She also had to hear all judicial cases *involving the sacred oaths* of the state" (Berger and White 1999, 87, emphasis mine). Her leadership required that she impart the knowledge and wisdom that she embodied as "mother of the clan" (Stoeltje 1997, 58). The function and legitimacy of her authority derive from her moral power as head of the matrilineage. Therefore, while Rattray said of the Ashante queen mother that she is "the personification of motherhood" (123, 85), the office of motherhood and its qualities are distinctly more than that of a protective nurturer.[7] The queen mother's overriding authority was spiritual and moral.

The queen mother was also "entitled to, and did have, her own separate court" (Berger and White 1999, 87).[8] That she maintained her own military forces indicates the independence of this regent, while her military might clearly dissociates her role from that of a mere counselor or maternal support. Just as a male woman-king is symbolically made to encompass both genders, the queen mother "is symbolically in some respects not a woman, but a person with the innate quality of a woman who moves in a man's sphere of action" (Gilbert 1993, 9). Her royal attire not only distinguishes her from commoners, but differentiates her from other women as well. She wears her ceremonial cloth "draped in the traditional manner (much as a man) rather than a sewn blouse worn over a cloth wrapper" (6). So the queen mother bears the insignia of masculine power as much as she embodies her innate female power. The gender ambiguity of rulers of both sexes is thus made to reflect the qualities of amorphous spiritual beings and ancestors to share the fulsomeness of their power and moral authority.

In precolonial states of the Asante (Ashanti) Empire of present-day Ghana, the queen mother (*Oheme*) ruled with her male junior (*Asantehene*). Together the regents had jurisdiction over males and females respectively but "in recognition of the *Ohema*'s significant status, her stool [the seat of power] (*Okonua panyin*) was considered the senior one" (Ogbomo 2005, 51). That seniority of office was best captured by her capacity to advise, because the wisdom achieved by moral discernment is paramount. In contemporary Ghana, the office of the queen mother endures. Perhaps because power is usually conceived in the nominal sense, as an instrument that must be visible in strongly structural forms of authority, some maintain that today the Akan queen mother "has little direct state authority and her legal jurisdiction is limited and ill-defined" (Gilbert 1993, 9). However, it is apparent that her critical duty is still to assert her moral supremacy and vigilantly maintain justice. The "new king swears his oath of allegiance first to her," and it is only she who can unstool an unjust king (8). Presiding over ritual situations, she serves as spiritual protector against the immoral use of power. She is invoked in arbitrations as the ultimate judge, "creator and destroyer," making decisions on the basis of her moral authority as representative of the "weeping" ancestors who grieve over the betrayal of mandates (8).

Today the queen mother of the Akuepem oversees ceremonies pertaining to women and, most tellingly, is responsible for organizing the ritual performance called *Aworabe*, "a ritual to keep away disease or bring rain in which *nude women pound the street with pestles at night. This rite drawing upon women's dangerous creative power is rarely performed today* and the present Queen Mother does not participate in it" (8; emphasis mine). The parallels to Egbiki are evident. The consistent constellation of critical gestures, especially female nudity or genital exposure and the pounding of pestles, constitutes the essence of the evocation of FGP. Worth noting is that the queen mother herself does not take part in the women's ritual of FGP. Rather, as the structural ruler presiding over worldly matters with tangible forces, she bears the same gender ambiguity as a woman-king. Therefore, she relies on the Mothers to deploy their female genital power in the invisible realm on behalf of the community. The performance does not displace structural rulership; its authority is of a different order altogether.

In Nigeria, among the Igbo east of the Niger River, the dual-sex system was originally ruled by two monarchs, a male *Obi*, concerned with the interests of the male community, and female *Omu*, charged with oversight of female concerns. However, the Omu reigned supreme as the "mother of the whole community" (Okonjo 1976, 47).[9] The Omu had her own council of female titled nobles (the *ilogo*) who "could challenge male authority . . . until men capitulated to their demands" (48). These actions were not based on antagonism but rather were intended to reinforce harmonious relationship and adequate representation of the respective needs of both sexes.

In an interview in the early 1970s, the Omu made mention of a particular duty of moral oversight with which she and her cabinet were charged: "If there is drought, we curse whoever caused it. If there is sickness and people are dying, my cabinet *goes naked in the night with live brands to curse* whoever brought it. If there is sickness in the next town, *I do something* with my cabinet to insure that sickness does not enter this town. *There are medicines we make at the entrance to the town.* These are just a few of my duties. I am the mother of the people" (50). The reference is clearly to that commanding rite that I am calling "female genital power."

The preeminence of FGP as the overarching moral force is so fundamental to West African cosmology and the prominence of female genital power is so pervasive in society that some refer to the bilateral system of rulership sustained by the Asante and related Akan peoples to this day as a "covert gynocracy" (Pritchard et al. 2010). The appeal to FGP continues still in contexts both "religious" and "worldly."

Stateless Societies, Dual-Sexed Systems, and Collective Self-Rule

To this point I have been highlighting ways in which women in traditional African societies enjoyed positions of power within the structures of the state. Western history generally privileges these hierarchical social orders and judges the empires, kingdoms, and states, which most closely parallel the political achievements of the West, to be more advanced and a measure of "civilization" in Africa and elsewhere. Discussing African women's history, Margaret Strobel remarked, "Unless the group had a queen or queen mother or female chief, [both oral and written accounts of African history] usually ignore women" (Strobel 1982, 510). In the colonial period, "government documents tended to report women only when they are problems, as carriers of venereal disease, as prostitutes or illegal beer brewers" (510). An exclusive focus on empires, kingdoms, and other institutions of structural power would recapitulate the view of society that precluded colonialists from acknowledging the degree to which African women were powerful and enjoyed the status, rights, and privileges attendant to it in precolonial society. Moreover, these biases distort the view of African civilization in other substantial ways. Ifi Amadiume (1987) claims that what has been especially eclipsed is the predominance and importance of the so-called stateless societies. Not coincidentally, it is in such societies that women enjoyed the greatest autonomy and authority.

This nonhierarchical and power-sharing type of social organization long endured as the most prevalent form of governance in Africa and still persists as local custom today. However, classifying such societies as stateless reproduces the kind of epistemological violence perpetrated by colonial imperialism that rendered women, as political entities, invisible. The negative qualifier *stateless* necessarily forces one to conceive of these societies in terms of what they lack. Identifying them as acephalous, literally *without* a head or ruler, similarly casts them in negative terms and conveys the implicit judgment that such societies are inferior, lacking in strategy and self-conscious agency. With the formulation also comes the presumption that without a ruling head these states would necessarily have been smaller or less powerful than kingdoms. In fact, such societies were often more powerful and of greater size than the much-vaunted kingdoms (Amadiume 1987, 24–26). A concomitant insinuation is that such forms of governance were preliminary, or primitive, destined to be superseded by the more efficient style of governance embodied by the hierarchical state. Underscoring that such societies were self-consciously devised to reject structural hierarchy in favor of a more egalitarian system of governance, Amadiume recommends classifying such societies instead as anti-state. This classification has the merit of emphasizing that they were intentionally devised as an alternative to hierarchical rulership. But, I suggest that it perpetuates the basic mistake of casting this form of social organization in terms of a negation. Rather than underscoring their antithetical stand, I propose a classification that underlines the collective and cooperative nature of these systems and particularly the way power is shared between the sexes and cycles through age sets that govern collectively.

One option might be to refer to such societies as systems of *collective bilateral self-rule*, or simply as "dual-sexed collectively governed" societies. The "dual-sex systems characteristic of most African societies" were structured as complementary self-governing and mutually sustaining bodies, with each sex managing its own affairs (Moran 1989, 454). In such systems, women are not conceived to be "the complementary opposites or the appendages of men. Instead, women and men seem to constitute different orders of human beings" (454). As far as the women are concerned, "given the cultural constructions of gender . . . men simply cannot represent women and their interests and vice-versa" (455). Therefore, women's associations tend to their own political and economic interests and wield their greatest influence through their collective mobilization of their networks.

Even in dual-sexed systems that operate through parallel structures of governance, women's authority ultimately prevailed through the women's associations. In the case of the Grebo of Liberia, for example, the elected leader of the women's council, the *Blo Nyene* (literally "Earth Woman"), has the power to veto decisions made by the men's council (453). Her ultimate veto power over the political decisions of men gives her the kind of superseding authority that the queen mother enjoyed over male regents in the more hierarchically arranged sovereign states. The title "Earth Woman" associates her with the primordial divinity and source of all sustenance, while suggestively paralleling the office of the Earth Priest who typically oversees the religious duties that attend to land and agricultural fertility. As we have seen, these, in turn, authorize structural authority. Therefore, even in an overtly patriarchal and patrilineal society, it is female power that serves as the foundational underpinning.

A similar phenomenon was documented among the Igbo in precolonial Nigeria by Ifi Amadiume in her groundbreaking work *Male Daughters, Female Husbands* (1987). The state of Nri was organized around divine kingship. However, the town of Nnobi was maintained as an independent religious center that paid homage to the river goddess Idemili, whose cult was "superior to the cult of ancestors" (19). Its central shrine was occupied by a titled woman called "The Great Woman," the *Agba Ekwe*, who symbolized concepts of womanhood derived from the goddess (54). Although the Nnobi were a clan organized as a dual-sexed system, with men dealing with male affairs and women with female affairs, the women's council, *Inyom Nnobi*, ruled supreme, standing "above the descent-based organization" (57). This is because it too was headed by the Agba Ekwe. She was also known as *Eze Nwanyi* (female king) (174). As in the case of the leader of the Grebo women's society, she held the most forceful instrument of political authority—the right of veto. Unlike titled men, whose positions of power could be challenged, "the position of the *Agba Ekwe* ... was never disputed" (55). The overriding arbitrating power granted to the senior titled woman would have been granted on the basis of this elder's moral authority. This is made clear through ritual gesture: in matters of deadlocked quarrels, it was the Agbe Ekwe who "had the last word when she stuck her long pointed staff in the ground" (67).

At the clan level Nnobi society was organized according to patrilineal descent, yet the female line held a place of privilege. Children of *daughters* occupied a special category within the patrilineages. Identified by the title *nwadiana*, these offspring of women enjoyed special "honor, respect and indulgence" (63). At the same time, there existed a privileged *matricentric* bond among siblings who were "children of one womb." The "spirit of common motherhood" instilled an especially strong code of conduct, one based on truth, mutual respect, and justice (58). This intimate bond was enforced by "supernatural sanction," *Ibenne*, a deity without shrine, believed *to punish immorality or betrayal of the members with an unforgiving fatal blow* (62, emphasis mine). While Amadiume suggests that such traditions point to a prior and latent matriarchy, I suggest that they demonstrate an active and enduring *matrifocal morality*, identifying which bonds are most profound and what values are to be most revered. These values are fiercely enforced with the merciless sanction of FGP.

Women's Associations, Secret Societies, and Social Sanctions

What African women may have lacked in terms of structural authority, they made up for through the command of their innate spiritual force. This is "manifested in the general belief that, even though women did not have the real symbol of authority in the form of an *ofo* [an object held by titled people], their mere gesture of protest, either by knocking the pestle used for pounding food, or their hands, on the ground, could be very effective in causing sickness in the village" (182). Here again we see the pounding of the pestle or striking the earth as an invocation to the primary goddess herself for succor and the implementation of a curse that, launched as a moral rebuke, is without mercy or compromise.

Like others writing on the Igbo, Amadiume cites the notorious unwillingness of elderly women to convert to Christianity and their active resistance to the missions that attacked indigenous religious cults, mentioning in particular the "dancing women's movement of 1925" (120). Almost twenty years later, when a zealous Christian defiantly killed a python in violation of taboo, it provoked a manifestation of "indigenous female militancy" vividly recalled today. The women "marched half naked to the provincial headquarters, Onitsha, to besiege the resident's office. [Receiving an inadequate reaction] they returned to Nnobi, went straight to the man's house and razed it to the ground. . . . Two weeks after the incident, the man is said to have died" (122). Elsewhere Amadiume recounts the incident and specified that the women "put a curse on him and the following morning, he was dead" (130). While there is no mention here of genital exposure by the outraged elders, the defense of sacred values by "half-naked" women evoking a curse suggests that they were drawing on this same moral power.

Because theirs was a magico-spiritual power to expel evil as well as a juridical prerogative, women elders were often called upon to intervene in other situations of social crisis, such as epidemics, deemed the result of witchcraft:

"Among the Isoko at Iyede (Niger-delta) whenever an epidemic or frequent deaths . . . occurred, the male elders called upon the women's organisation [sic] to perform rituals. *Stripping naked at night the women toured the village cursing evil doers*" (Ogbomo 2005, 68, emphasis mine). As in the case of Egbiki, men were expected to hide and refrain from seeing this, and violators were punished. When the most general interests of society are in the greatest jeopardy, the rite of FGP is called for, commanding a power greater than the governing wisdom or even the physical might of armies could offer.

The combination of innate spiritual power, moral supremacy, and worldly savvy is one not easily countered. The force is best illustrated by an incident in Nigeria in 1977. When the Women's Council of Nnobi agitated to protest the increasing infringement of women's rights and duties, police arrested their leaders. In response, women were called to "war" and "the pagans were allowed to come fortified with all their sorcery" (153). Recognizing that the women's "institution was too powerful . . . *like a state within a state*," the police released the leaders to avert violence (153, emphasis mine). The association of collective action and militancy with ritual and "mystical" aspects of "pagan" tradition, such as aggressive medicines, constitutes the full measure of female genital power.

More overtly "religious" in nature than the women's councils are the so-called secret societies and other "power associations" (McGovern 2011, 74) that cut across the vertical axis of social organization. Elders who control esoteric forms of knowledge traditionally dominate these associations, the membership of which is restricted to one sex. Alliances of this kind in traditional West African civilizations include masking societies, which bear the responsibility for transmitting the deepest values of society through ritual and its associated plastic arts as a visual canon. Other such "power associations" include the secret societies of blacksmiths, hunters, and midwives (57). Throughout West Africa the concept of secrecy is less a matter of withholding information or knowledge than it is an issue of its proper management in the hands of agents authorized to handle its power. Knowledge must be shared only at the appropriate time, to those prepared to receive it in the spirit that ensures that it will be put to use in the intended manner (cf. Bellman 1984). The secret constitutes the manner in which knowledge is communicated and the authorization to transmit it appropriately. The duty of societies that control such esoteric knowledge and sacred power is a religious as much as a social obligation, underscored by the secrecy that surrounds initiation to manage the exercise of its practices.

All-female secret societies long served as a wellspring of collective women's power. Their secret was that they embodied foundational moral authority as a mighty spiritual arm. An example is the secret society of the Ibibio women of Nigeria, *Ebere*, literally "women of the land." It functioned to "safeguard Ibibio women against the tyranny of their menfolk" and protect "'the spirit of womanhood,' while the complementary male secret society was to defend the territory of the Ibibio people as warriors" (Ifeka-Moller 1975, 139). Here again we see an analogy actively drawn between warriors and women's spiritual warfare.

Another purpose of the secret society is to cultivate a new generation of youth and indoctrinate them as capable adult members of society. Initiation into the society transmits knowledge and inculcates values through a long period of segregated instruction and ritual. One of the best-known societies of this kind is the ancient, widespread, and enduring male society, *Poro*, and its female counterpart, *Sande*.[10] These societies, introduced to the region by the Mende people as early as the eleventh century, are vast networks extending across a geographic expanse that outstripped any of the ancient empires or states. The case of the Mende chief Madame Yoko illustrates the point. Taking command after the death of her husband, she ruled in Sierra Leone from 1885 to 1905. While "Mende women had a long history of political activity, which included becoming chiefs of towns," Madame Yoko's rise to power and control of significant territories was attributed to Sande (Berger and White 1999, 89). Even today the Poro and Sande societies transcend ethnicity and nationality as well, extending from Sierra Leone to Liberia, Guinea, and Côte d'Ivoire. Their deep cultural roots and widespread political influence are so great that such associations might be classified among the stateless societies.

Some scholars have maintained that women's societies were limited to relatively few instances and provided only nominal structural power while reinforcing the kind of hierarchy that favored male domination in society at large. Ifeka-Moller, for example, argued that women's societies "adopted the dominant ranking system of men when creating their own hierarchies of officials" and in so doing recapitulated the "pervasive power of men" (Ifeka-Moller 1975, 134). However, a parallel structure of governance does not indicate subservience. While both the male and female associations of this kind controlled "the secrets of political power and reproductive health" (Chauveau and Richards 2008, 519), the female counterpart is generally acknowledged to have been stronger (Bledsoe 1980; MacCormack 1979). It is a well-known ethnographic fact that in Africa the eldest and most senior among women are often initiated into exclusively male societies and may even ascend to their highest rank. For example, the all-male masking society of the Dogon of Mali (*Awe*) is headed by a matron who bears the title *Yasigin*. She is also referred to by the name of the primordial ancestress and mythic founder of the mask, *Satimbé*. Significantly, the power of these masks does not reside in the sculpted wood face covering or headdress, but rather in the raffia fibers of the costume dyed red to represent the female blood (cf. Griaule and Dieterlen 1965; Pernet 1992). Just as the age set relies on the women elders for empowerment during wartime, the secret societies, in inducting a matron as their titular head, reveal their dependence on the knowledge and power that the women command to the greatest degree. The phenomenon suggests that women elders represent the essential values and mandates that sustained the whole of society.[11]

The superiority of Sande over Poro is also evident in this way. Like Poro, Sande is a masking society. It presents a rare instance in which women make and don the masks that represent them and the cultural ideals they embody. Through its iconography, the principal mask, *Sowei*, communicates ideals of womanhood and female power. Its helmet style, completely encompassing the head, and the smooth distended forehead of the face are reminiscent of the swollen belly of a pregnant woman. The elaborately plaited coiffure is intended to reinforce the identification of woman with Great Mother Earth and her abundant flora, and detailed plaiting renders homage to the river goddess. The archetypal carvings at the crest, comprised of three or five segmented petals, spread like an exotic flower. Protruding unabashedly like the spread labia, the female sex is glorified as that most secret and sacred locus of female power (Boone 1986; Grillo 1999, 11).[12] The head of the Sande society is also called "Sowei," and this matron is not only a member of Poro, but holds the highest rank among all its members.

Above all is the secret of the women elders, an embodied knowledge that exceeds all other means to confront evil and restore society to wholeness. When the postmenopausal matrons perform their nocturnal dance, their manifestation overrides the vertical structures of rulership, including gerontocracy.[13] Their imprecations are stronger than all mere secular rulings and even surpass the authority of other spiritual powers. They represent the predominant force that cuts across all planes of existence and embody morality as the source of power on the African frontier.

Age Sets and the Associated Authority of FGP

The most widespread form of stateless governance in West Africa is the age set (or "age-class") system. Youth are organized into age-based peer groups that take no account of clan or lineage. While the age set system comprises both men and women, only males are initiated collectively. The rite of passage is designed to undercut any social rank or distinctions among its members to inculcate solidarity and cooperation, since throughout the course of their lives they will carry out their mutual duties as a group. As the eight age sets are promoted in rank (for example, every eight years through a sixty-four-year life cycle, or "generation," as in the Adioukrou case) they take on a different charge, beginning as warriors and ending as arbiters in juridical matters before retirement. Thus, the senior class of elders assumes responsibility as the principal governing body, serving in the capacity of decision makers and judges during the final years of its generation. At the conclusion of their term the successive generation takes their place, confirmed in a ceremony of collective promotion of all the age grades. The retired elders, if they live long enough, are reinitiated with the incoming youth in the new junior class in the subsequent "Festival of Generations" eight years later. Among the Abidji of Côte d'Ivoire, "Each age class is the 'husband' of the younger age class and the 'wife' of the elder class" (Memel-Fotê 1980, 60–61).[14]

There are marked differences in the details of the way that the different groups of the southern Lagoon region (*lagunaires*) celebrate the initiation into the new generation. Nevertheless, all of their Festival of Generations ceremonies do share common features, highlighting what is sacrosanct. One feature is the commemoration of ancestors and the consecration of initiates during a secret visit to the sacred springs.[15] The other is the pageantry of wealth during which the initiates are publicly paraded through the central axis of the village. The young men don expensive cloth wrappers (imported *kente* cloth) and tie silken scarves around their foreheads or chests. They wear heavy necklaces and other gold jewelry laden with traditional ancestral ornaments that have been commissioned by the family and handed down through successive generations to indicate the collective wealth of the matrilineage. Their skin is daubed with a yellow chalky substance representing gold dust. These details reiterate "the attire worn by the women who brought up the rear of the procession in Akye ceremonies, and suggests that the men were intentionally copying female attire" (Visonà 2010, 157). Visonà calls this "cross-dressing." I suggest their dress is not about mimicry as parody but is rather a ritual means to invest [Latin: *investire*, to clothe] the young male warriors with the powers of the matriclan that they are being called to defend.[16] As Visonà rightly notes, "Specific aspects of the preparation and the final appearance of the war captains, the leading warriors of each age-set, suggest that female qualities have deeper religious significance," and men are visually represented in association with them during the initiatory spectacles (158). The war captains, significantly "chosen from specific, prominent matriclans" (138), are attended by their mothers and grasp worn pestles. Most significantly, "*around the head of every Akye war captain was the quintessential female item, a woman's [red] loin-*

cloth," which, according to the elders, "*brought strong female forces into constant contact with the warrior's head*" (158, emphasis mine).

Among the *lagunaires* and peoples of the forest zone in the southeastern Côte d'Ivoire, the terms used to designate the institution of the age set and the showy ceremony of their initiation are very similar, indicating a deeply rooted common source: for the Abê as well as the Akyé-lépin people in the Lagoon region, the term used is *fokwé* (or *fokué*). The Akyé say *fonkwe*; Abouré use *fakwe*; the Akyan, *fotchwe*; while the Adioukrou refer to both the age set and initiatory ceremony as *fatchwe*. This simple linguistic survey demonstrates that "under this term *fokwé*, we are dealing with an institution that is truly regional" (Memel-Fotê and Brunet-Jailly 2007, 711). More significant is the fact that the term *fokwé* is also widely used as the local name for the rite of appeal to FGP as a form of spiritual warfare. For example, the Tchaman call their "traditional women's religious mystique" "Fokwè," and the Abbey refer to it as "Fakwè" (Bahi 2006, 99). The semantic similarities among the terms for the institution of the age set, the ceremony of initiation into a new generation, and the ritual of FGP reveal something fundamental about their common nature and purpose: their grounding in the moral authority that belongs to the Mothers and their commitment to serve the society founded on it.

In her observations of numerous age set initiations among Lagoon peoples during the 1980s, Monica Blackman Visonà (2010) observed a preliminary rite performed by Akye women in the village of Memni at dawn: "The women chanted, rang bells, and danced slowly in a circle. . . . I followed a group of about twenty of these women to the end of town, where they entered at the graveyard . . . to pour out libations. . . . Finally the women asked me to stay behind while they walked down the road leading out of town. There they threw away the refuse they had collected in the street" (145).

Later, her interpreter explained that "this was a ceremony called Gbona Api (from *gbon*, to curse), and that it was danced by women who were 'strong' (who had supernatural power) to curse sorcerers" (145). Clearly this is a version of the rite of appeal to FGP performed as a protective cleansing and comparable to Egbiki, the women's ritual eviction of evil through their curse. The secret aspect of their performance, shielded from her observation, likely involved nudity and the powerful appeal to their genitals. Visonà's further inquiries and the elaboration of the significance of Gbona Api made explicit the consonance with other performances of FGP: "When Gbona Api is performed at night, the women wear only loincloths, strike the ground with used pestles, and chant 'Bekania.' This links their protective ceremony with the nocturnal dances of the Baule and other Akan peoples (Vogel 1998, 59).

In many Akan regions, women who are faced with a major crisis such as disease or warfare will walk through the community naked or stripped to their loincloths. Men stay inside their houses so that they will not see the women's procession" (145).

The Gbona Api ritual precedes and protects the initiation of the Akye age set just as Egbiki precedes and protects the Adioukrou youth performing the dangerous feats of Kpol. But the degree to which FGP is the underpinning of the age set is most clearly exemplified by the close association of the women's rite as spiritual combat and the final ordeal required of age set initiates in precolonial times: an expedition to an enemy village to bring back the bloody heads of victims. During the men's expedition, back in the village the women, naked and smeared with kaolin clay, sang and danced to offer "magical" support of the warriors' mission (Memel-Fotê and Brunet-Jailly 2007, 712). Upon their return to the village the initiates also danced in the central square. Once they were ritually purified and shaved, the youth "inaugurated a new season of their existence, that of full citizenship, patriot warriors, having a place of autonomy and deliberative voice in the political assembly of the village" (713). With their simultaneous performance of mystical combat, the women elders not only protected the new generation of warrior-citizens but initiated them as protectors of the matrikin who surrounded them in the formal parades.

The Ivoirian ethnographer Harris Memel-Fotê claimed that "of all social structures the age classes seems *the least sacred*. . . . Given the fact that it has no genie, nor place of worship, nor interdiction, nor clergy . . . [and] insofar as they integrate and transcend the clans, the age classes are the structures that correspond *most to the general interests of society*" (Memel-Fotê 1980, 135, emphasis. mine). However, the fokwé, as an initiatory society, not only teaches techniques of war but, through its close alliance with the female elders, also empowers youth to handle military force as a spiritual as well as a protective arm of society. In a discussion of women's affairs in Côte d'Ivoire with Mme Geneviève Bro-Grébé, who was at the time a minister of the Ivoirian government and former executive director of the Ivoirian Network of Women's Organizations (RIOF), she volunteered that among the Akyé-lépin, and more precisely in her natal village, Grand-Alépé, the women's traditional rite is used more extensively as a protective intervention made on the spiritual plane: "In my village they call it *Fokwé*. . . . When there is a danger, women strip naked—but that's at two o'clock, or three o'clock in the morning that it's done because men must not see. Legend says that it brings misfortune to men who look upon it. So, it's done very late in the night to exorcise, chase away, evil" (Interview, April 2010). The village's website therefore asserts that "the Fokué [sic] is a practice that is simultaneously a cultural, structural and *sacred* institution" (Village de Grand-Alépé 2012, emphasis mine). Therefore, the knowledge that the female overseers of the initiation embody, and the spiritual power that they lend to the age set by symbolic association, give the fokwé a religious inflection. The women elders provide a *sacramental* quality to the youths' initiatory investiture as warriors.

Together, the age set and the rite of FGP represent the twinned defense of home—one military and the other spiritual. Given the overlapping terminology, Memel-Fotê implies that the age set system called "fokwé" later lent its name to the women's rite; however, I suggest that it was the reverse. Women's spiritual power had primacy and remained the focal point for social order, while the age sets, instituted to support that order, were governed by women's moral authority.

Mmobomme: FGP as Spiritual Warfare

In addition to shaping the structures of rulership in West Africa, the idea that women elders dominated the moral and spiritual domain positioned women to intercede in times of social calamity or upheaval with FGP. Its magico-religious force supersedes all worldly evils. An important case is that of *Mmobomme*, a "distinctly female form of spiritual warfare" performed by the Asante and other ethnicities categorized as Akan, a cultural group situated along the coast of the Gulf of Guinea (Akyeampong and Obeng 2005, 30). In times of war, Asante women would perform daily ritual chants, proceeding through the villages in partial nudity and pounding empty mortars with pestles as a form of "spiritual torture of Asante's enemies" until the male soldiers returned (30). Just as Egbiki's curses expel the evils of witchcraft, Mmobomme aimed to strike a mortal blow to the enemy. Documentation by "at least twenty sources written by European observers between 1784 and 1903 covering the whole region between the lower Bandama River (in what is now Côte d'Ivoire) and the Volta" indicate that women performed mmobomme widely (Jones 1993, 548).

Most interpreters recognize the religious nature of the women's acts, but in so doing ascribe to them merely symbolic significance. For example, underscoring that the women's "magico-religious gestures" imitated warriors' acts, Jones deems the rite to be a mock battle, intended largely to provide spiritual support to actual warfare: "*omen carried fufu pestles to the crossroads outside the town, in order to remove misfortune. They might also stage a mock battle*: in 1784, for instance, the women of Accra fought one another with wooden sabres while their men were at war; in Akropong a century later the women, having tied cords and other objects around their feet, fought one another with whips shaped like guns" (552, emphasis mine).

Yet, as we have seen in Egbiki, the act of carrying, pounding, and discarding pestles is critical to women's spiritual battle against evil, with consequences equally dire hanging in the balance. Therefore, the pestle here appears to be more than a symbolic element of a "mock battle," but an actual arm used in a real battle fought on a spiritual plane.[17] For this very reason, "'in Asante, at least, the women responsible for mmobomme were obliged to lead the same sort of ascetic life as the men in the war camp—eating no tomatoes, for instance, and bathing only in cold water' (Ramseyer and Kuhne 1875, 292–93)" (Jones 1993, 556). That is, the women, whose action was deemed to have actual instrumental force, were not only engaged in support of the real war fought by men, but in a parallel kind of warfare.

If women's spiritual warfare is made consonant with male battles, their spiritual power is nevertheless superior, for it not only kills the enemy, it also purifies bloodshed. The Ndenye (an ethnic group in southern Côte d'Ivoire classified as Akan) perform Mmobomme when a pregnant woman dies, for "a pregnant woman is like a warrior who fights against death" (Perrot 1987, 168). So too, among the Bété, a patrilineal group in the south-central region of Côte d'Ivoire, FGP functions to ward off such a menace: "The death of a woman in childbirth is seen as a threat to the community as a whole and is therefore followed by a ritual ceremony in which *naked women drive men out of the village and assume power for a few days, subjecting the men to hunger and isolation*" (Perrot 1982, 32n1, emphasis mine). Only the rite of FGP had the purifying and sanctifying power to restore the grounds for wholesome society.[18]

Adjanou in Côte d'Ivoire: Warfare and Conscription

Among the Baulé (Baoulé), one of the most populous ethnicities in Côte d'Ivoire, women elders call their rite of FGP *Adjanou*. Enacted to evict evil and banish death, Adjanou offers protection whenever the collective is imperiled. At the same time, it is an act of spiritual warfare comparable in form and substance to Mmobomme: "The extreme case was that of Baule women, who at such times of crisis performed a dance (*adjanu*) in which their body was covered in white cloth and *only the genitalia were exposed*—a reversal of the normal state of affairs, when *such exposure was considered (by men) almost as dangerous as menstruation*" (Jones 1993, 557, emphasis mine).

As early as 1894 the French ethnographer Maurice Delafosse documented *Adjanou* (*Adjanu*). On that particular occasion, women gathered to perform it as a ritual of public excoriation of Okou, a local man who had violated the community's moral code. Treating him as the Asante women who performed

Mmobomme treated war enemies, the Baulé women stripped and chanted curses. Their song reviled Okou with overt sexual insult, accusing him of bestiality and impotence. Even as they abased him by ridiculing his inadequacy, they demonstrated their own potent "bottom power." "The women concluded the ceremony by making violent thrusts of the buttocks in the direction of the enemy country, singing: 'My arse (mon derrière) for Okou'" (550).

The public denunciation of a single individual may seem to be a negligible expression of power. However, such public rebuke could bring down leaders. As Amadiume noted, "If dictators emerged in the leadership they could not monopolize [power] . . . there were devices for removing them . . . [including] the Women's council and women's movement" (Amadiume 1997, 103). Moreover, the overriding moral authority of the women elders over the age set is most forcefully demonstrated by their use of FGP to shame men in this same way in order to press the men into military service. In precolonial Côte d'Ivoire, through dance and ritual techniques used in the war-dances of *fokwé* and the curses of Egbiki, the women would scorn and abuse able-bodied men who remained in the village during wartime. "The objects of attack were not only the enemy but also any man fit to bear arms who had remained at home. . . . *During their dancing the women would encircle such a man, shower him with ridicule and abuse*, and then perhaps beat him with sticks, stones, whisks cut from palm fronds or whips made of cotton threads. Women in Asante sang special songs (called *kosa-ankomee*, 'coward') which could drive war-shirkers to suicide. Alternatively, . . . *they might castrate him*" (Jones 1993, 553–54, emphasis mine).

The women's collective action enlisted men to support the principles and structure of matrifocal society, on pain of a humiliating social death. Clearly more than mere supporters of male warriors, the Mothers' moral chastisement actively conscripted men for the defense of home.

Matrifocal Morality: An Alternative to the Theory of Matriarchy

In her groundbreaking work *Reinventing Africa*, Ifi Amadiume contends that Western interpreters of African history, even feminists, go to great lengths to avoid reaching what for her is the obvious conclusion that abundant evidence supports the early and persistent existence of matriarchy. She rails against European feminists who make "derogatory dismissal" of maternity as essentialist and limiting to women's choices: "The very thought of women's power being based on the logic of motherhood has proved offensive to many Western feminists. . . . In the African system of matriarchy, it was women's means of empowerment" (Amadiume 1997, 114). It is this attitude that keeps Western interpreters from recognizing the principles that she claims are foundational to African society: "love, nurturance and protection derived from womb symbolism" (82). For Amadiume, the classification is warranted on the basis that West African societies have been founded on "a strong ideology of motherhood, and a general moral principle of love" (101). Yet we see that it is not love, at least not the warm sentiment of gentle care that Westerners generally associate with maternity, that the female elders manifest in their offices or collective rituals. Nor is their empowerment founded in actual motherhood. Rather, it is the principles of justice and respect for the most intimate social bonds for which the women stand and fiercely defend with ruthless righteousness. These bonds are rooted in the primacy of the mother-child unit and matrilineal kinship. It is the *moral principle* and not the social structure that is most vigorously enforced. The most compelling articulation of these principles and their most potent sanction is the terrible curse imposed through FGP. Therefore, I suggest that it is not matriarchy—the structural organization of society that privileges female authority—but matrifocal *morality* that undergirds African society.

Under patriarchy, women are so dominated and subordinated as to be objectified and reduced to instruments of exchange, but in the African systems that Amadiume calls "matriarchy" women never subjugated men in this way. In those systems in which women occupied great rank, African men enjoyed a parallel place in the structures of the social order. Even in overt matrilineal societies, men are afforded offices of governance. To reject the term *matriarchy* is not to dismiss the authority and power of African women in history but to recognize that under that authority there was greater balance between the sexes. We must look further than overt social forms and functions to the more subtle, "subjugated knowledges" that have informed the many complex forms of governance throughout the region over time. I suggest that the key to their organization lies not in structural arrangements at all, but in what Victor Turner (1969) famously called the invisible "anti-structural" bonds that make society cohere. More specifically, I propose that the stateless societies were founded on an ethical principle, one that forges allegiance, establishes cooperation based on justice, and fosters the means to thwart the menace of evil from every quarter. That founding principle is *matrifocal morality*. It is an irrefutable ethical demand, rooted in those most primary familial bonds, and vigilantly maintained through the sanctions of FGP.

As early as 1978 Wendy James made a similar proposal, suggesting that the term *matrifocality* best described the arrangement of a system as strongly focused on female power as that of the Asante, who are ruled by a queen mother and are matrilineal. She employs matrifocality to signal "the *moral primacy of biological motherhood* in the definition of social relations" (James 1978, 150, emphasis mine). The premise that I propose instead, *matrifocal morality*, modifies the perspective slightly, shifting from a focus on the centrality of the mother's position and the structure of matrilineal descent or rulership to a moral position that informs the ethical relations in all societies, regardless of the system of descent or the sex of the ruler. What defines that moral position is a matter that lies beyond the personal, affective ties to the basic family unit, however. As James herself recognized, "Even in the strongly and notoriously patrilineal societies of Africa, we may also find clues to the presence of underlying matrifocal ideas" (155–56). It is the precise nature of those *ideas*, extending beyond that of women's child-bearing capacity, that must be more fully articulated.[19]

A conceptual model to demonstrate the construct of matrifocal morality might be elaborated in the figure of a DNA helix in which two lateral strands stand for the discrete but parallel domains: the two "different orders of beings" in the dual-sexed order, men and women. In this analogy, these vertical axes are comprised of men's and women's councils, initiatory societies, and the hierarchical ranks within them. In these sequences, seniority is a controlling factor. What joins these two sides like the rungs of nucleotides in DNA are the generations of children, male and female alike, who come together in age sets. This secondary structure is interactive and responsible for the shape that the society assumes. In societies governed by collective self-rule, each generation comes of age and assumes its collective office to govern society as a whole. The rungs show the dual-sexed system to be linked inextricably. But their operation can only be fully explained by another, less structural, factor.

A tertiary structure (with no physical correlation in an actual DNA model) is an additional straight vertical axis suspended like a plumb line between the two lateral strands. This central strand represents an invisible but compelling matrifocality and its moral demands. It serves as the ballast in the midst of competing interests. This stabilizing force is vigilantly monitored and most vigorously enforced through the act of FGP. Its power is like the invisible stacking force that is at play in DNA, attracting the bases above and below it on the same strand and providing overall stability.

Ifi Amadiume comes close to suggesting such a schema, proposing that beyond matrilineage or patrilineage is "a third classificatory system, the non-gendered collective . . . based on non-discriminatory matriarchal collectivism, as a unifying moral code and culture" (Amadiume 2002, 43). The concept of matrifocal morality embodied in the "non-gendered," or rather *supra-gendered*, Mothers spells out precisely what this third system is and on what basis the moral code unifies various types of societies in West Africa.

As Amadiume made clear, the fundamental affective bond in West African society is not the nuclear family (father-mother-child), but the more primary social unit, that of mother and child. The tight stacking of the maternal bond and the obligations to siblings of one womb also informs the overall shape of society. It pulls the balanced order to one side, twisting the structure in such a way that its interests prevail. In matrilineal societies it is especially clear how the two strands of the dual-sexed order twist in a spiral descent as inheritance follows a transfer of goods through a familial line according to the identity of the mother of the inheriting male. Since inheritance is not passed directly from father to son but moves through the maternal line, matrifocality forces the staircase to turn to accommodate the diagonal direction of succession, and descent is slanted toward the female side. As a nephew inherits through his mother's brother and then passes it on to his sister's son, goods are literally rotated through the generations, with wealth and power revolving through maternal lines that connect the men (those who inherit or pass inheritance) and women (sisters and mothers who are the determining figures in the line of descent). The twist of inheritance across male and female domains more tightly coils the threads of society, drawing the fabric of interdependence tighter. Yet even in societies more complexly organized, the moral plumb line is represented by the senior member of the matrilineage or women's council who adjudicates and makes the supreme pronouncements of law.

In *Reinventing Africa*, Amadiume acknowledges this tendency for even dual-sex systems to tilt toward the matrifocal side. She therefore challenges the prevalent view of the dual-sex system as a "a 'harmonious dualism' between men and women," arguing that it "embodied two oppositional or contesting systems, the *balance tilting and changing all the time; that was the gender politics*" (Amadiume 1997, 93–94). Demonstrating the existence of "a flexible gender system, and a third non-gendered classificatory system," she implies that it mediates gender antagonism and "minimizes conflict" (129). By contrast, I suggest that it is not the recognition of the Mothers themselves as a third nongender that mediates conflict but the pervasive values of matrifocal morality that guide the dynamics of society.

Thus African social systems were hinged on an invisible principle, giving to its many forms a characteristic twist that is difficult to identify structurally. Matrifocal morality provides society with a stable system as long as the covert line and the principles that sustain it are respected. When social stability is threatened, the elder women, representing that central force, mobilize to restore order of this dynamic. With this model as a guide, the age set system too, so varied and complex, can be understood as the political scaffolding built to support the fundamental and compelling moral code. It is in defense of its principles that the young men go to war, while the women elders incite and support those young men with their own spiritual warfare, the rite of FGP.

Of course, the analogy is imprecise, but this DNA-like model provides a concrete vision for the kinds of social operations whose complexity and subtlety have caused them to be overlooked (by colonial administrators) or to be deemed too unwieldy to survive development. Providing for extended kinship ties, as required under matriliny, presumably poses a distinct disadvantage in a competitive economy based on individual effort, and for this reason, in the early years of development economics in Africa after national independence, it was suggested that increasing wealth and economic differentiation would inevitably lead to its demise. By comparison, patrilineal descent is so simple, its rules so straightforward, and its sustainability through one male's potential to bearing heirs with many wives so much less potentially problematic than a line dependent on one woman's fertility, that the persistence of matriliny cannot be readily explained without appealing to a compelling principle. As Mary Douglas observed, "The general impression of these analyses is that among kinship systems matriliny is a cumbersome dinosaur. Its survival seems to be a matter for wonder" (Douglas 1969, 123).[20] Despite the pressures of colonialism, Christianization, and globalization, matriliny has endured. Yet identifying the invisible principle responsible, and around which society pivots, is by no means a simple matter: "Society is more than a diagram, and where the matrilineal principle is enshrined, for whatever practical or symbolic purpose, the nodal position by women must be more than a diagrammatic matter. There must surely be evaluative connotations, *even a theory of the central focus provided by women* ... [and this] invites us to look further, not necessarily for 'female rule' in a crude power sense, but for equally strong affirmations of the central qualities, even the primacy, of women's position" (James 1978, 149).

The theory that illuminates the central focus that the Mothers provide is matrifocal morality. It is not an instrument of matriarchy, in diametric opposition to patriarchy "in a crude power sense," but a central and grounding principle that renders the social dynamics synergistic rather than conflictual. It is as much embedded in social structure as it is derived from a code of ethics. It is the integral but invisible balancing constraint on the patriarchal structure, "checking the development of totalitarian patriarchy and monolithism" (Amadiume 2005, 96). Matrifocal morality stands as the firm backbone of African societies, their complex rules of descent, self-governing rulership, and intertwining dual-sex systems.

With this brief historical survey and few examples, it is clear that the concept of matrifocal morality and its sanction through FGP has shaped structural rulership in West Africa and has served as a means by which women have both exercised political influence and enforced critical spiritual values undergirding society. In what follows I show how FGP was used across West Africa during the colonial era as an arm in the struggles against foreign domination, especially in situations that threatened women's traditional rights or infringed upon women's domains and prerogatives. Their appeal to FGP pushed back against the new structural impositions that ignored women as a social force, marginalized women as economic players, and undermined gender relations in a way that disenfranchised African women. These mobilizations continued even after independence as women sought to reassert the moral force of justice and make the postcolonial state accountable to foundational local knowledge. Drawing on documentation of those courageous interventions, I underscore that the struggle has always been at once a worldly as well as an unworldly spiritual battle, waged on the invisible plane, to rebuke the assault on the moral fundaments of African civilization.

3. GENDER AND RESISTANCE

The "Strategic Essentialism" of FGP

Honor to my mother
Mother whose vagina causes fear to all
Mother whose pubic hair bundles up in knots
Mother who sets a trap, set a trap.
—YORUBA INVOCATION, in Margaret Thompson Drewal,
Yoruba Ritual: Performers, Play, Agency

*Perceiving Women: Gender Ideology
and the Problem of Essentialism*

As a morally focused and grounding institution, FGP was a fundament of traditional social, religious, and political systems in West Africa. It established home, the place where identity and mutual responsibility are forcefully asserted and defended. Into this situation came colonialism and the Christian missions, whose gender ideologies challenged the very fundament of African society and whose institutions made women invisible. Colonial administrative records and historical accounts usually mention women only when they were causing trouble, failing to conform to Christian ideals of womanhood and Victorian conventions of comportment, or when African women actively resisted newly imposed subjugation. One significant kind of trouble the colonials encountered was the aggressive use of FGP.

In 1913 an editorial comment on the scandalous behavior of local women appeared in the British colonial newspaper the *Gold Coast Nation* offering a glimpse into one of the many instances in which African women resisted their displacement and domination with their naked rite: "We call the immediate attention to the Town Council to *two or three semi-nude women parading the streets from early morn till dewy eve.* It is, we presume, the duty of a Municipal Government, if it is a Municipal Government, to care for *the insane and half-witted* of both sexes. *The exhibitions we complain of are disgraceful in the extreme* and speak volumes of the unsatisfactory condition of Town Councils in the Colony" (*Gold Coast Nation* 1913, emphasis mine). The ritual rhetoric of FGP was lost on colonials, who could only see their shocking spectacle as an act of madness. The women's public nudity inverted the conventions of female modesty, but theirs was no madness; it was an exposition on the unhomeliness of the colonial state in the form of traditional rebuke.

While colonials failed to see African women as agents, recognize their roles of authority, or include them in avenues of power, the women increasingly made themselves visible by marshaling a strategic response. Throughout the colonial period African women mobilized their networks to take collective action in public protest. The evocation of FGP as the focal point of their uprisings brought the traditionally occult and nocturnal expulsion of evil into the public arena, making a stunning visual argument that the source of evil and the object of their spiritual battle was a very worldly power. It was a vivid castigation of the imperial order and condemnation of its radical incompatibility with the values of home.

As African women continued to resist colonial incursion and social injustice, scholars—especially female scholars—took note. For over four decades, scholars have recognized the existence of comparable cases of women's collective mobilization and protest across sub-Saharan Africa in which women made use of ritual bearing symbolic and structural similarities (Ardener 1975; Hunt 1989; Jones 1993; Lawrance 2003; van Allen 1972). Various instances of traditional mechanisms for shaming and social redress in response to abuse or sexual insult, the recourse to spiritual warfare, and incidents of rituals of female sanction in the context of political protests have been noted and compared, each offering a differently nuanced glimpse into the way that women embodied rebuke and enforced traditional values. However, the analyses were not sustained over a wide enough terrain, geographic or theoretical, to identify the most essential features or to decipher the full significance of the phenomenon. More problematic than the scope of study, however, has been the problem of gender and, more specifically, gender essentialism.

Essentialism assumes gender differences to be fixed and innate, assuming certain behavioral traits to be "natural" and inextricably tied to biology, especially reproduction. Claims about woman's essential nature or femininity are postulated on the grounds of sex, usually reducing women to the gendered roles they appear destined to play in culture as mothers. Gender essentialist ideology thereby reinforces a binary view of society in which women were always cast in a subordinate, nurturing role. Early Western feminists rejected such essentialism as demeaning. Postcolonial thought further challenged the way Western thinking readily homogenized all women into a universal category, effacing important cultural and even class differences. It maintains that any analysis of gender difference must be situated historically to investigate how gender is constructed in relation to power. For some, the category of gender itself is ultimately suspect, making cultural behavior appear naturally linked to sex differences, and argue that gender is nothing more than a performative trope. While gender criticism has provided openings for new readings of historical, sociological, and ethnographic material, the resulting interpretation is not free of its own distorting warrants. More recent gender criticism has exposed the enduring tendency of Western thinkers to make universalizing assumptions and project homogeneity on all women and especially on "the lives of women in the third world, thereby producing/re-presenting a composite, singular 'third world woman'—an image which appears arbitrarily constructed, but nevertheless carries with it the authorizing signature of Western humanist discourse" (Mohanty 1991, 33, cited in Joy 2001, 18). This pertains perhaps especially to works about African women.

Ironically, although early feminist scholars noticed comparative instances of FGP and were eager to make African women more visible, they may have been too encumbered by their own gendered interests to illuminate the phenomenon. They largely focused on the incidents as expressions of antagonism between the sexes, as rebellion against constrained social roles, or as resistance to women's political oppression. In so doing, they largely reflected those scholars' primary commitments: "At its most insidious, the literature on collective action is marked by a tendency to use African women's political protest and rebellion as a means of articulating western feminist strategies" (Hunt 1989, 363). Rather than perceiving *women*, what these studies actually illuminated were the motivating interests of the female scholars themselves as the "*perceiving women*" (Ardener 1975). That is, the gaze was reflexively turned back onto the observer to such an extent that the interpreter's interests became the real object of scrutiny.

By the 1990s, scholars were asking, "How can we write [women's] histories such that in making women 'visible' we do not blind ourselves to the historical processes that defined, redefined and engendered the states of the visible and the invisible?" (Biddick 1993, 390). In response, some urged reading for specific meanings in context and in recognition of "discrepancy, even contradiction, in the cultural norms and social roles" within any given society, "even if sexual difference itself is a recurring theme" (Scott 1999, 206). The attempt to problematize and historicize the category "gender" is therefore not new, and has since been ably accomplished by Western scholars and African scholars alike

(Amadiume 1987; Butler 1999; Joy 1998; Oyẹwùmí 1997a; Scott 1999). The latter increased awareness about how the discursive constructs about women and gender have been awkwardly or ill-applied to African cases and the stakes involved. They were especially effective in demonstrating that in Africa "in terms of social classification biological sex does not necessarily correspond to ideological gender" (Amadiume 1987, 112). None, however, provide a model that illuminates what is at the core of FGP in a way that links the cases across time and place to identify it as a single phenomenon. Even those who may see something suggestively comparable in the repeated instances of African women's mobilization and ritual actions may be shy of making any generalizations about women or claims on their behalf. As one such scholar studying Nigerian women's movements and their resistance to colonialism wrote, "We still have not fully understood the proverbial messages embedded in the songs, dances and verbal rhetoric of southeastern women in 1929 . . . we may be applying . . . 'retrospective significances' to these events, trying to make them more relevant to our own understandings and categories (including gender) than to those unrecorded ones of Ohandum [woman's association members] themselves. At worst we may be bending the meanings and values of Ohandum" (Bastian 2002, 272).

Gender essentialism may be an elision in the minds of the interpreters of women's acts, but is it also the case among the ritual actors who join together in solidarity by virtue of their sex? As Ifi Amadiume forcefully argued, "Middle-class White feminists have dismissed essentialist feminist theory or essentialism as limiting and stereotyping. Unfortunately, their arguments do not fit well with the African reality. For example, the traditional *African women's movement thrived on essentialism, using women's bodies and social roles as ideological and political symbols*" (Amadiume 1997, 179, emphasis mine). But to what does "women" refer?

A central aim of this chapter is to employ "gender" in "a theoretically sophisticated and critical mode" to argue that in making appeal to FGP, African women draw on their *own* "strategic essentialism," a self-consciously constructed gender of a third kind (Joy 2006, 14).

Following Amadiume's lead, this chapter takes up a close reading of various cases to suggest that at the core of West African women's social solidarity and collective action is their own "essentialist" self-understanding. It is *essentialist* insofar as it is defining, for both their identity and function; the special properties of the actors are the basis for their solidarity as well as the efficacy of their action. These female elders are able to perform FGP by virtue of qualities that are innate in cultivated persons of their age and sex (though not all make use of it).[1] Their self-definition and agency is based on a distinctive "local" understanding of gender that still has currency in the popular social imaginary. It is *strategic* in that it is manifest in collective action, executed to defend the moral domain that is their purview and the political rights attendant to their identity as the guardians of moral right and social justice. Not only is the execution of FGP a tactic of resistance by historical actors, it is also an expression of their own gendered identity articulated with performative eloquence. Their embodied and engaged self-understanding enables them to fight critical political battles and the gender ideological battles that are implicated in them. Therefore, traditional ritual exposure of their genitals is not only a key feature of their moral rebuke and spiritual warfare, but a key to their self-definition. It is this strategic essentialism that makes the various cases comparable.

Drawing on Foucault's genealogical analysis, this chapter undertakes a comparative reading of cases of FGP in West Africa, picking at the bits of ignored, discarded, or seemingly incidental details to reveal the consistent, defining principle that lies at their core. The aim is to show that these rites instantiate what Foucault called "subjugated knowledge" (Foucault and Gordon 1980, 81)—that is to say, "historical content that has been buried and disguised" by newly imposed regimes of thought (especially Western gender ideologies) or that have been suppressed or overlooked by those preoccupied with development, modernity, or globalization.

While many of the documented cases of FGP have been presented in anthropological literature either as isolated rites or local political acts of resistance, my aim is to "enlarge conventional understandings of women's political agency, and transcend the 'resistance' models that have often constrained understandings of women's roles as political and historical actors" (Lewis 2005, 382). A *gendered* reading of these incidents offers a deeper understanding of their dynamics and import. It shows that FGP engages gender strategically, as a mode of subversive disturbance. This approach suggests that African women's use of FGP itself offers a critical, "volatile mixture" (Joy 2006), embodying a unique appraisal of gender while engaging spiritual and moral matters in an astute and worldly way and under the most pressing political exigencies.

Among the first to attempt a broader sketch of comparative material, Shirley Ardener (1973) cites a 1929 paper by Edward Evans-Pritchard documenting women's ritualized obscenity among various peoples of southeastern Africa.[2] Among the Azande, lewd songs and gestures were common during joint economic enterprise (such as sowing, smelting, or beer making) and religious ceremonies (initiation and funerals). However, there were also women's rituals of social redress that involved genital exposure and "obscene expressions of abuse"; moreover, these were autonomous. On such occasions, the women were reported to *"tear off their grass covering from over the genitals and rush naked* after the intruder, *shouting obscene insults* at him and *making licentious gestures"* (Evans-Pritchard 1929, 320, emphasis mine).[3] Ardener underscored that the so-called "obscenities are merely signals conveying a message which is not obscene" (Ardener 1973, 436). She recognized that the purpose was not only to protest infringement of women's prerogatives but also to assert an essential womanhood, separate from women's reproductive power and distinct from motherhood: "[Ritual obscenity] arose in cases where *neither women's rights nor their functions as mothers, was the basic issue:* this was of another kind. I venture to suggest that it was the *dignity of a concept* which they considered valuable and beautiful—the dignity of their sexual identity of the order of that which I have called 'femineity' *and of which the symbol was their unique sexual anatomy"* (436, emphasis mine). The observation that the concept being defended was one *beyond the sanctity of motherhood* was especially astute. Unlike most other interpreters who insisted on the essentialism of these ritual actors "as procreators and mothers," Ardener perceived African women to be committed to the dignity of their sex conceived apart from biological reproduction or the estate of motherhood.

The often-reiterated reading of maternity as the motivating impulse and organizing force behind the women's collective mobilizations does not do justice to the religious conception about the nature of power or sufficiently attend to West African gender ideology that informed the whole fabric of indigenous culture. Yet the association of the female genitalia with women's reproductive function and maternity seemed to many all too "natural" to be questioned. Social historian Nancy Hunt (1989) lamented that Ardener's line of analysis was not pursued by other scholars. "Unfortunately [Ardener's] argument about the use of sexual insult as a symbolic 'means of enhancing dignity' has been lost in most of the subsequent historiography. The argument becomes a mechanistic one of tracing temporal continuities or arguing about conservative tendencies rather than *using the phenomenon of sexual insult as an entry point* by which to enquire into *the content of female belief and identity* underlying protest" (364, emphasis mine). Picking up this dropped thread of inquiry, this chapter traces such instances of female rebuke and brings into focus two critical aspects of their myriad manifestations to bring into sharper relief the seemingly elusive essence of FGP.

First, the gender in question is not woman as such but postmenopausal elders as persons embodying a different category of gender altogether. However compelling is the maternal instinct, and no matter how important maternity was and continues to be in Africa for women's social status, it is not women's common lot as actual mothers that defines those who engage in this form of sanction. The second, related aspect of the phenomenon is the *aggressive* nature of the rite and its stylized gestures of menace that demonstrate that its purpose is spiritual *warfare*. The actors do not act with maternal care or nurture. F G P is a merciless arm wielded whenever the defining morality of society is defiled.

Comparative Cases in Nigeria: Moral Insult as the Seat of Colonial Rebellion

In precolonial Nigeria, as elsewhere in West Africa, women organized to express their collective outrage over the abuse of a particular woman (as in a case of domestic violence), the verbal abuse of women generally (particularly any insult to a women's private parts), or an injustice that infringed on women's rights or prerogatives. Usually, these offenses were committed by men.[4] The mandated response was a ritual of condemnation and retribution displaying paradigmatic features of F G P. Among the Igbo of southeastern Nigeria, this ritual of sanction, appropriately called "Sitting on a Man," wielded considerable social control: "To 'sit on' or 'make war on' a man involved gathering at his compound, sometimes *late at night, dancing, singing scurrilous songs which detailed the women's grievances against him and often called his manhood into question, banging on his hut with the pestles women used for pounding yams, and perhaps demolishing his hut or plastering it with mud and roughing him up a bit*" (van Allen 1972, 170, emphasis mine). Of course, the late-night invectives against an offender, accompanied by the threatening gesture with their pestles and the aggressive verbal and physical assaults on the offender, all reiterate the quintessential actions of the performers of Egbiki whose actions are directed against witches.

In a landmark essay published in 1972, Judith van Allen drew parallels between this Igbo traditional ritual and one of the best-known instances of African women's collective mobilization: a series of uprisings in 1929 among the Igbo and Ibibio women in southeastern Nigeria against the threat of an impending British taxation of women's property (such as livestock) and income. The women's collective action had its most violent manifestation in Aba, a colonial administrative center. Taken by surprise by the women's seemingly sudden violent resistance, the British referred to the incidents as the "Aba riots." However, simultaneously alluding to their more strategic organization and to the deeper significance of their action, the Igbo and Ibibio called these actions the "Women's War" (Igbo: *Ogu Umanwaanyi*).

The symbolic consonance between the Women's War and the more circumscribed ritual of censure, "Sitting on a Man," shows that the uprising was in essence the same practice only on a grand scale and with a political agenda with national import: "Thousands of women showed up at native administration centers dressed in the same unusual way: *wearing short loincloths, their faces smeared with charcoal or ashes*.... Traditional dress, rituals and 'weapons' for 'sitting on' were used: *the head wreathed with young ferns symbolized war, and sticks, bound with ferns or young palms, were used to invoke the powers of the female ancestors*. The women's behavior also followed traditional patterns: much noise, stamping, preposterous threats and a general raucous atmosphere were all part of the institution of 'sitting on a man'" (van Allen 1972, 174–75, emphasis mine). The women's spectacular show of force was a literal revelation to the British. When the women gathered at Aba, not only did they "sit on" warrant chiefs, Africans who collected taxes and oversaw the implementation of other policies for the British, they broke in and released prisoners from jail and burned down buildings. Police and soldiers had to suppress repeated uprisings, and—in what one can imagine was an ultimate show of desperation—even called in the Boy Scouts as reinforcements.

For the British, the incident was a transitory riot. For the Igbo, the women's militant mobilization was a concerted act of warfare. The casualties were as calamitous as in any war, in fact: "Clashes between the women and the troops left more than fifty women dead and fifty wounded from gunfire" (174–75). Despite the fact that "the lives taken were those of women only—no men, Igbo or British, were even seriously injured," the British persisted in believing that the events had been orchestrated by men, and attempted to identify male instigators (175). Their blindness to women's agency persisted.

The deeper background of this remarkable incident indicates the degree to which the delicate balance of gendered interests maintained in traditional society had been disrupted by colonialism. The cash-crop economy and wage labor "brought increasing differentiation in the nature and rewards for work done by the two sexes," instigating or exacerbating tensions in society between men and women (Strobel 1982, 513). Two years earlier, immediately following the abolition of forced labor, a tax levy was imposed on men's wage income, the bulk of which women paid with "smouldering discontent" (Ifeka-Moller 1975, 131). According to the findings of the colonial Commission of Inquiry into the uprisings, the additional tax would have posed an untenable economic burden on women.[5] Just as important were challenges to traditional gender ideology that colonialism presented. In Nigeria as elsewhere in West Africa the colonial administrations usurped the most fertile land, conscripting its use for cash crops (coffee, cocoa, bananas). Privileging men as its purveyors, they deprived women access to arable plots, both disrupting the subsistence economy that women traditionally controlled and undermining women's economic autonomy. The usurpation of land typically under the purview of women or representatives of matrilineages, the inauguration of wage labor and economic policies that systematically disfavored women, and the creation of political institutions that rendered women invisible threatened the core of matrifocal morality. Women took recourse in FGP to signal their opposition and defend this core of society.

Writing in direct response to van Allen's thesis, Caroline Ifeka-Moller (1973) charged that the parallels between the local ritual and the war were nevertheless overstated, confusing two very different social processes. She maintained that the extensive, "inter-community mobilization of women" during the anticolonial uprisings surpassed the confines of local rituals of sanction not only in terms of their *scale* but also in their *inter-ethnicity* and the *pitch of violence* (318). Yet none of these factors is as significant as the symbolic consonance between the two phenomena and their ultimate comparable grounding in moral outrage over injustice. By Ifeka-Moller's own account, the women's behavior during the events of 1929 exhibited a "spiritual" dimension and a "remarkably ritualistic style" (Ifeka-Moller 1975, 133) for which she fails to account. Not only did the women destroy property and loot factories, they also "dressed in the garb of war, sang of death and blood, *gestured most obscenely and became spirit-possessed on occasion*" (Ifeka-Moller 1973, 318, emphasis mine). Such self-consciously contrived ritual and ecstatic comportment is clearly gratuitous to a merely political cause. The compelling continuity among the symbolic features of the local ritual and the wider sociopolitical movement can only be understood in terms of their deeper meaning, rooted in the local rituals of FGP.

The 1930 report of the colonial Commission of Inquiry also detailed the very particular ritual rhetoric that featured so prominently in the "women's war." One witness testified that "many women were dressed in sack cloths and *wore nkpatat (green creeper) in their hair*, carried sticks and *appeared to have been seized by some evil spirit*" (Ifeka-Moller 1975, 129). Another reported that at the trading center, Itu, "the women were *led by an old and nude woman* of great bulk. They acted in a strange manner, some *lying on the ground and kicking their legs in the air, and others making obscene gestures*" (129). An English lieutenant said that in another uprising in Opopo on the Niger delta, "some were *nearly naked wearing only wreaths of grass round their heads, waist and knees and some wearing tails made of grass. . . .* Some of these [reinforcements arriving by river and land to join the crowd] were *carrying machetes*" (129, emphasis mine).

These details make clear that the women were using the techniques associated with women's rituals of rebuke and redress associated with FGP, situating their power in the spiritual realm. That they carried sticks and machetes indicates that theirs was not a conciliatory purpose engendered by maternal concern—their aim was resistance, and their purpose was war, on both a material and spiritual plane. The reference to the uprising as a "women's war" in the Igbo language (*Ogu Umanwaanyi*) itself suggests that indigenous observers recognized continuity between the uprisings and the tradition of spiritual warfare, such as Mmobomme, which was the purview of women who alone had the power to intervene in the most dire of social circumstance. The action was pitched on a large-enough scale and force to meet the imperialist force with equal measure.

Confusing Conflations: Woman/Nature, Fecundity/Fertility, Womb/Vulva

Certain confusing conflations regularly appear in the literature that discusses various instances of FGP, all relating to sex and gender, and have posed problems for interpreters attempting comparison. The first is the presumed universal identification of woman with nature, a seemingly natural idea that presents woman as child-bearer who brings forth the social body, while man, by contrast, is the fashioner of culture. The second is the conflation of the symbolic association of female fecundity with agricultural fertility, a consistent theme of myth and ritual, with expressions of FGP. The third problem is related. The procreative power of the womb is not sufficiently distinguished from the physical seat of the elders' power, the vulva.

Gender criticism made overt the longstanding implicit truism in anthropological literature that "woman is to nature as man is to culture." It challenged this stereotypical projection of Western gender ideology onto other cultures as a blinding artifice. Amadiume not only disavows the equation of women with nature and men with culture in the African case, she goes so far as to underscore that in several West African cultures the very opposite has been true—that men were imagined to be creatures of the wild who must be tamed, cultivated, and controlled, pressed to the service of the sociable community of women (Amadiume 1997, 155). However, the enduring thematic association of woman with nature has presented obstacles to the interpretation of common ritual symbols deployed in FGP.

For example, Ifeka-Moller readily assumes that the vines with which elderly women regularly adorn themselves during these rites represent women's association with wild nature (1975, 144). In other contexts it is clear that vines and leaves associated with women and women's domains rather represent civilizing forces. In Dipri, for example, the particular vines and plants used for healing are those associated with the waters that the genie inhabits and are considered female. Similarly, among the Bron (Abron, Abrong) in the Tanda department of Côte d'Ivoire, bordering Ghana and Burkina-Faso, the elderly women performing the ritual of FGP called *Mgbra* carry the leaved branches of the Mgbra plant, associated with waterways, and don their heads with palm fronds, a common symbol of the founding of civilization in Akan territory (Ba Morou Ouattara, email communication on August 17 and 22, 2017, trans. mine). Therefore, vines are not intended to associate women with the untamed bush but rather with the source of civilization and the cooling, healing powers to sustain it. These, in turn, are correlated with the moral mandates that the women enforce.

A related source of confusion is the fact that in Africa the symbolic association between female fecundity and agricultural fertility is, indeed, a widespread theme in cosmogonic mythology that is reinforced in many forms of religious ritual. As we have seen with the myths of the origin of Dipri and Abidji civilization, for example, the yam is symbolically equated with the human body as it is gestated in the womb of the earth in mounds likened to women's pregnant bellies. This thematic association of woman, womb, fecundity with land, agricultural productivity, and social foundations is at the source of the earliest religious traditions that honor the Earth as a goddess and recognize the matrilineages as the only legitimate owners of the land. However, the very predominance of the theme may have obscured the very *different* meaning of the appeal to the female genitals, especially when the rite of FGP was executed as a protest against policies regarding land use.

Claiming that among the Igbo of Eastern Nigeria sexual values had remained largely unchanged between 1889 and 1930, Ifeka-Moller suggests that women's very self-identity was threatened by economic changes under colonialism. However, for her what was most disruptive was not men's new freedom from duty to the matrilineage or women's loss of control over land. Rather, she argues that in the early boom years the colonial palm oil economy brought unprecedented prosperity and that the new "emergence of female wealth" (Ifeka-Moller 1975, 144) aroused in women the anxiety that they were "becoming 'as men.' . . . *They feared that they were becoming infertile . . . and that the land itself was 'dying'*" (142, emphasis mine).

The idea that economic independence was new or menacing to women's identity runs counter to the well-known status of Nigerian women as the "owners of the market," the domain over which the women's councils had control and where women dominate and excel (e.g., Drewal and Drewal 1983).

Ifika-Moller's interpretation also seems to run askew of ethnographic accounts of Igbo tradition. Igbo on both sides of the Niger River operated according to the traditional dual-sexed system in which male-female complementarity was shared in all social processes—political, juridical, economic, and religious. While a male monarch, the *obi*, ruled the male community, women's concerns were subject to the rulership of the female *omu*, the "mother of the whole community" (Okonjo 1976, 47). The *omu* and her female cabinet, the *ilogo*, comprised of titled women, oversaw traditional female domains, including the market. Therefore, women's economic interests were not separate from spiritual and "religious" concerns, over which women had ultimate dominion. Nevertheless, the anxiety expressed in these terms points to the fact of rapid social change and challenges to traditional gender ideology under colonialism and illustrates how the threats to women's status and role were *projected onto the land*, the very foundation of home.

Indeed, there were "sharp discrepancies between what were traditional prescriptions for land use and the political realities" under colonialism (Diduk 1989, 347). For example, among the Akan, whose ethnic subgroups span a wide geographical expanse from contemporary Ghana to Côte d'Ivoire, "woman is the owner of the land and the whole of the wealth of the ancestral inheritance. The heir is only a steward and curator. He keeps it for the group. The true owners of the tribal realm are women. . . . [Therefore] the final word belongs to woman. Without her consent, any decision [regarding the disposition of land] is nul and void" (Dikeble and Hiba 1975, 383). The new policies systematically marginalized women from their decision-making authority over land use and denied them access to land, but also ignored women's traditional *spiritual* purview.

What is especially salient, however, is that the women activists who rose in response were *postmenopausal*, a state that is "consistent with a cultural precept that ascribes deference, mystical prowess and fortitude to the elderly" (Fonchingong and Tanga 2007, 126). Having surpassed their reproductive function, they are beyond the reach of supernatural assaults on fertility that witches reputedly target and that presumably the worldly evils of colonialism had also impacted. More to the point, the elderly women themselves embody and invoke comparable magico-spiritual powers. The act of calling upon FGP is considered so potent that younger women, still in their reproductive years, must be protected. This is the case among the contemporary women's society in Cameroon, Takembeng, which performs the rite of FGP as political protest. "Marchers are older women, although in my experience premenopausal and middle-aged women also participate . . . it is only postmenopausal women who expose their sexual organs, defecate, urinate, and so on. . . . *Takembeng women take great care to shield younger women from such actions*, moving them some distance away from their naked 'mothers'" (Diduk 2004, 35–36, emphasis mine).

When a member of the Takembeng was asked why *nudity* was an effective strategy for political action, the sixty-year-old informant responded that "they considered themselves '*kings* of the Earth' and 'architects of life'" (128, emphasis mine). The chosen imagery is particularly telling. Their power reigns over the entirety of creation, likening FGP to that of (male) rulers, with dominion over the whole earth making them tantamount to the gods. Indeed, power is demonstrated in woman's procreative capacity. But motherhood is not the power on which they draw. It is the asexual, gender-surpassing, supernatural power that the nudity of these elders evoke with their most potent weapon, FGP.

Essential to FGP is nakedness and the revelation of "women's secrets," her genitalia. The seat of the elders' power is therefore not the womb but the vulva (clitoris, labia, and vagina). Among the Ejagham of Southwest Cameroon, the oldest women's secret society, *Ekpa-Atu*, deploys the supernatural power, *njom*, believed to reside in the *bodies* of those elders, and makes clear that it is neither the womb nor its generative capacity that is its source. "The *vagina* is the part of the body to which this faculty is attributed. [Therefore] women's nudity is cause for great anguish for men. [Appealing to] their sex is the most powerful way for women to make their rights respected by men. *The power of their genitals is the secret of Ekpa-Atu, the women's society, active in the maintenance of their rights*" (Röschenthaler 1993, 183, emphasis mine). Traditional Yoruba iconography explicitly represents this same assertion about the seat of the Mothers' genital power: statues representing the Earth Mother, venerated in the Ogboni society as *Onile* ("Owner of the Earth") as well as the Great Mother, *Iyanla*, by the Gelede society represent her as "a naked woman with *aggressive characteristics*, such as *wide open labia* and what seems a *clitoris in erection*. This last detail would indicate . . . that the woman is 'as strong as a man'" (Witte, 1985–86, 305, emphasis mine). The famed helmet Sowo mask of the extensive and influential women's society, Sande, also conveys the secrets of womanhood in cryptic iconographic form. The sacred *sowo-wui* mask depicts a female head and ideal traits and qualities of woman. Its stylized coiffure is devoid of adornment other than the crest, typically comprised of three or five segmented petals. This can be interpreted as the splayed labia and clitoris. Far from a lewd allusion or shocking breach of decorum, the depiction is a glorification of the vulva as a representation of women's secret and sacred power.[6]

While young women may represent the creative potential of reproductive fertility, the Mothers embody an occult force of another kind, one that they unleash to devastating effect. The Tikar of Cameroon refer to this principle in a striking adage. "It is said that whenever a comet or shooting star appears, it is a sign that a woman has spread wide her legs to send forth her evil and direct it against men" (Ngoundoung 1999, 225). Tikar traditional ritual songs also relate that the dangerous female powers have a cosmic origin: "Salacious metaphors present the vagina as a sky that is brewing a terrible tornado, *an image of war* sent by invisible forces" (225). Therefore, when the elders display these sacred and secreted parts, bending over, standing and lifting their wrappers, or sitting with legs splayed, they are calling on the cosmic and moral force that abides in that epicenter.

What links distinct rituals drawing on FGP—those that sanction men for insult or moral injury and those that are potent measures to protect the community from supernatural malevolence or the evils of political catastrophe—is the ritual deployment of this preeminent power. The menacing destructive force that the female elders emit from their genitals is a mighty arm of spiritual warfare.[7] "In opposing colonialism all over Africa, women acted in the traditional manner *to defend the society of which they were the embodiment* . . . they did not rely on destructive weapons. In situations of extreme oppression, danger and anger, women *fought with their bodies by exposing that which is held sacred* and throwing excrement on themselves" (Amadiume 1997, 165, emphasis mine). The matrons' aggressive defense of the sacred principles of justice and moral righteousness with the weapon of FGP is what makes the two incidents of very different scope and aim—sitting on a man and the Women's War—ultimately comparable.

Comparative Cases in Cameroon:
The "Symbolic Template" of FGP

Noting significant parallels among the distinct women's rituals of three different ethnic groups in West Cameroon, Shirley Ardener (1973) compared their prototypical acts and traced their deployment from precolonial times to postcolonial protests. For her the contemporary mobilizations were patterned after the "symbolic templates" of traditional ritual. Moreover, the shared symbolism was able to "generate events from time to time in unexpected ways"—that is, to engender solidarity across various ethnic groups and marshal women's political uprisings (428). The instances also indicate the range of concerns that warranted the women's vigorous intervention. The first was occasioned by a rumor that the British colonial government was selling women's land to immigrant

Ibo from Nigeria. The second was the careless destruction of farms by cattle belonging to the nomadic Fulani to whom the British had granted the right of seasonal pasturage. The most serious source of contention was a colonial mandate for contour farming (plowing and planting across a slope following its various contours) to replace the women's traditional and less labor-intensive pattern of vertical planting straight up an incline. The intention was to prevent soil erosion, but the edict was made without consultation with women or consideration of their physical ability to comply, and those who failed to obey were to be fined (Diduk 1989). All the edicts infringed on land-use, the domain of women as the traditional food producers, and overturned the balance of the dual-sexual economic order. Not only did they marginalize women and threaten their livelihoods, the process upset the moral order. This double offense triggered the women's aggressive response, which drew from local custom that honored "women's secrets" embodied by their sex, and culminated in protests of a similar magnitude to the Nigerian Women's War.

According to colonial court records, the "native law of *titi ikoli*" by the Bakweri peoples made it a punishable offense "to insult the lower part of a women" or to reveal "women's secrets" (Ardener 1973, 425). "Titi ikoli" referred to the female vulva and in the Bakweri language suggested a thing "beautiful and above price" (426). At the same time the term referred to the customary women's collective militant action mandated in the event of any physical or verbal abuse of a woman or insult to womanhood. The women would converge upon the offender and sing *lewd songs accompanied by "obscene gestures,"* while the male reprobate would hide his eyes and other men would "beat a hasty retreat" (423).

The neighboring Balong shared this culture and ritual of collective retribution against an insult to women's private "bottom parts." In the event of an offense, they would "send a young woman round the village with a bell to warn men to stay indoors. [The women] will be angry and they will take all their clothes off. They will shame [the male offender] and sing songs. They will sing Ndungtuf Jinwefiga wa (I knock my toe, it hurts, meaning 'man curse me, I vex')" (427). While these observations are brief, the details vividly reiterate the dangers associated with viewing the naked ritual practitioners and present further evidence that the songs were not only meant to shame the man but were intended to bring distress upon, *curse*, or "vex" the wrongdoer. In essence these are *moral condemnations* more than economic protests or militant acts. The ritual rebukes aiming to restore the essential dignity of women shared key symbolic features with the religious ritual Egbiki: the taboo against men looking upon the female actors' nakedness, stripping and singing songs, and cursing the targeted offender.

The third case of FGP in Cameroon is the Anlu ritual of the Kom people inhabiting the Grassland Plateau at some distance inland. The Kom are matrilineal, and, consequently, "females occupy a prominent role" (427). "Anlu" is etymologically derived from the verb "to drive away," also categorized as a women's collective "disciplinary technique" employed against any man who insulted a woman's vagina or committed offenses of a sexual nature against a female. While Ardener insinuates that it is men who are driven away, I suggest that the etymology may also refer to the original moral purpose of such rituals, to drive away "evil," any natural force (illness and death), spiritual agency (witchcraft), or worldly action (insult or war) that threatens the good of the whole of the community.

Details of Anlu present both striking parallels to Egbiki and subtle differences. Its start is signaled by a woman who issues "a high-pitched shrill" that calls others to come running. The women are told of the offense committed in impromptu songs, giving rise to "wild" dancing during which "appeal is made to the dead ancestors of the offender, to join in with the 'Anlu'" (Ardener 1973, 428). The group retreat to the bush and return just before dawn, "donned in vines, bits of men's clothing and with painted faces, to carry out the full ritual." Singing and dancing, they proceed to the offender's compound, where they pour urine and excreta. "*Vulgar parts of the body are exhibited* as the *chant rises in weird depth*" (428, emphasis mine). One might argue that the significant *difference* between Anlu as ritual of rebuke and the invocation of Egbiki is the Kom women's shocking deposit of urine and feces, which may seem nothing more than a gross insult to answer the offender's affront with an indignity of equal proportion. But Egbiki also illustrates how bodily waste is used ritually in matters of moral offense to expel evil and trap malevolent witches. In both Anlu and Egbiki the excreta is charged with women's "bottom power."

In 1958 Kom women deployed that power when an overzealous local appointee of the British, a certain Mr. Chia, overstepped his local authority and sought to enforce the colonial order to implement contour farming. In response, "Mamma Abula" spat on him while the surrounding women let out a shrill ululation, "the Anlu war cry," and began dancing and singing (429). Mr. Chia fled but the women heaped vines and branches at his door, hurling insults and cursing him. From there Anlu enacted a performance of protest; the women went to the hills to set up a "demonstration farm" that used traditional methods in public defiance of the decree. By the next day, thousands of women had joined the fray, and the violence escalated. The women's coalition marched on the market, destroying men's stalls and driving them out of that prototypical female domain. In at least one episode the women took up *cutlasses and sticks* as arms in actual battle. In the ensuing months, the women set up their own court to deal with land use cases, but Anlu continued to rage, bringing police to arrest their leaders. To protest their sentencing, "two thousand women left for Bamenda, wearing vines, and with unwashed bodies painted black" championed their cause (430). The protests begun with FGP as a means of personal rebuke escalated to show its more far-reaching potential as an actual instrument of war, one that utilizes spiritual medicines (vines, branches, and sticks as well as women's bodies) to effect the worldly situation through unworldly means.

These uprisings were not restricted to the Kom. The symbolic consonance among regional women's traditions and their common moral purpose was able to "override allegiance to kin and tribal groups," and women from various villages and even neighboring groups would join to enforce sanctions (426). Among those who joined were women of the nearby Kedjom chiefdom, who drew on their parallel society, Fombuen. It "conferred respect and prestige upon women," enforcing adherence to their moral code through "disciplinary techniques," also called *fombuen*, and these were the vehicle for their mobilization (Diduk 1989, 341). The shared character and purpose among the women's associations and their respective rituals was clearly recognized by the African women themselves. Kedjom women were "quick to point out that, like the Kom, they made use of [fombuen] as a form of public ostracism and ridicule. . . . It is no coincidence that *lu* in the Kedjom language also means 'to drive away'" (342). African women's solidarity across ethnic lines is not unusual. Such solidarity would play out later as the women's traditional networks and rites were strategically leveraged in nationalist liberation movements.

The march on Bamenda was not merely an isolated event, either. Numerous acts of protest and marches over a period of at least eight months amounted to a remarkable cumulative force: "From May 1958 until January 1959 Kedjom women protested to their chiefdom political leaders and *repeatedly marched* in large numbers some twenty kilometres to the provincial capital of Bamenda" (339, emphasis mine). The women's persistent incursions ultimately triumphed, winning the release and dismissal of charges against their leaders. Ultimately, a female Anlu elder was seated on the local council monitoring land use, making this a rare instance in which the women took on structural power as an outcome.[8] Eventually even Mr. Chia wisely concluded, "Be careful with our mothers" (Ardener 1973, 431).

In 1932, when the French colonial governor of Togoland, Robert de Guise, announced a new tax levy on Ewe market women in Lomé, it was not only a difficult financial burden for these household providers but was also viewed as an affront to the rights of women, who had been to that time excluded from taxation (as they had been excluded from the political process in general). Their objections and warnings of reprisals, expressed via their male representatives in the indigenous city council, went unheeded. When the tax was implemented in January 1933, leaders of Duawo, a clandestine resistance movement, lodged a petition with the more senior minister of colonies. Infuriated by this challenge to his authority, de Guise arrested two of the leaders. "Within an hour, *as if from nowhere, market women . . . moved through the city* from the various markets in and outside Lomé, congregating outside the prison. *Marching, dancing, and singing, they chastised and threatened* the French and their African collaborators" (Lawrance 2003, 47, emphasis mine). As the throng grew to a crowd of several thousand the tone became increasingly menacing, causing de Guise to release the prisoners and eventually suspend the tax increase. The women's intervention did not end there, however. They ransacked the home of the council secretary, viewed as a collaborator. "Its wells were polluted, his name was cursed, and his family was *shamed by gorovodou priestesses exposing their naked buttocks and grinding along the ground of the enclosure* (a form of cursing known as *gbitété*)" (48, emphasis mine).

The following month military reinforcements were called in to purge the simmering resistance. Alleged protestors were arrested and civilians brutalized. The killing of seven people by a "deranged" soldier was seen as the culmination of this campaign of intimidation and repression. "It fell upon the women to oversee the purification of a city polluted by violence and death" (49). Women of the Vodou sect, gorovodou, were joined by others from the neighborhood to perform the cleansing ceremony, *dodédé*, called upon in times of extreme social crisis, such as epidemics, "to chase away disease and 'sweep clean' the pollution" (57). A Bè priest explained that the ceremony was sometimes combined with gbitété "as a vehicle of emphasizing blame" (57).

Lawrance sees in these events three separate movements and distinct types of display of women's moral authority. For him, the first, involving marching and singing, was a "broadly cultural and performative" expression of Ewe gender identity; the second, a display of "vulgarity and offensive gestures," was a shaming mechanism, while the third, the act of cleansing, qualified as a "spiritual and moral" act (53). I suggest these are all components of the single broader phenomenon, the deployment of female genital power. Together they enact the spiritual power and moral right that govern African society. While Lawrance presents the performance of dodédé as a reworking of a Vodou purification ceremony, the women elders' ritual expression of righteous indignation and indictment is simultaneously a spiritual matter and a worldly concern, targeting political and military evil as much as the offense of spiritual pollution.

As Lawrance briefly notes, the practice has endured in the postcolonial situation and has been repeatedly rehearsed as a visible form of resistance to the dictatorial dynasty of the former president, Gnassingbé Eyadéma, and his son and successor, Fauré Gnassingbé. And as recently as September 2017 thousands of shouting and ululating Togolese women, half naked and slapping their genitals and breasts in angry gesticulation or seated with open legs, demanded the immediate resignation of the president. "In a video circulating on social media, they can be seen dragging their buttocks on the ground at the entrance to police post" (MyJoyOnline.com 2017).

The documentation of FGP as political resistance shows not only its certain roots in the local women's societies and their common ritual of sanction, but also reveals that the material interests that the women defended were bound up with the offense to women as the *moral guardians* of society. Slighted by both the colonial administration and the male elite who benefitted from the injustices of colonial policies, the women took recourse in FGP as the most fitting and effective measure of redress. From their use in traditions of personal excoriation to their more extensive enactment in the public sphere as a mode of civil disobedience, through their escalation to the most militant form of violent confrontation, there is an unbroken succession of ritual performances in which women draw on their unique power as a militant force of righteous indignation and moral defense. Reading them as one phenomenon reveals the inextricable relationship between the religious and ethical aims and the more overtly political, worldly ends of women's collective mobilizations across West Africa.

Aggression: A Defining Quality of FGP

Persistent essentialist assumptions about the universality of woman and the naturalness of passivity and nurture as a defining quality of female gender impeded the understanding of FGP. The decidedly aggressive nature of women's ritual appeals presented a puzzling contradiction to those ideals about the feminine or expectations of women as mothers and still poses one of the greatest obstacles for an appreciation of this ritual expression as one defining female power.

A striking example of African women's disruption of gender expectations, and even certain local ideals and conventions, is the way the Kono women in Sierra Leone made use of the traditional institutions of the widespread women's secret society, Sande. While Sande is notorious for its masking tradition, which depicts ideal womanhood in terms of cool, self-possessed containment, the women of Sande showed themselves to be combative militants in defense of traditional women's rights and moral justice. In 1971 they used Sande to mobilize a protest against "the increasing competition for land and labor between their subsistence and cash-generating activities and the commercial farming of men" (Moran 1989, 451). The women made the preparatory rites preceding the society's initiation proper the occasion for a ritual of sanction that followed the paradigmatic *modus operandus* of FGP throughout West Africa. They paraded through the streets, donning leaves and hurling abuse at male authorities. They dragged and beat two subchiefs who had wrongly allocated land to men for cash cropping and protested men's claims to exclusive land ownership upheld in the courts. "Many women argued that there was no room left in Kono District for the women" and threatened to migrate to Guinea (Rosen 1983, 39).[9]

In an attempt to account for the aggressivity of women's collective actions, some interpreters have argued that their behavior follows the pattern of the classic "ritual of rebellion" (Gluckmann 1954) and demonstrates a latent but fundamental antagonism between the sexes. Ifeka-Moller argues that the shifting gender ideology under colonialism exacerbated this tension, threatening Igbo women who traditionally saw themselves as "domestic, pacific and dependent" (Ifeka-Moller 1975, 138). Like the members of Sande, they supposedly considered the "ideal woman" to have "a peaceful disposition . . . [that] mediates successfully in disputes" (138). For this reason "medicine used to resolve conflicts was said to be female and cooling" (138). But seeing "subservience" in cooling mediation does not properly appreciate the degree to which such capacity was generally regarded in West African traditions as a sacred value that ultimately translated into overriding power for women. For the neighboring Yoruba, for example, "the humble, submissive attitude of female figures" depicted in traditional iconography represents "cool domination of the creative and awesome *ase* [the vital force and cosmic spiritual power] of the mothers and perseverant self-control, much more than submission and male dominance" (Witte 1985–86, 308). The attitudes of restraint, containment, and "cooling" modulation are all indicative of the superior cosmic force embodied in every adult woman that "can bring death and disaster as well as fertility and well-being to human society" (305). This is the very force that the Mothers marshal through FGP.

As we have seen, during times of war, while the men were in battle women would perform FGP as a complementary act of warfare on the spiritual plane. In the absence of the men they also assumed stylized male behaviors, demonstrating what Adam Jones (1993) called "gender inversion." Drawing on documents dating to the early nineteenth century, Jones cites cases among the Baoulé and their Anyi neighbours in Côte d'Ivoire in which women would don men's clothing or carry long sticks or imitation weapons carved of wood and parody male behavior while the warriors were away.

> Women adopted the name of their husband or of a male relative and addressed one another with salutations normally reserved for men. Seated on the ground, they would tell tales of their alleged exploits in battle, each one giving lewd details of the (masculine) pleasure she would have in sleeping with the women she had captured. In addition . . . the women poured libations of water, drank water in the way men would drink palm wine or spirits, and then thanked the chief's wife with the words "Father X, thank you." Elsewhere women temporarily filled the political offices occupied in peacetime by their husbands, unless the latter were among the very old men who had remained at home. (Ramseyer and Kuhne 1875, 33; Jones 1993, 553n52)

Jones interprets such details as evidence of "status reversal" and surmises that "the thinking which lay behind mmobomme was somewhat similar" (Jones 1993, 559), symbolically enacting gender inversion. However, FGP does not seek to usurp male power or prowess, for it draws on independent and innate forces that are far superior. The women's parody of men seems rather to have *reinforced* social structure and men's place in it. Far from staging an actual contest of power, the women effectively held men's place in society open for them by occupying their position *provisionally*. The women's ritualized behavior was therefore not meant to contest male authority or replace men. Rather than antagonism, we may see in the self-conscious play a wry *performance* of gender. In an account by Delafosse, a French colonial in Côte d'Ivoire who observed these rites at the turn of the nineteenth century, the ludic quality of the women's lampoon of male behavior is apparent: "When drinking the water, the women allowed a little to trickle down on both sides of the mouth, just as a man would let palm wine 'flow through the whole beard on to the ground'" (553). Instead of gender inversion or outright opposition, such humor signals a minimizing disregard, and perhaps even indulgent tolerance, of men among them. In this posture of critique, the women's position of cultural and moral superiority is made visible.

While the women's mimicry as place holding suggests that women can supplant men, it is important to note that the reverse is never the case. As Jones himself notes, "Although mmobomme women might in some cases adopt men's roles, there *were no men to play the part of women*" (559, emphasis mine). This is a reiteration of women's ultimate preeminence. The rite of FGP most clearly demonstrates that only women's overriding power can drive out the menace that men are impotent to repel. At such times of crisis the female elders exhibit their unequivocal spiritual predominance. "When a woman dies in childbirth, it is believed that all other pregnant women are in danger. They therefore gather at one end of the village, wearing only a loincloth and holding branches. . . . The women set out to 'wage war' against the power which has caused a pregnant woman's death, shouting imprecations and begging the tutelary deities to protect them. They insult the men of the community, who are obliged to hide and whom they temporarily replace" (556).

It is significant that even during their collective mobilizations at wartime women "did not simply adopt . . . male 'models' [of war] uncritically. They also parodied them" (Diduk 1989, 344). For example, during their anti-colonial protests in 1958, Cameroonian women also donned men's dirty clothing, carried sticks to represent guns, and imitated male warriors. That the male clothes were soiled, torn, and smelly and their bodies smeared with dirt signaled a critique of men as beings marginal to the central tenets of a cultivated society. Their "comic caricature of male behavior" casts men in a disparaging way (344). It shows them acting outside the parameters of the moral order that is at the core of society. The women's displays exaggerated male behavior, and they took obvious relish in caricaturing and critiquing men. These sarcastic ritual parodies did not set women in competition with men, but distanced them from male domains and behaviors through ridicule. The women were therefore certainly aware that gender is to a certain degree *performative* and their comic depictions were subversive. They disrupted the "naturalness" of normative conceptions of gender roles, showing they "can be assumed at will, often with the intent of parodying established norms" (Joy 2006, 15). Most importantly, they contrasted the superior values that determine the crux of female ontology to men's while reinforcing their own self-conscious essentialism.

The fact that African women adopted aggressive behavior and military organizational structures during their collective mobilizations and protests has suggested to some that the female societies that performed rituals of FGP were *competing* with men and challenging male dominance. But significantly, when the women "went to war" against infringements upon their rights, they "did not demand to participate in male authority structures" (Diduk 1989, 343). Once their demands were met, the women's uprisings subsided. In other words, at least initially and in their precolonial contexts, women were not challenging a male-dominant social or political system. Their goal was to prevent encroachment on women's domains by calling for the fundamental respect for the values they embodied, a respect that in turn guarantees women's rights.

Confronting Gender Ideology in the Christian Missions

As we have seen, the governing structures and policies introduced by colonials seriously undermined women's autonomy and economic independence. Missionaries' Victorian attitudes and values about women's roles further curtailed women's possibilities even as they opened avenues of power to men. Even a cursory review of the influence of the Christian missions in West Africa on gender roles and social status reflects the way religion and gender have been mutually informing and mutually reinforcing.

A strong priority of the earliest missions in West Africa, both Protestant and Catholic, was the making of Christian families (Toungara 2001, 41; Leach 2008). Records of the Anglican Church Missionary Society (CMS) dating back to 1804 show a very particular ideology of gender was imposed on the system of education introduced to Africa through the mission schools—one that reflected the Victorian ideals of the white middle class, from which the CMS largely drew its recruits. While boys' schooling was subsidized by European missions, established for the training of catechists and priests, girls' schools were created belatedly and were not funded externally, but had to be self-supporting industries. Initially, and for quite a long period, it was the wives of CMS missionaries who were responsible for establishing girls' educations. For example, in Nigeria, "no male missionary had anything to do with the education of Igbo girls" (Bastian 2000, 147). Girls' schooling was inaugurated essentially to provide suitable marriage companions for the young male African converts, who were the principal targets of the missions.[10] The sole objective was to groom girls to take up their prescribed place in founding monogamous marriage and the nuclear family unit.

The European leadership was undoubtedly informed by the prevailing attitudes of the times and therefore regarded the education of women and girls as both a waste of valuable resources and beyond the purview of their mission. It was only after it became obvious that the young male converts could find no suitable wives that European women were encouraged to adopt the effort. The expressed aim of these women was to inculcate ideals of feminine virtue to African girls: "domesticity, conjugal fidelity and selflessness" (Leach 2008, 335). From the outset, then, girls' schooling was markedly different from that of boys. Not only were girls and boys educated separately (as proximity was viewed as temptation to sin), the girls' curriculum was academically restricted and dominated by sewing. Sewing was a means to prepare girls for Christian marriage, seen to impart patience, restraint, and order. Producing suitably modest clothing, the enterprise was also associated with the control of sexuality. *Gendered dress encouraged gendered roles and vice versa.* "Nakedness was associated with sexual promiscuity, immorality and heathenism; the flaunting of the female body was particularly offensive" (342).

From the missionaries' perspective, Christian schooling liberated girls from the so-called heathen practices of polygamy, payment of bride price, initiation ceremonies, and female circumcision, all of which were viewed as evidence of sexual licentiousness and demeaning to women. In Côte d'Ivoire, for example, Catholic missionaries lobbied French colonial administrators, whose policies attempted to respect African customs insofar as they did not conflict with "the basic principles of French civilization," to pass legislation that would guarantee women the exercise of free will necessary for Christian conversion (Toungara 2001, 42). They argued that traditional marriage customs were tantamount to slavery, which the French had outlawed as a violation of civilized principles. The decree that criminalized child betrothal by patrilineal elders without female consent and suspended bride price was nevertheless instituted quite belatedly, only in 1939. Ironically, such changes had damaging ramifications of their own. By restructuring African women's lives to conform to their imported gender ideals, missionaries unwittingly curtailed women's traditional social and economic independence, "marginalising—and in some cases impoverishing— them" (Leach 2008, 344). For example, both colonial administrators and missionaries promoted the Christian ideal of the nuclear family by granting men absolute authority over the marital household (making all property and income communal and subject to the husband's control). In so doing they neglected African women's economic self-determination, a right especially safeguarded in matrilineal societies. "Under the guise of protection, family codes reinforced patriarchal authority over women and children, and, in some cases, left women with less power than they had exercised under customary law with regard to their property rights and traditional economic responsibilities" (Toungara 2001, 54).

Christian values contravened customary expectations in other ways that particularly challenged girls. Christian rules of chastity before marriage ran counter to Akan tradition, which expected them to conceive before marriage as an essential proof of fertility. In the Akuapem state in Ghana for example, "the imperative [to demonstrate] fertility outweighed" the Christian mandate for women to defer sex in order to demonstrate "sexual subordination in marriage" (Dankwa 2005, 114). Therefore, the promiscuous behavior of so-called shameless women, sinful in the eyes of the church, was motivated by a set of social pressures on young women to secure social rank as a marriageable woman and to attain the respectable status of motherhood. Any shame that might be associated with conception despite having no regular suitor was transitory. "The disgrace lasts until the child is born. With its birth a girl becomes a mother and thereby resumes respect" (114). By contrast, a woman's eagerness to conceive subjected her to permanent exclusion from the church. Considerable hypocrisy regarding sexual license and infidelity prevailed; while "fallen" women were deterred from returning to a congregation, men were readmitted once they had paid their church taxes (114). Meanwhile, the lives of Christianized girls were hardly free. In the isolated girls' schools they were under constant surveillance, and every moment was scheduled or occupied by chores, including doing missionaries' laundry. From school they would enter Christian marital households where they were expected to be the subservient helpmates to their husbands, sometimes chosen for them by missionaries, who, not unlike patrilineal elders, "expected their charges to make alliances of duty rather than 'love matches'" (Bastian 2000, 152). The "model of domestic support and dependency" to which converts capitulated also undercut the separate social spheres in which women circulated and where they played active roles in society (152). While traditional women could become priestesses, prophets, healers/diviners, take up roles as "market queens," or be members of other title societies, Christians remained isolated in marriage (149). Moreover, they were severed from women's self-governing associations, which were a focal point for resistance to encroachments on traditional cultural values.

At the end of 1929, groups of Igbo women of southern Nigeria "began, in their own parlance, to 'move' about the eastern countryside," gathering political momentum to their increasingly militant political resistance to British colonial domination. The movement transcended local identity; the Igbo Women called themselves *Ohandum*, or "Women of All Towns" (261). "Since men and some colonized women had not heeded the earth deity's message, . . . *Ohandum* had to make a more direct set of gestures, putting their own bodies on the line to illustrate what social life ought to be" (267). While the women's rhetoric, "*not all of it verbal*," was subtle and not adequately or accurately transcribed into the colonial record, it is clear that the women made appeal to the "rhetorical flourishes and gestures" of FGP (267). They "sang 'abusive songs' . . . even going so far as to 'slap their tummies' in a derisive fashion" (260–61). "Slapping their tummies" and exposed crotch is a classic "obscene" gesture of rebuke consistently exhibited in rituals of protest that deploy FGP. It is significant, too, that both during the women's uprising and the interrogations of participants by colonial administrators in its aftermath, the crowds of women "would attempt to dominate the colonial bureaucracy itself by means of performance art, demonstrating the absurdity of bureaucratic form by parodying them" (265). In this context it is clear that the women were drawing on the traditional performative parody of men to contest their oppression and challenge the legitimacy of male authority as one without moral foundation.

While African elites in traditional society shunned early missionaries, Christian converts fared better under colonialism, serving as plantation managers and second-level administrators. Hoping "to gain security, wealth, and prestige by affiliating themselves with Christianity," Akan women in Côte d'Ivoire as well as Yoruba women in Nigeria then encouraged their daughters to marry Christian men (Toungara 2001, 43). At the same time the Christian women, who at first eschewed the women's associations as "outmoded" and rejected their practices as "pagan," eventually came together in groups that mimicked them (Bastian 2000, 149). One might say that the missionary vision succeeded to a remarkable degree, for despite the isolation and ostracism that new converts initially experienced in West African society, the descendants of these newly invented Christian families eventually became the elites of the newly independent African nations—the civil servants or workers in European commercial firms, including women who served as teachers, lawyers, judges, pharmacists, and midwives (Toungara 2001, 45). In Nigeria, "the Igbo-speaking Christian schoolgirls of the early 1900s became the elite, Christian matrons of the 1930s and the mothers [of those men and women who eventually] took an active part in Nigeria's struggles for independence" (45).

Ironically, despite women's active role in nationalist liberation struggles in Africa, women did not find relief from oppression after independence. The African men who had profited from the colonial androcentrism and Christian patriarchy perpetuated their discriminatory practices in the institutions of the neo-colonial state, justifying them as practices in keeping with modernity and development, even further curtailing women's rights and prerogatives. "In the post-independence period, African men in control of new governments legislated in their own interest" (54). Women's lot has not improved in any large measure since.

Comparative Cases in Liberia: Blowing Whistles and Linking Arms

Surely one of the reasons that the ritual form of women's protest endures is precisely because its spiritual and moral motivations elevate their petitions beyond the mere political spheres of interest and shield the actors as religious mediators in a way that other forms of civil disobedience or unrest could not. In 1983 the Grebo women of southeastern Liberia marched to the capital city, Monrovia, to protest the levy of a new tax of ten dollars per person by the government, under a relatively new military rule. Approximately 240 women walked fifteen miles from the interior to the coastal regional capital, *ringing hand-bells and blowing whistles, "traditional instruments of . . . the council of female elders"* (Moran 1989, 446, emphasis mine). They first stopped at the home of the regional chief, who received them with serious ceremony and respect, before moving on to protest the administrative superintendent in Monrovia. They were met by "stern, male officials" in military uniform, flanked by armed soldiers (446). But despite the fact that their collective congress was a violation of the ban on political activity, the officials heard their complaint. Recognizing that "the *form* of their protest fits a pattern of female political action well documented for West Africa," Moran asserts that this pattern "illuminates *the cultural construction of gender, power and representation* used by Grebo women to evaluate state-level policy" (444, emphasis mine). It is precisely because the women's political resistance took the form of that respected tradition that it was granted greater latitude.

The power of FGP to trump all political protocol was most dramatically demonstrated by Leymah Gbowee, the coordinator of the Women of Liberia Mass Action for Peace, who spearheaded an end to the fourteen-year civil war in Liberia in 2003. The regular demonstrations by the coalition of Christian and Muslim women had been instrumental in pressuring the government of Charles Taylor to enter into peace negotiations with the warring rebels, Liberia United for Reconciliation and Democracy (LURD). But when the formal peace talks were finally underway in Ghana, under the auspices of ECOWAS, the male representatives seemed to be enjoying the perks and privileges of the spotlight and posh hotels rather than seriously negotiating peace. When the parlays dragged on, Gbowee and the delegation of Liberian women who had traveled to attend the proceedings as advocates for peace staged a sit-in, linking arms to block the doors to prevent participants from leaving until they reached a resolution. When authorities came to arrest Gbowee for "obstructing justice," her indignation reached such a pitch that she announced, "I am going to strip naked" (Reticker 2008). Recognizing the seriousness of the threat, the police immediately backed down. Moreover, Gen. Abdusalami Abubakar, the Nigerian statesman appointed by ECOWAS to moderate the talks, emerged from the building and ensured that the women were allowed to remain. This marked the turning point that forced the talks, in Gbowee's words, "to be real peace talks and not a circus" (Reticker 2008).

Deadly Warriors, Not Maternal Peacemakers

In Cameroon in 1981 and 1982, as well, the women's use of *fombuen* imagery to protest the abuse of government authority afforded them a critical and privileged platform for social critique, "since public protests [were] not otherwise tolerated by the Cameroonian state" (Diduk, 1989, 339). In the 1990s, the Takembeng in Cameroon worked in conjunction with other campaigns of civil disobedience to protest government taxes. The women distributed tracts that denounced the government's wanton killings, arrests, and victimization of citizens, citing their indignation "as life givers" (Fonchingong and Tanga 2007, 124). While the women decried the lamentable political abuses "as mothers," their interventions did not rest on maternal feeling but relied on their moral power activated in ritual: "As indicated by an informant, aged sixty, the group *performed traditional rituals before any outing*" (124, emphasis mine). These would surely have been the ritual appeal to FGP, as their acts of public protest clearly demonstrate.

The iconographic details are especially telling, for the symbolism is most definitely not that of the maternal peacemaker: "Their hair was mostly grey and they circulated almost nude, teeth clenched with a large blade of grass gripped in between their mouth symbolizing 'no talk but action'" (124). Moreover, the leaves in the women's mouths purportedly "enforce total compliance" (128). The gesture is therefore intended to be more than symbolic; it is a magico-religious act that is expected to elicit concrete results. The women also grip a traditional plant "meant to register disapproval at certain 'unholy' practices" (128). In other words, the women were not as mothers seeking conciliation, they were conducting themselves as warriors preparing for spiritual combat.

Fonchingong and Tanga subscribe to the idea that in the public domain the women "*[use] their bodies as symbolic and metaphoric devices to subvert the dominant discourse of womanhood*" (128). However, the "dominant discourse of womanhood" that FGP overturns is that of woman-as-mother, and especially the Western idealization of mother as passive nurturer, for their active militancy and threat demonstrates nothing of the tender mother, meek and mild. The authority they wield is not that of their maternal office but their sacred role as fierce enforcers of moral justice. Aiming to shed light on the women's *modus operandi*, Fonchingong and Tanga contend that "[the women's] presence involves *maternal* authority to restore peace, threatening and *using bodily exposure against violators* from whom it is meant to shame and stop" (125, emphasis mine). The authority may derive from matrifocal morality, but it is far from "maternal" in the sense of motherly caring, nurturing, or even peacemaking. Stripping themselves naked in view of the security forces, the "grey-haired elders" invoked the curse that befalls any who violate the injunction not to look upon them in this state. Nor is it shame but fear that elicits the strong response the women sought in the political context through public exposure. When the Cameroonian women marched in Bamenda in 1991 to protest at the provincial governor's mansion, it was reported that "their passage . . . meant every place had to remain closed and everybody had to desert the streets" (125). The efficacy of the women's ritual rhetoric relied on its widely recognized meaning in the popular social imaginary. In response to Takembeng's actions Cameroonian soldiers "registered their shock and disbelief" because "watching the nakedness of those they considered their mothers" desecrated cultural norms; "most of the military men . . . who are familiar with the sacrosanct aspect of tradition were rendered helpless" (127). Understanding the dangerous ramifications of having been exposed to the Mothers' curse, they sought ritual cleansing in a ceremony "to wash off the ill luck" (127). An intriguing local newspaper account reported that those who confronted the women defiantly "died under mysterious circumstances. . . . The deaths were attributed to the chanting spells and incantations" of the Takembeng (127). Another such instance was related by first-hand informants: "As two informants aged 49 and 55 years recounted, [the women] stripped themselves naked and the gendarme officer instead of retracting watched on intently. Some minutes later, his rifle dropped and he collapsed and died a few hours later. The women attributed his demise to *a curse* since he had despised their nudity by staring intently" (129, emphasis mine). The curse unleashed through the deployment of FGP is ostensibly as deadly as that wielded by the armed soldiers.

Reports of the efficacy of FGP are not unusual. After two years of conflict over administrative succession in Kembong, in the Cross River region of Cameroon and Nigeria in 1987, the women elders of the *Ekpa-Atu* society poured "magic water with which they have washed themselves" at the doorsteps of the men who were defying traditional rules (Röschenthaler 1993, 184). "Four [of those] very influential men . . . died in accidents. The man who ran for office was the most affected . . . he lost his money without knowing why. He aged and no longer behaved normally" (190).

Strategic Essentialism: A Continuous Tradition of Worldly Resistance

Recognizing the Takembeng practices as a historical "punitive ritual" to sanction social infractions, Fonchingong and Tanga suggest that its use in the political domain constituted an entirely new application. The "transformation of the Takumbeng from an indigenous female secret society to a modern protest group . . . restored protest as a women's legacy"[11] (Fonchingong and Tanga 2007, 134). But where these authors say the women's "actions are visible crystallizations of the latent ideas of their predecessors," I argue that the principle of FGP has remained active in the social imaginary and that its rites have been regularly called upon not only as a measure for social redress but also an effective form of civil society (134). Their strategies have not been "re-adapted to suit the exigencies of the period," but are enduring practices that have been consciously deployed in the face of injustice (134).

That is, various instances in which this power is evoked must not overshadow their common source or the continuity of the underlying phenomenon. Once one recognizes FGP as the underlying principle and power, it becomes clear that the women's vigilant activism was never disrupted. Tracing the details of FGP in history shows it to be a longstanding feature of African civil society. Takembeng is not a "transformation" or adaptation of an ancient tradition, but merely a contemporary instance of it, standing in continuity with that legacy. The Mothers have regularly been spurred to action by moral indignation, and their aim has always been social redress.

The ritualized interventions of Takembeng women today follow conventions of traditional moral censure, and, like other West African women who resorted to them in anti-colonial struggles, they deploy the rites of FGP as a worldly political strategy of resistance. Their ritual rhetoric situates Takembeng action among the myriad other women's societies that express their moral outrage in these terms. The women strip naked and march as warriors going into battle wielding sticks "as though they were guns" (Diduk 2004, 34). They carry the "medicines" to conduct spiritual warfare and ensure protection, such as knotted grasses and plant stalks symbolic of renewal and restoration. They also defecate in public. Most critically, its members make clear that their principal actors are not just "women," but women in the later stage in life. These Takembeng activists are known as the "Mami Takembeng," the Mothers.

Susan Diduk (2004) is one of the few to recognize that these acts are rooted in a "precolonial ideology" of gender that differs significantly from the stereotyped projections of womanhood in patriarchal Western culture, though no less essentialist. That is, fundamental traits ascribed to these African elders are still considered *innate*. As we have seen, African women's associations and the rite of FGP reflect a social imaginary, shared by many West African cultures, in which gender and the qualities attributed to females are not fixed but change at different stages in life. An African postmenopausal elder surpasses any normalizing ascription to her as woman or woman-as-mother through longevity, attaining a new status and accruing special qualities. Ifi Amadiume demonstrated that in certain African traditions men and women could fulfill the same social functions in ways that were not tied to gender: "With this possibility of non-gendered status and role, a woman need not be masculinized in order to wield power" (Amadiume 1997, 113). She claimed that it places them in another gender category altogether that she calls "neuter." "They had a collective neuter gender that could mediate this difference for role and status fulfillment . . . [such that] their social system was not based only on an indefinite separation of the sexes" (115). I suggest that the Mothers who wield FGP rather reflect the spiritual authority of the gender doubleness that they attained with age, which places them on a par with the gods. This explains why a female elder may ascend to the highest rank of male secret societies, while the reverse is never the case for a male.

As Diduk asserts, "It is precisely the 'essentialist' definition of women . . . that allows [the female elders] to act so powerfully" (2004, 39). The basis for the women's associations and their collective mobilizations is not a dogmatic, universal natural law applicable to all women, or even any given woman throughout her life, for "the nature of women is understood as changing over the life cycle and differing between communities" (40). The power that accrues to a woman of a certain age enables her to surpass gender as the measure by which respect and deference are accorded. Age is more determinative of access to power—both social and spiritual.

Unlike some early feminists who presumed that all women suffered the same oppressions of patriarchy and could unite in solidarity on the basis of the universal given of their womanhood, the African women enacting female genital power make no such universalist assumptions. "Popular perceptions of postmenopausal women are essentialist to the extent that such women are thought to embody spiritual powers that are *not shared by women who are still reproducing*. These views, however, are not universalist. They do not assume that postmenopausal women in other societies hold similar powers" (40). Most critically, this essentialism is rooted in "local" (i.e., African) conceptions of identity and power: "Their appeal to taken-for-granted cultural premises of morality as the natural preserve of women, lends Takembeng both credibility and efficacy" (30). The kind of essentialism on which FGP is founded is also performative; it lays claim to a particular capacity and form of agency. The source of the female elders' authority is the widespread acceptance that by their very nature they wield "a mystical power of reprisal" and invoke it at the peril of the transgressors of the moral order (39). It is therefore a "strategic essentialism."

The women who join together to exercise FGP as a means of intervention in contemporary political affairs take advantage of their collective strength to present a unified front in defense of a singular purpose, but they also recognize and respect discrete differences among them. "Membership of the protests . . . cuts across quarters, ethnic groups and especially socio-economic distinctions" (Diduk 1989, 35). The solidarity of the women elders is founded on the strength of their fundamental commonality as moral guardians. At the same time, they do not efface all local identity under the universalizing banner of "woman." "In Kedjom . . . when women 'come out' over a common issue, they still generally march sequentially: in other words, women from one fondom [local district] march together, followed later by women from a different fondom" (34). The most critical distinguishing marker among women is age and the status that the elders bear as the Mothers.

Gendered Violence: Territorial Occupation and Rape

FGP has featured prominently throughout the West African region in nationalist struggles, but the Mothers' outrage was not only pitched against colonial aggressors and their colluders. Their vigilance and moral rebuke continued after independence and feature regularly in protest against postcolonial African governments on the contemporary political landscape. The continuity in the unhomely impositions and disruptions of the moral order is most vividly apparent in the history of violence against women. The association of bodies and land again emerges as a theme, for territorial occupation by force becomes inscribed on women's bodies in political domination and conflict as rape.

During the 1950s Cameroonian rural women themselves drew an association between colonial control of fecund land, political repression, and the threat to their own reproductive fertility, leading them to boycott European birth clinics as an act of resistance. They complained to the United Nations that "while the men are away in the bush [fleeing arrest for nationalist activities], the French colonialists come and maltreat women, untold numbers of whom have been killed, including some who were pregnant" (Terretta 2007, 79). The women boycotted the newly established colonial birthing clinics, maternity wards, and dispensaries, reputed to be sterilizing women or causing them to miscarry as part of the colonial "project of eradicating the nationalist movement by eliminating future generations of nationalists" (81). This preoccupation with the protection of female fertility as a means of defending national interests was not an unfounded fantasy, but grounded in the fact that the French forces called in to "pacify" the population perpetrated horrific acts of sexual violence and torture. The social topography of political domination and control was mapped onto bodily topography through sexual violence. Rape was used "as a weapon wielded by soldiers under French command" (83). Wives of political prisoners were intentionally targeted. Petitions made at the time to the UN by the Democratic Union of Cameroonian Women (UDEFEC) detail barbarities including the kidnap, gang rape, and murder of women in army camps and the rape of girls under age nine. A particularly brutal and symbolically significant case was the torture in 1955 of a UDEFEC leader, Marthe Bahida, whose "genitals were burnt with a red hot iron" (84).

Gender and Resistance in the Postcolony: A Pan-African Phenomenon

That Cameroonian women's international outcry failed to ignite moral indignation. More terrible yet, the postcolonial state has perpetuated the political strategy of taking possession over land through the violent possession of women's bodies. Postcolonial politics in Africa has subjected women to a double colonization under male hegemony, showing that there is nothing "post," in the sense of being finished with or beyond, the values or methods of violent domination. Across the continent women have been the primary victims in the ongoing violence plaguing the continent in the repeated waves of civil war and their territorial struggles. But they have also been at the forefront of protests that condemn the state, which has lost its moral compass. In this fight for moral authority women continue to evoke the traditions of collective mobilization and deploy FGP as their most powerful weapon.

In Mali in 1991 a popular insurrection fueled the coup d'état that ended the dictatorial regime of President General Moussa Traoré. However, it cost the lives of more than one hundred civilians, mostly university and secondary school students. "Standing in the place where those students marched when Bamako was under siege of fire and blood, the President made a speech saying, 'When there are no more shrouds left, the skirts of your mothers will replace them' (news.abamako.com). It was a warning that any further resistance would even bring more deaths. In the face of the killings of their children and especially in light of those words, the women [rose up]" (Bintou Koné, email communication of September 7, 2017, translation mine). One of the women whose child was killed "stripped naked and took her deceased child in her arms while cursing the power of General Moussa Traoré. Such acts (especially if conducted by an elderly woman) in most countries of Africa announce the end of the ruling power in place. The monument of martyrs, at the entrance to the first bridge in Bamako, bears strong witness to this act on March 26, 1991, known as Black Friday" (Koné, email communication of September 7, 2017).

Challenging the suggestion by some that no Muslim women would deploy the rite of FGP or engage in its shocking transgression of female decorum, the young Malian scholar who provided the example of Bamako's Black Friday offered this response:

> Women's genital power is something that must not be underestimated. When a conflict is at its peak and when youth come under threat, the women make themselves heard through their *fierce engagement*. This engagement can lead to behavior in which no woman would participate under normal circumstances. When a situation becomes desperate, she will overstep all the conventions established by society, by ethnicity as well as religion [Christianity or Islam]. It is not because a woman is from a particular religion, ethnicity or social status (noble or other caste) that she will not behave in this way when the situation demands. The act of stripping has nothing to do with religion (which the ritual even surpasses), since the pain [of moral indignation] is so great that [nudity] is the ultimate weapon. It is the last resort for stopping the abuses or putting an end to a situation of extreme danger. (Koné, email communication, September 7, 2017)[12]

Women were also at the forefront of postcolonial resistance in Togo. A coalition of political parties and civil society groups, the "Let's Save Togo" Collective (CST), was created to oppose the repressive authoritarian rule of President Fauré Gnassingbé and demand an end to decades of the regime that had begun when Gnassingbé's father, Gnassingbé Eyadéma, seized the reins of power in a coup thirty-eight years earlier. The son's election in 2005 was marred by allegations of fraud and violent protests, during which four hundred citizens were killed (*BBC News*, April 29, 2015). In 2012 CST lobbied to enforce the 1992 constitutional provision that limited the presidential mandate to five years with one renewable term, as well as the right to freedom of assembly and the defense of human rights. When their nonviolent protests were interrupted and demonstrators arrested, the women leaders called for a sex strike as a means of pressuring the government to free the detainees. Failing that, they planned a "demonstration in the nude" in the capital city, Lomé, "to show that women counted and that they did not accept what was happening" (Bonai 2012). As participants were gathering in the Bè-Château quarter of the city for that demonstration, military police entered the quarter to suppress it. In response, outraged women elders "did not hesitate to show themselves naked before the police and security forces, as a means of cursing them" (M05, August 22, 2012). The protesters were met with tear gas and rubber bullets, and a number were seriously injured.

Unperturbed, CST organized a woman's march aimed at denouncing "poor governance, the high cost of living and unemployment that aggravate the already precarious situation of Togolese women, the use of women's associations and their leadership to the detriment of women's interests, the refusal to respect human rights and particularly the rights of women, and the confiscation by the National Information Agency (ANR) of funds belonging to market women" (Koffi 2012). But women's interests were not their only focus. As defenders of society at large, Togolese women deployed FGP to condemn the state's assaults on the populace. In April 2013, following the government's violent repression of peaceful student demonstrations, members of the opposition called for the most radical response that only the Mothers could provide: "a parade of women in their costume of damnation" (Godson 2013). On May 18, 2013, women elders gathered in front of the national police station in Lomé and bared their breasts to "curse the country's authorities" for having caused the death of an opposition leader under detention (JeuneAfrique 2013). "With arms raised to the heavens, they cried out 'Hélu' (Curses) on those who oppressed and killed their people" (Anctogo.com 2013). A YouTube video shows the "indignant and furious" Togolese women shouting in front of the gates of a police station. Many are seated spread-eagled, a position traditionally considered unseemly for women, offensive and taboo precisely because it exposes their secret and sacred parts. They slap their bared breasts and tap their genitals as if to activate that seat of moral power (Kouevi 2013) while hurling invectives and making "incantations to conjure an evil spell" (TogoVisions 2013a).

Filmed and available to an unlimited online public, this appeal to the traditional idiom of outrage and condemnation is more readily seen as a form of political remonstrance in keeping with other interventions of its kind across Africa. In a recent incident in Uganda, filmed and posted to YouTube, one sees the outraged women elders wail and shout, then strip and hold their breasts, some even rolling on the ground and raising their legs in front of government officials and armed guards, while the men who accompany the women shield their eyes and the officials avert their gaze in shame (Byaruhanga 2015). In the Democratic Republic of Congo women elders are shown singing and strutting in a political march as some lift their wraps to expose their legs and crotch, while others bend over and flagrantly display their bottoms, their genitals barely covered by a g-string (Jambo Jambo News Channel 2014). With such ritualized public displays of the denuded genitalia, African women make their own stark self-representation. They embody the moral values that have been betrayed and violated. At the same time, by activating their "bottom power" they reassert their claim to power's most authoritative and enduring source.

In Côte d'Ivoire, which has only recently come through more than a decade of civil war and horrific violence, the struggle to assert the values of the Mothers endures. This will be the focus of Part III. But to place it in context, we first address the degree to which those values have been foundational to the most basic organizing features of African civilization: ethnicity and alliance.

ABIDJAN, CÔTE D'IVOIRE—In April 2011 women demonstrated to condemn the killings of seven women during a peaceful International Women's Day march. The poignant
placard reads, "[President] Gbagbo—It's a woman who gave you birth. You have no
heart" (for discussion, see chapter 6). Photographer SIA KAMBOU/AFP/Getty Images.

◀ Three leaders of the 1949 Women's March to Grand-Bassam: Marie Koré, Goly Gbaou-
zon, Léonie Richardo. Once gathered at the colonial prison, women stripped to perform
Adjanou, the rite of female genital power, to rebuke the French and demand the libera-
tion of national leaders. Source: NET, CIVOX, "Histoire/Hommage à Marie Koré, Goly
Gbaouzon, Léonie Richardo: Femmes Pionnaires du Combat pour la Libération de la
Côte d'Ivoire," www.civox.net. Accessed March 15, 2017. http://www.civox.net/Histoire
-Hommage-a-Marie-Kore-Goly-Gbaouzon-Leonie-Richardo-Femmes-pionniaires-du
-combat-pour-la-liberation-de-la-Cote_a4635.html.

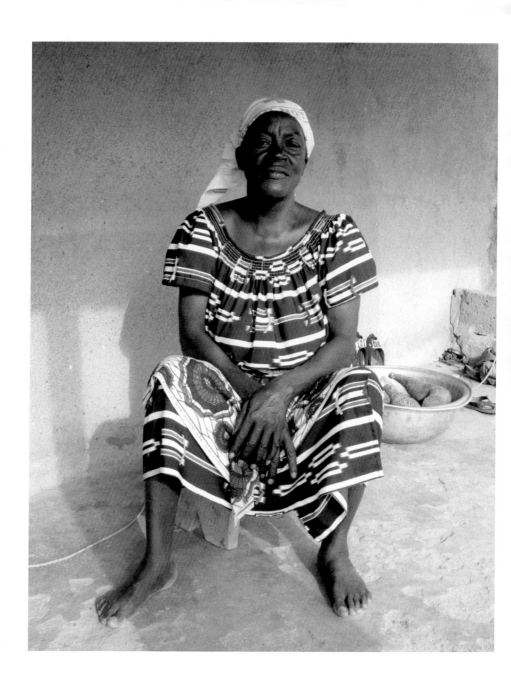

SAHUYÉ, CÔTE D'IVOIRE, 2010—Portrait of Kamenan Adjoba, one of the women who perform Egbiki, the ritual deployment of FGP at the time of Dipri to trap witches and chase away evil and death (see chapter 1). Photo by Laura Grillo.

◄ NIGERIA, 2009—Angry women in Emure Ekiti use rite of FGP to protest. Among the Yoruba, it is said that the power of the Mothers is greater than that of the gods (see chapter 1). Jacob Olupona relayed to the author that when a Yoruba woman crouches in the position of childbirth to curse, as depicted here, it is a threat so mighty that it calls for immediate repentance or doom (private communication, March 2013). Source: http://dailyindependentnig.com/2015/03/women-protest-naked-ekiti (accessed July 19, 2015; no longer available).

TOGO, 2013—Togolese women deploy FGP to demand the release of detained prisoners in front of the National Security headquarters in Lomé. This still from a video shows the furious, indignant Togolese women effecting their curse on government authorities for having caused the death of an imprisoned opposition leader (see chapter 3.) Source: Extract from YouTube post: Louis Kouevi, Indignées et Furieuses les Femmes du CST, Torse Nu, hurlent "Attention Faure, Libere Nos Enfants," May 2013, https://www .youtube.com/watch?v=X_W5xURdKZ4.

TREICHVILLE, ABIDJAN, CÔTE D'IVOIRE—Adjanou dancers, smeared with kaolin clay and bearing branches protesting the Republican Guard. "Adjanou" is the Baulé name for the rite of female genital power, which the Abidji and Adioukrou call "Egbiki." Here the women effect the rite as a public rebuke and curse against violations of the moral order (see chapter 6). Source: http://www.radiosun.fr/sun -news/5760-abidjan-manifestation-des-femmes-danseuses-dadjanou-violemment -dispersees (accessed November 25, 2011; no longer available).

TOGO, JANUARY 11, 2013—Women from the Bè quarter of Lomé stripped to rebuke the military police who attempted to prevent a demonstration by a local union against the dictatorial Gnassingbé regime (see chapter 3). Source: TogoVisions, *Les Femmes de Bè Se Dénudent pour Exprimer Leur Colère Contre Les Abus Policiers* [November 1, 2013], https://www.youtube.com/watch?v =jhFxacUdLTw (accessed January 25, 2016). Used courtesy of Alfred Attipoe, TogoVisions.

GRAND-BASSAM, CÔTE D'IVOIRE—Statue commemorating Women's March of 1949 (for discussion, see chapter 7). Photo by Laura Grillo.

◀ ABIDJAN, CÔTE D'IVOIRE, 2015—Stripped and crouched in the position of child-birth, a distraught, incensed elder curses the military police who beat and gassed women victims of war who had come to claim their overdue compensation from the National Commission for Reconciliation and Restitution. Source: Video "Manifestation Devant la Conariv: Des Victimes de Guerre Battues et Gazées par la Police." Linfodrome.ci, October 6, 2015, http://www.linfodrome.com/societe-culture/23015-manifestation -devant-la-conariv-des-victimes-de-guerre-battues-et-gazees-par-la-police. Courtesy of videographer César Djedje Mel.

GRAND-BASSAM, CÔTE D'IVOIRE—Memorial statue of Women's March of 1949 (*front*). Source: The Official Site of the Office of the Mayor of Grand-Bassam, Côte d'Ivoire, http://mairiedegrandbassam.ci/fr/projets-en-cours.

Part II. Worldliness

FGP IN THE MAKING OF ETHNICITY, ALLIANCE, AND WAR IN CÔTE D'IVOIRE

●

Frontier societies are apt to derive not from a single society
but to draw upon and re-synthesize several idiosyncratic
local expressions of common cultural principles.
—IGOR KOPYTOFF, *The African Frontier:*
The Reproduction of Traditional African Societies

Return to a Puzzlement

Chapter 1 introduced the traditional celebration Dipri and, applying a hermeneutic approach, sounded the mysterious depths of witchcraft and women's allegedly innate access to this spiritual power. Chapter 4 returns to the particular context of Côte d'Ivoire and Dipri but approaches it differently and uses it toward different ends. We begin with a fundamental puzzlement: although Dipri is an important "new year" festival, commemorating the founding of civilization, it is not universally celebrated among the Abidji, but is maintained by only one clan of Abidji villages.[1] Equally perplexing is that the tradition is shared by the neighboring Adioukrou to the south, though by only two villages—Orbaff and Yassap—that again comprise a small subgroup. What makes this more puzzling still is that Abidji society is patrilineal, while the Adioukrou are matrilineal. It is clear then that this critical traditional festival, while harkening back to a mythic ancestor and the very origins of social order, cannot be seen as an assertion of ethnic identity, and certainly not if ethnicity is presumed to refer to the homogeneity of a singular people with one common line of descent and unique character.

Yet given their structural differences, an alliance and joint celebration of Abidji and Adioukrou would not have proceeded naturally, either. Traditionally the Abidji are governed by the senior member of the founding lineage under the guidance of a council composed of other elders.[2] The Adioukrou society, by contrast, is a more overtly acephalous one, governed by collective rule. Each Adioukrou village organizes its citizens into eight "generations," or age sets, into which members are initiated in early adulthood. The most senior age set governs collectively for the duration of the generations' eight-year cycle. On what basis, then, would a strategic alliance between these two peoples have been forged? What is the common feature of social life that allowed them to bond?

The answers are relevant to the situation in Côte d'Ivoire today, whose social and political dynamics are not atypical on the continent: the country has gone through civil war, and the protracted political tension and turmoil are drawn along ethnic and regional lines. While some nationalists and many political analysts in the international community decry those allegiances as antiquated and irrelevant in the context of today's increasing globalization, ethnic identity endures here, as everywhere in Africa, as an inextricable feature of social life. Given the extreme number of ethnicities comprising Côte d'Ivoire's population and the heterogeneity of those groups, there is surely something valuable to be learned about nation building from the history of the peacetime alliances that were negotiated among them as migrant groups arrived, consolidated, and settled here.

Unfortunately, the public history of Africa is usually conducted from the top down. Not only is the focus the fate of the state, it has mostly been framed in terms of the "crudest designations of historical periods: of 'pre-colonial,' 'colonial,' and 'post-colonial,'" a narrative in which the West figures as the determining agent (Lonsdale 2000, 14). As Lonsdale suggests, what may be more indicative of the significance of Africa's past and most determinative for its future are those features of social history that lie in "the gap," that have been obscured by preoccupation with only those features that echo the West. As we saw in the preceding chapter, the persistence of the appeal to FGP across these epochs invites us to conceive of African history from a different perspective. Reviewing it from the perspective of female power demonstrates an approach from the bottom up, and here the pun is intended, for in Nigeria the common idiom that refers to the innate spiritual power of women instantiated in their genitals is "bottom-power" (Olupona 2011, 222).

Chapter 4 turns to the complex history of Côte d'Ivoire, the way that migrants coalesced to form its ethnic groups, and the way that these groups negotiated strategic alliances among them. Retracing the history of these frontier societies in what was once the relatively open expanse of the forest might suggest a straightforward historiography and may at first blush seem trivial and unrelated to the subject of FGP. However, it represents an attempt to seek in the story of the origin and organization of the Abidji and Adioukrou clues to those "internal visions of power" (Memel-Fotê 1980, 12) that have shaped African society, but that remain obscured by academic preoccupation with empires, kingdoms, and formal states.

Chapter 5 turns to the dynamics of contemporary politics in Côte d'Ivoire and considers the way that the engine of war was fueled by the manipulation of both ethnicity and alliance. I look not only to the hard facts of the regional divisions and power contests but also to the "imaginary premise of all politics" (Lonsdale 1986, 141), the moral ideals, and embodied techniques that may be just as determinative to the shape of the crisis. Here I entertain the ideas of Mike McGovern, who explores the "metacommunicative 'play' frame" (2011, 27) of the Ivoirian conflict, the self-conscious rhetorical work of those involved, to ask how the performative knowledge of the women elders figures in this serious play.

4. FOUNDING KNOWLEDGE /
BINDING POWER

The Moral Foundations of Ethnicity and Alliance

From now on, I am the guardian of tradition. I am your keeper.
I am committed to watch over your achievements . . .
whatever the situation, I will never flee.
—NANAN KOSSUA PRAO ABABIO, Queen Mother
of the Abron of Transua, Côte d'Ivoire, in Philippe Delanne et al.,
Arts au Féminin en Côte d'Ivoire

. . . newcomers establish their rule by superior knowledge . . .
—IGOR KOPYTOFF, *The African Frontier: The Reproduction of
Traditional African Societies*

Accounting for Ethnic Diversity in Côte d'Ivoire:
A Frontier Society

One of the most striking features of the social landscape of Côte d'Ivoire is
its cultural diversity. By most counts there are at least sixty distinct ethnic
groups considered indigenous to its territory and, according to some, more
than one hundred ethnicities comprising its populace today. No matter the
exact number, what is most significant is that "social anthropology attests to
the [existence of] a proliferation of truly distinct peoples in the pre-colonial
era, grouped in territories and *conscious of their historical, political and cultural
identity*" (Memel-Fotê and Brunet-Jailly 2007, 216, emphasis mine).

It is well known that this indigenous populace was informed by omnidirectional migrations coming in multiple waves over time. Perhaps the clearest indicator of their various origins is language. The linguistic features of the languages
spoken by the earliest inhabitants of the region were so distinct that even in any
given subregion there would have been no mutual comprehension among them.
Today, the various Ivoirian ethnicities are generally categorized linguistically
into three segments that largely correlate with the geographical regions where

the related groups are clustered: those inhabiting the preforest/desert area in the north are collectively identified as Mandé; the ensemble of linguistically related groups to the west are called Kru, and the southeastern lagoon peoples are categorized as Kwa. Three different lineage systems further differentiate these segments: the Mandé and Kru follow a patrilineal system; the majority of the Kwa groups follow the matrilineal system or a system of dual descent, in which patrilineal and matrilineal constellations are active in a single society.

These clusters of peoples can also be disaggregated according to one of four distinct political systems by which they were governed, as these were still in effect in the early twentieth century, and their attributes are still discernible in the social organization of village life today. In the first instance, political power belonged to the lineage of the village founder and was exercised by an elected member of that lineage. This system was in force among matrilineal groups as much as patrilineal ones. According to a second system, power was allotted to an elite personage, generally a rich man, whose economic power was leveraged for the prosperity and security of the village. Since the patronage of such a "big man" determined young men's access to both land and the wealth necessary to obtain a bride, this autocratic gerontocracy was particularly restrictive. A third system tempered the reigning power of such a rich or influential man with the principles of plutocracy and gerontocracy. That is, a council of elders would rule alongside the lineage head who served as chief. The Abidji are among this kind. The fourth type of political system reserves power for the collective. It is ruled by an age group (*fokwé*), a group born into the same generation and that takes on a different social role at each successive stage in life.[1] The Adioukrou exemplify this system of power. All these systems have been classified as stateless because these local, egalitarian polities remained politically independent. In all cases, such polities belonged to confederations that were organized voluntarily, while the military and juridical authority was placed in the hands of an ever-changing governing age set.

In his groundbreaking work *The African Frontier: The Reproduction of Traditional African Societies* (1987), Igor Kopytoff put forward a new perspective from which to understand the complexities of African history and cultural identity and account for the composite nature of the ethnicities in places like Côte d'Ivoire—territories that once comprised the frontier for African civilizations. His thesis is that "many, indeed most, African societies were formed around an initial core-group" that broke away from a metropole, or at least a more mature and established polity, and moved into the periphery (Kopytoff 1987, 7). That frontier was a relatively open terrain that offered the migrating groups independence from those dominating polities and thus the opportunity for self-definition and governance. In contrast with the previously widespread stereotype that all societies in sub-Saharan Africa were founded as independent tribes, whose origins were singular and whose racial composition was uniform, the frontier model, more grounded in scholarship, shows that most populations are the result of ceaseless mobility and accommodation to encounter. The thesis offers a means by which one can better understand the formation of what Kopytoff calls "ethnically ambiguous" societies, those with multiple origins as is typical of so many groups in Côte d'Ivoire. It helps to loosen the construct of ethnic identity from the burden of any claim to homogeneous origin or a singular history that goes back "to the dawn of time."

The thesis also explains the great cultural diversity in Côte d'Ivoire. The West African rainforest belt cuts a corridor across its territory, and the core of the country "remained a major forest frontier until the twentieth century" (Chauveau and Richards 2008, 516). For centuries that forest zone was a haven for the regular influx of immigrants who found refuge and habitable land there. The lyrics of Côte d'Ivoire's national anthem refer to this history: "We salute you, O land of hope/Country of hospitality."[2]

The reasons for migration were usually dire and were tied to moral conundrums: epidemics (associated with witchcraft or with genies refusing human settlement), homicide, war, or incidents of adultery that caused a founding ancestor (and sometimes his/her entourage) to flee. Those coming from the southeast were typically fleeing wars being waged against the hegemony of the Asante kingdoms. From the fifteenth century, trade in gold, kola, and slaves fractured the Akan states into warring entities and triggered the migration of vulnerable and threatened populations westward, across the Comoé River and into the southeastern region of contemporary Côte d'Ivoire. Akan culture strongly informs Baoulé society as well as smaller neighboring groups, including the Abidji and Adioukrou.

As peoples met, negotiated relations, joined in alliance, adopted cultural features, and intermarried, these composite groups "formed from an ethnically heterogeneous base" established new identities (Memel-Fotê and Brunet-Jailly 2007, 219). Even among those ethnicities recognized to have indigenous origins in Côte d'Ivoire, the current populace is known to derive from multiple origins and assimilation. Political alliances, intermarriages, cultural superimpositions, and schisms of former confederations lent even greater complexity to the profile of the newly consolidating groups and the long history of Côte d'Ivoire's ethnic multiplicity.

In his recent book analyzing the crisis in Côte d'Ivoire today, *Making War in Côte d'Ivoire*, Mike McGovern alludes to this history of consolidated identity to claim that ethnicity is more ephemeral and fluid a notion than has been represented by those involved in the Ivoirian conflict. Following Kopytoff, McGovern suggests that the various ethnic groups indigenous to Côte d'Ivoire—and particularly those in the southern region—were constituted as "provisional and multi-ethnic patchwork" entities and only relatively recently hypostatized (McGovern 2011, 64). On this basis, he argues that (unlike their northern counterparts) these groups consolidated identity on the basis of an "'anti-historiographic' ideology of autochthony," a false claim to indigenous identity and land. These matters are not negligible artifacts of history. In recent years contests over who had legitimate rights to citizenship, fueled by just such challenges to the authenticity of ethnicity and belonging, ignited the Ivoirian civil war.

In actuality, Kopytoff makes the subtler argument that while the ethnicities within the forest zone have heterogeneous origins, they are *not* "patchwork" societies haphazardly stitched together, but coherent polities that self-consciously consolidated elements from various source traditions. Identity was not provisional and opportunistic but forged by design, through the inventive symbolic work of myth ("official histories") and ritual (such as Dipri), which function similarly to consolidate identity (Kopytoff 1987, 4–5). Awareness of a complex history and allegiance to a social identity are not mutually exclusive. The work of tradition—always innovative and accommodating to history—reconciles the real with the ideal and obscures contradiction in favor of coherence. As Memel-Fotê explains, "Oral tradition as a form of collective memory, or a more or less complete and faithful representation of the past, is at the same time a projection of actual society. In it, one can see the structure, the inadequate technologies, the contradictions and conflicts that it endeavors to *camouflage or to resolve to the benefit of theoretical unity*" (Memel-Fotê and Brunet-Jailly 2007, 62, emphasis mine). Thus ethnic identity is not merely ascribed, but is actively negotiated and intentionally constructed.

Dipri exemplifies this phenomenon. On one hand, the fact that both Abidji and Adioukrou retain two very different myths about Dipri's meaning and about the origin of sékè faithfully represents the actual past: it demonstrates that the tradition has multiple sources and strands. On the other hand, the contradictions are camouflaged by the composite nature of the festival itself, for its various elements—the bath at the river, the initiation, the cult of the ancestor and collective funeral, and the spectacular magic manifestations of trance and spontaneous healing—are presented as a coherent whole and consistently practiced in every village that celebrates Dipri. While the history of the two groups is known, the symbolic rhetorical work of the ritual is itself an endeavor to mask or minimize that past in favor of a theoretical unity, the alliance among the villages that practice it.

Because the ethnic groups of southeastern Côte d'Ivoire are the product of history and constructed rather than natural entities, McGovern also suggests that "it was often quite simple for individuals or groups to change linguistic and thus ethnic identities through the middle of the twentieth century" (McGovern 2011, 46–47). While alliances could be closely cemented through trade and marriage or imposed through military conquest and the cultural hegemony of the conquering group, his claim that a shift of identity was a simple matter or a facile affair is certainly overdrawn. His conjecture may be driven by postmodern skepticism of the category of "ethnicity" itself and motivated by an interest in unsettling the antiquated essentialist conception that ethnicity is innate. Like many postmodern analysts, he avoids the universalizing singular (as in "the Adioukrou") or resorts to quote marks to signal that it is a reified construct. This emphasis on the instability of ethnic identity is certainly aimed at undermining one of the driving ideologies of the civil war in Côte d'Ivoire, that of Ivoirité.

That invented term, meaning "Ivoirianess," referred to the claims of the primacy and privilege of indigenous populations to determine the political fate of the country. It became a rallying cry of nationalists who wished citizenship to be based on indigenous origins and who resisted granting voting rights to recent immigrants. Ivoirité inflamed a dangerous political ambiance of xenophobia in a country whose expatriate population is, by recent measure, as high as twenty-six percent. For McGovern, however, any commitment to indigenous ethnic identity is "rooted in a fictional and romanticized image of the past. Groups have migrated, conquered one another and intermarried for as far back as we have historical data—oral or written—describing the region that became Côte d'Ivoire. . . . The reality is that identity and belonging were fluid and contested both before and after colonial incursion" (84).

Indeed, as suggested by the brief portrait of the country presented so far, the multiple groups in Côte d'Ivoire that self-identify as indigenous are not primordially existing groups linked by biological heritage. As in all history, circumstance and the aleatory gave rise to those communal identities. They are the products of "accidents, the minute deviations—or conversely, the complete reversals—the errors, the false appraisals, and the faulty calculations that gave birth to" them (Foucault 1977, 81). The ethnicities are indeed *cultural* constructions. Nevertheless, they persist and continue to have value and import in Côte d'Ivoire today. Local identity endures, and its fealties drive both alliances and conflicts at deep levels and in ways that certainly still inform the worldly affairs of politics in Côte d'Ivoire. Although the traditions of the contemporary ethnic groups of Côte d'Ivoire are not timeless, they have been centuries in the making. These cannot be readily dismissed as inauthentic or ignored as irrelevant for not having a historicity that goes any deeper than the national identities of most Western countries. Therefore, I use the term *ethnicity* and *ethnic group* as do Ivoirians, to refer not to a people with primordial origins or defining physical characteristics but rather to a political polity with which people actively identify even while maintaining self-consciousness about how the collective came into being as a sociocultural entity.[3]

While the history of the peoples of Côte d'Ivoire and the southern forest region in particular is complex, it is neither unknown nor unrecoverable from the murky recesses of oral tradition. Tracing the details of this history of migrations, settlements, and the consolidation of the various ethnic identities in the region is necessary to show in the first instance that Abidji and Adioukrou are neither fictions, nor groups that recently consolidated for opportunistic ends, but real social entities with long histories and deep roots. Because ethnic identity is being challenged today by politicians promoting globalist agendas and postmodern theorists alike, it is subject to erasure. What is even more vulnerable to eclipse is the tradition of women's knowledge and power. However, their moral vision and intervention are particularly relevant today both as the traditional ground of ethnicity and as a call to national peacetime alliance that transcends ethnicity. In recovering the story of ethnicity and alliances in the forest, the founding knowledge of the Mothers and the binding nature of FGP as a moral stance come into view.

*Founding Knowledge: Matrifocal Morality
and Regional Coherence*

Paradoxically, despite the cultural diversity and historical complexity of the forest region, many observers, including Kopytoff, ascribe to this subregion a sense of continuity and coherence. Memel-Fotê, for example, notes that in Côte d'Ivoire "beneath a diversity which should neither be denied nor neglected, was unity" (Memel-Fotê and Brunet-Jailly 2007, 217). The cause or source of this unity, however, remained unexplained and inchoate. "From the Comoé to the Sassandra [the major rivers in the western and eastern regions of Côte d'Ivoire respectively], from the ocean to the savanna, from one region to another in this zone, and *a fortiori* from one society to another there were transitions, links, and apparent continuity. . . . Everything suggests the hypothesis of *one* social formation, in cultural terms one civilization, whose diverse societies are its multiple faces" (218–19). What might account for such a sense of cultural coherence in a crazy-quilt region comprised of multiple societies peopled by repeated waves of omnidirectional migrations and loosely stitched together by mutual accommodation?

The frontier thesis supposedly explains what is today a coherent culture area. According to Kopytoff, in African prehistory the "ancestral African population was relatively concentrated . . . constituting what one may refer to as *an 'ecumene'*" (Kopytoff 1987, 10), a habitable world defined by a persistent culture. He suggests that "*the fundamental principles underlying the construction of new societies were forged and re-forged* in the course of African history. These *principles* persisted into the later stages of political development, but these later stages are, in themselves, *beyond the scope of this analysis*" (8, emphasis mine). Without identifying what these fundamental principles might have been or what key features might have been shared by the founding populace, Kopytoff nevertheless proposes that from this original core habitat the "frontiersmen were bringing with them a basically similar kit of cultural and ideological resources" that account for the "striking degree" of cultural unity throughout sub-Saharan Africa (8).

For Ife Amadiume (1997) the most critical feature of that presumed Ur-tradition, the cultural foundation of African civilization, is the dependence on the primary kinship bond: that of mother-child. It establishes the precedence of matriarchy and is the reason that even in the most hierarchal patriarchies a remnant of matrilineality remains as a vestigial entity, giving clue to its earlier stage of social organization. While Kopytoff never goes so far as to suggest that society is based on matriarchy or even matrilineal organization, he does recognize that new relationships forged in the frontier were fashioned as "pseudo-kin" networks "modeled on kinship ties ('blood' being the usual idiom) [as] the basis for its existence and for the introduction of new members" (Kopytoff 1987, 41).[4] Therefore, kinship is just a metaphor for the bonds of ethnicity, which in fact was determined on the basis of something other than blood or descent.

While both these hypotheses shed "some revealing even if flickering light" on the possible reasons for the "profound similarities among the political cultures of far-flung African societies" (8), I suggest that what constitutes the core similarity among the many frontier societies is not a feature of sociopolitical organization but a less overtly structural principle. More essential to founding a settlement and to negotiating relations with newcomers is the *moral domain*, the sphere in which women's insight, privilege, and power prevailed.

Regardless of pattern of kinship relations or hierarchical social order, West African traditional societies gave primacy to woman, not only as the quintessential progenitor and inaugurator of the first moral bond through motherhood, but also as the personification of the ancestors' founding knowledge and the administrator of their righteousness. My hypothesis is that this matrifocal morality was the kernel of the original *ecumene* carried into the frontier. At once a comprehensive doctrine and a seminal code of conduct, matrifocal morality served as the common premise on which new society consolidated and alliances were negotiated.

Matrifocal morality is both an episteme and an ontology so widely shared that it lends to the region a cultural coherence, readily acknowledged by travelers and scholars alike. Yet as the very ground of knowledge and the metaphysical vision on the basis of which one understands the nature and relations of being, it is so diffuse as to be unrecognizable without recourse to an alternative means of inquiry. A genealogical investigation of the kind introduced by Foucault examines surface manifestations for clues to this elusive foundation. "Genealogy does not resemble the evolution of a species and does not map the destiny of a people. On the contrary, to follow the complex course of descent is to maintain passing events in their proper dispersion; it is to identify the accidents, the minute deviations—or conversely, the complete reversals—the errors, the false appraisals, and the faulty calculations that gave birth to these things *that continue to exist and have value* for us (Foucault et al. 1984, 81, emphasis mine). Looking to the domain of the moral and to the spiritual powers that supposedly enforce its mandates, one can see what lies beneath the otherwise ill-defined cultural unity and what provides the structure at the core of what is otherwise a plethora of complex models of social organization.

As we have seen, the wide geographical spread of the ritual of FGP suggests a common underlying substrate among the many "ethnicities" across West Africa. Understanding FGP as a *founding knowledge* better explains the cultural coherence of the forest region. It also lends insight into the *binding power* that enabled the newly constituted polities to form alliances.

Ethnic Consolidation on the Frontier: Adioukrou and Abidji Origins

The history of the Abidji and the Adioukrou, counted among the indigenous ethnicities of Côte d'Ivoire, clearly shows them to be comprised of a heterogeneous population that consolidated their distinct cultural identities over time. Moreover, the people themselves are aware of it: "All traditions accord to affirm that the founding ancestors had multiple origins and that the ethnic unity was historically worked out from a primal diversity" (Memel-Fotê 1980, 63).

Situated in the southeastern region, Abidji territory is clearly demarcated geographically, which was the basis for its cultural consolidation. To the south, the Pébo Forest separates it from Adioukrou territory. To the north the Mafé River separates it from the Aboudé village of Oress-Krobou, with which Abidji maintain traditionally good relations. To the west the Méré Forest and great Bandama River separate Abidji from Agni-Baoulé territory. The arrival of the Abidji, who were the first settlers of these lands, likely dates back 250 years. Two main waves of immigrants later infused the Abidji populace and culture: the Alladian, from the southern Ebrié lagoon region, and the Ashante from the east. It was from this second wave that the Abidji Ogbru subset was constituted, the clan that celebrates Dipri (Lafargue 1976, 21–22).

The Adioukrou territory lies further south. Principally situated along the Ebrié lagoon on the Gulf of Guinée, its more recent confederation of villages was established in the forest to the north, with Yassap at the furthest parameter. While considered indigenous, as the earliest settlers in their territory, they are also a composite people informed by multiple waves of newcomers from every direction: eight waves of migrations established the Adioukrou population and are officially recognized in their own historical accounts of their consolidation. Dida-Bété matriclans from the immediate northwest formed the foundational core (Memel-Fotê 2007, 220, 244). In the sixteenth century migration brought Alladian and Avikam from the lagoon region, and the first Adioukrou confederation of villages was formed. From the east came the Ebrié (Kyaman). Also, from the epicenter of Akan territory in the east came the Akedzu, who joined the Adioukrou in Lahou in the seventeenth century. Northern influxes, and particularly Baoulé (Baulé-Elpmwin) immigrants, date to the eighteenth century. Like the Abidji, the Adioukrou are considered a subset of the Akan and, more specifically, belong to an ensemble called "Agwa." "Agwa" means both "refuge" and "respite," an etymology that suggests that their alliances provided both protection and hospitality (Memel-Fotê and Brunet-Jailly 2007, 244). They represent the kind of artificial (though for that no less real) "corporate kin groups" that Kopytoff suggested were the actual basis of ethnicity in the African forest frontier.

Vestiges of Matrifocality in Abidji Origin Legends

The Abidji are classified as belonging to the Akan, a broader category of African ethnicities with common cultural features and origins in the east, in the region that is contemporary Ghana. Akan political organization is based on the matrilineage, headed by male and female coregents who occupied stools, the literal seat of power, understood to be the spiritual locus of the ancestors. Writing of Akan societies in Côte d'Ivoire, Dikeble and Hiba underscored the female source of all power: "Among the Akans, political power comes from the *adia-bia* stool, *which belongs to the woman*. That is why [those in Akan society] affirm that authority belongs to woman. She is the holder of *all power, spiritual and temporal*: she is the origin of law" (Dikeble and Hiba 1975, 382, emphasis mine).

Many ethnic groups relate a version of the master narrative, the famous legend of the Akan Queen Pokou (alias Abla or Abra Pokou, c. 1730) who, fleeing the Asante confederacy in Kumasi (Ghana), led her people westward to the Comoé River. There she saved them from the pursuing enemy by sacrificing her son to a river spirit that parted the waters and let them cross into Côte d'Ivoire, where they founded the Baoulé. The contemporary town of Sikinsi was originally an Abidji village with Asante origins, and its legend follows the pattern of the Asante mytho-history. A war between neighboring villages broke out as the result of a quarrel over adultery. In the face of defeat the entire population fled to the west, pursued by warriors representing the wronged party. At the banks of the Comoé River, diviners indicated that the chief, Sikinsi, was to sacrifice a child to enable the people to cross. Sikinsi asked his sister for her child, but she refused, and so his wife delivered her baby to save her people. When the child was thrown into the waters, they receded to allow the group to pass, but then flowed again, stopping the enemy's pursuit (Lafargue 1976, 26). The narrative recapitulates the narrative of Queen Pokou's retreat with one significant reversal: in the Asante case, the sacrifice of the queen's child reinforces the matrilineal tradition, while the Abidji legend underscores the sister's refusal and makes Sikinsi's own sacrifice the justification for their actual patrilineal tradition. Nevertheless, Sikinsi's wife is the heroine, for her offering is voluntary.

Sahuyé also traces its origin to the Asante and more particularly to the Baoulé. According to its founding legend, the ancestors were a brother and sister named "Ebri Tchimu" and "Ebri Adya." Because Adya's son committed adultery with Tchimu's wife, Tchimu killed his nephew. The adultery and murder are all the more shocking given the intimate and privileged relationship usually enjoyed between the maternal uncle and his sister's son in matrilineal societies. Adya decided to avenge her son's death and asked for the help of the Baoulé queen, Abra Poku, offering her a quantity of yams that had been hollowed and filled with gold. The queen provided Adya with an army, and a war erupted. The defeated Tchimu fled with his people to the west, under a leader named Abesé. At the river, a child sacrifice was required as an offering. Tchimu's *own wife gave up her child*, and they then successfully crossed. The name of the place where they eventually settled was Sahuyé, which means "the trouble is ended" (28–29).

This legend also combines strong matrifocal elements with the twist that justifies the Abidji adoption of a patrilineal system. The double transgression is such a great breach of the primary matrilineal bond and its sacrosanct moral nature that it results in war and the definitive break-up of society. The queen's army supports the defining matriarch (mother and sister of the offenders) and her call for retaliation against the murder of the matrilineal heir. It is indicative of the might of female power in response to moral outrage against offense to the matrilineage. Even the detail of yams filled with gold is significant, for the yam is often likened in African ritual rhetoric to the human body born of woman. So the matriarch's entreaty for military reinforcement is made in symbolic terms that call to mind her primacy.

In *structural* matters of social organization, Abidji are patrilineal. Despite this, there are indications that matrilineal and matrifocal principles persist and are forcefully asserted in key institutions underlying the very sustenance of the patrilineage. Abidji reserve a place of privilege for the *Dyanofwè*, a special designation for a sister's son. A man considers his Dyanofwè as his own child. Therefore, he is traditionally responsible for providing this nephew with a portion of land to cultivate and in the past even provided the necessary bride wealth so that he could take a wife. More importantly, this maternal uncle can transmit to his nephew the cult of the genie that is associated with his lineage. In turn the Dyanofwè owes his mother's brother the critical social obligation of burying him, implying that his structural position predominates over the paternal lineage, even the uncle's immediate offspring. "When the maternal uncle dies, it is the Dyanofwè who builds the platform for his funeral bed, digs the tomb, carries the coffin to the cemetery, and buries the deceased" (Lafargue 1976, 70). The fulfillment of these obligations ensures the spiritual well-being of the deceased. The bond between these matrikin is of a spiritual and moral nature.

Ironically, even contemporary cultural interpreters, like McGovern, discuss the critical dynamics of matrilineage only in terms of "the uncle-nephew relationship" (McGovern 2011, 72). By featuring the male actors, the phrase disguises the central feature of the relationship and the organizing principle behind it: matrifocality. For both these persons social identity is first and foremost established through their relationship to a woman. They are either the *mother's brother* or the *sister's son*. Matrifocality means more than a recognition of the maternal line or the ascription of the most authoritative role to the mother's brother (11n16). As this special relationship with the Dyanofwè demonstrates, it is especially an ethic based on a set of *values*.

Marriage is another feature of patriarchal social structure that is compromised in Abidji society by the privileged matrifocal relationship between the Dyanofwè and his mother's brother. In Abidji society a male may not marry a woman classified as belonging to either his paternal or maternal line—that is to say, his sisters, cousins, or any woman whose *mother* is a descendant of either line. Such a union would be considered incestuous. The particular emphasis on the taboo of the marriage within the matriline is in itself indicative of its primacy. "In cases of an infraction, the plantation of the incestuous couple will become sterile since the seeds will be 'spoiled' and the children, if there are any, will be deformed . . . they will waste away and die after much suffering" (Lafargue 1976, 71). The exception is that "the maternal uncle can give his [classificatory] 'daughter' to his sister's son as a wife," *provided that the bride's mother is not from the direct lineage of the groom* (71). Here again, the Dyanofwè is allowed to circumvent restrictions that would preclude a favorable marriage, in particular one that entwines the patriline and matriline. In this ruling the bloodline that is protected from incest is the matrilineage. Nevertheless, the threat of the consequences of an incestuous marriage remains. Therefore, appeal is made to the overriding powers of "an old woman" (71).

That old woman pounds certain leaves mixed with water, saturates a belt or bracelet in the infusion, has the bride wear it to ward off the danger, and has the partners serve each other the juices as a prophylactic.[5] The implication is that the medicinal infusion has magical, preternatural properties, for the old woman is the one who controls the moral mandates and the ramifications of transgression and can intervene by supernatural, spiritual means to her desired effect. She manufactures the spellbound stuff with the pestle, for it is not only a primordial tool for transformation, reworking the raw products of the earth into cuisine, but it is the quintessential instrument of female conjuring. As with Egbiki, the elderly female agent has the unique capacity to override moral transgression and its threat of sterility and death with her magical prowess.

Yet another indication of women's essential authorizing force is the benediction performed by an elderly woman when an Abidji couple marries. At that time "the only rite that has any religious character" is performed by "*an old aunt*, who takes a cup and pours libations on the ground, addressing the women ancestors of her lineage, saying 'you were married and you have lived in peace'" (76). It is not insignificant that this old aunt is "*the eldest of women from [the bride's] lineage*" (77, emphasis mine). For even though a bride goes to live with her husband, the matrilineage retains a hold over the woman and her offspring by virtue of the primacy of that bond and the moral force that it signifies.

Lafargue notes the unusual character of this sacerdotal act, given that in Abidji tradition it is only men, and more particularly the heads of the male lineage, who are authorized to perform sacrifices and libations. He explains that because these old women are not compensated in exchange for their daughter, taking no part in the dowry offered for her, they "risk being poorly disposed towards their 'daughter' . . . and *making her sterile by magical procedures.* One therefore gives them the rite of nuptial benediction [so that] . . . *the one from whom one might have feared receiving a curse is constrained by performing a blessing*" (77, emphasis mine). His interpretation reads like a recapitulation of the fairytale of "Sleeping Beauty," the maiden whose tribulations were caused by an old female fairy who, failing to receive an invitation to the wedding of Sleeping Beauty's mother, curses the progeny of that marriage with a kind of "sterility" so deep that the young girl becomes entirely frozen in a deathlike stupor. While it is true that in the Abidji case, the matriarch's power is similarly ambiguous and therefore must be harnessed for "the good," it seems that more than the fear of slight and retribution is at work. More important here is the implicit recognition that the ongoing success of the patrilineage depends on the power of the elderly matriarch to override the threat of death. This is a power ubiquitously ascribed to the Mothers. It is the same capacity that is invoked with the rite of *Egbiki*, through the appeal to FGP.

Adioukrou Origins: Matrifocal Magic and Genii-ology

Adioukrou culture is infused with the elements of Akan civilization at every level: "on the material plane, according to the customs of housing, diet and clothing as well as techniques of production; on the social level, with the dominance of the matrilineal reign; on the mental plane according to its mythology, vision of the world and religion" (Memel-Fotê 1980, 100). In all respects, worldly and structural as well as spiritual and "anti-structural," it is a matrifocal society that gives primacy to woman as source of all power.

As with most matrilineal societies, the Adioukrou legends of origin relate that the social founder and negotiator for settlement was a woman. The word *Adioukrou,* spelled phonetically as *odjukru* or *odzukru,* actually refers to a citizen of that society. The term that more properly designates the entire society or culture and its territory is *Lodzukru.* It has various etymologies, each associated with a legend of the group's origin. The most common explication traces the name to *Lodz,* the name of a woman, and also to *sodz,* sickness. According to one version, an old woman named Lodz suffered from sores but was healed by a mysterious being who appeared with plants with which she was healed (*ewl*) in an unexpected manner (*kpru*). Therefore "*Lodz ewl kpru,*" meaning "Lodz was miraculously healed," became the name of the people she founded (83).

Another legend says that a young Dida man went into the forest and came upon three daughters of a genie. *Ja Lodz* was one of them. She fell madly in love and followed the youth to his village and refused to return to her genie-father. The furious genie caused her to be ill, but her sisters pleaded for his mercy. Relenting, the father appeared to *Ja Lodz* in a dream to show her the plants she needed to heal herself. When she applied the juice from these medicinal plants to her body she was unexpectedly healed, and the people said "the illness (*sodz*) that had cast a pall over you (*ukr'm*) is no more (n . . . ng)": "*sodz n'ukr'ng.*" The descendants of Lodz are therefore the *Odzukru* (84). While the etymology is perhaps less convincing here, the story is interesting in that the claim is that the group are the direct descendants of *a female genie of the forest*, a being who typically allows for the negotiated settlement in an otherwise wild land. It is also significant that this primordial ancestress is healed by plants given by a genie, for it recalls the similar myth of the origin of sékè celebrated at Dipri.[6]

In a third legend, Lodz was a very beautiful married Dida woman who took a lover. As a result of her adulterous affair, Lodz gave birth to a daughter. Fleeing the fury of the husband, the couple and child crossed a river and took refuge in a forest. But Lodz became plagued with mysterious wounds and couldn't go on. So her lover left her and her daughter to go in search of food. At this moment of crisis a genie appeared to Lodz and told her to go to a certain encampment where she would find the cure. There she met an old man who went into the forest and gathered some medicinal plants for her. The genie then reappeared to show her how to use them as a remedy. When Lodz's lover returned, he found her suddenly healed: *Lodz ewl kpru* (85–86). The couple settled there and established the *Oboru*, considered the primordial Adioukrou matriclan (69).

The significant recurring elements in these versions are (a) illness or wounds and unexpected healing, (b) the intermediation of a genie of the forest to bring about the healing, and (c) that it is a woman (in one case in the form of a love-sick female genie) who is the founding ancestress of this matrilineal people. These accounts of the intimate link between genies and the founding ancestress and her matrikin in Adioukrou society are not merely a quaint folkloric tradition, but a strategic discursive maneuver, for only the accord of a genie authorizes a group to inhabit a territory, and only its benediction can enable their settlement to thrive. Through such legends the Adioukrou demonstrate that matrilineal genealogy converges with "genii-ology," the intimate association between ancestress and the spiritual source of legitimate power. This "firstness" of woman, as progenitor and settler with the moral claim of primogenitor, makes the Adioukrou not only matrilineal but also matrifocal.

In the Adioukrou language the word *eb* means "home." More literally it refers to the act of planting the first tree, the primordial act of establishing a settlement in the otherwise undomesticated space of the forest. The palm grove (*sar*) was, and still is, the quintessential sign of civilization for the Adioukrou. The *sar* and the material resources extracted from it (palm oil, palm wine, palm kernels for soap) belonged to the matrilineages, grounding each village socially and securing it economically. The palm plantation was also politically determinative, delimiting the village borders as well as the frontiers of the tribal confederation (*lebutu*). The symbol of social cohesion, the palm grove was the "most authentic expression of the *projection of social values on adioukrou space*" (Koby Assa 1981, 110, emphasis mine). Home was therefore also a moral topography.

For the Adioukrou, as for other Akan in southeastern Côte d'Ivoire, "Woman is the owner of the land and the whole wealth of the ancestral inheritance. The heir is only a steward and curator" (Dikeble and Hiba 1975, 383). While other collective units of society—the patriclans, age sets, or the village itself—were entitled to hold other forms of wealth such as livestock, money, valuable objects like cloth and jewelry, or slaves, the matriclans alone were entitled to control all these assets combined and always commanded the greatest share (Memel-Fotê 1980, 265). The matriclan also was the ultimate arbiter of any decision regarding the disposition of land, and therefore, "the final word belongs to woman. Without her consent, any decision is nul and void" (Dikeble and Hiba 1975, 383).

Once the land was exploited and dedicated to a matrilineage, it was indivisible, and any trespass would "provoke immediate conflict" (382). The youngest generation of the age set, indoctrinated as warriors in service of the matriclan (*bosu*), defend it. During war, women "maintain the purity of the territory in order to ensure victory; they dress in white and smear themselves with kaolin . . . they organize the *momomé*, a dance that is intended to chase away all impurity from the village. . . . The women keep watch; they dance and sing all night . . . to signal peace or armistice, it is a woman dressed in white who is sent to the negotiations" (386). My Adioukrou informants called this act of spiritual warfare by the same name as the rite preceding Dipri, *Egbiki*. By whatever name, the defense of land, village, political alliance, and justice was as much a defense of the moral values of the matrilineage as the material space that it claimed. Linking the spiritual values to social law, the ritual entreaty of FGP is a vigorous defense of the moral righteousness that is the foundation of both religious and worldly affairs.

As the founder of home, woman is also founder of the law. Law is not only a legislated code of conduct, but also the administration of what is just. "All [legal] judgments are made in the name of a woman. Justice, among the Akan of south-eastern Côte d'Ivoire, is symbolized by a woman because woman incarnates equity and impartiality. She is the supreme judge and her decision is without appeal" (384). In Adioukrou traditional society in particular, "spiritual values are not excluded from these social values. Justice is so essential to the constitution of home (*eb*) that any *transgression of law is interpreted as an affront to or trampling upon home itself*" (Memel-Fotê 1980, 118, emphasis mine).

The word *eb* also connotes the fundamental social values that enable one to live in social harmony. These include not only sentiments like love and loyalty but also the strong force of law and adherence to righteousness. An Adioukrou citizen was not only a person claiming autochthony, but one cultivated in the social space and according to its values. Only such a person can be called *eb-ij*, literally, "person of home."[7] Yet even Memel-Fotê, the foremost interpreter of this society and himself an Adioukrou, fails to identify with any precision what might constitute that determinative sensibility or underlying ethical value that defines *eb*. Struggling to name it, he can only offer the assertion that Adioukrou culture rests on a "unified vision of the cosmos, certain fundamental religious principles" and "*an ethic difficult to discern*" (Memel-Fotê 1980, 100, emphasis mine). He calls this nebulous ethos a type of "humanism," based on the traditional principle that a human being is the primary source of wealth "because a person, unlike gold, can answer the call of distress" (100). More specifically, it is the human being integrated into the matrilineage that is its wealth.

The social significance of the Adioukrou matriclan (*bosu*) is so great that genealogical knowledge of the lineage is still strictly preserved and confirmed at times of "great family assemblies" (54). Memel-Fotê gives the example of the matriclan "Mise-la" whose origin is Avikam, a lagoon people from the area of Grand-Lahou to the southwest. According to legend, Mise was a wealthy Avikam woman who took an Adioukrou lover. From their union were born seven children, three of whom were daughters. They each founded a matriclan and established one of the three villages comprising the first Adioukrou confederation, Bouboury (54–55). Even today the descendants of these matriclans pay homage to their Avikam relations. In so doing, they reinforce the strategic worldly alliance between them as much as the moral bond of maternal kinship.

Eventually, however, like most of the surrounding lagoon societies, the Adioukrou developed a system of bilateral filiation, and the term *eb* became synonymous with *patriclan*, the male ancestors in the paternal line. Nevertheless, these patrilineages remain subordinate to the matriclans. "Each village only knows the genealogy of the segment of patrilineal filiation that is its own. Often that line is little known, in contrast to what happens with the matriclans, which are the principal object of the *selu*," the specialist entrusted to retain historical information about the female line of descent (169).

The principal duty of the patriline is to oversee two rites of passage for the youth who come of age, signaling that they are contributing members of the *bosu*. For males the rite of initiation, called *lowe*, is collective. It prepares men for the performance of their duties in the age set. "The institution of the *bosu*, the maternal line, existed prior to the age classes, which in turn preceded the institution of the *eb*" (118). As we have seen, the fokwé puts those youth at the disposition of the matrilineage, making them into warriors who will defend home. The initiation of females into the "generation" of the age set, *dediakp*, is conducted individually, usually at the time of first menstruation. More important for a woman is the festival of maternity celebrated at the time of her first delivery, *wawr* (Memel-Fotê and Brunet-Jailly 2007, 20).

Wawr, not marriage, is the principal right in this matrifocal culture. It is a celebration of a woman's victory over a nine-month battle and her elevation to the status of mother.[8] It involves a retreat during which time the mother is fed, washed, massaged with oil, and allowed to rest, restricted from any economic or sexual activity. In former times it lasted three months. Today it may last only a week, more a symbolic gesture than an actual time of recovery. Wawr ends with a formal and triumphant "coming out" parade in which the new mother and child are presented to society and honored with a sumptuous feast. She is smeared with black clay, a mark imposed on men during their initiation (*lowe*). Her child contributes to the matrilineage its "greatest wealth." Moreover, the man responsible for conducting the Wawr ceremonies is the father of the new mother, not the father of the newborn child. While the paternity of the child is acknowledged, Wawr accords no honor or concession to his patrilineage. Rather, it pays homage to the matriline and celebrates its extension.

One might well argue that the comparable male institution is not *lowe* but *Angbandji*, an individual celebration of a man of a certain age who has acquired sufficient wealth to be considered a person of consequence. This parade and feast is a preliminary rite that enables him to celebrate *Ebeb*, the investiture of an age class with the authority to govern and the retirement of those who have completed the full cycle. Those are elevated to the ranks of respected counselors, the *ebebu* (lit. people of ebeb). Yet in *Angbandji*, a man comes out surrounded by the women of his matrilineage, while at the time of Wawr a woman is paraded alone. Moreover, to participate in the festival of Ebeb and attain the status of ebebu, a woman does not have to undergo this prerequisite ceremony to demonstrate her worth to the matriclan. An elderly woman *is* the embodiment of matriliny and stands for the principles on which society ultimately depends. For this reason, although the males of the age set occupy the overt positions of leadership, the matrilineage remains the guiding force. Therefore, "in old age a woman participates in family councils and can occupy the office of president" (Memel-Fotê 1980, 129). Ultimately the ritual of Angbandji situates a man who is coming into his full power at the time of the Festival of Generations as a product of the matriline and shows that he and his wealth are essentially in service to that female society.

From this analysis we see that a straightforward genealogy confirms that the nature of *ethnicity* in Côte d'Ivoire is composite and constructed, but a genealogical inquiry into their "*internal* visions of power" has shown that the principles that organized these diverse peoples into coherent polities were moral and matrifocal. Tracing such minutia enabled us to find indicators of the underlying principle of matrifocal morality in play, shedding light on "what we tend to feel is without history" (Foucault 1977, 76), namely the real and effective agency of African women in the establishment of worldly relations. Doing so allows us to dispense with "that grand fictive machine that is ethnicity" as something "fully constituted from one knows not what darkness of time" (Terray 1983, 1275) and to demonstrate that ethnicity in the frontier societies of Côte d'Ivoire was rather self-consciously constructed and negotiated on the basis of the moral principles of firstness and the recognition of the primacy of woman.

The same *moral knowledge* that served as the basis for the formation of ethnic groups also operated as the force that bound them in *alliances* in both peace and war. Collaborative covenants *between* ethnic groups in the region allowed for peaceful trade relations and strength to defend home on the forest frontier. The efficacy of those worldly alliances depended on the principles that inhere in the Mothers as their paramount source and most potent agent.

Binding Power: Alliances on the Moral Frontier

The period between the fifteenth and seventeenth centuries was a time of intensive migration and settlement of the forest frontier, the center of which was the territory of present-day Côte d'Ivoire. Kopytoff contends that, "when immigrants moved out of the metropolitan political system to the frontier, they left behind them institutions that had a moral legitimacy and entered what was, *morally, an institutional vacuum*" (1987, 26–27, emphasis mine). By such a reckoning, however, when a segmented and displaced group encountered a settled community on the frontier there would have been no basis for establishing peaceful relations with them. Without a common commitment to certain core moral principles, the frontier itself would not have been sufficiently hospitable to allow for mutual accommodation and settlement. The region would have been a literal battlefield of contentious clashes. I suggest that rather than entering a moral vacuum, migrants carried into the frontier that basic *founding knowledge*: that all social structure and political organization must be authorized by spiritual power and inaugurated through woman as its primary source and most effective mediator.

As even legends of origin relate, the metropolitan source communities were not necessarily models of civic organization that the frontier society would have sought to reproduce. Some splinter groups headed out into the unknown hinterlands to escape their jurisdiction. Therefore, the model for frontier communities would likely not have been based on a rejected organizational structure, but rather on an ideal. Kopytoff, too, surmised that "the impulse that carries people to the frontier" would have been the desire "to secure a way of life that is culturally legitimate and desirable but that is, for some reason, *unattainable at home*" (33, emphasis mine). The frontier represented the opportunity to revitalize those central values on which societies were *ideally* founded—the justice and moral order established by the ancestors. More than the structures of matriliny, patriliny, chieftainship, or kingship, what was reproduced and perpetuated was a commitment to an organizing principle—and that was a moral one.

As Kopytoff himself observed, only the persistence of a fundamental guiding principle could effectively account for the cultural coherence in the culturally heterogeneous region: "The similarities across Africa are too complex to have simply arisen from direct diffusion, yet they are too great to have developed through repeated coincidence, again and again, independently. We must see the societies in question from a new perspective, as having been *constructed— not out of whole cloth but from a cultural inventory of symbols and practices* that were brought from a metropole and *that pre-dated any particular society* being observed" (34, emphasis mine). FGP is the essential feature of that common cultural inventory. While some of its most powerful instances can be traced to the important metropoles, like the Asante royal state or the Mali Empire, the symbols and practice of the rite are independent of the markings of any particular ethnic identity or great society; FGP is rather a manifestation of the most primary overarching cultural values upon which every group depended. Those values—justice, righteous indignation over moral offense, and the fierce defense of moral authority—were most strongly asserted through women's naked assemblies, but have remained unrecognized as the basis for coherence on the frontier: "At present one can only note pragmatically certain themes that appear again and again in the African ethnographic literature and that would form part of the cultural 'baggage' that African frontiersmen would have repeatedly brought with them to their new settlements" (35). As the founding knowledge/ binding power on which new frontier societies relied, matrifocal morality and its enforcement through FGP are the essential contents of the "baggage" carried into the frontier.[9]

The common appeal to matrifocal morality also answers a problem with which Kopytoff was confronted and that the diffusionist model alone did not resolve: "Logically, continuous diffusion *should* create a spread across the face of the land of a *mish-mash* of cultural traits. But what we find is *something else*: a structured distribution of cultural patterns, some being very widely distributed and others being more locally confined" (15, emphasis mine). I contend that while the *political* cultures between the newcomers and local hosts might have been very disparate, the *moral* distance between them was negligible. More than any structure of kinship or rulership, what was reproduced and perpetuated on the frontier was the adherence to the principles of solidarity and egalitarianism and righteous indignation in the face of their violation. On this basis one can better understand how polities forged in the frontier self-consciously remained distinct in identity, organization, language, and custom, while their commitment to this core moral ideology was able to confer a certain quality of cultural uniformity among them.

Absorbing Outsiders, Acquiring Kin: Expansion on Moral Grounds

During the settlement of the forest frontier the matriclans operated and developed as a "mechanism for absorbing outsiders," incorporating into the newly consolidating communities fresh immigrants to reinforce the populace (Akyeampong and Obeng 2005, 29). In this early period "the matriclan was conceived of in terms of alliance rather than descent"; only later did the bloodline become a more important signifier of lineage and legitimacy (29).[10] The integration of immigrants into core egalitarian communities as defined by the matrilineages may have been a strategy for escaping the hegemony of the kingdoms and tributary societies from which some of the forest populations originally fled.[11] The invigoration of the matrilineages would have bolstered the egalitarianism of matrilineal societies, forged strategic alliances that enabled their survival and defense, and "weakened the monopoly of aristocratic chiefs" to which the disparate groups might have otherwise been subjected (Chauveau and Richards 2008, 520).

The fact that the impetus for many of the migrations into the forest region was a social crisis triggered by injustice or oppression further suggests that the moral would have featured as a principle for new foundations of society. It explains the tendency for frontier societies to remain "stateless" by design, more egalitarian than the polities of the metropoles from which the migrant populations were seeking refuge and respite.[12] The kind of power that organized and sustained the notoriously complex social structures of stateless societies betrays a concern for maintaining power as a dynamic rather than an entity in the hands of a person who might abuse it.[13] While one finds in the great states rites that invest rulers with female power, in frontier societies, the threat of the exercise of FGP rather holds secular authority in check. Until matrifocal morality can be seen as the factor shaping the forest zone, the sensed commonality will remain inchoate and treated as the result of "cultural givens of hoary antiquity and undeterminable origin" (Kopytoff 1987, 39).

Because matrilineage depends on the fertility and successive live births from one woman, it is always more precarious than patrilineage, where new members can be supplied by multiple women. And while a man can extend his reproductive life in the hopes of having a son, a woman who enters menopause without daughters leaves her matriline impoverished, and the wealth of that matriline cannot be passed on to her grandchildren. This vulnerability "makes reinforcement of the lineage an imperious necessity" to its survival (Perrot 1987, 168). Kopytoff too argues that "acquiring adherents who could qualify as kinsmen" was strategic because it fostered a relationship of obligation, making them more reliable (Kopytoff 1987, 44). But rather than inquiring into the *obligations* that bind kin groups, he underscores the *sentimental* quality of those relations: "In Africa, such terms as 'mother' and 'sister' convey sentiments of warmth, nurture, and attachment" (38). Yet as we have seen, "mother" is also a title of utmost respect and deference to her primordial power. While female elders are called "the Mothers," it is a recognition of the firstness of woman in the chain of humanity and society's subordination to the principles women embody.

One strategy for acquiring new kin was by adopting "those 'without lineage,' whose children can no longer be traced to their paternal lineages" (Perrot 1987, 168)—in other words, slaves. Societies like the Adioukrou and Abidji were less involved in slavery than the more hierarchical states outside of the forest frontier. Nevertheless, slavery was a regular feature of society even in these more egalitarian polities. Adioukrou matrilineages in danger of extinction integrated foreigners and slaves as "kin," either by marriage or adoption.

The more common strategy was to strengthen the matriline through exogamous marriage. The offspring of such marital alliances stood to benefit from a double inheritance, thereby enriching the collective holdings of the matrilineage. Therefore, Adioukrou showed preference for marriage into the patrilineal Abidji society (Memel-Fotê 1980, 589). To illustrate: the children of an Adioukrou father and an Abidji mother would inherit from their mother's patrilineage according to Abidji rules, but those same children would be socially integrated into the father's matriclan and Adioukrou by rights and could work the land of the matrilineage. In the case where the mother was Adioukrou and the father Abidji, the children automatically belonged to the matriclan, heirs of the maternal uncle (120). Nevertheless, these children would inherit from the father's patrilineage, as well. Given that for the Adioukrou the human being is the greatest treasure, marriage with an Abidji clearly offers advantages. The matriclan will benefit from the progeny and may even acquire additional wealth through inheritance from outsiders.

From Genealogy to "Genii-ology": Alliance on the Spiritual Plane

Marriages and the offspring they produced also fostered important spiritual alliances. Regular intermarriages between the Adioukrou of Yassap and the Abidji of Gomon, for example, gave rise to the patriclan *Ejikpaf*. "As a general rule, the patriclans bear the names of their tutelary genies. Religion is thus an element of a person's social identification" (Memel-Fotê 1980, 168). Consequently, a close affiliation between patriclans can be discerned from the fact that they maintain a cult to the same genie. This patriclan specializes in "magic" (173). "It is more or less certain that the Adioukrou patriclan called Ejikpaf shares its origin with the Abidji from the village of Gomon. Ejikpaf in Abidji means 'genie.' This clan dominates the village of Yassap (*Jasakp*). . . . Yassap and Gomon share the same harvest ritual, celebrated each year at the same time, as determined by Gomon. A genie of the water associated with this ritual is, for the Abidji, the principal genie of the village" (Memel-Fotê 1980, 54). The harvest ritual to which Memel-Fotê refers is, of course, Dipri, and the genie is Kporu. This explains the celebration of Dipri, in part, as a rite limited to a particular clan, bound by marriage, blood, and moral obligation.

Lafargue too notes the remarkable fact that "this magical 'power' [sékè], so dominant in the Abidji Ogbru villages, . . . therefore [actually] *originated in Yassap in Adioukou country*, [and they] would have transmitted them to their allies in the Abidji villages of Sahouyé [sic] and Gomon, who in turn would have diffused them to other Ogbru villages" (Lafargue 1976, 36, emphasis mine).[14] In fact, he goes so far as to say that only after the alliance was formed with the Adioukrou of Yassap did the manifestation of Dipri's magic enter Abidji territory (150).

Kopytoff explained that one means of making an association with newcomers enticing within the frontier society was to offer "'medicines' to attract and retain adherents" (Kopytoff 1987, 62). The opposite was surely just as true. That is, the newcomers may have enticed a host community to offer protection and alliance in war by sharing their protective medicines and spiritual powers. A strategic alliance with Gomon would have led Yassap to offer the magical means of protection in war, the heritage of Sèké. So while the Adioukrou Festival of Yams was superimposed on the Abidji New Year celebration of Dipri as a tutelary gesture, the Adioukrou initiation to the "genie" Séké would have provided for the transmission of the "medicine" associated with that cult. It added another layer to the event, making it more than merely a territorial hierarchical authority but the full expression of a moral bond and the forging of an inviolable alliance between groups on spiritual grounds.

Dissent and Relocation: Expansion on Moral Grounds

Societies with collective self-rule clearly resisted hierarchical state authority, spreading power instead across the *eb* (clans, lineages, and age sets). Yet in collectively governed society, "there is little to stop the young from forming new communities in the forest" (Chauveau and Richards 2008, 517). According to recurrent themes in many legends of origin in the region, splits often did happen because of quarrels over adultery, witchcraft, or other moral affronts (cf. Perrot 1987).

Dissent on moral grounds constitutes another part of the story of how one segment of Adioukrou forged special alliances with the Abidji and came to share in the spiritual powers that are the centerpiece of Dipri. Once again following the clues of disparate details of ethnicity and alliance, we can recover the subjugated knowledges of matrifocal morality and female power at work, giving shape to the history of the region.

The Adioukrou comprise two confederations in a state of semi-permanent rivalry: The Bobor and the Dibrm confederations, whose villages Bouboury and Debrimou served as their respective seats. The Bobor confederation was consolidated first, in the sixteenth century, with the incorporation of Alladian immigrants from the south.[15] The establishment of the alliance correlates with the inauguration of the institution of the age set. In the seventeenth century Debrimou seceded and formed its own confederation. Orbaff and Yassap were among the villages belonging to this group. The story of why the Adioukrou are split into separate and hostile camps is a *moral* tale and a matter of mytho-history.

According to one tradition Debrimou was founded by two brothers, sons of the legendary founding ancestress of the Adioukrou, Lodz.[16] The two hunters set up an encampment in the forest and found that it was so fertile there that when others asked about it, they answered "Kibrm, don't ask!," meaning that it was beyond description. This is the origin of the name "Dibrm," or "Debrimou." During one hunting expedition, the elder brother, Sès, went off in search of water, while Niagne stayed behind. Sès discovered the river Selikpo (associated with the genie Selikp who is adored in Orbaff and Yassap). But when he returned to camp he found that Niagne had eaten without waiting for him. To do so, he had made sacrifice to the genie of that place. Later, when the encampment expanded to become a village, the brothers fought over who had the right to oversee the first celebration of Ebeb that would initiate the age set and hence establish its formal system of governance. The judges of Bouboury determined that Niagne, although younger, had primacy, since it was he who had been the first to sacrifice to the genie at the time of his first meal in that territory. This story of two brothers who encounter a genie in the forest while hunting mirrors the tale of the origin of Dipri, although that story is Abidji and relates to the founders of Sahuyé and Gomon. As we shall see, this is no coincidence.

The judgment overturned the presumption of the privilege of gerontocracy, imposing instead a system of seniority. Under this system, rank is a function of the degree to which one has mastered esoteric knowledge/power, usually by undergoing various degrees of initiation. On this basis under certain circumstances a younger person may rank above an elder.[17] More than a physical condition, "age" therefore is a social category, or more precisely it is a spiritual one. In this case, Bouboury's ruling reiterated that *spiritual knowledge* takes precedence over the structured order and hierarchical principles of social organization. Their decision underscored that the founding of Debrimou was determined by that most significant gesture of settlement—the homage to the genie—and dependent on the power granted through a covenant with that spiritual host. It was an assertion of what was a general principle on the frontier: that "precedence is not an absolute fact of chronology. The claims to primacy . . . were not based on the fact that they were the very first inhabitants but that they had wrested a civilized social order out of a socio-political wilderness" (Kopytoff 1987, 56). Therefore, society is, quite literally, morally grounded. To inhabit the ground and make a settlement depends on an inviolable bond.

The judicial determination in the case of the two brothers imposed a logic about the nature of authority, but sowed dissent. Bouboury was entitled to make the ruling as the senior village, the elder of the confederation, but in some respect the decision subverted the grounds for their own authority over Debrimou, a frontier village and subordinate community. From that time, Debrimou (and especially the clan associated with the elder brother) challenged the primacy of Bouboury, eventually splitting to found its own rival confederation. The secession dates to 1690 or 1711, depending on which age class and subset is used as the point of departure for making the calculation (Memel-Fotê 1980, 106). The simmering tension between the two confederations endured over three hundred years and was exacerbated in colonial times, when the French appointed an Adioukrou from Debrimou (the junior confederation) as the regional chief of their indirect rule.[18]

Dipri as a Tributary Act: The Moral Foundations of Strategic Alliance

Given the fomenting tensions with Bouboury and because they were the farthest outlying villages in the Dibrim confederation, Orbaff and Yassap sought an alliance with the Abidji for reinforcement and protection in the event of a war.[19] As newcomers to the territory, the breakaway Adioukrou villages would have been granted this protection and privileged access to land only by acknowledging the primacy of the Abidji as the first settlers and by submitting to the reigning lineage, which maintained the cult to both its ancestor and the genie. Both were accomplished through the rhetorical work of Dipri.

The submission of the newcomer to the "owners of the land" is such a fundamental moral principle that, as we have seen, it governs relations with the Earth goddess and the genies as much as relations among human societies. The ancient and still current principle that governs first comer–late comer relations is that "one cannot refuse an outsider who needs land as a means of subsistence. The 'stranger' must respect the bundle of duties associated with his social incorporation in the local community and consequently contribute to the reinforcement of the economy under the locally prevailing social order" (Chauveau and Richards 2008, 52). In the context of the Abidji-Adioukrou relations, the "bundle of duties" to which the newcomers were obligated must certainly have included indoctrination into the cult of the ancestors of the Abidji hosts. Chauveau and Richards underscore that the "stranger owes his *tuteur* [patron] perennial gratitude (an obligation transferred to his heirs), expressed through the gift of agricultural products" (525). That those Adioukrou were under a perennial obligation to their Abidji patrons explains their reference to this spectacular event of Dipri as the Festival of Yams. This phrase underscores the debt that is recognized and honored through the performance of the rite and emphasizes the sacrifice of the first harvest as its most critical aspect.

Among all the Ivoirian groups classified as Akan, the Festival of Yams is an important independent ritual celebrating both the ancestors and the new harvest, but for most it has nothing to do with Sèkè. While these groups conduct the festival "at different, uncoordinated times of the year spaced through time from one society to another," it is significant that "in Orgbaf and Yassakp [Yassap] they obey the sacred calendar of the Abidji" (Memel-Fotê and Brunet-Jailly 2007, 716). By submitting to the Abidji calendar and subsuming the Festival of Yams to the Abidji celebration of Dipri, these two villages pay homage to their hosts by linking their own ancestral festival with that of the Abidji while fulfilling their ritual obligation to them.

The principle of primacy in the sense of being first and therefore having natural authority over newcomers is undeniably one that shaped the cultural landscape on the frontier. It is part of the moral scaffolding on which society was erected. Yet one kind of firstness that ethnography typically overlooks is the ever-repeated assertion that in the history of humanity Woman came first and that it is she who is therefore the natural authority, the one who literally embodies the moral domain and to which even the most senior and powerful social representative owes obedience and respect. A tribute to the spiritual and moral preeminence that women represented was therefore essential to formal alliances.

Female Powers and Moral Bonds

Parallels between the legend of the founding of the Dibrm confederation and the *second* myth of the origin of Dipri exist, and the reason is now more apparent. The tale is a story of two brothers in the forest and a genie who grants one of them special rights (to settle land) that the brothers share. As we saw (in chapter 1), the myth of the origin of sèkè comprises these same basic mythemes: a genie in the forest grants one brother rights (to the powers of a plant) that are to be shared with his brother. The strikingly similar structural configurations of these two narratives suggest a common source. The Adioukrou origin of sèkè explains it and also explains why there are two such disparate myths associated with Dipri. The myth of Bidyo and the miraculous appearance of the yam from the body of his sacrificed child is about the establishment of the territorial rights of the Abidji and the founding of society. It validates the *vertical* structures of society: the hierarchy of the lineages, the ancestral cult, and the right of primogenitor over the land. The second myth narrates an encounter with a genie who offers a leaf with miraculous powers. It is about the origin of sèkè and the power of *kpol*. It makes no territorial or hierarchical claims; its focus is esoteric power and the moral obligation to share it for the benefit of kin and ally. In this way, it underscores the *horizontal* bonds of society, the domain in which woman's role as source and protector is paramount.

The discovery of sékè by the Adioukrou brother hunters explains why the Adioukrou call the whole spectacular event *Erng-ok*, meaning "to bathe in the water,"[20] or *Kpol*, referring to the trance and the compelling force of the genie. The elder who officiates at the river "carries a palm branch, and wears rings on his ankles whose sounding *prevents any dread encounter*. The palm branch represents spiritual life and *through its manipulation witches are supposedly able to shackle or free a soul*" (Memel-Fotê 1980, 297). The allusion to the threat of evil and the dangers of supernatural entrapment that could befall an unprotected neophyte is a sign of the deeper purposes of initiation. But as we know, that capacity is uniquely ascribed to the Mothers and their appeal in Egbiki to FGP.

The initiation proper is a secret rite excluded from public view. Nevertheless, the consonance between the known details of the initiatory ceremony and an initiation conducted among the neighboring Anyi peoples (also a matrilineal group classified as Akan) are suggestive and lend insight into the connection with female power. Anyi spiritual mediums (*komye*) are all female. At the time of initiation into their vocation, the novitiates are sworn to serve the water genies. An initiate must wear a "sort of loincloth, held by a belt made of a string of pearls. She cannot use a mortar and pestle . . . she is forbidden sexual relations . . . she must obey her 'mother' (her mistress in initiation) unrestrictedly. When she addresses her, kneeling as a captive before her, she must use the utmost respect" (Perrot 1996, 173). The parallels with the dress and restrictions imposed on initiates, as well as the injunction against the use of the pestle at the time of Dipri, are evident. The obedience to the "mother," the initiating elder and spiritual guide, is translated in Dipri to obedience to one's actual mother, from whom a youth must obtain prior permission to participate in the rite, at risk of peril to his life. The ceremonies that bring a new *komye* out into public service at the conclusion of her formal apprenticeship involve ordeals in which she must demonstrate her capacity to "see" by clairvoyance the hidden acts of others, and also "'see' and avoid all the traps that her adversaries have set 'invisibly' on her path to test her talents," including putting before her "deep holes [that] open under her feet" (174). This kind of test is similar to the one that the Sékèpuone put before the new initiates of Dipri. It is ultimately the great danger that the women who perform Egbiki must be prepared to face, as well.[21]

The Egbiki rite demonstrates that even while the male patriclan Ejikpaf "specializes in magic" (Memel-Fotê 1980, 173), the most exceptional "means of conjuring spells, and also the most singular power, is employed by women" (Lafargue 1976, 190–93). The rite is an exercise of the supreme and overarching power that the Mothers alone can wield. While the genies and genii-ology helped establish alliances between clans, the paramount force of FGP binds even groups unrelated by territory, ethnicity, or custom. Female genital power is an evocation of the inviolable moral order itself.

Oaths and the Binding Force of Female Power

Strategic alliances in the multiethnic forest zone of precolonial Africa ensured peace and security of trade among otherwise unrelated people. While they were necessarily political they were also religious and moral. The moral notions of inviolability, immunity, and inalienable rights were shared in the forest zone and understood not only in terms of negative prohibitions but also as positive attitudes and conventions in support of the preservation of life and the dignity of persons. These translated practically into two fundamental obligations: the duty to extend hospitality to the stranger and the obligation to protect social justice, first and foremost in terms of respect owed to women (Memel-Fotê and Brunet-Jailly 2007, 365). The duties of civility owed to the stranger or even to free male allies were conditional, restricted to periods of peace and enforced only in the territory of the host. By contrast, the absolute and unassailable rights owed to women knew no limits. "First, [protection and courtesy] was extended to the entire female sex without exception or regard to age or status: girls and women, indigenous or newcomer, free and slave. Next, it was permanent" (366). This fundamental principle, in force among southern Akan societies and beyond, explains in part the free circulation of women who undertook trade across ethnic boundaries. These privileges were founded in the basic premise that "women share in the sacrality of the earth. . . . The female subject is the place where ancestors and gods, continuing the creation of life, participate as founders and agents" and on this basis are venerated (366).

The symbolic allusion to women's presence and binding power is made in formal pacts as well: "Two sorts of relations determined exchanges: the control of the channels of communication and traffic linked to *territorial sovereigns* on the one hand, and the *alliances* that various formal pacts established on the other. To these prescribed relations were added a type of *unbreakable political-religious relationship that, while not formally prescribed, was inalienable:* the *inviolability accorded to women*" (Memel-Fotê and Brunet-Jailly 2007, 355, emphasis mine). Formal alliances between groups were effected ritually, through "blood pacts." Such a pact was made between factions of the Adioukrou and Abidji with whom they did not share clan affiliation. According to oral history, Adzeb, an Adioukrou from Yassap, and N'Dja, an Abidji hunter from Elibu, swore that they would spill neither each other's blood nor that of their descendants.[22] They cleared a trail and brought each other food and other products that their two groups would trade. N'Dja supplied bananas, yam, and tarot while the Adioukrou traded atiéké,[23] palm nut oil, and tobacco (Memel-Fotê 1980, 382). Although it is not mentioned in this passage, it is likely that a blood sacrifice was made in such cases. It also suggests that the procedure followed a prototypical rite of oath making that involved digging a hole, making sacrifice in it, and swearing to the Earth goddess.[24]

Blood pacts also served to open a trade route. The parties involved would "dig a hole and fill it with the things [that were to be traded]; or simply, they built a pile as a 'sacrum,' *oshu*. One after another they made the rounds of the pile or hole and swore mutual protection" (Memel-Fotê and Brunet-Jailly 2007, 362). The sacred oath itself involved blood, literally spilled in a sacrifice, as well as female blood, for the oath is sworn on a "dirty rag," a woman's loincloth, or more explicitly, her menstrual cloth soiled with blood. To make the pact, the cloth was seized by members of each party and ripped in two.

On January 31, 1898, G. Thomann, a European trader in Côte d'Ivoire, witnessed such a pact made between the Neyo, who were part of his convoy, and three clans of Bété people: the Bété-Guidêko, the Bété-Bobwo, and the Bété-Sokuy:

> To seal the trade treaty in an irrevocable fashion, the indigenous peoples wished to conduct a fetish ceremony which in that region replaced the exchange of blood. . . . *They borrowed from a married woman a cloth used for intimate purposes (diépro), then a representative of each peoples held an end of the dirty rag.* The two operators repeated once more the clauses of the treaty, then together tugging on the cloth, they tore it. Each one then placed their piece of the stuff on a brand prepared in advance and watched while the cloth was completely reduced to cinders. A young cock was then brought by the Gogui chief who with a knife broke a corner of the beak. Held by the feet, the animal poured out his blood drip by drip on the ashes of the *diépro*. When they were sufficiently impregnated, the indigenous people from both camps rushed upon it and, soaking their hands in the disgusting mixture of ashes and blood, smeared each other with it on the neck and back. (G. Thomann 1903 in Memel-Fotê and Brunet-Jailly 2007, 364, emphasis mine)

Female blood was thus the most potent form of effecting a social bond. In Akan society generally, and in the kingdom of the Asante of Ghana in particular, "the greatest Asante shrine, the Golden Stool, was periodically *contaminated* with menstrual blood *to sharpen its power*" (Akyeampong and Obeng 2005, 33, emphasis mine). If we replace the word *contaminated* with *infused*, one can readily see that the potent blood from women's genitals is empowering and lent to the stool, the sacrosanct symbol of the nation, both vigor and moral force.

Any breach of a sacred oath would result in a metaphysical sanction of the highest order: death. The manner of death one could anticipate was signaled symbolically by the elements contained in the ritual pact. Among the Adioukrou and Abê, for example, after swearing mutual protection one would drink water infused with salt and hot pepper.[25] It was understood that a breach would result in death by drowning or diarrhea. The instrument of sanction invoked by the central presence of a woman's "dirty rag" is certain and bloody death, just as the effective appeal to FGP as spiritual warfare brings about the certain and bloody death of the enemy. Moreover, the act suggests the total destruction of the very grounds of their respective peoples, signaled by the smearing of their bodies with the "disgusting mixture" that consists of the female blood of the matrikin combined with the sacrificial offering of themselves and their generation in the form of the broken-beaked young cock.

By appealing to the female genitals, such an oath or covenant was made binding: "The sacred plays a role as an instrument to ensure order in three ways: curses, accusation of witchcraft and blessing. Properly speaking, the curse— *ofn*—is the means by which sanction of the gods and the dead, supreme judges, is called down upon the insurgent who transgress the law or breaches an oath. A disgrace (*abu-ejr*) in the form of an illness, accident or death is the logical consequence and expected result of an *ofn*. A popular and solemn weapon of superiors in relationship to inferiors, the curse protects rulers against contestation and subversion" (Memel-Fotê 1980, 373).

As we have seen, all three instruments of social order are present simultaneously in the appeal to FGP. Its evocation is itself a trap that will *reveal the identity of a witch* even as it punishes that evil-doer, it is the most powerful *curse*, stronger than any spell or act of sorcery, and it is *the most effective protection* with an overarching reach extending across the whole of village and society. As the most primary, potent, and paramount embodiment of the moral order, the female genitals represent the source and instrument of righteous agency.

In these pacts we see FGP operational as a strategy, a technology, and a discourse all at once. In such gestures, the "power is neither given, nor exchanged, nor recovered, but rather exercised, and . . . only exists in action. . . . It is above all a relation of force" (Foucault and Gordon 1980, 89). By appealing to the moral righteousness of woman and to her genitals and blood as the symbol of the terrible consequence of moral violation, the pact is a strategic exercise of relations of power. The Mothers make symbolic use of the technology of FGP as an ambiguous force, simultaneously reinforcing social cohesion and peace even as it threatens the malediction of any who threatens that order. In this way, FGP is always, essentially, a coercive arm of worldly political power as much as it is an expression of an ideal spiritual aspiration for the use of that power as a benediction. Even in the performance of such rituals where women are absent, the allusion to their power is a way to reinscribe it in social institutions. It shows FGP to be a common ingredient of local knowledge—both as a foundational understanding implicitly shared and as essential to *savoir-faire* that makes something happen. It shows it to be an essential component of power relations and, for that reason, a critical component of these institutionalized forms of knowledge that rely on informed expertise and mastery of execution to produce real effects.

Conjuring up the Will to Engage

The concept of FGP and its application on the worldly stage of society and politics is a very particularly African, and therefore *local* and idiosyncratic, construct. It is one of those critical "idioms in which successive African immigrants have in past millennia conjured up the will to engage in their local struggles for mastery" (Lonsdale 2000, 12). By unearthing from the weight of structural details the more anti-structural principles that have been so often overlooked, we have seen how the deep and mysterious founding knowledge/binding power associated with women elders undergirds the surface and most overt structures of social hierarchy as well as the moral order.

The aim of the next part is to show that the idioms so critical for the founding of African civilization are not only still alive in the contemporary local imaginary but that the subjugated knowledges of matrifocal morality are persistent ideals and still in play in the contemporary contests about the nature and sources of power and its proper exercise. As we shall see, the Mothers continue to conjure up the will to engage the founding knowledge and binding power that they embody, and still mobilize to effect their FGP in the fractured situation of civil war.

5. WOMEN AT THE CHECKPOINT
Challenging the Forces of Civil War

No sociology of political change in progress since colonization is
possible without preliminary anthropological study.
—HARRIS MEMEL-FOTÊ, *Le Système Politique de Lodjoukrou:
Une Société Lignagère à Classes d'Âge (Côte-d'Ivoire)*

Justice, among the Akan, is symbolized by a woman because woman incarnates
equality. She is the supreme judge and her decision is without appeal.
—JOSÉPHINE DIKEBLÉ AND MADELEINE HIBA,
"La Femme dans la Vie Politique Traditionelle des Sociétés à Etat
du Centre, de L'est et du Sud-Est de la Côte d'Ivoire"

Nationalism and Tribalism

During the years following African independence and the rise of the new
nation-states, the "hated twin" of territorial nationalism was tribalism (Lonsdale 1986, 131). While nationalism promoted local sovereignty, called for political self-determination, and promised participation in the global economy,
tribalism was (and still is) associated with backward-looking isolation and
self-defeating internal competition. Even today analysts of the common contemporary strife in Africa typically portray ethnic identity and regional alliances along ethnic lines as the rivals of national unity and assume they are responsible for inducing violent conflicts.

Despite the widespread assumption that ethnicity is a problem to be overcome if the African state is to achieve stability, statistics actually reveal no
correlation between ethnic heterogeneity and civil war.[1] Stanford scholars
James D. Fearon and David D. Laitin concluded in their 2003 study that "it
appears not to be true that a greater degree of ethnic or religious diversity—or
indeed any particular cultural demography—by itself makes a country more
prone to civil war" (Bass 2006). More surprisingly, literature on civil wars
also suggests that countries with greater heterogeneity are less prone to civil

war than those with a significantly polarized populace; "social diversity can have several offsetting effects that may reduce the risk of large-scale violent conflict" (Elbadawi and Sambanis 2000, 247). In more polarized societies, it is easier for rebellion to arise and find broad support, but a more diverse population requires regular negotiation and cooperative participation in governance. "Ethnic diversity may be a potential asset to Africa," since a negotiated equilibrium among groups can lend credibility to nascent democracies (263). Defying stereotypical expectations, a growing body of work indicates that ethnic diversity is therefore actually "a deterrent rather than a cause of civil war" (254).

Comparative studies of the incidence of civil war concluded that violent conflict in Africa, as elsewhere, has less to do with ethnic demography than with lack of accountability in governance. The greatest indicator of the probability of civil war is not poverty but lack of political freedom and representation, while an expanded level of political rights reduces the risk of conflict to almost zero (257). Moreover, political reform appears to be a *prerequisite* for steady economic development, rather than the *consequence* of a stable state (261).

Côte d'Ivoire, like too many other sub-Saharan African countries, was torn apart by civil war, and much has been made of ethnicity, regional alliances, and religious divisions as the underlying cause of civil strife. Indeed, the populace has been divided according to seemingly clear axes: "Mandé/Dyula" vs. "Akan/ Baoulé," Northern vs. Southern, Muslim vs. Christian. Both journalistic and scholarly accounts of the course of the Ivoirian conflict typically hinge on these very factors. One interpreter of the hostilities put it especially forcefully and prescriptively: "the article . . . argues strongly that since ethnicity is at the root of the Ivorian civil conflict, de-ethnicisation of politics will serve as appropriate therapy for a conflict-free Côte d'Ivoire where an Ivorian, irrespective of his/ her ethnic and religious backgrounds, will be seen and regarded as a genuine and bonafide citizen of the country" (Badmus 2009, 45). Other studies call for more nuanced analysis and offer alternative explanations for the factors driving civil war. They indicate what even analysts who focus on ethnicity as a root cause of violence also allow that in most conflicts in Africa, division among ethnic groups has been politically manipulated for pragmatic reasons by parties seeking to obtain or retain power. "The conflict in Ivory Coast is a by-product of deep-seated cleavages revolving around ethnicity, nationality and religion. Politicians tapped into these differences to consolidate their monopoly on power, and in the process, pushed the country toward civil war" (Ogwang 2011).

In light of all these findings, a reconsideration of the meaning and value of ethnicity and ethnic alliance seems more urgent than ever. We have seen that ethnicity is neither a romantic fiction nor a mere opportunistic liaison recently constructed for political ends, but a historical reality and a critical feature of the social landscape. With this in mind, it seems imperative to consider what these traditions may contribute to the contemporary state, and what the state, in turn, owes them. "Ethnic politics is stigmatized as tribalism. . . . But we must also ask whether the destruction of ethnic associations, among Africa's most vital social institutions, will not also destroy some of the main guarantors of the popular right to argue about political accountability" (Lonsdale 1986, 141). One of those "main guarantors" of accountability has been the widespread local principle of governance based on moral commitments, enforced by metaphysical sanction, and vigilantly maintained by the ritual interventions of the founding Mothers. As we have seen, the women elders authorize rulership and check its power. Their vigilance and activism are "part of the moral calculus of power" (128). It can be argued, therefore, that the test of both political accountability and the moral authority of governance in Africa is the condition of women in society and the degree to which they, who monitor justice for all society, are satisfied.

As traditions are effaced by the systems and interests of the colonial and postcolonial state, women have been losing ground. This has happened both literally, as they have lost control over territories and the economic independence that access afforded them, and figuratively, in terms of the degree to which social systems are accountable to the standards that they embody and uphold. This chapter introduces the dynamics of Côte d'Ivoire's recent civil war to demonstrate that, while largely overlooked by journalists and scholars alike, the rhetorical work of the female elders who perform FGP is critical among other discursive tropes at play.

Ethnicity and Alliance in the Cash Crop Economy: The Roots of Conflict

One of the more recent studies of the worldly situation in Côte d'Ivoire is Mike McGovern's *Making War in Côte d'Ivoire* (2011). A work of cultural anthropology that also offers a cogent interpretation of the history leading up to the civil war, it is a study of social dynamics in the fraught decade after the coup d'état of 1999 and before the highly contested presidential elections of 2010, a period known as "no peace, no war." To explain the violence McGovern looks beyond the usual tropes of ethnic conflict, nationalist xenophobia, and the drama of decolonization and turns attention instead to the "heightened and self-conscious level of the rhetoric used by many actors" on both sides of the warring factions: the "Young Patriots," who supported the republic and the state headed by former President Laurent Gbagbo, and the rebel forces that overturned that government (27). For me this rhetoric includes the unspoken rhetoric of women, who are by and large ignored in McGovern's analysis.

Early on McGovern signals that one must treat ethnic identity apart from other "incentives, motivations and justifications" involved in the escalating conflict in Côte d'Ivoire (25). The most inflammatory tinder that fueled the conflict was the way that ethnicity was manipulated in service of national elite politics. McGovern recounts how the Ivoirian state encouraged immigration to supply workers for the coffee and cocoa plantations that subsidized its coffers, calling its political strategy an "internal colonization" (87). It is essentially the story of how interethnic resentment became hardened into a brittle policy of state that fractured the country, both along an east/west divide and, as hostilities escalated, along the north/south axis, as well. It begins in the south-central region, in territory identified with the Bété peoples, where the contestation over land, a focus in the civil war, became especially acute.

Like other ethnic groups in the forest zone, the Bété have a complex history, and its founding populace was comprised of many distinct subgroups. They are classified as belonging to the Krou language cluster and share cultural links with peoples in the southwestern quadrant of Côte d'Ivoire between the Ivoirian cities of Daloa and Gagnoa, such as the Dan, We, Guéré, Guro.[2] Although the founding population of the Bété had migrated to the area as early as the seventeenth century, during the colonial era it was increasingly informed by an influx of Dyula and Voltaic immigrants from the north, as well as Baoulé from the east who were impelled by the French to farm coffee and cocoa in the region. By the 1930s locals in the Gagnoa region, feeling increasingly displaced and targeted by French colonial discrimination, launched a resistance movement. Their intractability became associated with their very identity. Following Jean-Pierre Dozon (1979), McGovern relates that French colonials supposedly ascribed the name *Bété* to them as a pejorative label ("bête" meaning stupid or pig-headed in French vernacular). For this reason, he asserts that Bété identity, like the name of the group itself, was essentially a *colonial* fabrication, forged among unrelated groups who claimed status as an autochthonous people in an effort to resist the encroachment of Baoulé, whom the French favored.[3] That is, for McGovern, Bété ethnicity is merely an artifice created to lay claim to land. On this premise he argues that this society, identifying itself as indigenous, "can only anachronistically be called 'Bété' . . . before the twentieth century" (Launay 1986, 286). By extension, he implies that all southern ethnicities in the forest zone were thus constructed as cultural inventions, composed through strategic alliances for political expedience. For him, Bété history is unique only in that its composition is so recent, so politically inflected, and so linked to the civil war.

While it is true that the tensions between Bété and Baoulé were defining for the conflict, the establishment of a consolidated Bété ethnic consciousness is not merely "an epiphenomenon of the colonial labeling process," as McGovern suggests (286). Such a claim is itself an extension of the manipulation of ethnicity by the postcolonial state that drove wedges not only between the semi-desert and poor region of the north and rainforest and plantation-rich south, but between big-planters in the southeast (Akan and Baoulé) and those who contested their claims to land in the southwest (Krou and Bété). What the focus on the authenticity of ethnicity and the inter-ethnic nature of the conflict disguises is that the civil war was a product of the state's "nation-building project [that] was essentially a process of alienating and deconstructing existing identities, allegiances that were based on entrenched demarcations of traditional territorial spaces" (Araoye 2012, xiii–xiv).

After independence in 1960, Côte d'Ivoire's cash-crop economy rapidly expanded. The country has been among the largest producers of coffee and leads the world in the production and export of cocoa, producing an estimated 33 percent of the world's supply as recently as 2012. During the early years, autochthonous elders provided newcomers with access to ancestral lands for cash-crop farming through traditional conventions. These covenants were understood to be revocable leases and, according to custom, operated as traditional "Tutorat" in which the hosts extended rights of land use to newcomers but retained the ownership of the territory as a traditional holding. However, under the first president, Félix Houphouët-Boigny, the Ivoirian state legislated a new land policy, the "policy of *mise en valeur*, in which the government granted land to anyone who put it to use" (McGovern 2011, 80). The policy aimed to supply the labor necessary to pioneer forested lands to which the state had laid claim and to facilitate the expansion of cash-crop farming that it controlled.[4] The state kept the borders wide open to encourage the influx of migrant farmers into the fertile southwestern region. Meanwhile, the government courted the support of the rural youth by serving as the patron of an alternative path for them into the urban sphere, offering free schooling and expanded employment opportunities in Abidjan and other urban centers. (In this respect, the *mobility of youth*, a factor of the eventual turmoil, was in part also manufactured by state policy.) This strategy held sway until the late

1970s, when the state's ability to absorb young Ivoirian elites became saturated (Fauré 1993, 317).

The newcomers who benefitted from the new land policy were not only foreigners, but especially Akan (Baoulé) big planters from the southeastern region, many of whom originated from aristocratic matrilineal lineages. Under pressure for new land, Akan youth extended their activities to the central-western (Bété) region. As contributors to the wealth of their matrilineal families, the Akan youth did not represent a challenge to the authority of the elders or the traditional system, which as we shall see, was the case for youth from other ethnicities (Chauveau and Richards 2008, 521). According to some, under the leadership of Houphouët-Boigny, who was himself a Baoulé, the Bété were actively targeted for manipulation. "The government encouraged people from the dominant Baoulé group and others from around the country to settle in the far west in order to dilute Bété dominance there and profit from the cacoa [sic] and coffee plantations there. Bété identity is now influenced by these indigenous/outsider, rural/urban contrasts rather than by pre-colonial factors" (Minority Rights Group 2015).

In exchange for the rewards associated with its policy of "agricultural colonization," the state expected the immigrant populations to support Houphouët-Boigny's state party and its local agents (Chauveau and Richards 2008, 530). The strength of that support was not insignificant, given that since independence in 1960 foreigners had been given the vote as long as they registered on the electoral roll (Fauré 1993, 326). Thirty years later, at the time of the first competitive presidential election held in 1990, an estimated 40 percent of the population was comprised of foreigners, and the majority of these were from Burkina Faso (326). Throughout Houphouët's reign, his party, the Parti Démocratique de Côte d'Ivoire (PDCI), was able to maintain a monopoly, both political and economic. But this long-time strategy of earning political capital through land reapportionment sowed the seeds of resentment and xenophobia that would later figure largely in the Ivoirian civil wars of 2002 and 2011. The party's "official championing of votes for foreigners obliged opposition parties to adopt slogans that were distinctively xenophobic" (326).

As early as 1970 a multiethnic coalition rose up in the southwest region to rebel against the land policy and "foreign" incursion.[5] Denouncing Houphouët for having "sold the country" and "promoted a fateful tribalism" that favored the Baoulé and Dyula, they marched to Gagnoa, where they declared succession and established a new state called *Eburnea* (Grah Mel 2010, 294). The rebellion was harshly suppressed, and among those participants arrested and jailed was Laurent Gbagbo. Released after two years, he went on to become a professor and was active in a teachers' union. A volatile union strike caused him to flee Côte d'Ivoire. While living in exile, Gbagbo founded an opposition party (the Front Populaire Ivoirien, or FPI). "The FPI was *founded in defensiveness over the incursions of outsiders into their homelands*, which were also the richest agricultural lands in Côte d'Ivoire and a major source of its revenue. The party was also *nurtured by resentment* over years of economic and political exclusion. Perhaps not surprisingly, the FPI took on ultranationalist and xenophobic overtones from the start. In the west, the notion of *Ivoirité* came to mean not just the exclusion of northerners from national politics, but also the reclamation of indigenous lands" (Minority Rights Group 2015, emphasis mine).

Gbagbo returned from exile in 1988 and was the first to stand as a rival to Houphouët in the first multiparty election in 1990. He would eventually become the third president of Côte d'Ivoire, serving during the civil war in 2002 and the prolonged period of unrest that followed; after a hotly contested election and violent aftermath in 2011, Gbagbo was ultimately removed from office by force and tried by the Hague for war crimes. This flash-forward allows one to see that the seeds of civil war were sown early and deeply by state manipulation of ethnic demographics and land use connected with it.

Ivoirité: Return to Autochthonous Privilege and the First Civil War

After the death of Houphouët-Boigny in 1993 and under his successor, Henri Konan Bédié, the direction of public policy on land rights shifted again. A new land law [*domaine foncier rural*] not only restored the authority of autochthony, it definitively excluded foreigners from land ownership.

The return to autochthonous privilege came in the guise of new patriotic zeal and was articulated as a nationalist ideology known as *Ivoirité*. Bédié first coined the term *Ivoirité* (or "Ivoirian-ness") in 1995 to stir a sense of authentic belonging and participation in nation building that would unite the heterogeneous population of Côte d'Ivoire. Later, however, it came to refer to a politics of exclusion inaugurated by a hastily drafted electoral code that defined citizenship more narrowly. More specifically, the code required that only a citizen could run for the office of president, and that both parents of that candidate had to have been born in Côte d'Ivoire. This specification targeted the disqualification of Bédié's rival for office, Alassane Ouattara, the former prime minister and a northern Muslim whose father was rumored to be from Burkina Faso. "Ivoirité" became a xenophobic rallying cry on the part of nationalist patriots against the "foreign" encroachment on Ivoirian territory, resources, and politics.

The first civil war erupted in 2002 with a mutiny mounted by troops, most of northern origin, rumored to be backed by the state of Burkina Faso. While the government maintained control over the south and the economic capital, Abidjan, the new rebel forces took the main northern city, Bouaké, as their new base. French troops were deployed to block further rebel incursions. After a cease-fire, France helped broker a peace agreement (the "Linas-Marcoussis Agreement," or MLA) and establish a new coalition government. Three issues seemed to be causing conflict, all rooted in ethnicity and the definition of *home*: the modification of *national identity, eligibility for citizenship, and land tenure laws.*

While most of the initial fighting had ended by late 2004, the country remained split between a rebel-held north and a government-held south. A tentative truce was called until elections could be held. These were alternatively promised and delayed until 2010, five years after Gbagbo's term of office was supposed to have expired.

Intergenerational Tension, Styles of Warfare, and "Woman Damage"

McGovern entertains these political facts in another register. He considers the obscured cultural dynamics in play—both those habits of mind and ways of being that are not entirely conscious and the stronger rhetorical patterns of tradition and ritual expression. He suggests that at its most basic level, the civil war can be seen as a contest of youth and elder statesmen. The rule of seniors that was overturned was not only the traditional systems in which elders controlled land. It was also a coup against the old guard of the Ivoirian national political elite who sustained the leadership style and mode of the "Old Man," Côte d'Ivoire's first president, Félix Houphouët-Boigny, who had ruled for more than thirty years with "paternal authoritarianism" (Fauré 1993, 320). It is not uncommon for analysts of the Ivoirian dynamics therefore to see an intergenerational struggle between youth, who felt robbed of the promise and possibility of the once prosperous nation, and the generation of elders whose corruption and stranglehold on power deprived them of it. McGovern, however, suggests approaching the conflict in Côte d'Ivoire "elliptically," analyzing the dynamics of warfare as the product of two overlapping sets of relations. The first of these is the "intergenerational tension" endemic to all social structures but that, depending on the type of traditional society, leads to rebellion and war in different ways. The second factor is a divide between those whose identity is tied to land and who claim to be indigenous, and those with a supposedly more portable identity, uncoupled from any fixed territory. What is not given consideration in this analysis is the place and role of women elders, and in particular those who appeal to FGP. This is a significant oversight for, especially among Akan and other matrifocal groups, women are the traditional owners of the land. Moreover, women have been political agents of a different kind, for when they invoke their spiritual warfare, even in the overtly political arena, their rebuke consistently rises above the parochial interests of a particular ethnicity or governmental regime.

According to McGovern, the different styles of governance in traditional societies placed differing demands and expectations on youth and offered them dissimilar rewards, as well. In his analysis these disparities created intergenerational tensions that figured prominently in Côte d'Ivoire's civil war. He distinguished two types of warfare: "pillage" and "entrepreneurial capture" of territory by siege.[6] In small-scale societies more characteristic of the south, seniors ("Big Men") rule over juniors and maintain the legitimacy of their authority on the basis of their rights over the land. In peacetime the dynamics between the generations "run parallel to [traditional] relations between landowners and newcomers" in the forest frontier (McGovern 2011, 56). It is a tributary relationship, and the stability of society depends on the submission of youth to those right relations. At the same time, this gerontocratic hierarchy relies on youth to defend that social order in times of crisis and to defer personal aspirations. At such times, "young men who were denied the possibility of upward social mobility [had] to claim social advancement by force" (53). Their aim was not to overturn the system, but merely to gain control for themselves. McGovern characterizes this type of violent siege as pillage. By contrast, what McGovern calls "principled wars" are driven by "clear objectives," namely "empire-building," more typical of the "jihadi empires and states" of the Sahel region (54). For McGovern, "those who conquer for principled reasons can actually lay claim to their own acts of violence as underpinning their peacetime legitimacy" while those who merely pillage can derive no legitimacy for their new rule (54). On the basis of this idealized view of warfare, he sets the "deep history of state formation" of the eighteenth-century jihadists and the nineteenth-century slave raiders of the north against what he calls "opportunistic, non-ideological and entrepreneurial" warfare among southern "stateless" societies (56–60).[7]

McGovern's paradigm betrays a considerable partiality toward state structure and monotheistic religious ideology as civilizing forces and toward northern cultures and societies supposedly modeled accordingly. Ironically, the model of gerontocratic hierarchies overturned by pillage that McGovern associates with southern traditions actually more readily applies to the northern systems that controlled youth by controlling their access to women. When the northern youth failed to submit to the demand that they work for elders to earn bride wealth, the "Big Men" referred to their consequent loss of power as "woman damage" (Chauveau and Richards 2008, 518). Tragically, the type of violence that was in play in Côte d'Ivoire during the civil war evinced a more literal and most egregious form of "woman damage": the violation of women's bodies through sexual violence and the destruction of the foundations of social order by the intentional assault on its moral and matrifocal foundations.[8]

In the forest zone, the intergenerational tension leading up to the civil war had an entirely different dynamic than the mere opportunistic power grab that McGovern describes. As the urban centers failed to deliver on the promise of prosperity and ready employment, Bété and other youth from the newly colonized region returned to find that their elders had provided "strangers," non-Ivoirians and Ivoirians alike, access to ancestral lands in their absence. It was a double betrayal. However, rather than turning against those elders, youth from the southwestern region redoubled their identification with tradition to defend their rights to ancestral lands over the claims of foreigners who had farmed them in their absence during those boom years. Rather than turn against elders, they focused their resentment on the usurpers who seemed to betray the traditional mandates of deference that newcomers owed their hosts. The perception that the newcomers were usurpers of agrarian resources dovetailed with the nationalistic ideology of Ivoirité that was also stirring a terrible zeal among urban young patriots from the southeast supporting Gbagbo's government in Abidjan.

Those urban uprisings were not a rebellion of juniors over elders, nor did they represent what McGovern calls the "entrepreneurial capture" of territory. It was rather a defense of the old guard. When the young patriots encircled the Hotel Ivoire to protect the Gbagbo regime from French military forces, which they perceived to be backing the rebels, those youth were defending traditional political turf. Youth uprisings, street skirmishes, and ethnic terrorism erupted in the neighborhoods of Abidjan. The violence targeted populations of northern origin and European expatriates alike. The shocking attacks garnered a great share of media attention, for their unthinkable brutality unexpectedly betrayed what had been a point of pride for Ivoirians: the heritage of tolerance for ethnic heterogeneity and a tradition of mutual respect. But the activism of *rural* youth, triggered by contestation over land acquisition, was just as brutal and "the most active, durable and violent" during the long intra-war period (523).

In addition to these intergenerational tensions and the different styles of war-fare that supposedly distinguished northern and southern youth, McGovern identifies another, overlapping factor supposedly affecting the dynamics of war in Côte d'Ivoire: portable identity. According to this construct, *portability* does not refer to the experience of extreme mobility of the generation of youth displaced and molded according to the interests of the state, but to the nature of personhood that McGovern ascribes uniquely to the northern Mande. McGovern draws striking contrast between the way that personhood and iden-tity are constructed by the northern Mande compared to the Bété and other peoples in Côte d'Ivoire's southern forest zone, whom he equates with them. For McGovern, the Mande sense of personhood is derived from the prestige of an imagined affiliation with a precolonial empire and a concomitant sense of superiority (52). It is supposedly characterized by a sense of individuality forged by "striving to overcome one's destiny" (53), something that those iden-tifying with indigenous claim to the land presumably lack.[9] These differences in self-understanding presumably distinguished the supposedly noble "entre-preneurial capture" of northern youth from the mere "pillage" of southern youth caught up in the civil war.

McGovern seeks to buttress his premise on the grounds that "Northern Mande speakers' memory of illustrious ancestors goes back hundreds of years and is consecrated by professional genealogist-praise singers called *jeliw*" (49). Claiming the Mande have a unique interest in the past and "in a second-order evaluation of history's uses, its transmission, and its interpretation" as "histo-riography" (51), he contrasts them with the Bété, whom he likens to "many other groups from the country's south" (52), as "more characterized by the 'anti-historiographic' ideology of autochthony that takes present interests and for-mulates a hypostasized prior identity that fits the purpose at hand" (64). In other words, for McGovern the Bété and other southern ethnic groups were either unaware of their history and the composite nature of their identity, forged over time, or intentionally created a fictional ethnic identity in the in-terest of laying claim to the land.

Ironically, McGovern goes on to acknowledge that until the nineteenth century the Maninka/Dyula lived in an "anarchic and insecure" region and that it is only the "*memory* of states and early adherence . . . to Islam [that] became important symbolic resources for people of northern Mande origins in the twen-tieth century" (60).[10] In this sense, it is as much a hypostasized prior identity as any supposedly contrived southern claim to indigenous grounding (although by his own reckoning it seems that the history of the consolidation of southern groups goes back further than the Dyula claim to statehood). Nevertheless, McGovern argues that while northerners have a pronounced sense of individuality, the identity of those from the stateless societies in the forest zone is inextricably tied to "relations to ancestral land" (52), making identity both "highly localised" [sic] and "non-portable" (50). In essence, McGovern's portrayal recapitulates the antiquated imaginary division that was once deployed to distinguish world religions from the so-called primitive traditions. It sets *history* and identity rooted in *time* in opposition to *tradition*, in which identity is rooted in *space*. Authentic identity grounded in temporal history is represented by the state and its chronicles of conquest, while identity derived from identification with tradition (presumed to be timeless) amounts to myth—that is to say, groundless invention. His thesis suggests that preoccupation with time moves people and nations forward, while identification with space leads to rigidity and nostalgia. The idea that the northern Mande have a unique type of portable identity seems invested in distancing them from a presumably closed society, delimited by space and inherently backward. This differentiated treatment of time and space in which all spatial organization is made to appear to be anti-historical also seems to parallel the differential treatment of women and men by Western colonial powers, where men were included in the history-making "project of existence," while women were identified with nature (space) and treated as the "fixed, the undialectical, the immobile" (Foucault and Gordon 1980, 70).

Yet as we have seen, the collectively self-ruled societies of the southern region were *no less cognizant* of their origins and *no less exacting chroniclers* of their histories and the ancestral filiation. Among the Adioukrou, for example, this knowledge goes back five hundred years, to the sixteenth century. Discussing the depth and complexity of Adioukrou oral history, Memel-Fotê cites three groups of traditional specialists whose role it is to conserve and transmit this self-knowledge: the *Selu* who maintain the genealogies of the founding matriclan, the masters of the talking drum (*brem-ar-es-el*), and the sages or "master reciters" (*odadu*) who are what he calls "historico-literary chroniclers" (Memel-Fotê 1980, 45). Together they represent the principal pillars of Adioukrou sociocultural order: genealogy, the system of the age set, and the ritual calendar, respectively. Through these masters of oral history villages can reconstruct with great precision events going back four cycles of the age set (45). The genesis of the system of age sets that governs Adioukrou society may have originated as far back as 1414, though by a second reckoning, one that begins the cycle with a different age set as the inaugurating group, it most reliably dates to 1575 (58–59).

Such details clearly show that the criteria for differentiation between northern and southern peoples lack validity. Southern peoples have no lack of historical knowledge or interest in the past as historiography of their identity. Nor are such ethnic groups invested in an erasure or dissimulation of the history of the multiple migrations and alliances that resulted in their consolidation. On the contrary, as we demonstrated in chapter 4, alliances were forged on moral grounds, in keeping with the rules that enabled first comers to lay claim to land through spiritual alliance with the genies, the primordial owners of that land. Those spiritual rules also provided for land use for newcomers as long as they respected the duties that reinforced that original bond. In other words, the rules that identified indigenous peoples with the land were not incompatible with mobility, and even helped to foster relocation and a kind of resettlement that was grounded in justice and peace, not pillage. Far from immobile and fixed, such ethnicities are constructed on moral principles of settlement, productive occupation, and meaningful symbolic relations to territory. Moreover, as we have seen, it is women who most forcefully embody both the guardianship of the land and the moral knowledge that oversee its just apportionment.

Joking Relations, Worldliness, and War

McGovern ascribes to northerners unique "techniques of the self" that supposedly enable them to break free of the oppressive traditions and that presumably would otherwise keep them fixed in time and space. One is *sanankuya*, the institution of joking relations. *Sanankuya* prescribes that Mande, who are otherwise strangers, exchange jibes in a form of stylized abuse in accordance with their relations between their respective totemic clans. McGovern sees this as evidence of their "mobile identity," one that aligns with cosmopolitan notions of personhood in which the individual acts as an independent subject free from the constraints of a collective moral situation. By contrast, he portrays the purportedly fixed identity of southern ethnicities as decidedly unworldly: "In forest-region villages and chiefdoms to the south, clans stand in a hierarchical relationship within a village or chiefdom. However, such relations have to do with the accepted order of arrival. . . . This ideology of identity is highly localised and is not portable, as *sanankuya* relations are" (McGovern 2011, 49–50). I argued above that the rules governing relations between first comers and new comers are in fact highly conducive to mobility and portable, even malleable, identity. Here I will demonstrate that this formalized custom of joking relations is not unique to northerners but also exists in the south.

As the result of a blood pact between the Abidji and Dida, the intimate relations between them are considered inviolable and eternal. The relationship is signaled by a rhetorical tradition known as *Tokpè*, the ritual exchange of insult.[11] According to the custom of Tokpè, an Abidji, no matter his village, clan lineage, or rank, is considered the slave of a Dida. No Dida will miss an opportunity to lord it over his Abidji companions with joking abuse, threatening to invoke his presumed right to lay claim to anything he desired. The tradition continues with good humor, jest, and plenty of threats to seize valuables by this right. While attending the Adioukrou Festival of Yams (Kpol) in Yassap, I was accompanied by a professor of sociology, a Dida, a former student of Memel-Fotê. As we sat with a group of renowned Sékèpuone, the professor teased them that although he was younger and not an initiate of Kpol, they were his slaves and owed him reverence. The elder laughed and immediately called on his wife to bring him the best food they had to offer. Such discursive strategy is cathartic, dispelling latent hostilities between potentially competing factions, and establishes the kind of frankness and transparency usually enjoyed only in the intimate space of home. These exchanges betray at once the ethos of the warrior, aggressive and ready to defend one's right, and respect for moral prescriptions that underlie all relations of peace. The exchanges in the verbal ritual of Tokpè can therefore be merciless: "The most brutal verbal violence emphasizes indignation, if not fury, provoked by a political, social or moral transgression judged to be unacceptable and ineluctable, an overturning of values that should be in force without question" (Oger, quoted in Cossette 2013, 91). In this way they mirror the embodied ritual of FGP. Both rituals simultaneously maintain peace and enforce moral bonds by aggressively invoking insults and threats. Tokpè does not free the individual from the constraints of a collective moral situation, but rather reinforces them. Nevertheless those moral bonds facilitate relations between strangers, persons of differing ethnic identity who may meet on foreign turf.

Women's Mobilization: A Portable Identity of a Different Kind

McGovern's schema appears designed to infer that it is *northern* youth who are uniquely able to overturn the stultifying conventions of the past by seizing territory and putting it toward "entrepreneurial" ends, the building of a modern society. It suggests that the entrepreneurial capture of young northern rebel forces in Côte d'Ivoire should be understood as a liberating break from repressive ahistorical traditions, the triumph of "greater" religion, and a demonstration of the capacity for empire building. For McGovern breaking with the past means undercutting local tradition as an impediment to modernity and the promise of the new global order. Such views may well serve as an apologia for the incursion of the northern, Moslem rebel coup in Côte d'Ivoire and the postcolonial state. However, they do not do justice to the fuller cultural situation. By taking into consideration women and the trope of FGP in play in the dynamics of war making and alliance building, we consider one of those "vital social institutions" that Lonsdale suggests are the most forceful guarantors of political accountability (Lonsdale 1986, 141).

Although mobile young warmongers may capture land, their occupation is *not sufficient to establish legitimacy* over it. As McGovern himself acknowledges, in precolonial Africa tradition prescribed how the relations between autochthones and strangers were regulated. "There were strict rules across this region [that] required that strangers steer clear of politics," although if this ideal were to go unheeded, "the very same set of structured relations helped to set things right again so that humans, ancestral spirits, and the indigenous earth, water and other local spirits could re-establish *a productive working relationship without which communal life was perceived to be unfeasible*" (McGovern 2011, 74, emphasis mine). The reference to the positive and moral aspect of traditions, and especially those associated with territory, is important. To gain legitimacy necessary to rule, conquerors of what McGovern calls the "once 'true' autochthones" had to renegotiate their prerogatives over the land through "the alignment of physical and esoteric powers ... often considered essential to the prosperity of a village or chiefdom" (74). This is where the interjection of women's special ascription of power may have its greatest import. As we have seen, in African traditional thought, moral authority is a measure of the legitimacy of political rulership. FGP confers this authority and most forcefully curtails the abuse of worldly power.

In a significant personal anecdote McGovern relates an experience of being stopped along with fellow minibus passengers at a military checkpoint, a place where extortion, robbery, and even sexual abuse were known to commonly take place in Côte d'Ivoire. The incident is exceptional, however, because "several older women" effectively intervene and begin to "berate the soldiers and police. . . . '*We are your mothers* and we are tired. . . . Give us our papers and give the driver his papers *before we curse you*.' After a slight pause that did not do much to help them save face, the soldiers decided that our papers were in order and we were on our way" (188, emphasis mine). While the point of the narrative for McGovern is to illustrate that "checkpoint extortion stood metonymically for the entire system of 'neither war nor peace'" in Côte d'Ivoire (189), the incident is especially a formidable testimony to the contemporary efficacy of the threat of FGP. It portrays the capacity of the Mothers to counter the intimidating physical menace of the young military men with a threat of force of a different kind: a deadly curse that such women alone have the unique capacity to inflict. The exchange opposed young men with elderly women, physical threat with spiritual threat, guns with the spiritual weapon of the female sex. The most significant detail of this anecdote, then, is that in this contest of power, *the old women prevailed.* The women's message was understood, and the soldiers' acquiescence was unmitigated.

So effective was this intervention that it caused McGovern to "wonder why such revolts are not more common" (188). The answer, of course, is that their act, while brave, was no mere feat of heroism, but an exercise of power that only a select group could command. The soldiers' ready submission attests to the fact that respect for "the Mothers" and the spiritual power that they incarnate is not an obscure artifact of an antiquated tradition as an untainted world apart, but still operates as an integral part of the local epistemology that informs contemporary social life. It is part of the "webs of meaning and habits of mind" (131) that constitute cultural reality in this part of the world and render it comprehensible. Their appeal was to an overarching ideology. Significantly, the ethnicity of the women and the soldiers was not a critical factor of the exchange. The idiom of FGP runs deeper than language and extends beyond the supposedly parochial worldview of any particular ethnicity. It even transcends regional distinctions and political interests, as the soldiers represented the Gbagbo government and their purpose was ostensibly to intimidate northerners. The incident provides evidence that the concept of FGP endures as a civilizing force greater than the amoral powers of politics.

Today the foundation for social stability may yet find its anchor in that same invocation of the moral domain and the accountability that the Mothers demand. As we have seen, the various instances of women's collective movements and use of the rites of FGP as a political vehicle throughout Africa arose at different historical moments, involved different agents, and had a variety of immediate causes. Yet they shared a motivating principle that has a long pedigree in West African history. Each case in which women's collective uprising made appeal to the ritual of FGP arose independently and in its own context, but all of these instances set in relief an ideal moral vision as the mobilizing factor. Without identification with any particular territory, and transcending ethnicity, cases of FGP point to a truly portable identity.

It is only in a footnote that McGovern refers to women, noting that they are "particularly vulnerable to rape, yet they have been anything but passive" and are not the stereotypical peacemakers women are presumed to be in times of war (112n17). He cites as his example the First Lady, Simone Gbagbo, who was active in the polarizing politics associated with her husband's regime. I contend that the example of women's collective mobilizations better represents what women themselves stand for—literally and figuratively—in times of extraordinary social disruption and threat to the community, in situations of brutality and injustice, and in contexts where the state rules with insouciance for the welfare of its people. Theirs is the embodied moral imagination active on the contemporary scene as it has been for centuries, a vigilant presence ready to intervene to challenge impunity and to awaken conscience and ethical judgment.

The female elders who threatened to wield the mystical powers of FGP were also clearly exercising their gerontocratic prerogative to suppress the violent usurpation of power by youth. The act is not an oppressive subjugation, however, but an effective enactment of the constraint of morality on power. Morality, like power, is not a thing that can be possessed, but a relation that "always occurs in the interstice," as subjects are caught up in the "meticulous rituals of power" (Foucault and Gordon 1980, 138). Their intervention drew on *savoir*, the implicit knowledge commonly shared. It is knowledge of the local in action. But it also demonstrated considerable *savoir-faire*, a worldly sensibility and a capacity to use it.

Worldly Acts and Immortal Longings

For McGovern any commitment to the idea that territorial borders have ever been clearly established or tied to particular ethnic groups is to participate in "the fantasy of 'turning the clock back to zero,'" an imagined time of origins. He contends that in the context of civil unrest it "creates at least as many problems as it solves" (McGovern 2011, 63–64). But it is one thing to decry the nationalist ideology of *Ivoirité* that fueled tensions between long-time residents and new immigrants, fostered a dangerous xenophobia, and led to horrendous racist violence. It is another to suggest that ethnicities that have been solidified for centuries and cultures with which Ivoirians still strongly identify are "fictional and romanticized image(s) of the past" and therefore negligible (84). As McGovern himself acknowledges, "All humans are trapped in webs of meaning and habits of mind that are not of their own making. To abandon these entirely is to risk incomprehensibility" (131).

The crisis in Côte d'Ivoire has become a stage on which the "intangible heritage" of deeply rooted principles, values, and attitudes that have safeguarded civilizations for centuries is being made visible. "Periods of insecurity . . . tend to bring otherwise unstated principles underlying peacetime life to the fore" (58). For a certain stratum of society, and perhaps especially for matrilineal or matrifocal groups in the forest region, matrifocal morality reveals itself to be that most essential *founding knowledge* and *binding power* that grounds society in justice and respect. The Mothers who stand up to soldiers armed only with their moral force reflect what Lonsdale calls the "immortal longings" of the community (Lonsdale 1986, 141). Simultaneously spiritual values and worldly political aims, they appeal for accountability. These are the longings for dignity and justice that drove pioneers into the forest zone in the first place and on which they forged their new civilizations.

Where McGovern seems to wish to dismiss invented, imaginal dimensions of society (and ethnicity in particular) as historically unfounded and therefore inauthentic, these long-negotiated alliances and binding values, continually rehearsed in canonical acts of ritual, in fact carry the deepest convictions on which identity is based. For that reason, ethnicity continues to operate as a critical feature of the social landscape and cannot be excised from the worldly project of nation building.

If a second civil war in Côte d'Ivoire was delayed for almost a decade, it was because of the Ivoirian self-image as a sophisticated people, beyond the "barbarity" that characterized conflicts in Liberia and other African nations (McGovern 2011, 207). Along these same lines, Ivoirians repeatedly asserted to me that because theirs was a country that had always been ethnically heterogeneous and was a culture that tolerated intermarriage and migration, they would never be as susceptible to the hostile rifts that rendered other civil wars so brutal. Yet their argument was not that theirs was a culture of superior religiosity or grand empire, nor was it made on the basis that they were so postmodern as to be above ethnic rivalry. Rather, they underscored that their own cultures shared a "notion of decency" and basic "respect for the human being" that could never be breached to such a degree. This is also the point that women so forcefully extol when referring to FGP. The Mothers' appeal to the image of civilized and legitimate behavior is still viable in the social imaginary. The vulnerable elderly women who were stopped with McGovern at the checkpoint were diametrically opposed, both physically and symbolically, with those young men who wreak havoc there and in the streets as "roving gangs of regional warriors," perpetrating horrors—murder, torture, amputation, rape—on a vulnerable populace (109). While those young male players represent the high visibility, high stakes, high voltage politics, elderly women make their critique felt through the moral undercurrent of society, using "bottom power." Their allusion to FGP was enough, in this instance, to invert the usual locus of power, and showed it to be most legitimately invested in neither the structural institution of the state and its armed forces nor in the brute strength of youth, but in the Mothers and the morality they embody.

Part III. Timeliness

URGENT SITUATIONS
AND EMERGENT CRITIQUES

•

What has to be done, therefore, is to invert the logic of emergency . . .
it is not the emergency of problems which prevents the formulation of long-term
plans but the absence of any plan that subjects us to the tyranny of emergency.
—JÉRÔME BINDÉ, "Towards an Ethics of the Future"

A Timely Battle in Intimate Spaces

Journal, April, 2011: *"By miracle, I reached my sister-in-law in Abidjan by phone
this morning. She's been barricaded in Angré, terrorized by constant gunfire and
the threat of marauders banging on doors, pillaging and raping. Bodies lie outside
in the street, some gathered and burned under tires. 'The stench!,' she says. Communication is scant; no TV/radio. Only occasional phone contact. Automobiles
are stripped and destroyed by men proclaiming vengeance on Gbagbo by punishing
the population. Some claim Ouattara forces are guilty or complicit; others blame
young thugs and criminals loosed from prisons, roaming ungoverned. She's 'lucky'
she says; she has water, rice, charcoal, canned goods, and gas lamps (there's no electricity). She and three women who took refuge in her house sleep in the corridor
to avoid stray bullets, and pray they'll be spared the savagery of men who 'are no
longer human beings.'"*

This entry scribbled in my journal barely begins to document the urgent
situation that followed the contested elections in Côte d'Ivoire. Like all civil
wars, the conflict there was a fight for the control of territory. As Foucault

pointed out in conversation with Colin Gordon, land is so much more than earth. It is turf. "*Territory* is no doubt a geographical notion, but it's first of all a juridico-political one." Gordon replied, "The *region* of the geographers is the military region (from *regere*, to command), a *province* is a conquered territory (from *vincere*). *Field* evokes the battlefield" (Foucault and Gordon 1980, 68–69). Almost everywhere women's bodies have been symbolically associated with earth and land, bearing the properties of fecundity and (re)production, and as we have seen, in African traditions they not only share in the primacy and potency of the earth but are also the paramount vehicles for making land habitable and communities safe from malefic forces. It is perhaps inevitable, then, that women's bodies are targets of violent siege, conquest, and command in war.

Civil war is, by definition, a breakdown of civility and the destruction of civil society, a situation that puts citizenship at issue and makes civilians "fair game" in the contest of power. The particular kind of incivility visited upon women, however, was acute precisely because of the hold that matrifocality has on the popular social imaginary and the degree to which the fundamental basis of land and home is established in the female body. "Violence committed on the private domain of a woman's body" is a particularly effective weapon, striking the hearts and minds of the population, "freighted as [the female body] is with representational duties to signify: home and hearth, kinship and tradition, past and future" (Al-Kassim 2008, 176).

During the Ivoirian civil war and its protracted aftermath, women were regularly victimized by sexual violence. The field of battle, already an intimate one in the case of a civil war waged on home turf, becomes more intimate still when it is perpetrated on women. Rape and other sexual torture violently rend a woman's body and her body from herself, even as these crimes rip the seams of society. These most intimate violations are public acts of invasion intended to "unhome" the victims and the surrounding populace. Rape as a weapon of war is often explained as a tactic of humiliation. In Côte d'Ivoire rape also assaults the very source of civilization, and for matrilineal societies, it attacks the female foundations of social identity. Rape "'ruins' not only women and their wombs, but the broader bio-social economy that they would otherwise re-create and sustain" (Apter 2012, 41). Sexual violence perpetrated on women situates the battleground at the epicenter of African power/knowledge: the female sex.

While their bodies have borne the horrifying trauma of assault, women have not only been victims; they have also been the vehicles of forceful response. In Côte d'Ivoire women have repeatedly resorted to the ritual invocation of FGP to confront and protest the violations against women and the abuse of authority by the forces vying for control. Their ritual puts in relief that which is presumed to be unimportant/immaterial because it has been ignored, or inexistent because it has been occluded—women's own moral authority. For this very reason, it is especially important to recognize that the deployment of FGP, as a refusal of exactly this kind of incivility, has always been at the heart of African civil society.

The emergence of ancient tradition in situations of contemporary political crisis should not be confused with anti-history. In contrast with the supposed *timelessness* of religious tradition and the presumed ahistoricity of myth and ritual, the interventions of the women making appeal to FGP are especially timely. Indeed, the enactment of FGP has always been an *urgent undertaking made in the most critical of times*. While it is a *strategic* response to an emergency situation, the ritual of FGP also recalls to collective memory foundational ethical imperatives; the Mothers seek to enforce the moral prescriptions that have sustained African society historically to restore the justice that peace demands. Their manifestations openly assert that "the long-term strategy requires reviving ethical thought" (Bindé 2001, 97). The evocation of FGP demands a "sober quest for long-term solutions" (91) based on the recollection of the ethical imperatives that the Mothers embody.

6. VIOLATION AND DEPLOYMENT

FGP in Politics in Côte d'Ivoire

The Adjanou dancers were kidnapped . . . gunned down, coldly executed. . . .
The blood of those brave women cries Justice, Justice, Justice.
—F. TAKY, "Hommage Aux Danseuses d'Adjanou: Assassinées Pour Avoir Dansé."

Silence! It is the hegemony of women to which men should bow;
the power of women affirms itself. May men acknowledge its power, predominance,
supremacy. Any man who defies it is cursed for a certain death. Any man who dares resist
it will be under a spell. The power of women affirms itself. It is undeniable,
we have the power. It is our predominance that manifests itself.
—FAFWÊ WOMENS' SONG, Bouaké, Côte d'Ivoire, United Nations Population Fund

The coup d'état in 2002 split the country into government and rebel factions, divided geographically not only along a north-south axis, but also between east and west. Active hostilities were formally quelled with a cease-fire in 2003, followed by peace agreements negotiated with the assistance of France, the United Nations, the African Union, and the body representing the surrounding states in the West African region (ECOWAS). A fragile detente was maintained for years, with the support of the UN Operation in Côte d'Ivoire (UNOCI) as well as a French peacekeeping force. During the turbulent period between 2004 and 2007 known as *"No Peace, No War,"* elections were postponed more than six times, and despite several negotiated settlements, disarmament totally failed. With tensions high and all political activity focused on the contest of power, the civilian population paid the price. Criminal gangs, armed with Kalashnikov rifles, hunting rifles, knives, and machetes, regularly attacked civilians in their homes and fields and as they traveled to markets.

Abuses against civilians went beyond harassment, intimidation, and pillaging; they regularly included rape and gang rape of women of every age and escalated to torture and mutilation (especially sexual torture, including sexual slavery, induced abortions, and forced acts of incest), cannibalism, murder, and massacre (HRW 2007, 51, 58). International organizations like Amnesty

International (AI) and Human Rights Watch (HRW) documented that all levels of both government agents and rebel forces were complicit in criminal assault on the civilian population: "The power of the gun prevails. . . . Criminal gangs, militiamen, police, gendarmes, and rebel forces subject locals to an unrelenting stream of abuses, including banditry, assault, extortion, and the *rape of women, girls, and even babies*" (Wells, Hassan, and HRW 2010, 3).

Based on interviews with survivors, witnesses, local civil society groups, and workers from international humanitarian organizations, human rights monitoring agencies compiled extensive reports that provide reliable evidence that rampant sexual violence has been a widespread weapon of war in Côte d'Ivoire since 2000 and that thousands of girls and women have been victimized. Their most comprehensive reports were produced in 2007, but the subject has been regularly revisited as renewed attention focused on another wave of atrocities during the postelection violence.[1] Both Amnesty International and Human Rights Watch documented that throughout the Ivoirian conflict combatants and militia perpetrated ongoing sexual violence on a massive scale with impunity. "Hundreds of women and girls have been sexually assaulted, raped, and gang raped [by groups of masked bandits who attack vehicles at roadblocks]. . . . Women and girls are systematically pulled off transport vehicles, one by one, and marched into the bush where they are raped while other bandits stand guard. Victims include very young children, including babies, and women over seventy years of age. During home attacks, husbands are tied up and forced to watch as wives, daughters, and other female family members are raped" (Wells, Hassan, and HRW 2010, 5).

In 2004 the UN Security Council mandated a formal inquiry into the allegations of sexual violence during the civil war as crimes against humanity, asking the Ivoirian government to organize a commission of inquiry on the matter. The report of that body, submitted to the UN High Commissioner for Human Rights, corroborated the sexual abuse of women of all ages, "accompanied by cruel, inhuman and degrading treatment, rape in the presence of partners/ children, forced incest, sexual harassment, indecent assault, abduction and sexual slavery" (Amnesty International 2007, 9).

The incontrovertible evidence shows that throughout the conflict *both* pro-government militias and the armed opposition were guilty of these crimes. Their systematic assaults were used to terrify, abase, and befoul the civilian population. "As symbols of the 'honour' of their communities, women were raped to humiliate them, the men in their families and their entire community" (6). The abuses were politically motivated, as the perpetrators targeted women of particular ethnic groups or from regions perceived to sympathize with the opposition. Women and girls were raped and subjected to gender-based torture to extract information and punish and intimidate the populace. Amnesty International summarized the terrible evidence succinctly: "Rape has therefore been used strategically and tactically as a weapon of war to fulfill many of the objectives of all parties to the conflict in Côte d'Ivoire" (6).

Due to the prevailing culture of impunity, the intimidation and threat of reprisals by perpetrators, the fear of ostracism by families, and the cultural taboos surrounding sexual purity and violation, most violations went unreported (HRW 2007, 13). It seems certain that, despite the already horrific substantiated record that thousands of women have been victimized, the scale and brutality of the sexual and physical violence perpetrated against women during the conflict in Côte d'Ivoire has been vastly underestimated.

Rape as a Weapon of War: The Assault on Women and the Roots of Civilization

Rape has always been a weapon of war, a way of seizing the heart of communal power and subverting it through terror and shame. While turf is the ostensible target of civil war, it is the body, and not the land, that is the field upon which force is most keenly felt: "The most obvious and striking feature of [ethnic] violence . . . is its site and target—the body [is] the site of the worst possible infliction of pain, terror, indignity, and suffering in comparison with property or other resources. Yet it is clear that the violence inflicted on the human body in ethnic contexts is never entirely random or lacking cultural form" (Appadurai 1999, 309).

Just as ethnic violence is "violence between previous social intimates" (305), sexual violence overturns the intimate act of intercourse from a socially sanctioned expression of solidarity (the bonds of love, family, and community) to an assault on physical, psychological, and social coherence. The violation of women is profanation of intimacy itself—the invasion of the most secret, intimate part of the female anatomy, the place of reserved access, the most revered and sacrosanct source of life and communal renewal. In ethnocidal violence, knowledge of how morality and memory is inscribed is intentionally exploited in "'routinized symbolic schemes of nightmarish cruelty'" (Malkki, quoted in Appadurai 1999, 309). This same perversion of cultural knowledge drives sexual violence. Rape in war is "a grotesque form of intimacy with the ethnic other" (317). The "closed identity" of ethnicity, matrilineality, descent, lineage, tradition, honor, dignity, local ethnics is forced open in rape. In a region in which women are not only persons with an ethnic identity but also the moral core/

corps of the social lineage, a violation of women's bodies has maximum symbolic impact as an assault on the community as a whole. This type of violence is calculated to strike at the very roots of the social order. For this very reason it has been a strategy of warfare in the region for as long as there has been matriliny. "The fact that women form the framework of the lineage is made evident by a feature of war in Akan country: one of the objectives of military campaigns and incursions is the capture of 'princesses' (*dihye*), mothers and sisters of the king, in order to deprive the enemy lineage of heirs and to attack it in its reproductive capacity (underlining that it is in order to appropriate it, that the conquerors marry their captives)" (Perrot 1979, 220).

In its report on the many atrocities perpetrated on Ivoirian women during the years of political conflict, HRW noted that the sexual violence appears "designed to punish and terrorize entire families and communities" (78). They acknowledged the degree to which assault on a woman affects the collective in traditional African culture, understood as an offense to the ancestors and the spiritual order.

> The entire village is concerned by rape because the rape affects its collective identity, especially the rape of a child. According to some Ivorian customs, ancestors of the village are believed to become angry when a rape is committed. They believe this can bring bad luck to and damage the prosperity of an entire village. To avoid this fate, sacrifices are necessary, often involving a white sheep or goat, running water, and Kola nuts. . . . Larger, community rituals appear to have less to do with purifying the victim's body and more with assuaging ancestors. While the goals of rebuilding spiritual order in the community and public shaming of perpetrators are important, it is essential to note that the goal of these rituals is rarely to listen to and validate the experience of the survivor. Moreover, there is almost no confidentiality in such traditional or tribal mechanisms for dealing with rape. (120)

This one brief mention of the cultural significance of rape and traditional means of redress in the report by HRW is commendable but clearly inadequate. Confidentiality is moot if the offense is not internalized as a stain of shame borne by the victim privately but recognized as an intolerable outrage on the whole of civil society, one that demands the mobilization of the community in response. Such solidarity deflects the focus from the victim to the perpetrator and relieves the victim of internalized guilt. The use of FGP as a mechanism for dealing with rape may not be a feature of every society, or it has been so long suppressed that it is no longer practiced in some regions. Yet it has not been forgotten everywhere. Its resurgence on the political scene shows that not all traditional practices are harmful or dismissive of women's personal dignity.

Tracing FGP in history and the history of protest in Côte d'Ivoire is not to subscribe to the idea of an uninterrupted continuity of women's power (which is certainly challenged by the actual circumstances of the daily lives of many women, even in matrilineal societies). Rather, the object is to show that despite the repeated incursions and disruptions of the traditional systems of justice and redress or the discontinuities and accidents of history that challenged the place and power of African women in society, there remains deeply embedded in the social imaginary a set of rules and mechanisms for enforcing both.

These rules and mechanisms repeatedly emerge in history, especially in the most unfavorable circumstances. Only when society is threatened by cataclysm or faced with calamity does FGP emerge from its secreted night performances to take center stage as a daytime manifestation in the streets and the political arena. There it reasserts itself as a conscious critique with compelling moral force. If FGP persists as a social reality it is because its agents recognize it as a real power capable of enforcement and as a value that is not only still worthy of assertion, but perhaps now especially timely.

"My Womb Is Torn": Sexual Violence in Côte d'Ivoire's Civil War

Most analysts concur that the roots of the nature and scale of sexual violence in the Ivoirian civil war can be traced to December 2000, when the Supreme Court ruled that Alassane Ouattara, the leader of the opposition party—the Rassemblement des Républicains (RDR)—be excluded from candidacy for president. Demonstrators rose up in protest, and the response by Gbagbo's security forces was swift and violent. They specifically targeted the Dyula community, perceived to be universal supporters of the northern opposition leader, and especially women as its most vulnerable mark.[2] Several women were arrested immediately during the demonstrations in the streets of Abidjan. Others were denounced by Gbagbo supporters as participants in the protest marches and taken from their homes later. Once in detention at the Police Training School, the women were stripped, maltreated, violated with wood batons, and raped by police in the presence of superior officers. Amnesty International reported that in a wave of subsequent reprisals against Ouattara supporters, "Dioula women were also publicly handed over by security forces to civilians who raped them in front of a mob of other people" (7).

In Abidjan, militias supporting the Gbagbo regime, such as the Jeunes Patriotes (Young Patriots), were equally implicated. Along with the army and police, the militia systematically targeted populations presumed to hold sympathies with the RDR and made women the pawns in their campaign of intimidation and humiliation. Human Rights Watch also documented harrowing acts of sexual abuse, torture, and rape conducted by the militant pro-government student group Fédération estudiantine et scolaire de Côte d'Ivoire, FESCI (Federation of Students and Pupils of Côte d'Ivoire).[3] Members of FESCI used violence to control accommodations and commerce on the university campus in Abidjan and especially intimidated those believed to support the opposition; FESCI members sexually harassed, verbally abused, demeaned, and accosted female students perceived to be opponents of President Gbagbo. One female leader of a rival student organization, the Association générale des élèves et étudiants de la Côte d'Ivoire (AGEE-CI), was kidnapped, interrogated, urged to confess AGEE-CI's collaboration with the rebels, and then brutally gang-raped (HRW 2007, 83–84). Another female student who was gang-raped after interrogation detailed her similar ordeal at the hands of FESCI members to Amnesty International: "They then said I was playing with fire and that instead of giving out tracts I should have stayed in my proper place at home and looked for a husband. . . . They put a canvas bag over my face and one of them pressed my throat so that I couldn't scream while one of them was raping me" (Amnesty International 2007, 10).

Despite the fact that an official investigation, conducted after NGOs raised the alarm, confirmed that the women's allegations were true, no one was ever charged for these crimes. The total failure to prosecute members of the security forces sent the message that "women could be targeted for political or ethnic reasons with total impunity" (10). This opened the way to similar attacks that "increased alarmingly both in number and in gravity since the armed conflict began" (21).

Amnesty's comment on the incident summarizes the way *youth have pitted themselves against women* in a significant move away from the traditional grounding of African civilization. This case shows not only that violence against women was perpetrated by pro-government militias and condoned by their leaders; it also illustrates the degree to which sexist stereotypes and misogyny have infiltrated the contemporary social imagination in youth who have little to no grounding in or identification with African traditions that respect women and revere female power. The youths' adoption of the belittling attitude and active diminishment of women is reminiscent of the way their forebears took advantage of sexist colonial practices that sidelined and disenfranchised women to advance their own economic and political interests, eventually adopting European attitudes that further demeaned women.

Horrific as the crimes were, the most serious and intense concentration of assaults on women occurred between 2002 and 2003, following the outbreak of the civil war, when the armed rebellion succeeded in dividing the country into two distinct territories, the government-held Christian south and the rebel-held Muslim north. At that time, the northern rebel group, known as the MPCI, consolidated with opposition factions in the west (MPIGO and MJP) under the banner of "Forces Nouvelles" (New Forces).[4] The civilian population was caught in the violence as scapegoat, target, and pawn. "Civilian militias, tolerated if not encouraged by state security forces, engaged in widespread targeting of the immigrant community, particularly village-based Burkinabé agricultural workers in the west. The conflict also sparked a sharp escalation in inter-community, inter-ethnic violence in the west and elsewhere, often pitting presumed non-native groups, such as Burkinabé, Malians, or Dioula, known derogatively as the allogènes (namely foreigners), against the presumed indigenous groups (known as autochthones), such as the Guéré, Bété or Krou" (HRW 2007, 19). Against this backdrop, women suffered brutal victimization. "An aid agency active in both government- and rebel-held areas in western Côte d'Ivoire registered over 2,700 women seeking information and assistance in 2005 as victims of sexual violence, mostly for residual trauma related to violations committed between 2002 and 2003" (22).

Although a series of peace agreements and the presence of a UN peace-keeping mission led to an official cease-fire in 2004, no political resolution was reached, and the country remained split. The UN monitored a buffer zone, known as the "Zone of Confidence," that ran the width of the country from east to west, but during the protracted stalemate, forces never disarmed, and conditions of security for civilians degenerated. Government forces conducted raids on predominantly Dyula neighborhoods in Abidjan, such as Adjamé, and subjected women to sexual violence as reprisals for government opposition. Following a protest march by the RDR in 2004, for example, soldiers attacked the immigrant community and raped a woman of Malian origin in front of her husband (71). Sexual assault was to become a regular occurrence and typical feature of the conflict. The rebel forces were no less brutal, despite their initial promises that they would spare the civilian population. When the MPCI took control of the northern town of Bouaké, female relatives of pro-government security forces, including police and gendarmes as well as the army, were singled out, sexually attacked, and explicitly told they were being punished for the political affiliations of their family members (29). In other cases, relatives of government officials, especially Baoulé, were raped (55).

Roadside checkpoints operated both by government and rebel forces throughout the country became focal points of terror. Vehicles were routinely stopped, passengers' belongings pillaged, and women pulled out and brutally raped. Because "the petty trading that occurs on market days is primarily conducted by women," they were compelled to travel to sustain a meager living and thus were vulnerable to repeated attacks (Wells, Hassan, and HRW 2010, 27). A civil leader who worked in the rebel-held west during the most brutal period between 2002 and 2003 documented many cases in which women and girls were abducted from checkpoints in the region surrounding the town of Man. "When women went to do errands in the market the [rebel] soldiers would kidnap them on their way back at checkpoints" (HRW 2007, 46). Checkpoints remained dangerous sites of predatory assaults long after the official end to the first civil war and throughout the long period of political stalemate. "Between 2009 and 2010 HRW documented that at least eighty-one women and girls had been sexually assaulted in just twelve separate bandit attacks of vehicles at road blocks" (Wells, Hassan, and HRW).[5]

Throughout the decade of "no peace, no war," armed marauders roamed in lawless bands, and civilians were the victims of their banditry and terror. Amnesty International reported that these groups operated under a loose chain of command "and seem to have been primarily interested in looting. In this context, *women were often treated as objects to be looted along with material wealth*" (Amnesty International 2007, 12, emphasis mine). Many women were taken captive and made to serve as sex slaves in military camps. Survivors described being considered the "property" of a combatant, which in some cases afforded them protection from assault by others (HRW 2007, 41).

Women refugees fleeing from the zones controlled by the rebels gave testimony of widespread sadistic attacks. The rebel forces "raped women, forced fathers to take their own daughters or even their aged mothers, in the presence of the whole household. They eviscerated pregnant women to learn the sex of the baby . . . their fetuses were eaten by those cannibals" (Bro-Grégbé 2004, 52, 94). The women, "the first victims of the armed conflicts," suffered long-term consequences from these atrocities. Not only severely traumatized, many were exposed to the AIDS virus; HRW confirmed such reports:

> Rebels in Côte d'Ivoire carried out horrific sexual abuse against women and girls in areas under their control, including rape, gang rape, sexual assault, forced miscarriages, and forced incest. Women and girls were subjected to sexual violence in their homes, as they sought refuge, after being found hiding in forests, after being stopped at military checkpoints, as

they worked on their farms, and even in places of worship. Sexual violence was often accompanied by other acts of physical violence such as beating, torture, killing, mutilation, or cannibalism. Numerous women and girls were abducted and subjected to sexual slavery in rebel camps, where they endured rapes over extended periods of time. Resistance was frequently met with punishment, even death. (HRW 2007, 23–24)

The ONUCI Human Rights Division verified that such shocking horrors had been carried out by rebels along with their supporting militias, the "Cocos taillés" (lit. "trimmed coconuts," referring to their characteristic shaved heads), as well as Dozos, traditional hunter/magicians who turned themselves into a fighting force during the war (Amnesty International 2007, 52).[6] Meanwhile, in the western region, the Liberian and Sierra Leonean mercenaries who had been recruited to serve in the rebel-held west were reputedly the most savage assailants. Women were abducted and taken to camps to serve as domestics and sex slaves and subjected to terrifying atrocities linked to sexual violence. One female teen related how she was the victim of cannibalism: "They'd rape me three or four in the night, they would put their guns next to you and if you refuse they kill you. . . . They cut off a piece of my leg and they did the same thing to two other girls. They cooked it in front of us and ate it and said they wanted to taste human flesh" (HRW 2007, 37–38).

An internal power struggle in 2003 between the MPCI and the combined forces of the western groups, the MPJ and MPIGO, resulted in the eventual expulsion of the expatriate fighters, considered to be the most consistent perpetrators of such unthinkably sadistic crimes. Ironically, that effort "gave rise to a short but brutal surge in violence against women," during which time many sex slaves were killed either by their captors or by Ivoirian forces in reprisal against the captives for "dating" the expelled warlords (45, 51). Even during the relatively stable periods of détente, the long intermission between civil wars known as "No Peace, No War," the regular assault on women continued. "Sexual abuse during this period—from late 2003 to 2006—was often associated with key political and military developments in Côte d'Ivoire, including riots, large-scale violence, and inter-ethnic clashes. Of the 15 cases of sexual violence documented by Human Rights Watch during this time, six took place during such periods" (61).

The long-awaited presidential election, intended to settle the conflict and unite the country once and for all, was finally held on October 31, 2010. The international community acknowledged Alassane Ouattara to be the winner, but the Ivoirian election commission contested the validity of the electoral roles and, because the results were not released by the deadline, the Constitutional Council declared the results invalid. Consequently, Gbagbo refused to cede power. The ensuing six-month standoff caused an eruption of renewed violence not only between the armed factions but also on the civilian population. Many had already lost their lives and civil rights during the decade-long wait to exercise democracy, but the postelection violence was even more intense and devastating. Gbagbo surrendered on April 11, 2011, but not before the fight for power had cost the country dearly. Nearly one million Ivoirians were displaced and over 3,000 people, most of them civilians, were killed. With such a toll, that infighting officially became known as Côte d'Ivoire's "second civil war."

The initial military offensive attacked key targets in Abidjan. Many of the violent clashes between security forces and civilians took place in Abobo, a suburb heavily populated by Muslim settlers from the north and a stronghold of Ouattara supporters. HRW reported that pro-Gbagbo forces targeted immigrants from Mali, Burkina Faso, and other West African countries and detained and attacked civilians on ethnic and political grounds. Ouattara spokesmen called for the assaults on civilians in Abidjan to be investigated by the International Criminal Court (ICC), but meanwhile, HRW accused Ouattara's forces of perpetrating some of the worst human rights violations against civilians. They carried out a month-long "onslaught of abuses" in the west on the Guéré ethnic group, suspected of supplying Gbagbo's militia (Wells 2012). The attacks culminated on March 29, 2011, when pro-Ouattara forces and their Dozo militia seized control of the western town of Duékoué.[7] There they retaliated against the population by razing their surrounding villages, maiming, disemboweling, and executing women, children, and the elderly, and committing rape (Wells 2012). Dozens of women were held captive and repeatedly gang-raped, and during these assaults their attackers made reference to their ethnicity; "one said as he grabbed a girl, 'Your Guéré husbands wanted war with us, so we'll give them war'" (HRW 2011a). Hundreds were massacred. A communal well was later discovered to be a mass grave for many of these victims.

The International Committee of the Red Cross (ICRC) condemned the assault on Duékoué as "particularly shocking in its size and brutality," while the UN human rights experts declared that the enforced disappearances, killings, rape, and other sexual violence constituted international crimes that should be subject to the International Criminal Court (ICC). Nevertheless, the assault on helpless civilians continued. In July 2012, the Dozos and a contingent of Ouattara's Republican Forces attacked a camp of internally displaced persons in Nahibly, near Duékoué, repeating the horrific abuses experienced in that town.

The survivors of the horrors of sexual violence, sadistic gender-based torture, and especially protracted victimization endure serious and long-term injury, both physical and psychological. "Women and girls had guns, sticks, pens, and other objects inserted into their vaginas. Others were abducted to serve as sex slaves or forcibly conscripted into the fighting forces. Many women and girls suffered serious, at times debilitating, physical impairments as a consequence of the sexual abuse they endured. Some suffered tears in their genital and reproductive tissue; others suffered from botched abortions following their sexual assault. Countless victims suffered from sexually transmitted infections and were put at high risk for the transmission of HIV/AIDS" (HRW 2007, 135).

The physical injuries women sustained in assaults caused miscarriages, infertility, enduring abdominal pain, and internal injuries like uterine prolapse, fistulas, and associated bleeding and discharge. One woman who had been gang-raped by rebels in 2003 told Amnesty International, "I don't have periods any more, I can't see properly, and *my womb is torn*" (Amnesty International 2007, 24). Many others died of AIDS. The psychological trauma was just as devastating. Survivors reported long-term posttraumatic stress (including flashbacks, headaches, insomnia), shock, and depression, even suicidal tendencies. During interviews with HRW many survivors "spoke to the deep cultural revulsion around the issue of sexual violence. Most could not clearly designate the word 'rape' in a local language" (HRW 2007, 99). "Women preferred the term O Kôhô, which means "ruined" or "dirtied" and underscores the notions of rupture and of destruction of a person after she has been raped. In Yacouba in the Dix-Huit Montagnes region, the term used is Yanshiyi when a child is raped, and Yene Whompi when a woman is raped. Both terms allude to destruction and violence" (99).

The rage, shame, and loss of self-esteem caused by rape made normal sexual relations difficult to sustain, ruined marriages, and destroyed families. Many suffered social stigmatization as a result of their rape, especially if they gave birth as a result. Some were ostracized, abandoned by husbands, and made homeless. The consequences are profound; in such desperate circumstances, some turned to prostitution. The mother of one such victim said, "She's already been destroyed; she's on drugs and she drinks" (Amnesty International 2007, 28).

Deployment: The Appeal to FGP as an
Urgent and Timely Response

Ivoirian women have not only been victims. During the war and after, women spearheaded the most visible demonstrations of protest against abuses of power and calls for basic rights. Their brave collective uprisings must be underscored just to be noticed and understood for what they are, for as one commentator on the powerful place of women in the Ivoirian struggle noted, using the words of the Burkinabe historian, writer, and politician Joseph Ki-Zerbo, "When one does not know what one is looking for, one does not know what one finds" (N'Zi 2010).

As early as September 2002, within days of the attempted coup d'état by the rebel forces, Geneviève Bro-Grégbé, the former Ivoirian minister of sports, who had also served as the executive director of the Réseau Ivoirien des Organisations Féminines—RIOF (Ivoirian Network of Women's Organizations), organized a coalition of NGOs, women's auxiliaries of various political parties as well as women leaders in civil society, calling it the Collectif des Mouvements des Femmes Patriotes (Collective of Movements of Women Patriots). Its goal was to mobilize an effort to support the Gbagbo government and call for peace (Bro-Grégbé 2004, 27, 48). Explaining the rationale for mobilizing women, Bro-Grégbé underscored traditional ideology respecting women as the source of life who bear sustaining protective function in society. "Woman whose first function is to give life is the one who protects and preserves it . . . because it is often in peril for her own life that she gives birth, woman knows the cost of life better than anyone. . . . *Ultimately, woman, [is] the channel through which moral values, such as truth, sincerity, love, forgiveness and respect for others is transmitted and perpetuated*" (93, emphasis mine).[8] Other, more spontaneous and traditional initiatives, however, more overtly embodied the tradition of FGP as an indignant rebuke and threat directed at those who perpetrated injustice on the community.

Martyrs of Civil Society: Adjanou Dancers of Sakassou in 2002

In 2002, at the urging of "young patriots" to resist the attack that ignited the civil war in Côte d'Ivoire, Nanan Kolia Tano, female chief of the Baoulé village Douakandro in the region of Sakassou, organized five elderly women to ward off the cataclysm. They executed the rite they call *Adjanou* (in Baoulé meaning literally "between the legs"), an appeal to FGP described by Nanan Kolia Tano as "a 'mystical' dance" performed in the nude. They danced for seven days. The sixty-five-year-old chief related that "at the end of this mystical week, the rebels arrived suddenly in the village and carried away the dancers who would never again return" (Djinko 2003).

According to witnesses and newspaper accounts of a subsequent investigation into the incident, the rebels from the Movement patriotique de Côte d'Ivoire (MPCI) under the leadership of Guillaume Soro came from Bouaké and entered the village of Assandrè, where they ransacked and pillaged the home of Amany Goly François, the former director of tax administration under the first president, Houphouët-Boigny. One of the women began to sound the bell that "according to the practice of the Adjanou, calls all its members to perform the dance" (Kouano 2013). The rebels arrested an elderly woman, Koffi N'goran, for having sounded the bell "because the act would lead to the curse of the Adjanou dancers" (Kouano 2013). In other words, they were well aware of the significance and presumed power of the rite. She was beaten bloody, humiliated, and taken to the rebel base. Family members eventually paid the rebels to release her, and she fled to Yamoussoukro, the capital city in the heart of Baoulé country.

On December 2, 2002, the rebels returned to Assandrè to seek out the Adjanou women, but by that time they had all fled. Instead they arrested a male elder, Kouadio Yao, presumably for allowing the women of the village to perform "Adjanou, which they considered a dangerous fetish" (Kouano 2013). The rebels then proceeded to the nearby village of Assafou. A member of the commando said, "At the entrance to the village our car overturned causing the death of one of our group. It is clear that it is the Adjanou women who caused it by their diabolical dance that they performed when we approached" (Kouano 2013). The soldiers abducted five of the Adjanou dancers. Only the chief escaped their roundup. The rebels raped, tortured, and killed all the others (Kouano 2013). The women were executed by machine gun and their bodies thrown in a ditch on the road to Katiola in the northern region of Bouake (Taky 2014). The victims, all mothers and grandmothers, are remembered as martyrs, and their names and ages are regularly recalled in tributes to their noble efforts and tragic end: Kouame Affoue, born in 1936, age sixty-six at the time of the abduction and murders; Yao Adjoua, age sixty-four; Yao Flondoh, age seventy-two; Yao Amoin, age eighty-four; and Lossi N'zue Jacqueline, seventy-seven years old (Djinko 2003; Lousse 2013; Taky 2014).

Referring to this incident during an interview, Bro-Grébé attested to the fact of the murders and that the motive had everything to do with the degree to which female genital power is acknowledged in the social imaginary as a dangerous and efficacious force:

> The rebels executed them—and it was a summary execution, you know, they were killed without any formal procedure—it's because they know, they are of an age to know, that that particular ritual was especially dangerous for them. That is why they were executed. And this ritual was done in several parts of CI. After that what happened? Even in the north, there was a time when the rebels were no longer getting along with the local civilian population, and they retreated to the sacred forest. The result was catastrophic. The rebels killed each other.

Yes, they killed each other.[9] So these are things that exist. They are important. That is why I say I would like to see Côte d'Ivoire valorize those traditions. It's precisely because the rebels knew that the ritual was dangerous for them that they tried to supplant them. But they can't. They are practiced everywhere in Côte d'Ivoire! . . . *It is a traditional value that must be perpetuated. Because it is the power of Woman. It is power. That is the power of woman. Even if we don't always see woman in the circles of decision-making, according to tradition, woman has a real power, and it's recognized.* (Personal interview, Abidjan, April 26, 2010, emphasis mine)

Those performers of Adjanou who were summarily executed are celebrated among the Baoulé as warriors and martyrs for the cause of peace. Their public recognizes that their act harkens back to ancient tradition and is an integral part of the history of the Ivoirian nationalist struggle for independence. One Ivoirian blogger made the connection clear: "In the old days, whenever there was a grave threat, Akan women were called to banish the evil spell, executing a dance that the Baoulé call Adjanou, and the Agni call Momemé. Armed with old pestles and sticks resembling rifles, they would cross the village from one end to the other chanting their songs, hammering the ground with their arms. It was conducted at night and performed naked. Their bodies smeared in kaolin, the women danced Adjanou" (Taky 2014).

This blogger, like others who pay tribute to the Adjanou dancers, makes a conscious association between the elders' performance of the ancient rite in Sakassou and the acts of the national heroines who marched in 1949 to Grand-Bassam to free prisoners held by French colonial authorities. "Had [the French colonial] Governor Laurent Pechoux given the order to kill the Adjanou dancers in February 1949, the PDCI-RDA would not exist, the prisoners of Grand-Bassam would never have been liberated and Côte d'Ivoire would never have known its pseudo-independence" (Taky 2014). Unlike those celebrated patriots, "these old women, guarantors of tradition . . . grandmothers whose only concern was to dance for peace, a substantial peace in our country, went to Eblôh without a grave" (Taky 2014).

FGP Deployed against French Minister Villepin in 2003

The iconic incident of 1949 was also foremost in the minds of those who witnessed the deployment of FGP the following year, when Ivoirian women again rose in patriotic zeal to draw on their mystical power in defense of the country. In 2003, when the French minister of foreign affairs, Dominique de Villepin, was sent as a special envoy to help broker a coalition government and, in his words "avoid a humanitarian catastrophe," it was rumored that he had come to demand Gbagbo's resignation. As a result, throngs of government loyalists congregated at the French embassy to protest what was perceived to be an overreaching intervention that smacked of colonialism. Two hundred women blocked Villepin's motorcade, chanting, "We want Gbagbo" (Duval 2003). In an act both insulting and menacing as a conjuration of female genital power, those naked women urinated on his motorcade, a spectacle to which a personal friend and informant of mine was an eyewitness (Anonymous, personal interview April 26, 2010; Gueye 2004). A report in the local press not only relayed the incident, but like Bro-Grébé's account of the deployment of Adjanou against the rebels, suggests that this ritual does indeed have uncanny efficacy: "The Europeans do not know that it is a very strong symbol in Africa when, in their fury, women show their female sanctuary in public while delivering strong words as curses. The last human beings in Africa would be seized with fear at such a spectacle. Thus, since his sad experience in Côte d'Ivoire when women urinated on the wheels of the car that was driving him, Mr. Devillepin has gone from bad to worse" (Gueye 2004).

Dr. Serge-Nicolas N'Zi also cites this case and draws an analogy to those of the patriotic women who executed Adjanou in Grand-Bassam to curse the colonial oppressors. For him, too, the act is not merely a signal of political resistance but a spiritual weapon whose devastating effect can be anticipated:

> Ask Dominique de Villepin, the former French Minister of Foreign Affairs, who found himself blocked by the women patriots of Geneviève Bro Grébé for an hour after he emerged from a meeting with the Ivoirian President, Laurent Gbagbo, in January 2003. *He was shocked, dazed and flabbergasted to find himself face to face with completely naked women and in the center of a concert of insults, curses and sputum.* . . . It is said that *Adjanou brings misfortune* down on the one against whom this dance is directed; the situation of Dominique [de Villepin] . . . is not far from being a case in point. (N'Zi 2010, emphasis mine)

Another blogger reported that Alassane Ouattara (referred to in the vernacular of the street as "Ado") and the French president at that time, Nicolas Sarkozy ("Sarko"), had also been the targets of women's special imprecation, and predicted a troubled future for them as a result. "ADO and 'Sarko, the restless evil one' were given the 'RED KODJO' treatment by Ivoirian women in Paris not long ago. A Kodjo is a cache-sexe [an article of clothing covering the genitalia, traditionally a cloth strung from beads tied around the hips] that is specifically used by women. The color red is a symbol of menstruation, among other things in this particular context. *The resulting curse will not be long in taking effect, since if it was by force of arms that Sarko and his partner vanquished Ivoirians, they will be gutted by other means"* (Gueye 2004, emphasis mine). Those "other means" are the means of women's spiritual warfare, the potent weapon of ultimate resort.

Geneviève Bro-Grébé herself referred to this incident as a spontaneous uprising in response to the women's perception of a mortal threat to society. When the Mothers appear civil strife is shown to be something more than a terrible social struggle. It is a signal of a moral evil that must be banished from the public space, which they accomplish with their daylight ritual of adjuration:

> There was a moment when, during the manifestation in front of the French Embassy in Plateau—there were women who stripped naked. Spontaneously. No one asked them to do it. . . . *In the south here we don't necessarily call it Adjanou. In my village they call it Foqwé. But what the women did during the crisis—they do it whenever there is a serious danger.* . . . At the height of the crisis, in 2002—September, October, November. . . . *people came from all these regions to the public square in Plateau to exorcise the evil.* So people came, the warrior chiefs, and danced in the public square. . . . Those are things that happened during that crisis. (Personal interview, April 26, 2010, emphasis mine)

The following year another spontaneous public display of FGP erupted on the political scene to signal moral indignation and social lament. Bro-Grébé relayed what she saw, alluding both to the heroism of the actors and the gravity of the act: "In 2004, when the tanks fired on Ivoirans, killing sixty people, there was one woman—we have a photo of her somewhere—*one woman who stripped naked.* Later it disrupted her home life; her husband chased her from the house. So this is to say that these things exist, but *it happens when there is a true danger."* (Personal interview, April 26, 2010, emphasis mine)

Black Tuesday 2004: FGP against French Forces at the Hôtel Ivoire

That particular enactment of FGP was an indictment of the tragic events of November 6 through 10 of 2004, during which, according to the official report by the Ivoirian Minister of Health, fifty-seven Ivoirian civilians were killed and 2,226 wounded (Canal+ 2004). It all began on November 3 when Gbagbo's government launched an aerial offensive against rebel forces that had refused to disarm, as provided for by their latest peace agreement. When French troops and those associated with the UN peacekeeping force, the Force Licorne, failed to react to this cease-fire violation, the Forces Nouvelles accused them of backing Gbagbo and attacked a French military barracks in the western town of Man (Amnesty International 2006). That same day, November 6, the Ivoirian air force bombarded a French barracks in Bouaké, the rebel stronghold. That attack killed nine French soldiers. In retaliation President Jacques Chirac ordered an air strike that destroyed the entire Ivoirian fleet, and the French seized the airport. Charles Blé Goudé, leader of the Young Patriots, called upon Ivoirians to defend the nation from reoccupation by their former colonial masters, and thousands heeded the call. Newspapers also galvanized patriotic intervention, reporting that Chirac had declared war on Côte d'Ivoire "after the failure of the rebellion that their country had instigated in order to bring down the government of President Laurent Gbagbo" (*Notre Voie*, November 8, 2004, quoted in Amnesty International 2006, 6). As the first crowd of protestors was crossing one of Abidjan's principal bridges and heading toward the airport, French helicopter gunboats opened fire on the unarmed civilians, hitting at least four victims, destroying two vehicles, and scattering terrorized marchers.

In the ensuing days, the Young Patriots seized the radio and television studios and fueled tensions with the xenophobic rhetoric of their broadcasts. These pro-Gbagbo youth themselves looted and ransacked opposition party headquarters and attacked the homes of their leaders. They also vandalized foreign property in Abidjan, notably the campuses of French private schools. More serious still was the violence they leveled against foreign nationals, and in particular French women. Amnesty International noted that "*there were several reports of women being raped. The victims were French women, other foreign women and Ivoirian women associated with the French, such as the wives of French men or nannies of French children*" (10). Once again, women's bodies became the locus of the contest for power and its violent conquest.

On November 7, 2004, as civil unrest in Abidjan grew acute, foreign nationals were evacuated by helicopter from the grounds of the Hôtel Ivoire. It was especially ironic as the iconic hotel, one of the earliest high-rises built in the heyday of economic prosperity and political promise, was a symbol of national pride, representing the early achievements of development as well as the country's reputation as a haven of international hospitality. Two days later, on November 9, French tanks rolled in to the elite neighborhood of Cocody in Abidjan and headed toward the presidential palace, while others were stationed at the nearby Hôtel Ivoire, which became a makeshift military headquarters.

Persuaded that the presence of French armored vehicles was a signal of their intention to overthrow President Gbagbo, thousands of unarmed demonstrators gathered in front of the hotel to protest (Rosenthal 2005). After an all-day standoff, the increasingly rowdy crowd crossed the line of demarcation between them and the local gendarmes who had been called in to keep them at bay. Some young men reached the tanks. According to a witness, "This elicited some applause from the crowd; they were enjoying every minute of it" (Amnesty International 2006, 16). This is when French soldiers shot into the crowd, killing scores and wounding thousands.[10] An investigative report by Amnesty International quotes witnesses to these events whose accounts describe the state of mind of the demonstrators in front of the hotel that day: "On Tuesday morning around six, we went to the Hôtel Ivoire; there was a white tape, barbed wire and tanks. The crowd grew bigger and at about 10 a.m. we broke through the white tape and called on the French to leave the hotel; *we sang patriotic songs, some people took their clothes off. It was total euphoria; we cursed the French*" (14, emphasis mine).

The evocation of FGP was significant for the French, as well, who understood it as a vile provocation. According to the French military, some protesters "made obscene gestures." An official of the Force Licorne justified their assault saying, "*Women took off their clothes in front of us and insulted us*" (14, emphasis mine). When the French opened fire, the Hôtel Ivoire, emblem of urbane cosmopolitanism, became the site of senseless slaughter. That day in 2004 has become known as "Black Tuesday."

Old Pots and Bullets: FGP in Defense of Living Conditions in 2008

In the next few years a tense détente prevailed, but the economic conditions of the fractured country plummeted, and women again showed themselves to be the vigilant monitors of social equity and justice and vigorous agitators for social well-being. The tradition of women's solidarity and the ritual display of female power was manifest in an uprising in Côte d'Ivoire on April 2, 2008, when women took to the streets of Abidjan to protest the sudden surge in prices of food and staples. It began in the neighborhoods of Yopougon and Cocody, with women chanting, "We want to eat, we want to eat," and quickly spread to other quarters of the city and even to some towns in the interior as participants sent the signal to others by cellphone to join the movement (Silué 2008). In several districts (Cocody, Riviéra, II Plateau, Port-Bouët, Yopougon) women blocked the major city arteries with branches, benches, cinder blocks, and trash cans, and even set tires on fire. *"Their faces smeared with kaolin, they were armed with old pots to make the maximum noise in the hope of being heard and eventually understood"* (Silué 2008, emphasis mine). These ritual details, given no further comment or explanation in the press, clearly point to the tradition of women's potent intervention in times of social catastrophe and their turn to the paramount forces necessary to evict from their midst the threatening forces of evil.

In the district of Port Bouët, the women met with violent reprisal. When they refused to remove the roadblocks they set up in protest, members of the elite forces, the Compagnie Républicaine de Sécurité (CRS) and the Centre de Commandement et de Sécurité (CECOS), opened fire and killed one young man who was accompanying the crowd (Silué 2008). The disproportionate show of force against the demonstrators rallying against inflation was shocking and ignited in the popular imagination an association between these women and those who had faced the repressive colonial authorities. "The recent women's march against the cost of living can be likened to that of the women to Grand Bassam in 1949," since both movements had been led by simple housewives who were motivated by the need for "the improvement of conditions of living for the entire population" (Silué 2008).

FGP Causes a Prefect to Flee in 2010

Two years later the deteriorating conditions of life were again the cause of a show of female genital power in CI. In February of 2010 over 3,000 people from twenty-one villages in the district of Didiévi marched on local headquarters to protest the cuts of electricity and water, measures understood to have been taken by President Gbagbo to punish the districts presumed to favor his political opponent. They declared that they no longer regarded Gbagbo as head of state and told the state's representative (*préfet*) Didier Kragbé that they therefore no longer recognized his authority, either. "The appearance of women [performing] *adjanou* in front of the precinct made the occupant flee and resort to sending in armed forces"; one hundred troops rushed to the scene (*Le Nouveau Reveil* 2010).

Cleansing the Country of Evil in Yamoussoukro in 2011

In February 2011 in Yamoussoukro hundreds of kaolin-smeared women dressed in white occupied the outer courtyard of the residence of the late president Houphouët-Boigny. Their aim was to perform Adjanou on the anniversary of the funeral of the "Father of the Nation," called an "Apostle of Peace," and through that rite condemn what the organizer called "the deplorable state of the country's affairs, now aggravated by the postelectoral crisis on the one hand, and the illegal occupation of this place by Laurent Gbagbo, his men and his military who have profaned this site" (*Le Mandat* 2011). According to Gnamien M'Bandama Kouakou Antoine, spokesperson for the Boigny family, the residence had become a "powder keg," a place of munitions and a camp for militia and mercenaries (Diallo 2011).

In Yamoussoukro, Houphouët-Boigny's natal village, it is reputed that Adjanou helped him win victory over the French colonials and bring the country to independence (Mintho 2011). Perhaps for this very reason the women's arrival triggered a strong reaction from the Forces de défense et de sécurité (FDS), the army serving the contested president Gbagbo, which initially barred their entrance. The women, ranging in age from sixty to over eighty, were nevertheless able to occupy the grounds, an act interpreted by at least one journalist as the women's successful "usurpation of power" (*Le Mandat* 2011).

While their aim was to appeal to Adjanou to "ward off the spirit of evil that had overtaken Côte d'Ivoire" and to dance continuously until peace once again reigned (Diallo 2011), their occupation was in fact an act of war, however peaceful in appearance. One journalist was careful to relate the significance of the rite and the gravity of the women's presence:

> They don't open their mouths to speak yet one understands their message, provided one has a discerning mind. The principal message is understood thus: "The hour is very serious; *a veritable spiritual combat* is taking place. This spiritual combat is undertaken exclusively by women who are well informed and strictly selected for it. It is thus not a matter for men who, moreover, must keep away. We are in the spiritual domain, and here (according to African tradition, especially Ivoirian tradition) *the strength and the power belong to Woman.*" . . . When the women execute [the rite] no man shows his face, or he risks drawing curses upon him that may even go so far as to cost him his life! During the dance, all the women . . . are naked. (*Le Mandat* 2011, emphasis mine)

They had danced for ten days when a soldier spied on them as a voyeur and photographed the scene, knowingly violating their sacred act and its taboos. The indignant organizer of the women, Madame Yvonne Kouamé, related the incident: "At 5:30 in the morning, while we were making the rounds of the private residence of Houphouët-Boigny, a soldier began to film us naked. We were so surprised because no one could imagine that a man would act in such a way" (Diallo 2011). To another reporter she said, "'We were right in the middle of dancing Adjanou when an individual in military uniform, a camera in his fist, filmed the scene. When the dancers noticed him and tried to stop him, he fled and jumped into a 4X4 vehicle with military plates. Incredible! It is a serious violation of our feminine intimacy and our sacred dance, strictly forbidden to men,' said the outraged leader" (*Le Mandat* 2011). The infuriated dancers "made their outrage known to the canton chief, all Baoulé chiefs and kings, as well as political administrative authorities by shouting and blocking the entrances to the palace" (Mintho 2011).

Thrashing the Enemy in 2011

That same month, February 2011, saw a violent confrontation between the Forces de Défense et de sécurité (FDS) loyal to Gbagbo and pro-Ouattara demonstrators in Abidjan. Several dozen women gathered at the headquarters of the Republican Guard to protest the "massacre" of their children and with the intention of executing the ritual dance Adjanou (Bolougbeu 2011). They were prevented from doing so, dispersed with tear gas and the shots of soldiers fired into the air. A few days later Adjanou dancers appeared in Treichville, a lively neighborhood in the city of Abidjan, to protest "their children's arbitrary abduction" by Gbagbo's Republican Guard; they brandished their *kodjo* (female loincloths) to "thrash the enemy" (Radiosun 2011). The "women's revolt" became an almost daily affair. After the Adjanou dance in Yamoussoukro, the number of women's marches escalated and spread to Treichville in Abidjan, where "in a heroic uprising, the women obtained the release of certain women arrested by Gbagbo's republican guard, and then on February 21 and 28 women marched in Grand-Bassam. On March 1 the women of Adjamé and Koumaassi in Abidjan took to the streets to demand that Gbagbo step down.

Despite the long duration and extreme brutality of the war, the plight of the Ivoirian population, and the appeal of the women for peace, the international media paid scant attention. But the shocking slaughter of seven women conducting a peaceful protest finally grabbed the international headlines. On March 3, 2011, women marched in the Abobo quarter of Abidjan to demand an end to the postelection violence. They assumed that "soldiers would be too ashamed to open fire" on women (Callimachi 2011). Ironically the peaceful demonstration against violence turned into a bloody site of the brazen killing of civilians. Government soldiers shot seven women dead. Their killing and surrounding frenzy, captured on amateur video and circulated on YouTube, made the massacre a vivid and shocking spectacle of civilian abuse that Ivoirians had long suffered (BBC News 2011c; CNN 2011). In an interview with BBC Radio,

Aya Virginie Touré, the president of the women's group allied to the party of Ouattara, described the gathering of women on the fateful day, clearly signaling their rebuke of the state in the traditional way:

> The march started on the third, in the morning. Literally people from all the neighborhoods in Abidjan—there are ten different districts—were marching. Altogether they were talking about twenty-five to thirty thousand women in the streets. They were excited, enthusiastic, joyful. They believed they were going to solve the problem. That's why they were happy. . . . . *There were some who were naked,* some wearing white, some black. *Some were holding branches. Or had branches as part of their outfits. Some were covered in [white kaolin] clay.* . . . *All of these outfits are traditional that they would wear—or not wear—to show how unhappy they are. This is African tradition.* This is the way to show how they are feeling inside, to reflect the state of their soul. (Bannister 2011)[11]

In an interview with the British newspaper the *Guardian*, Touré estimated that about five hundred of the women were either naked or wearing black. "In Africa, and Ivory Coast, this is like a curse. . . . That's why the soldiers were afraid and shot at them. Some also had brooms and leaves in their hands. They were cursing the rule of Gbagbo, putting a spell on him: 'If you were born of woman, step down; if not, you can stay.' This is why the soldiers were scared" (Smith 2011). The women were chanting, dancing, and whistling. When tanks and Humvees arrived on the scene the women began to cheer, thinking they were there as a show of support. But suddenly they opened fire on the crowd. "It all happened all of a sudden; no one was expecting it. Women started falling. . . . Seven women died that day. . . . I would never have thought they would shoot at women. . . . I had no idea this could happen," said Touré (BBC 2011). Another participant told the BBC World Service that more than 5,000 women had gathered at a particular roundabout that was the designated rallying point in Abobo. "Then we heard young girls shouting: 'Tanks are coming! Tanks are coming!' . . . And those who were in the tanks started shooting at us with machine guns. . . . We have no idea why they shot at us. We were just a gathering of women, nothing else but women" (BBC News 2011b). She bravely added, "We, the women of Ivory Coast, will continue our action" (BBC News 2011b). Sirah Drane, who helped to organize the march, had also seen the tanks and thought, "'They won't shoot at women.' . . . I heard a boom. They started spraying us. . . . Opening fire on unarmed women? It's inconceivable," she told reporters (Callimachi 2011).

Six days later, on the occasion of International Women's Day, hundreds of Ivoirian women gathered to commemorate the fallen women and draw attention to their fate. The throng of "women marched in three neighborhoods in Abidjan—Abobo, Treichville and Koumassi—to protest the bloodshed" (CNN Wire Staff 2011). It is worth noting that women on both sides of the political and ethnic divide marched that day, albeit in separate parades and quarters, "to call for a return to peace in the country that [had] been plunged in violence for several weeks" (CNNIC 2011). A leader of the pro-Gbagbo faction, Danièle Boni Claverie, affirmed the role of women in the effort to stabilize the political turmoil, stating, "We must commit to the quest for freedom and peace over the culture of violence and war ... peace must be the business of women" (CNNIC 2011). Those from the pro-Ouattara faction wore black or red as a sign of mourning for their slain comrades. But at that rally, as well, four protesters were killed.

While these slaughters had finally garnered media attention, and the Women's International Day memorial protest march was also given wide coverage, what local journalists referenced only obliquely, and the foreign press entirely ignored, was the religious foundation of the ritual rhetoric informing the acts of those early protestors and contemporary demonstrators alike. In these public manifestations, the women appeared smeared in white kaolin clay, a symbol of power whose source is the watery depths from which both women and spirits are said to emerge (Boone 1986). *In these many various manifestations the women consistently appeared wielding branches and implements for conjuring blessings and curses; they were draped with leaves associated with magico-medicinal protection, and some stripped naked, danced and gestured suggestively.* Failing to interpret such expression, journalists offer a merely political rendition of events and misconstrue their true significance (Grillo 2012). The ritual performances of female genital power made public in the political arena have been history-making acts of civil society. Through their ancient ritual rhetoric these women eloquently condemn political power unchecked by moral authority. In Côte d'Ivoire, the women's deployment of female genital power as a call to restore the moral underpinnings of the state shows the state's widespread sexual violation of women to be even more reprehensible, as it sets in high relief government's critical missing ingredient (Grillo 2012).

7. MEMORY, MEMORIALIZATION, AND MORALITY

> Cultures may then be represented as zones of control or of abandonment,
> of recollection and of forgetting, of force or of dependence, of exclusiveness or
> of sharing, all taking place in the global history that is our element.
> —EDWARD W. SAID, "Representing the Colonized: Anthropology's Interlocutors"

Impunity and Partisan Justice: A Case of State Amnesia

The unimaginable atrocities to which they were systematically subjected as targets of civil war left Ivoirian women and girls permanently damaged and in perpetual pain. The psychological trauma of terror and humiliation has been personally devastating, and has led to terrible social ramifications including stigmatization, rejection by husbands, and alienation from families. Women were consequently further victimized by poverty, sometimes turning to prostitution as a last resort of the broken and isolated. The suffering extended to the social body, as well. Many women were infected with HIV and died from AIDS; children were orphaned; communities were destroyed.

Under President Gbagbo in 2003, the state attempted to draw the curtain over the horrors of the civil strife by hastily inaugurating a policy of state-sanctioned forgetting: blanket amnesty for the perpetrators of the crimes of the first civil war. The women belonging to the Union générale des victimes de guerre de Côte d'Ivoire (UVGCI), the Union of Victims of War Crimes, responded with a vociferous outcry. They wrote to the National Assembly to express their opposition, saying that the amnesty law "humiliated, ridiculed and wounded their dignity as women" (Tanoh 2003). They threatened to protest and curse parliament by organizing a "*sit-in in the garment of Eve, that is to say, completely naked*" (Tanoh 2003, emphasis mine). In the words of Monique Kobri, the association's vice president, while the amnesty was intended to "crown the entrance of the principal actors of the rebellion into government," the sit in would turn that crown into "a crown of thorns, given what the *exposure of women's nakedness means in Africa*" (Araoye 2012, 56; Tanoh 2003, emphasis mine). Their outcry and threat went unheeded. Ironically, the mute enactment of ritual rebuke might have better succeeded in making their indignation heard. Four years later, in 2007, the union's members were still waiting for acknowledgment and accountability. All 2,000 of them filed formal dossiers with international tribunals and met with the international commission charged with investigating human rights abuses in Côte d'Ivoire to document the facts of their victimization.[1] Monique Kobri, who was by then the president of the UVGCI, warned that "many of the women have HIV, and others have been affected mentally and psychologically" and that without prosecution or restitution, they would continue to suffer as the war's "forgotten victims" (BBC News 2007).

When President Alassane Dramane Ouattara came to power in the spring of 2011, he repeatedly affirmed his commitment to impartial justice for war crimes and to the restoration of the rule of law. The public persistently recalled to collective memory the murders of the Adjanou dancers and expressed indignation that not only had immunity been extended to the accused killers, but some of them were promoted within the ranks of the military (O. A. M. 2011).[2] Once again Kobri decried the state's facile pronouncement of political reconciliation without justice for victims. Referring to them, she said, "One cannot speak of reconciliation while discounting a portion of the population" (Gneproust 2011). She reminded the public that the women who suffered victimization in 2002 were still calling for sanctions against those war criminals and identified with the women who suffered similar horrors and indignities during the postelection crisis: "We deplore the crisis of November 2010 and we are in solidarity with our sisters who lived through the same atrocities as we did. But we hope that the investigators take into account all those who suffered in order to allow all Ivoirians to free their hearts" (Gneproust 2011). Even though Monique Kobri's own husband and son had been murdered by rebel forces in Bouaké, she underscored that the union's struggle for justice could not be a political one, taking pains to dissociate it from any advocacy for Laurent Gbagbo: "I have been struggling since 2002 so that the injustice will be rectified and not for the cause of Laurent Gbagbo. I am not at all competent to defend him," she said (Gneproust 2011). Such persistent recollection of those patiently awaiting justice stands in relief against the government's amnesia.

If the culture of impunity precipitated the unprecedented assault on civilians and women during the conflict, the government's lack of accountability after the war ended and its failure to arrest, prosecute, and punish known perpetrators associated with the Republican Forces or allied militia groups prevented any hope for true justice. It seemed that the West and the international community that created the agenda for the postcolonial state had so fetishized democracy (at least the "soft" form characterized by elections) that it turned a blind eye when the new government's processes contravened constitutional provisions for accountability. While Gbagbo was transferred to The Hague and tried by the ICC for crimes against humanity, of the 150 other people charged with crimes committed during the postelection violence, none were associated with the pro-Ouattara camp.[3]

Not only was justice for women not forthcoming, but the armed forces of Ouattara's new government, the FRCI, renewed the cycle of revenge and brutal repression against former Gbagbo supporters, making reconciliation in Côte d'Ivoire even more elusive (Amnesty International 2013a, 1). The traditional hunters *cum* military militia, the Dozos, along with members of the national army, carried out "extra-judicial executions, deliberate and arbitrary killings, politically motivated arrests and torture" (1). Detainees were held for political and ethnic affiliations for long periods without access to legal representation or contact with families and were subject to "inhumane and degrading treatment" (1). Some were tortured to extract confessions (1). Perhaps the most significant abuse by government forces after Ouattara came to power was the massive and vicious attack on the Nahibly camp of internally displaced people that took place in July 2012.[4] Led by the state-backed Dozos, the raiders targeted civilians from the Guéré ethnic group, considered to have been Gbagbo supporters and therefore a "hostile" populace (1). The official UN death toll was 816 civilians, excluding the number of bodies later discovered in wells and mass graves (Le Monde.fr 2015). Men, women, children, the aged and infirm "were killed and injured by guns, machetes, axes, and clubs and by being burned alive. . . . Charred and abandoned clothing and possessions were everywhere," scattered in the wake of the refugees' frantic flight (Neve and Amnesty International 2013). Five months later, an HRW observer visiting the site noted that the fertile earth had begun to reclaim the terrain with its abundant vegetation, making it seem as if "the very memory of the Nahibly attack [was] itself fading away . . . [as] impunity only deepens and grows over" (Neve and Amnesty International 2013). The battle for territory was becoming a fight for the collective memory and for control over the narrative that would prevail in the history of the nation. That would require the erasure and systematic forgetting of certain events of the past as much as recollection.

Even two years after Outtara took power, Côte d'Ivoire remained in a fragile state, and the country was still deeply divided. Up to that time criminal proceedings had been led almost exclusively against those who had been aligned with Gbagbo. The decidedly one-sided system of justice that unfolded under the new government was documented by three human rights monitoring agencies in a joint report published in 2013 to raise the alarm. They charged that "the atrocities committed by the forces that supported or are supporting still the 'pro-Ouattara camp' (Forces Nouvelles later became the FRCI) and their auxiliary militia (particularly the Dozos), are today the subject of a single charge" (FIDH-LIDHO-MIDH 2013, 16). Significantly, that one accused subject, Amadé Ouérémi, was not one of the Republican Forces but a leader of a formally unaligned group of Burkinabé fighters.

Another two years had passed when Amnesty International again lamented that up to that point "not a single member of the national army or any other supporter of President Alassane Ouattara [had been] held to account for their actions" (16). On June 26, 2015, Human Rights Watch (HRW), the International Federation for Human Rights (FIDH), and nineteen other groups issued a joint letter to President Ouattara urging that the governmental body organized to investigate the grave postelection abuses of human rights should be allowed to conclude its work (HRW 2015). It was only the following month, with the first official indictment of leaders of the former rebel forces, that a step to rectify this partisan justice was made. Among those charged was Losséni Fofana, the commander of the Republican Forces accused of leading the assault on Duékoué that resulted in the slaughter of hundreds of civilians (Le Monde.fr 2015).

Even though justice was finally being pursued, women remained the consistently forgotten victims. In March of 2015 FIDH filed a civil lawsuit on behalf of forty-three women who were victims of sexual abuse during the postelection crisis, charging that the response of the Ivoirian justice system to their suffering had been entirely inadequate. Their lawyer and FIDH president called for justice "for women who have suffered rape . . . exercised independent of any political or electoral agenda" (FIDH–Worldwide Human Rights Movement 2015). They were later joined in the judicial proceedings by the Ivoirian Movement for Human Rights (MIDH) and the Ivoirian League for Human Rights (LIDHO) to represent over two hundred victims. When the United Nations decided to extend the mandate of the UNOCI for another year, through June 30, 2016, the UN Special Representative of the Secretary-General on Sexual Violence in Conflict also called for a new commitment on the part of the Ivoirian state to end sexual violence.[5] That end could only come with thorough recollection of the collective wound inflicted on women and the end of impunity for the perpetrators of such abuse.

This record of delayed and lopsided pursuit of justice is ironic, given that at the start of his term President Ouattara announced that he would make reconciliation the focus of his presidency. Looking to South Africa and the way the government there had fostered peace after its struggle against apartheid ended, Ouattara determined that Côte d'Ivoire would follow its model of seeking truth and reconciliation. After calling on South Africa's Bishop Desmond Tutu as well as other African leaders for advice on procedure, he established the Commission Dialogue, Vérité et Réconciliation (CDVR) and empowered it to investigate violations of human rights to ease tensions and promote national unity. In principle, the aim of such a commission is to promote restorative rather than retributive justice. Rather than viewing war crimes as offenses against the state, it focuses on the victimization of individuals and the community. In the interest of healing, the process seeks to provide a constructive response to wrongdoings and to build partnerships between former adversaries. But because South Africa's policy had been to grant amnesty to all who confessed to wrongdoing, it was feared that the application of such a model in Côte d'Ivoire risked perpetuating its record of immunity for known human rights violators (FIDH-LIDHO-MIDH 2013, 21). From the outset many warned that hasty foreclosure of the complaints could impede the integrity of the process in Côte d'Ivoire and fail to diffuse mistrust and hostility.

Perhaps for this very reason, the commission's first report, submitted two years after its inauguration, avoided addressing the violations of human rights during the war or the postelection crisis at all, focusing instead on the causes of the first attempted coup d'état in 1999 and the army mutiny of 2002 (La Rédaction 2014). According to the director of Freedom House, an organization monitoring human rights, the CDVR "should have concentrated on the essential: seeking the truth on what happened during the crisis and bringing justice and reparation to the victims. *But the victims were forgotten. . . . The commission never interviewed a single victim*" (La Rédaction 2014, emphasis mine). Consequently, while the commission had also been charged with establishing a dialogue between the political parties of the opposing camps, Ouattara's Rassemblement des Républicains (RDR) and Gbagbo's Front Populaire Ivoirien (FPI), it also failed to ease political tensions between them.

CDVR president Charles Konan Banny submitted the commission's final report one year later, in December 2015. Very different in focus, it also led to immediate and concrete results for the victims of war. It claimed to be based on over 72,000 interviews with victims, of which more than 28,000 were women (gouv.ci 2015). Moreover, on the occasion of the report's delivery, President Ouattara announced that a fund of ten million FCFA (approximately twenty thousand US dollars) had been established to compensate victims. The commission also took care to address the long-neglected domain of traditional religion and the cultural roots of reconciliation and peace. When he submitted the commission's report, Banny recommended the establishment of a "National Day of Remembrance and Forgiveness," acknowledging that the war was as much a spiritual as a criminal offense and had to be addressed at this level, as well: "The flow of blood . . . is considered everywhere in Côte d'Ivoire to be an immense catastrophe because it involved a rupture of three links, namely *the relation with the earth that is forced to absorb the spilled human blood, the respect for the spirits, and the link between human beings and the universe.* We foresee consecrating an entire month to this psychological and cultural exercise that will culminate with a national celebration" (gouv.ci 2015, emphasis mine). Yet just as the state seemed to have suffered from selective recall when it came to the violence perpetrated on the populace, causing women's victimization to be forgotten, its turn to indigenous tradition was equally flawed by a damning slight of women as the primary and paramount spiritual source of retributive justice. According to tradition, only women's power can purify the Earth of "spilled human blood," reconcile humans to the Earth and its spiritual overseers, and restore the "link between human beings with the universe" in a way that makes the land fit for human habitation. However, Banny and the CDVR had consistently sidelined the women elders who embodied this power.

An event previously organized by the commission was a case in point. Nanan Awoula Tanoé Désiré, who was serving as the CDVR vice president and who is also the supreme chief of the N'Zima-Kôtôkô people (Grand-Bassam), arranged for a purification ceremony to mourn the violence of the civil war and to seek redress and pardon from the dead. It was held in March 2012 in the cultural "palace" of Treichville, one of Abidjan's oldest popular districts. At the opening ceremony the supreme chief stumbled. It was a portentous omen. Banny then knelt down to invoke the forgiveness of the casualties of the war, but for the public the dead had already signaled their clear refusal. According to at least one local journalist, the ceremony's failure was not unrelated to the absence of two sets of female ritual specialists, the Komians (traditional Akan priestesses) and Adjanou dancers, those properly authorized and empowered to perform such rites (Djé 2012).

The neglect of these female spiritual authorities was more than a social gaffe or faux pas, underscored by the chief's literal misstep, however. It constituted a form of amnesia that is typical of the postcolonial state and demonstrates what

Africanists have come to refer to as a contemporary "memory crisis" (Antze and Lambek 1996; De Jong and Rowlands 2007; Werbner 1998). The omission of the women at this supposedly traditional ceremony exemplified the kind of "failure of memory, where the trace of indigenous cultural institutions and the interpretive traditions that upheld them are distorted beyond recognition" (Al-Kassim 2008, 168). By "forgetting" the Mothers and replacing them with the state's newly appointed, secular intercessors, the "traditional" chiefs, the CDRV presented the appearance of accountability to tradition, but was in fact evoking a new postcolonial subjectivity, the identification with the state that is beyond any actual tradition. The state's grandiose ceremonialism and its slight of the female authorities can therefore be read as an active attempt to usurp their spiritual power.

In the popular social imaginary such state amnesia points to the source of the ongoing troubles in Côte d'Ivoire even after Ouattara had assumed power. On February 2, 2012, the newly established president failed to show for an official rendezvous with the public in Abobo, the quarter where his candidacy had been heavily favored. The meeting was to be the occasion for Ouattara to express his gratitude for that support and especially to thank the "traditional dancers of the fetish called 'Adjanou'" who had "invoked the spirits ... to install the president-elect to the seat of supreme magistrate" (Adriel 2012). The neglected Adjanou dancers may have been personally affronted by Ouattara's absence; moreover, they warned that the political leader's neglect of his moral and spiritual duty foretold the government's doom, for "'one does not play with the genies'" (Adriel 2012). Their warning of the disastrous consequences of ignoring the proper channels of spiritual power may sound quaintly credulous to postmodern secularists, taken in its most literal sense. But given the significant role that the principle of matrifocal morality has played over the centuries in African civilization and the force that it still bears in the collective social imaginary today, even the most pragmatic political analyst can see that the neglect of the benediction of the Mothers opens the government to the charge of ruling illegitimately—that is, without moral authority.

Nation Building and the Achievement of Forgetting

The neglect, distortion, and erasure of indigenous cultural institutions by the state and its polity are not the result of any actual failure of memory. Rather, this phenomenon is recognized as an *achievement* of the state, the result of a strategy that Richard Werbner (1998) refers to as "remembering to forget." Forgetting is essential to nation building. In order to forge a new coherent impression of belonging, especially in an ethnically heterogeneous country that has been further fractured by civil war, the postcolonial state must repress differences. Turning away from the past, it offers a new narrative of itself as the future—as the inevitable culmination of the progress of history. Such a narrative presents the advent of the new state as a radical break from a "primitive" past, which in the Ivoirian case is all that is associated with the causes of the civil war and its violence.[6] That past is actively disavowed by the state through various mechanisms of manipulation of the collective memory. One of those mechanisms is the work of the commission for dialogue, truth, and reconciliation (CDVR).

The CDVR's avoidance of public testimony about human rights abuses, its suppression of the airing of grievances, and its hasty foreclosure of dissent through facile reconciliation all point to the state's will to forget the brutal aspects of the past and quickly dissociate itself from the violence of the civil war to gain political legitimacy. It demonstrates the strategy of situating violence in the "primitive sphere outside the boundaries of national memory" (Al-Kassim 2008, 168). Making itself an emblem of the triumph of the civilizing force of democracy over and against the fragmenting ethnic and religious allegiances of the past, the postcolonial state sidesteps accountability.

Refusing to conform to such a postcolonial script, women's traditional activism calls to mind the persistent injustices of the state as an ongoing form of violence perpetrated on its populace, especially female victims of war. The Mothers' persistent recollection of the past and their use of tradition as a relevant critique of the present challenge the state's self-exoneration. In Côte d'Ivoire the eruptions of FGP to condemn the brutality of forces on both sides of the conflict signaled women's refusal to reduce the civil war to "clichés of tribal kinship and communal atavism or essential inaptitude for democratic self-rule" (173). Their traditional rebuke of the state's immoral use of force undermines the depiction of the crisis as "only a throwback" to the primitive past (Cramer 2006, 229). Their embodied critique has been directed instead at the state itself as the source of the cataclysm that befell the country and shows all its "children" to be its suffering victims. By planting themselves on the streets and in the midst of normal civilian life, the women's act of civil disobedience reveals the structural violence of the postcolonial state to have a long pedigree from which it can neither dissociate itself nor free itself without the check of the Mothers.

The concerted determination of the state to avoid history, "that of not wishing to remember a past, of willfully disempowering a past . . . the deliberate rejection of 'the past'" creates a vacuum in the collective memory that the state fills by another kind of narrative, one that has been called "nostalgia for the future" (Van Dijk 1998, 157). Founded on global forces, markets, and models of development, the nationalist postcolony presents itself as the fulcrum of the inexorable press of history toward progress. This discursive strategy suppresses and "forgets" features of the past that impede the state's consolidating hold over the present. Forgetting all but the push toward progress, the state focuses attention uniquely on its raison d'être: the unification of the people and the consolidation of a common aim and end. "It is through this syntax of forgetting—or being obliged to forget—that the problematic identification of a national people becomes visible. . . . To be obliged to forget—in the construction of the national present—is not a question of historical memory; it is the construction of a discourse on society that *performs* the problem of totalizing the people and unifying the national will" (Bhabha 1994, 230). The work of the CDVR is again a case in point. In an effort to suppress the history of enmity and fratricide (and matricide) that culminated in genocidal slaughter and incomprehensible abuse, its first report neglected to address that violence at all. The subsequent rush to amnesty for perpetrators aimed at the "construction of the national present" in which all would be united in common cause of peace and totalizing identity under the new banner of Ivoirian citizenship. It demonstrates the kind of "nostalgia for the future" in which all is well and where the state's goal for progress proceeds uninhibited by memories of forgotten traditions, broken alliances, or the terrible suffering caused by civil war.

By contrast, the women's performances of FGP as a rebuke of the state problematize that totalizing vision of the state's trajectory and will. Rather than submitting to the new postcolonial script about the march of history toward nationalism or the consolidation of knowledge in global terms, the local critique embodied in FGP fosters what Foucault calls "an insurrection of subjugated knowledges" (Foucault and Gordon 1980, 81). The women's manifestations forcefully reject the substitution of the foundational values of home with those of the state's cosmopolitan elites. Drawing on deep traditions of resistance, they condemn the mechanisms of globalization that have no grounding in the local and no accountability to real persons living in local situations. They recall what the totalizing state would have the people forget: those who have been marginalized and victimized in the brutal contest for state control and the ongoing suffering of the local populace.

It would be a mistake to infer that this appeal to tradition displaces the state's nostalgia for the future with a backward-looking turn to an antiquated past. The Mothers' performances are not nostalgic in that untimely way, but are rather always timely manifestations. They are punctual interventions at moments of acute crisis, the very definition of a timely event. Moreover, they demand the immediate application of the fitting but "forgotten" ethical imperatives of power. This resistance to state amnesia and its concerted focus on the present directive toward the future makes their performance a form of dissidence. Their rebuke offers a relevant critique of the present in light of a significant past—the history of abuse against women that they refuse to gloss over and the history of a tradition of female power that demands retribution for such abuse.

The Monumental State: Memorialization
of the Mothers-of-the-Nation

State amnesia is symptomatic of one way that the state consolidates its own identity and power. The other way is by co-opting collective memory and putting it in the service of the state through the official channels of commemoration and memorialization. Through the physical monuments it erects, the state controls history and vividly inscribes its official account into the public imagination. A monument relates to "memory as a transgenerational act in public culture. But a paradox emerges: the proliferation of monuments produces invisibility, making monuments a kind of historical waste, the opposite of what they claim to be" (Bal 1999, xv). A vivid example of this paradoxical erasure of history is the Ivoirian monument commemorating the 1949 women's march to the colonial jail in Grand-Bassam.

Situated in the center of a roundabout at the Place de la Paix at the entrance to town, the white concrete statue features realistic figures of three women, fully clothed in traditional garb and head-wrappers, walking together. The woman in the lead, her mouth open as if shouting a directive, extends her arm and points the way forward. Her comrades follow. One is regal and resolute. The other, carrying a baby strapped to her back in the traditional fashion, extends a cupped hand as if to invite onlookers to join. The inscription on the pedestal reads, "To our valiant women who, with their historic march on the prison of Grand-Bassam on December 24, 1949, wrested back men's confiscated liberty," and is signed by Mayor F. Ablé and dated February 6, 1998.[7] Its sentimental depiction of women as (young) mothers and as mothers-of-the nation pointing toward its future commemorates their part in the struggle for independence but paradoxically renders the source of women's actual power invisible. They are not carrying branches or pestles, the arms of spiritual warfare, but are portrayed as literal mothers carrying babies instead. Their breasts are not exposed; the figures wear demur camisoles with butterfly sleeves. The gesture of the lead figure, with extended arm and pointed index finger, signals bold determination but nothing of the threat that they fiercely wielded with their embodied curse as weapon of war. While the actual marchers numbered in the thousands, neither the figure nor the inscription alludes to their legion. The inscription further reduces their role, suggesting they were a mere auxiliary to the *male* fight for independence. Finally, as an official installation by the mayor, the memorial recasts the women's march as a retroactive validation of the contemporary postcolonial state. It is ironic that in all these ways the memorial statue can be seen as a portrait of the "new form of subjection [that would] await the citizens of the modern postcolonial state" (Al-Kassim 2008, 168). Ultimately, the monument is not a commemoration at all, but the opposite, the production of an erasure of the actual manifestation of the women's power.

FGP in action is so much more than that insipid monument. Women's own self-representation in their performance of ritual condemnation not only refuses their erasure by the amnesia of the postcolonial state, it also rejects their conscription into the state's authorized version of women's role as mother-of-the-nation. When the elders perform their forceful dance, slapping their exposed breasts and crotch, they are defying the identity thrust upon them in war (vulnerable target for rape and subjugated sex slave) and even the more benign yet perhaps equally devastating one scripted for them by the international community (traumatized victim). Their self-representation proposes an alternative trope altogether—a way of imagining postcolonial belonging that does not capitulate to the subjugated role being scripted for women by the nationalist postcolony. It is itself the performance of a critique of misused power and the mobilization of a terrible force that cannot afford to be forgotten: the "monumental" force embodied by Woman as an innate moral power.

Monumental Slaughter: Civil War and the Destruction of State Monuments

If monuments are sites of nationally appropriated history designed to give visibility to nationhood and to create nostalgia for what the modern state seeks to become, their destruction is the most obvious way that the state might seek to control the collective memory of past regimes. In the days immediately following Gbagbo's removal from office, Ouattara's supporters toppled what they called the "grotesque" monumentalization of his predecessor's reign. Fascinating and instructive is the urban legend that supposedly fueled the drive to destroy various monuments in Abidjan: the rumor that human remains would be found entombed in those representations of state power. "What the people are saying needs to be verified. It seems that there were bones, that people were buried alive. . . . That's why I stopped to see for myself," said one witness to the demolition of a statue of St. John in a square of the same name in the elite neighborhood of Abidjan, Cocody (RFI 2011). The choice of this statue for demolition is significant, for Gbagbo was a professed Christian, and his support came from a Christianized populace stimulated by impassioned preachers proclaiming that his reign was ordained by God. Other monuments destroyed were more overt symbols of the pride of the Ivoirian state and its control of its borders, like the statue of twin elephants facing each other with lifted trunks that formed an archway over the airport road.

The trope of the state as a cannibalistic witch feeding its bloodlust and nourishing its power with sacrificial victims is not unusual in the popular social imaginary in Africa and has been the subject of other studies (Devisch 1995). The urban legend also harkened to the dark rumors that circulated in the days of the first Ivoirian president, Houphouët-Boigny, about the source of his intractable power and legendary control over politicians and the populace alike. Tales were whispered that he consulted indigenous priests and that he made offerings of human sacrifice to the fetish that consolidated and protected his power. "What did we not hear about [Houphouët's] crocodiles in the artificial lakes of his natal village Yamoussoukro and the terrible legends that even now surround their existence!" (Adédé 2011). Ouattara's followers too consulted their seers, who "revealed to them that these statues hid a mystical pillar on which the power of Laurent Gbagbo rested" (Adédé 2011). The toppled monuments erected during Gbagbo's era ultimately yielded no such grotesque foundations, but the spectacle of their destruction, fueled by moral indignation over the presumably inhuman(e) engine of the machine of his state, reveals the degree to which the idea of the spiritual source of power and the horror of its abuse is active in the social imaginary.

The civil war was a monumental slaughter. Its unthinkable violence looms large and casts a shadow over society unable to fathom the cost in terms other than the traditional idioms of absolute evil. In the image of a malevolent witch, the bloodthirsty and cannibalistic state has reaped a feast of soldiers and civilians alike and continues to feed on a terrorized populace to satisfy its need. In the idiom of traditional religions, the Mothers embody the only counterforce capable of putting an end to witches' appetite for human blood and keeping the power of evil in check. They overcome evil and death with FGP. While war can consolidate secular power and rulership, its violence also threatens the new order. To establish its moral legitimacy and the right to rule, the state must neutralize the blood it shed. As we have seen, this can only be achieved through purification rites in which women's blood is the potent ingredient. That blood is the binding force that consolidated alliances.

With the destruction and erasure of the ugly past, the new postmodern state, too, may begin to build its monumental history on a clean slate, both literal and figurative. Their erection of grandiose monuments seems to be a "necessary condition of the production of nationals" (Appadurai 1995, 215). Prominently placed in public centers, they configure the state's consolidating power. Just as the nation-state controls the actual space of its territory by enforcing its borders, it relies on the control of the space of the social imaginary. "The nation-state relies for its legitimacy on the intensity of its meaningful presence in a continuous body of bounded territory. It works by policing its borders, producing its 'people,' constructing its citizens ... constructing its *locales of memory and commemoration* ... [to produce a] homogeneous space of nationness" (215, emphasis mine). The destruction of monuments in the public squares literally clears the space of national memory to reconfigure it. With the erection of new monuments, the state constructs a view of history with which it wishes its citizens to identify and recall. But while the state monumentalizes its ideology in the hard matter of concrete and steel, the vigilant female guardians of the moral order continue to make their aging naked bodies the site of the living tradition of contestation, agitating against such stilted and spurious foundations of power. Where moral indignation over the abusive power of the state is expressed through the toppling of its monuments so that its legacy is erased from memory, the moral indignation of the Mothers demands recollection. Their traditional mode of protest is an active form of remembrance as a moral act.

State Control of Collective Memory: Domesticating the "Cultural Heritage"

Where the state cannot dispatch a vivid past through amnesia nor contain it with monumentalization, it may yet control the threatening evocation of collective memory of its populace by circumscribing and domesticating it as a "cultural heritage" for which it purports to serve as protective guardian. Rowland and De Jong (2007) contend that the UNESCO policy in Africa played a significant part in shaping this very role for the postcolonial state. Its World Heritage Convention, adopted in 1972, mandates that states protect and promote the conservation of monuments and natural resources as a treasure enriching all humanity. While it privileges those kinds of tangible sites, UNESCO also recognizes the existence of an "intangible heritage" that is equally worthy of preservation, namely, "oral traditions and expressions; performing arts; social practices, rituals and festive events; knowledge and practices concerning nature and the universe" (UNESCO 2016). What is problematic, however, is that the UNESCO policy conforms to the idea of globalization as an inescapable trajectory, one that will presumably culminate in the erasure of the local and, with it, cultural diversity. It is built on a notion of heritage based on loss. From such a perspective, the aim of preservation is not to enable cultural heritage to inform contemporary culture and the interests of the state, but rather to give license to the state to domesticate the collective memory and channel its power toward its own consolidation.

The reification of tradition and the strategic appeal to it as a means for gaining political control was a technique used by the French and British colonial regimes in Africa to contain and domesticate local custom. The most glaring example is the imposed local chiefs (supposedly representing tradition) and the application of indirect rule through native administrations to serve their aims. In more recent decades, state-subsidized representations of traditional culture have been similarly reinvented and put into the service of the postcolonial state. Transforming a potentially threatening memory of resistance into a timeless marker of national identity, the postcolonial state remakes it into a self-legitimizing emblem and charter for its own pedigree. A classic example is the way Kenya organized state-sponsored performances by Maasai warriors under the thatched roofs of huge open-air stages in Nairobi, transforming the proud heritage of Maasai resistance to colonial domination into a tourist attraction outside the government-controlled game parks. Even cases where state-subsidized preservation served less overtly political agenda, the effect is to relegate cultural performance to a timeless past with no bearing on the future of the modern nation. In Senegambia, when the Kankurang masquerade supposedly lost its "awe-inspiring authority" among urban spectators, the state appropriated and preserved the performance under the auspices of UNESCO as a "Masterpiece of the Intangible Heritage" (Rowlands and De Jong 2007, 27). Fulfilling the mandate of preservation, the state seemingly attends to a valuable cultural recollection while inventing for itself a future unencumbered by its memory.

As we have seen in the case of the contemporary Ivoirian state's substitution of female ritual specialists by traditional chiefs who act as its agents, state invocation of customary practices does not necessarily ensure they are preserved; it may signal an attempt to supplant them. And the Ivoirian state's monument of the women's march to Grand-Bassam appeared to co-opt the collective memory of the women's uprising and recast it as a legacy

of national pride. The *actual performance* of FGP is not so easily domesticated, however. The spontaneous uprising and evocation of FGP cannot be
scripted by the state as a timeless cultural artifact with no bearing on the
circumstance in which it is performed. Mobilized as critiques of their own
society, the women's performances are sporadic, provisional, and contingent
on current events. Without the context that evokes these performances of
rebuke, the Mothers' nudity could only become the subject of prurient interest or titillating curiosity. As an aggressive act of war and a solemn curse with
mortal consequence, the Mothers' self-conscious self-depiction in the stark
terms of menacing nudity inspires dread and stirs rage; its performance defies
domestication as theatre.[8]

The Temporariness of Performance and the Stirring of Moral Memory

Ironically, while the World Heritage Convention hails the value of culture as
an "intangible" heritage, cultural performances like FGP are not an intangible
at all, but substantially real and excitingly palpable as vivid spectacle. Like all
ritual, the performances are the actual, material embodiment of collective
memory. What distinguishes FGP and other significant cultural acts from
natural sites, texts, or monuments is not their *intangibility* but their *ephemeral*
quality. It is the *impermanence of performance* that makes ritual a different kind
of cultural legacy.

This temporary, provisional, punctual nature of the performances of the
Mothers who call on their female genital power is particularly apt today, for as
philosopher Achille Mbembe noted, "'Temporariness'—or the fact or condition of temporariness ... is a central feature of the neo-liberal age especially
for those who live in the 'shadow of the world system'" (Shipley et al. 2010,
659–60). While the postcolonial state clings to the structures of its immediate
colonial predecessors and manipulates memory to ascribe to itself "if not the
illusion, then the sense of stability, or continuity" (Shipley et al. 2010, 659–60),
the ancient appeal to FGP recalls those foundational values that actually forged
and sustained African society and reasserts their relevance today. Stepping out
of the "shadow of the world system," they make their presence unmistakably
visible and make a place for themselves and the living archive that they represent. However ephemeral and vulnerable they may seem, the invocations of
FGP are powerful precisely because the Mothers reclaim their "own humanity in the face of powerful dehumanizing and, at times, abstract and invisible
forces" like globalization (Shipley et al. 2010, 659–60).

The impermanence of ritual makes memory a fundamental feature of its production and reproduction. Performance is always a self-reflexive adaptation of past and remembered acts, applied to the present to achieve new ends. Enacted in the public domain, ritual stirs collective memory to act the present moment in a way that commemorative monuments cannot. The living performance of FGP presents a challenge to the postcolonial state because it cannot contain its form or its message. Its spontaneous eruption sanctions the state that has forgotten the moral foundations that have been the guarantors of African civilization and justice.

The World Heritage Convention underscores "the obligation by the State in Africa to promote and protect *the morals and traditional values* recognized by the community" (De Jong and Rowlands 2007, 18, emphasis mine). However, by delivering to the state a sacred duty that is traditionally the purview of the Mothers, the policy undermines the very heritage it purports to safeguard. The ritual of appeal to female genital power exists to sanction the state; the state cannot serve as its sanction.

Questioning the virtue of UNESCO's commitment to the state as the patron of cultural preservation in the age of the "post-nation," Jacques Derrida called for a "new ethics" that would lead to UNESCO "opening-up the self-validating aspect of the institution to the 'voice of the other'" (Butler 2007, 60). He called for attention "to alternative imaginations that are not necessarily based on the model of the 'Greek' archive but on *other 'traditions' that have countered the disinheritance by colonialism*" (Rowlands and De Jong 2007, 21, emphasis mine). The Mothers' naked defiance stands as such an *"alternative heritage discourse and memory-work* in the contemporary global context" (Butler 2007, 59, emphasis mine). Their embodied recollection of cultural memory does not bear the burden of memory on behalf of the state, as do monuments or other official representations of the past, but calls upon the memory of its legacy to "open up spaces for reflexive engagements" (27). FGP pushes back and resists the globalizing forces that are shaping the postcolony and the destructive ramifications of adopting them unselfconsciously. The Mothers' focus on the local archive does not mean their interest is merely one of "preserving" the cultural traditions that are fast disappearing in the face of modernity. Instead, the legacy of these activists directs the attention of the state to the ethical imperatives that are the neglected ground on which they stand.

Whereas UNESCO's project enables *the state to reframe traditions* and render them commodities for a globalized (Westernized, cosmopolitan) culture, the invocation of FGP *reframes the postcolonial state*, showing its mechanisms to be a hollow adoption of form devoid of the very intangible heritage that the women actively recall. For those enacting the rite of FGP, that heritage is a *moral* one. It demands accountability in rulership and justice with respect to women in society. Their performances are not a remnant of the past or an impediment to the benefits that globalization affords. Rather, they are essential recollections of the dignity of African civilization in the context of postcolonial politics that otherwise disregards local memory. The ritual of moral outrage opens the way for more meaningful governance—one that is ethically responsive to the foundational values that are the true legacy of its people.

Memory Crisis of Another Kind: The Crisis of Remembering

Narrative is often hailed as the hallmark of memory, and textual accounts are similarly deemed to be the surest register of collective experience. Narrative organizes experience into a coherent event and enables it to be communicated and its significance to be shared. A victim's account of trauma as narrative can have consolidating power. Its telling enables one who suffers the indignity of assault to turn herself "into a proper subject" (Bal 1999, x). But trauma cannot always be readily integrated into a narrative form. A traumatized victim often lacks the ability to master her suffering sufficiently to impose narrative upon it. "Traumatic memories remain present for the subject with particular vividness and/or totally resist integration . . . they *cannot become narratives*" (viii, emphasis mine). The history of the work of South Africa's Truth and Reconciliation Commission, the model on which the Ivoirian CDVR was based, was troubled by this psychological conundrum.

When the South African Commission sought testimony from victims, they were surprised that women were reluctant to come forward and bear witness. Given the opportunity to recount the horrors they had suffered, many women found they were unable to do the very thing that the commission required: give their suffering the coherence of an account. Many felt what they had suffered was literally unspeakable; there were no words or even concepts in the indigenous languages to translate adequately what they had suffered, and often their insufficient command of English or Afrikaans left them voiceless. Even with translators available, the cultural gap was too wide to make testimony possible for many. The shame of publicly exposing the intimate violations was too much for them to bear. Nevertheless, in order to bring the past under symbolic control, the appearance of their inclusion in the process was indispensable for the state. In her analysis of the work of South Africa's Truth and Reconciliation Commission, Dina Al-Kassim contends that pressure that the state exerted on women to make a public account of their rape and torture was itself a kind of state violence, "constitutive of a new unspeakability" (Al-Kassim 2008, 176).

Eventually, in an effort to accommodate the women's discomfort with making public disclosure, the commission agreed to receive reconstituted accounts by substitutes who spoke on behalf of the victims. The representative sample that was entered into the record as a result was, for Al-Kassim, as troubling as their enforced public exposure. The summary accounts obscured the scope of female victimization and simultaneously left them literally mute and unheard. The result was not unlike the effect of the monument of the Women's March in Grand-Bassam that purports to represent the women's manifestation but actually hides from public view their own powerful form of self-presentation and erases it from collective memory. While the symbolic inclusion of women victims in the South African Commission's report was intended to represent them to foster reconciliation, its minimization of their trauma failed to offer those women recognition, the empowerment, or the relief necessary for recovery.

Al-Kassim's analysis challenges the received wisdom that state-sanctioned confession is a viable means of achieving national healing and reconciliation. She demonstrates how even in the context of a process explicitly designed for the state to do the hard work of honest recollection and bear the burden of memory in the interest of national healing, the dynamics reflected "the more general problem of the location of women in the symbolic register of the state's articulation" (177). True healing and reconciliation requires a full examination of that which has been excluded from the official archive of national memory. The commission's failure to remember the full extent of women's trauma foreclosed the participation of those women in the citizenship that was supposedly being constructed through redress. Meanwhile, the traditions that might have once afforded women protection and might still offer a means of empowerment and social reincorporation are ignored.

In Côte d'Ivoire and across West Africa, those traditions in the form of appeal to female genital power are still a living archive—a matriarchive—whose potential to empower women stands at odds with the aims of the postcolonial African state, built on the systematic subjugation of that power and too long unresponsive to the demands for retribution for systematic criminal assault on women as victims of its war. As Al-Kassim charges, "The story of a state violence that reaches into a private domain is not only the story of state violence and political subjection; it is also the tale of layers and histories of a violent subjection of women" (176). In Côte d'Ivoire, too, the history of women's subjugation has been at least as old as colonialism and the influence of Christian mission that was its handmaiden. The responsibility for that subjugation has been passed on to the postcolonial state, which seems to have managed that legacy winningly. The slow and steady erosion of women's social, legal, and economic status may well have been a precondition of the massive intimate violations perpetrated on women's bodies in the names of both political factions vying for control of the Ivoirian state during these recent civil wars.

Memory and Trauma: Recovery and the Subjugated Archive

Unarticulated trauma, what Bal calls "(non)memory," creates a "tragically solitary" form of suffering (Bal 1999, x). The trauma endures precisely because it remains without witness and without response. For this reason, she argues, "trauma can paradoxically stand for the importance of cultural memory" (x). That is, the collective recollection of suffering can stand in for that all-important, relief-bearing witness and provide a framework through which victims may give what has befallen them some form of coherence. Ritual has a unique ability to address trauma precisely because it is nondiscursive and embodied. It represents what cannot be articulated, yet paradoxically instills reflection and fosters a responsive shift in its participants. As a collective act, ritual can break through tragic isolation without requiring that a victim narrate her trauma and can even be accomplished without any words spoken at all.[9] Where language fails, what is required is decisive action.

FGP may stand in as such an act of sense-making articulation of suffering and indignation. It doesn't reenact the narrative of rape, sexual slavery, or other tortures perpetrated on the women of Côte d'Ivoire. Instead, it literally "makes sense" of the violence through its sensational display of outrage and its rally for recognition and redress. It guards a space for the unspeakable, confronting evil with a force that is its equal in terrible power, in the form of a curse. While the women may sound that curse with shouts, songs, or incantations, it is their gestures that cast the spell. They wail and slap their naked breasts, they expose their buttocks or crotch, they part their legs while seated or lying on the ground, a position that defies all normal public decorum, or strip and kneel in the posture of childbearing to draw down the ultimate curse. Such acts put into full view the unthinkable extent of their outrage and condemnation.

Their embodied resistance to the violence of the postcolony (including the violence of the official narrative that minimizes or silences them) makes a persuasive case that the "intractability of woman's body [is indeed a terrible] thorn in the side of state narration" (Al-Kassim 2008, 185). Appearing in their most vulnerable state, naked women stand in stark contrast to the armor-shielded and arm-toting soldiers and the suited politicians encased in their black Mercedes-Benz motorcades. Yet in their nakedness, they recall not victimization but empowerment, mimetically evoking the mytho-history of West African civilizations based on matrifocal morality. They refer to these ancient and widespread cultural traditions in which female elders have been the source of all social bonds and civilizing alliances, the owners of the land, and the makers of war and peace.

To effect change, however, such "cultural recall is not merely something of which you happen to be a bearer but something that you actually *perform*" (Bal 1999, vii). The Adjanou dancers and other performers of FGP are conscious agents, effecting history through the activation of that collective memory and the evocation of an ethical response that it elicits. Their decision to recapitulate the disruptive ritual of rebuke that African women elders have performed for centuries is an act of recollection—self-consciously drawing on cultural memory and gathering the force of collective agency.

FGP simultaneously makes women's collective suffering visible and cries out for accountability and justice. Reintroducing woman in her most vulnerable state to the political scene, the act refuses the state's dissociation from the traumatic recall of women's sexual abuse. At the same time, the act refuses to cast women in the role of abject victim alone, for their naked incantation draws upon their most intimate, innate, and world-making power.

While women are often too ashamed of their victimization to testify or make claim for restitution as individuals, the brazen nudity and defiant gesticulation of women collectively enacting FGP turn shame on aggressors. The ritual of FGP constitutes women's refusal to be subjugated or effaced. The women's use of the naked female body to excoriate the political forces is a profound reversal of the way the naked and vulnerable bodies of women are abused by sexual assault. The enactment of FGP is therefore potentially empowering for victims who witness it. The ritual rhetoric is a fully articulated expression of indignation, so different from the unspeakable and unspoken accounts of the female victims of apartheid's violence or their abbreviated and summary accounts relayed to the commission. It is a powerful alternative to the profound silence of the South African women who refused to testify in the terms demanded by the commission, a silence that Al-Kassim called "'truth' as non-speaking" (Al-Kassim 2008, 177). The ritual gestures of public excoriation and shaming exposure that are the hallmark of FGP are a form of truth telling through nonspeaking as well, but theirs is a powerful articulation of rage and public condemnation of abuse. Moreover, it is its own aggressive force. More than a lament, the naked rite invokes the strongest curse. Forcing the perpetrators of injustice to break the taboo of looking on the Mothers' nakedness, the rite actively asserts women's power in their own self-representing terms; the strength of this collective depiction of women as the moral foundation of society and their collective demand for accountability requires response.

The vivid spectacle of FGP is a recovery of the subjugated archive whose recollection has the potential to restore to victims of war the dignity robbed from them by the violations they suffered without retraumatizing them or subjecting them to the indignity of public testimony.

Memory Work: Making Memory Work Again Now

Scholarly work on memory regularly underscores that both for the individual and at the cultural level, memory is never a fixed entity or settled matter. It is always operational, what is often referred to as "memory-work." What has been recorded is not stored in an unchanging form, but regularly altered and effaced to make room for what comes after, even while leaving a visible trace. "Culture is a palimpsest and in this respect resembles individual memory" (Assmann 2006, 25). This is to say, the collective memory that informs the intangible cultural heritage, like individual memory, is worked and reworked, recalled and recollected over time and changes in response to new experience. Therefore, "the frontier between stored and functional memory is constantly shifting" (25). Each occasion of FGP represents a challenge to what constitutes the "functional memory" in Africa today. As the women engage the "stored" (read "suppressed," "neglected," or "demeaned") memory of their power, they force it into view as spectacle and, with this aggressive self-assertion, rescue the practice and its significance from the buried and subjugated archive.

The women's rite is memory-work, the active recollection of what is stored in the collective social imaginary, and it works that memory for immediate effect. Calling the conventions and values of the collective back to mind, the performances attempt to bridge a fractured society through that "re-collection." Cultural memory of this kind is not just that which is communicated overtly but also "encompasses the age-old, out-of-the-way, and discarded" and "acquires a breadth of vision and of force" of its own (27). That is to say, the performance evokes the repressed, banished, or otherwise unacknowledged record of history, making it accessible. At the same time, the act is a sober condemnation of the very social amnesia that has relegated the value of women and their sacred power to a thing of the past in the first place. "Such a remembering is a paradoxical intervention in the history of violence, injustice and oppression" (23). The spectacle of FGP is a visual remonstrance that decries the violence, injustice, and oppression of those in power and a ritual that actively seeks to overturn such wrongs.

A Failure of Memory? FGP in the Eyes of Youth

Cultural memory is a transpersonal phenomenon that is shared with others, but also extends across generations, encompassing time and experience that cannot be recalled by any one individual, or even one portion of society at any particular instance. Cultural memory is the matrix upon which an individual's social identity is developed and is the source of functional, communicative memory. But things break down when individual functional memory and collective cultural memory become disconnected.

While I was in Côte d'Ivoire I wondered to what degree the public acts of the Mothers still spoke to urban Ivoirians and especially to the youth today. As we have seen, the multiple ethnic populations indigenous to Côte d'Ivoire, even in the precolonial period, already constituted a heterogeneous cultural landscape. This has been made all the more complex during the last half century by the economic prosperity and promise of early postcolonial development, attracting waves of immigrants and refugees across its borders. Since then, ethnic intermarriage and new generations born and raised in the sprawling metropolis have led to an increased cultural hybridity and uprootedness. Many young people living in the cities today no longer speak an African language, and some have never been to an ancestral village, even one considered home by their parents. Do these new hybrid populations still "have eyes to see" women's appeal to FGP in public protest as anything more than an act of barbarity or more meaningful than a rude assault on politicians? Can one rightly claim that FGP effectively recollects tradition for all its spectators, especially for the young who have had little encounter with traditional society and no direct inculcation into the deep cultural values and their symbolic emblems or embodied modes of expression?

As Homi Bhabha points out, "It is not adequate simply to become aware of the semiotic systems that produce the signs of culture . . . we are faced with the challenge of reading, into the present of a specific cultural performance, the traces of . . . institutions of knowledge" (Bhabha 1994, 233). The challenge of reading the signs and their meanings is not only a problem for scholars interested in ethnographic interpretation. It is also an acute problem in Côte d'Ivoire, where the semiotics of women's gestures must be read in order to command the force that they intend. If their eloquent discourse, encrypted as it is in the embodied rhetoric of a forgotten tradition, cannot be recognized and understood, it risks being nothing but an empty gesture in a fragmented and chaotic situation. While FGP may have lost its awe-inspiring authority for urban cosmopolitans, it may even have lost all meaning for many of the uninitiated urbanites, and especially for its youth.

The Collective Memory of Youth: Two Local Surveys

Sensing the increased alienation of youth from their ancestral traditions, I decided to try to conduct a survey. Although I was aware from the outset that my sample size would be far too small to qualify it as a study with scientific rigor, I felt it would nevertheless offer some objective indicators of what young people knew or might understand in the face of the rhetoric of FGP. My host in Abidjan introduced me to Mme Yésone, the proviseur (principal) of the Lycée Moderne Nangui Abrogoua, one of the largest secondary schools in the city. She generously allowed me to conduct the survey, which I prepared under the supervision of an Ivoirian expert in sociological methods. The students surveyed were all in the last two years of schooling before obtaining the baccalaureate degree and ranged in age from seventeen to twenty-three years old. The total yield was ninety-seven completed questionnaires.

Of the ninety-seven respondents, sixty-one self-identified as Christian (some specifying Catholic, Evangelical, Methodist, or Harrist), thirty-four were practicing Muslims, one identified himself as Buddhist, and one specified she practiced no religion.[10] The survey included multiple-choice questions that asked respondents to select the best possible meaning of certain gestures that appear in traditional African art and ritual and are indicative of female power. A majority of all the students polled (64 percent) answered all of these correctly, or offered a less ambiguous answer or clarification based on knowledge of their own tradition in the margin. That was a greater proportion than I had expected. For example, asked how to interpret the meaning of "a group of women pouring water in which they had washed themselves at the entrance of the village," over half correctly chose the answer "to trap witches." Of these, one-quarter also correctly answered at least two of the three other questions on African iconography in art and ritual, indicating a high degree of cultural knowledge. In particular, they correctly indicated that "if you were to see an old women in a group of protesters strip naked" one should interpret her intention "as a threat that she would use her innate power." Many also correctly identified the meaning of a woman striking the ground with a pestle as a "sign of a curse." That so many recognized and understood this most significant aspect of FGP as a public rebuke was a surprising and important finding, suggesting that the matri-archive still does operate as functional memory among Ivoirian youth.

When asked whether women today have as much, less, or more power than they did in traditional society, 44 percent of all student respondents felt that women enjoyed less power today than they did in traditional society; 36 percent felt that they had as much power, while only 19 percent felt that they had more power today. The divided opinion might suggest confusion about what constitutes "power," or it may signal ambivalence about what women's status in society today should be.

Overall, the results suggested that the heritage of FGP still informs the functional memory of contemporary society. The majority of the student body polled had enough knowledge to be able to interpret the manifestations of FGP with insight into their intent and significance. Still, I decided to attempt a survey among young people attending Kpol in Orbaff as a means to compare the urban youth, with relatively little attachment to village life, with those who were residents of the village.

Delivering and gathering the questionnaire under the animated conditions of the village in full preparation for an annual event proved difficult, and the sampling was extremely small. Nevertheless, some data was obtained. As might be expected of youth who are strongly connected to their ancestral village, it revealed a much greater awareness of the meaning of traditional iconography and the significance of women's gestures of power and moral authority. All were aware that a woman striking the ground with a pestle is "a signal of a curse," and all but one of the dozen sampled correctly identified the meaning of the ritual in which women pour water at the entrance to the village: "to lay a trap for witches." Three-quarters of the Orbaff respondents knew that the performance of FGP in Grand-Bassam in 1949 was an act that "underscored the moral authority of women" and further identified correctly that if an elderly woman in a group of protestors were to strip naked, her gesture should be interpreted "as a threat that she would use her innate power." Despite this insight, like the students polled in Abidjan, they were divided as to whether women today have more or less power they had in traditional society. The lack of consensus suggests that the question touches on complex and unresolved matters in a society that is still contending with the dismantling of tradition brought about during colonialization and the postcolonial project of nation building.[11]

FGP Online: Recollecting Morality or Ethnopornography?

It is often argued that the Internet, with its borderless, instant access, has created a global community, one that allows for a more inclusive, multivocal representation and dialogue. In fact, the Internet is a place where FGP is made manifest on a global scale, diffused by the media and private blogs as well as YouTube videos, giving the performances an immediate worldwide reach. But there, the performances that were once timely and provisional critiques become fixed electronically as permanent spectacles, available for viewing at any time and from anywhere.

At best, this extended reach has the positive potential of enabling academic investigators and casual web-crawlers alike to recognize the semiotic connection among many instances of FGP across Africa and to make connections that might not have been made before between otherwise discrete and isolated incidents. At worst, the new technology takes the place of colonial techniques (like the circulation of photographic postcards of naked natives) that would fix the bodies of the subaltern under the gaze of Western spectators. These now clichéd depictions of "the primitive" justified the subordination of the "other" as a means of reining in their wild excesses under the harness of modernity.

When the spectacular YouTube videos and arresting photographs of naked or semi-nude female bodies are presented out of context and without any explanation, their exposure subjects them to the insult of mere voyeurism. Under these conditions, rather than being seen as a defiant self-representation and self-consciously deployed transgressive technique, the appeal to female genital power is viewed through the lens of the colonial legacy as an indication of wildness and sexual excess. The images of nudity and defiance, circulated in the globalized no-space of the Internet, where there is no possibility of relation between observer and observed, might risk becoming viewed as objects of the "ethnopornographic gaze."[12] Their representation merely in terms of exotic, unbounded bodies could be interpreted as a form of exploitation that recapitulates the violence of colonial "othering." On such a stage the very message that the Mothers intend to convey would thus be overturned. Rather than expressing that the immoral use of political power causes social degradation and suffering, their images would be seen as degrading representations to support an immoral ideology of domination.

The commentaries of African viewers of these Internet postings illustrate just such responses. In April 2009, Yoruba women of the Ekiti State in Nigeria marched in protest against the stalemated gubernatorial election. While more than 300 women took part in the peaceful rally for democracy, the procession was led by "more than twenty elderly women among the group, whose ages ranged between sixty and eighty years [who] went half-dressed" (Ikeji 2009). The website report posted a photo of the event, including the culminating ritual of appeal to FGP itself: "At the Oke-Iyinmi roundabout, ten of the half-dressed women caused a stir when they formed a separate group to perform a rite, in which they were heard appeasing the gods of the land. While the rite lasted, the women rained curses on all anti-democratic forces and those disrupting the peace of the state" (Ikeji 2009).

The posted reactions range from validating recognition of the tradition and deep cultural knowledge to disrespectfully dismissive remarks to hostile rejection. Some are amusing, while others are serious and didactic. The first to post a response, presumably a young woman who identifies herself with the provocative pseudonym "Thirty-six inches of brown legs," recognized the meaning of the gesture and, despite her own self-objectification, readily articulated it in colorful vernacular: "*i hear if an elderly naked yoruba woman curses u . . . there is going to be an obituary out for u soon . . .* this is some scary shit. but im glad that people are standing up to this nonsense we call democracy in Nigeria" (Ikeji 2009, emphasis mine). Her immediate respondent, however, posted a rather ironic condemnation: "There is nothing that can happen to make people go that far. *Don't they have morals. Idiots!*" (Ikeji 2009, emphasis mine). The third anonymous blogger betrayed an anxiety that the spectacle would attract the objectifying gaze of the West that has long denigrated Africa: "May the Lord help us! *i hope this one never make* CNN" (Ikeji 2009, emphasis mine).

Other comments reflect frustration and rage caused by the disruption of cultural memory and the consequent incoherence and incomprehensibility among local subjects. When the gestures of the women elders are not recognized or understood, the local disintegrates. In its place is the unhomeliness of the postmodern condition: "Wow!! madness!! i tried to link the half nakedness to the election thingy but *the two do not even correlate.* I mean if it was like a sexual related protest or something in that respect, it'll be a tad easier to digest. these images *make us look like babarians around the globe* . . . nothing more, nothing less. and *If my grandma ever dared to participate in such, . . . let's just say it wouldn't be funny.*—April 30, 2009" (Ikeji 2009, emphasis mine).

Other posts demonstrate an even more deeply internalized colonial condemnation of African civilization, betraying what Ashis Nandy (1983) called, "The Intimate Enemy." This example, though more carefully articulated than the former, is more blatantly self-loathing:

No wonder other parts of the world sometimes see Africans as uncivilized, savages, uneducated group of people. There is no excuse for women coming out with their sagging breasts saying they are protesting. About what? protesting to be half naked or to be fully naked, it has nothing to do with any political affairs. Our ancestors lived like that, but this is modern day, the twenty-first century. I don't care about history, when I read the history of Nigeria, specifically the Yoruba history, I see nothing but many immoral and indecent acts. They do many insane things that is attached and called part of the culture, for example, the tribal marks that yoruba people sometimes have on their faces or bodies to differentiate them from other group of Yorubas is unnecessary, apart from the fact that it disfigures your skin. Such acts as protesting half naked for a wake up call, whether it's part of culture or have been practiced for years is inappropriate, in Africa and other parts of the world. We can get our point across fully dressed, and maybe it will even be more effective.—May 2, 2009. (Ikeji 2009, emphasis mine).

While the response is condemnatory on the grounds of contemporary decorum, others are blatantly misogynist: "All those old Mamas, with their drooping breasts, remove those very ugly images from youtube" (LeTogoVi 2013a). Such youth have lost any relational consciousness to the local. While their alienation may have been caused by an actual spatial dislocation, a separation from their ancestral villages where the local is produced, the unhomeliness that their commentary reflects is the result of a failure of cultural memory. It is a disconnection from the past as a relevant one. Their comments betray a kind of untimely meditation on FGP.

Nevertheless, the new connections through electronic media also offer an opportunity to make the necessary correctives through a public recollection of the meaning of the tradition:

> *A woman baring her naked breasts in protest of something, ESPECIALLY an elderly woman at that symbolises a curse.* And is deeply rooted in spirituality et al. We have let "enlightenment" and civilization blind us to where we all really came from . . . remember our ancestors knew and did something before xtianity and islam . . . and it worked . . . *it wasn't all bad. Somebody is talking morals* . . . i laugh . . . morals based on the fact that the oyinbo man taught our people that nakedness is a bad thing? better go and read the history of your country(ies) if you are african. *Listen to the elders and then come back and repeat that this women have no morals—* April 30, 2009. (LeTogoVi 2013a, emphasis mine)

A second website posted images of the same protest without explanation (Jeremy 2009). The accompanying images depict the semi-nude elderly women kneeling and raising their arms in appeal, thrusting them forward in a gesture of rebuke and crouching on all fours in the archetypal posture of childbirth. A similar series of responses followed, and several echo the recognition of the power of the tradition as well as the need to respect it: "If we feel uncomfortable with them now, then we have the cultures of those who brought us Christianity and Islam to blame. Personally I am completely comfortable with nudity. It should be respected as an age old form of protest"—Sugabelly April 29, 2009 (Jeremy 2009). One responded to the images with a concise summary of their meaning: "Fear an angry Yoruba woman that strips in protest, that is a stern admonition.—Akin, April 29, 2009" (Jeremy 2009).

Anecdotes were posted in response that also testify to the fact that FGP is still a living tradition and active in the popular social imaginary: "Many years ago in lagos, armed robbers visited (what else can you call it?) my brother's elderly neighbour. The minute she saw them she began to strip (in naijaspeak, 'nekkid ha self.' The previously fearless thieves immediately shielded their eyes (while still wielding their guns) saying 'Oh OH oh, mama, why are you doing this noOW? please stop it, mama, PLEEEase.' *Mama kept stripping.—The hoods fled for their lives.* Mama's strip came from the belly- from her gut. *She MEANT that curse, and the boys believed her.*—Anonymous April 29, 2009" (Jeremy 2009, emphasis mine). The "subjugated archive" is kept in circulation through recollections such as these and further mobilizing in virtual space: "Wow! I remember in Warri, Effurun actually, early 90's, there was a peaceful demonstration and *Mobile Policemen started using excessive force and some old women came out totally naked. The MPs ran for their lives.* Tradition, superstition, no matter how enlightened you are, there is something to be said for the power of the nakedness of an old woman in protest. 'person eye no de see old mama bia bia.'—Anonymous, April 29, 2009" (Jeremy 2009, emphasis mine).

The computer-mediated communication gives visibility to the acts of FGP and generates conversation about it. The chat reflects that the negative responses are informed by conventional Western stereotypes of women (the women elders were neither beautiful nor modest) and a colonial discourse about African tradition (their acts were irrational and "backward," threatening to a nation seeking identification with modernity). It also engendered forceful reiterations of local meaning and recollections about the efficacy of this living heritage in contemporary life. While some onlookers might not immediately grasp the significance of the women's gestures, and some of the culturally unindoctrinated even revile or mock them, I suggest that the dialogue itself constitutes a form of recollection. After all, memory is more "intersubjective and dialogical than exclusively individual, more act (remembering) than object and more ongoing engagement than passive absorption and playback" (Lambek 1996, 239). The online debate brings attention and scrutiny to a critical dimension of cultural memory that is increasingly repressed and ignored or, precisely because its meaning has been forgotten, denigrated. While the matters under review are not settled, the chat about these events has the virtue of opening up spaces of reflexive engagement about the subjugated archive.

Ultimately, the online discussions about the manifestations of the Mothers echo their very purpose. The aim of the public demonstrations is not to commemorate, memorialize, or reify the past but to make a memorable irruption into the present. The performances are "vehicles *for* memory rather than the frozen remnants of memory" (239). The cry from the soul for "Maman Côte d'Ivoire" is a cry for respect for all that the Mothers stand for when they stand naked before politicians today.

Reviving the Subjugated Archive

Postmodern theorist Homi Bhabha offers two metaphors through which we can appreciate the memory-work of FGP as timely memory, especially significant now. "The bridge" is a spatial metaphor for that which links the reified community of nation with the disseminated and forgotten populace at the local level. "The meanwhile" is a temporal metaphor linking the (forgotten) past with the (forgetful) future-looking ideology of the postcolony. The nation-state builds its unifying narrative, but "meanwhile" the people carry on with their diverse ways of being. The women who perform FGP forge the bridge between the gathered and the dispersed and carry on with their formidable tradition even in the midst of state amnesia or public disregard, actively recalling the archive of a living heritage as a relevant one.

The stance of the female elders in public protest mediates between those at the center of power—in the presidential palace, at the jailhouse, and in front of foreign military tanks—and those who are disseminated—the victims of the war and displaced refugees fleeing its violent reach, the locals who have been willfully disempowered and whose presence is deliberately overlooked. The performance injects the alterity of indigenous reality onto the postcolonial, postmodern political scene that otherwise homogenizes the people and forgets the particularity of cultural identity. Although women are not minorities, they have nevertheless been forgotten in the discourse of the state, rendered secondary players. Seen merely as mothers and wives, their original power is usurped, and women then also become the displaced—that is, on the margins of power, where once they were at the center. Remembering their place is a new gathering and a bridge between those who remember and those who have forgotten the centering principles of matrifocal morality.

Their ritual presence also makes visible "the meanwhile," indigenous ways that carry on despite being made extraneous to the structures of the postcolonial. Undeterred by the effacing discourse of nation building and resisting the state's attempts to co-opt them as the mothers-of-the-nation, the Mothers continue to carry out a time-honored tradition. While the state is busy meeting the needs of the metropole, "the meanwhile" carries on with the business of the local. The meanwhile is the active social imaginary that continues to play out in timely ways. It recalls the relevance of the past, its historical traditions, and their moral demands for the future. For that reason, their performative action is a critical means of remembering. While it may not be profitable for the motors of globalization, the contemporary African state cannot afford to ignore or dispel them.

The defiant action of the women elders is also especially timely. Their traditional protest is a bridge—not back to a timeless tradition or a retreat from history—but back to the assertion of African foundational morality as the only constructive way forward. With their very bodies, the women throw down the gauntlet of judgment and challenge those who would dare defy them to spiritual combat. This insurrection of FGP is not only "a powerful repository of cultural knowledge," but is one "that erases the rationalist and progressivist logics of the 'canonical' nation" (Bhabha 1994, 219). That is, the Mothers' public demonstrations refute the new postcolonial script about the march of history toward the consolidation of power in the nation-state and the authorization of knowledge by the globalizing force of technology on moral grounds.

The "intractability of woman's body, thorn in the side of state narration," defies domestication (Al-Kassim 2008, 185). The manifestations of FGP do not commemorate, memorialize, or reify the past as an ideal, but recapture the memory of a tradition of insurrection by repeating its irruptions into the present. Their performances are "vehicles *for* memory rather than the frozen remnants of memory" (Lambek 1996, 239). They actively revive the matri-archive and seek to impose its moral imperative.

CONCLUSION. AN INTIMATE REBUKE

A Local Critique in the Global Postcolony

> On Sunday July 24, 2011, in the square at Trocadero in Paris,
> operation "red Kodjo" was put into action.... Ivoirian women patriots,
> ever mobilized and determined, demonstrated their profound indignation
> and revolted against the tragic situation that their country is enduring.
> —TOGUI ZEKA, "Manifestation des Femmes Patriotes à Paris:
> 'Les Kodjos Rouges en Action pour la Malediction Effective.'"

Accountability: An Urgent Appeal, a Moral Demand

In a post–civil war society that is still seeking equilibrium, accountability is a critical and timely matter. As John Lonsdale remarked, "The idea of accountability seems noticeable for its comparative absence from the field of African studies. This is partly because it is a difficult concept to use, but also because some scholars have thought it to be irrelevant or even inappropriate to the African case" (Lonsdale 1986, 127). Nevertheless, matrifocal morality exercised in the form of FGP does hold authority accountable, and the Mothers' collective action has always been "part of the moral calculus of power" in Africa (127).

Today those victimized by the horrors of the war, especially women, are demanding justice on ethical grounds and doing so in the vernacular terms of traditional calls for such reckoning; FGP may be the strongest weapon of the women victims of war crimes who continue to cry out for acknowledgment and retribution. In October 2015, the Collective of Women Victims in Côte d'Ivoire (CVCI) gathered at the headquarters of the National Commission for Reconciliation and the Indemnification of Victims (Conariv) in Abidjan to demand the list of those victims who were to be compensated. While three of their representatives were received, the demonstrators waited outside peaceably for hours, but when the police used force in an attempt to disperse them, the situation quickly degenerated. One of them, Bakayoko Anzata, was seized by three officers and beaten with truncheons. In angry response, elderly women in the group began to strip and issue curses. The video embedded in the journalist's report and posted on YouTube depicts the appeal to FGP as a spontaneous manifestation of righteous indignation and a courageous contest between violent force and moral might (Mel 2015). First one sees three elderly and corpulent women who have already exposed their breasts further remove their garments while women standing behind them nod with approval, wail, and shout. Others gesticulate angrily and argue with military personnel. The camera pans to another elder standing bare-breasted before an officer. A fourth, stripped to the waist, intentionally struts toward the camera, lets out a battle cry, and thrusts both arms in the air. The camera moves farther into the crowd of women, focusing on yet another who is slowly disrobing with deliberate concentration. A toothless old woman in a pink dress and headscarf stands beside her, staring at the camera as if to warn against the offense of its intrusive gaze. The video then cuts to a close-up of Bakayoko Anzata, whose camisole was torn in her scuffle with police. The woman beside her bears witness to what happened. "Here she is, she's the one who they hit," she says, pointing to the victim. "The one who they undressed and struck, here she is. Turn and show them your body." We see that the flesh on the left side of her back between her bra and waist is marked with red welts. "They tore her clothing. . . ." The victim turns back to the camera, takes a piece of fabric and unfolds it and, holding it up to view, says, "He hit me and I tore off his epaulette. He told me to give it to him and I answered, 'I won't give it to you, in the name of God.'" Her voice trembles, and she jabs at the air. "As they killed my two big brothers, that is how God will kill them also. I didn't come here because of hunger. If I came here it is for the sake of justice. God will bring justice. God shall punish them. In the name of God! If they betrayed justice, the justice of men, they cannot betray the justice of God. One cannot escape that justice. That justice will find them, God willing. They will never again repeat what they did, never again." She waves her finger to emphasize the point. While this lament and appeal for divine retribution is expressed in the familiar terms of the Abrahamic faiths, it is no less a call for the kind of intervention that the Mothers make themselves and through a power as metaphysical as it is moral.

The scene then jumps, and the camera witnesses the execution of the curse of FGP. An old woman with naked sagging breasts stands before three young armed officers. She shouts and waves a finger of reproach and then gets down on her hands and knees in the ritual posture of malediction, the posture of childbirth. When she rises she hurls an angry remark in their direction with a gesture of contempt. Another elderly woman comes to lead her away while she continues her indignant imprecations. In a final take, yet another elder screams as if overcome by frustration and fury and tears at her shirt, while two younger women restrain her. They pull the shirt back over her naked bosom and try to lead her away, but she breaks free and struts forward with a look of menacing determination. The crowd behind her begins a shrill incantation.

The use of FGP in political resistance not only disrupts the state agenda, it reveals that underneath the fragile overlay of the state is the more substantial substrata of indigenous reality that the African state cannot afford to ignore. The women are not demanding democratic representation but decrying the inadequacies of the political dynamic from the vantage point of a much deeper and older tradition. As Bakayoko Anzata put it, "If I came here it is for the sake of justice." The women's pressing appeal cast in the form of an ancient tradition draws attention not only to their immediate plight, but also to a critical issue in the time of postcolonialism across Africa: the demand for the ethical grounding of the state.

Female Agency and African Civil Society

In the face of widespread pessimism about the fate of Africa under the direction of brutal and bankrupt postcolonial regimes, some historians of Africa turned their attention to "the flesh and blood struggles of ordinary people" to show how they could stand up to the structures of injustice (Lonsdale 2000, 7). In recent decades women's collective mobilizations have been featured in studies of African peasant revolts and the nationalist efforts that sprang up as a consequence. However, the myriad incidents appear in such studies "like weeds without any organizing principle other than their common humanity" (11). These fragmented depictions are given too narrow a geographic or temporal focus or are only considered in terms of their effect on the changing political landscape and mapped in terms of political victories or losses. Perhaps for that very reason, scholars and political actors alike have failed to consider the Mothers and their ritual rebuke as anything more than marginal players, auxiliaries to the central agents shaping society.

Writing as a political theorist in the 1980s and focusing especially on Côte d'Ivoire, Jean-François Bayart, for one, claimed that in Africa there was "no common cultural frame of reference" between groups that would even allow for the existence of the kind of horizontal associations that characterize civil society (Bayart 1986, 117–18). Given the ethnic diversity within Africa, Bayart supposed that there could be no "*organisational principle*' capable of challenging absolute state control" (117–18, emphasis mine). The heterogeneity of Ivoirian society in particular seemed to him devoid of any unifying vision necessary for broad collective effort, for civil society "exists only in so far as there is a *self-consciousness of its existence* and *of its opposition to the state*" (117, emphasis mine). In fact, the deployment of FGP has been a cornerstone of civil society throughout African history. If civil society is "the de facto binding, organizing principle of the political order" (Harbeson, Rothchild, and Chazan 1994, 4), then it seems clear that the *founding knowledge* and *binding power* instantiated by the Mothers eminently qualify. Matrifocal morality and the enactment of FGP as its enforcing sanction are imprinted on the local social imaginary, the "deep matrix for meaningful participation" (Steger 2008, 6), to such a degree that these principles and techniques constitute the "*private sphere* of material, cultural and political activities *resisting the incursions of the state*" that defines civil society (Fatton 1995, 67, emphasis mine). Casting the phenomenon in this way brings it into focus as a relevant, timely, and effective means of collective mobilization for the purpose of exerting influence on the state.

The performances of FGP in the political sphere are neither called for by political elites nor enacted by cosmopolitans. They are the product of "ordinary people" who bravely put themselves on the frontlines of contestation. They generate mobilization from the bottom up and, moreover, use their "bottom-power" to condemn breaches by the state by appealing to the local social imaginary. Ultimately what may make the deployment of FGP most effective as a form of civil society may be that very informal, impermanent, and fluid nature of the women's networks, for they are not dependent on the state for their existence, nor are they seeking a collaborative relationship with it. The kind of power that is exercised through the ritual invocation of FGP by the anonymous Mothers is best understood as a dynamic in which "power is neither given, nor exchanged, nor recovered, but rather exercised, and . . . only exists in action . . . it is above all a relation of force" (Foucault and Gordon 1980, 89). The relation they are seeking is recognition through accountability. As the rite itself makes plain, power is not only in the possession of those "in power," but is a force that must be exercised for the good if power is to have any legitimacy at all.

The Mothers' mobilization and public action challenge "state legitimacy, and does so without presuming any necessary connection between legitimacy and democracy" (Harbeson, Rothchild, and Chazan 1994, 4). The activism of FGP underscores that accountability is the ruler's imperative. The ultimate sanction is the forfeit of the right to rule. The presence of the Mothers on the political scene is a barometer of the degree to which the state is deemed legitimate by those for whom it matters most—the society it supposedly serves. The current situation in post–civil war, post-election Côte d'Ivoire is still precarious and will remain unstable unless the state attends to the demands of civil society.

The interpenetration of religious and political discourse is now acute and the focus of much academic interest of late, but this conversation largely continues to exclude indigenous religions, and this despite their ongoing vitality on the continent and the degree to which the intangible heritage of FGP still profoundly informs a shared epistemology across West African ethnicities and national borders. As Africanist Jane Guyer noted, "In spite of the spiritual power in indigenous and syncretic movements, it is generally the orthodox, and therefore internationally connected, religious organizations that hold political power within the 'establishment' of civil society: the Catholic Church, the Muslim Brotherhoods, the Christian fundamentalist movement, the Anglican bishoprics" (Guyer 1994, 224). Yet all these established purveyors of "the sacredness of power" exclude women from office. Even when these institutions insist on inserting religion into the worldly arena, they deny women authority as instruments of its power.

The spontaneous uprisings of African women may be one arena in which the spiritual authority of women as the paramount arbiters of worldly legitimacy is apparent and most forcefully expressed. The elders who resort to the traditional ritual appeal of FGP do so in self-professed solidarity with the plight of a whole swath of the population—the unarmed and disenfranchised civilian populace squeezed between warring factions, not only left to their own devices by the state but also actively victimized by its wantonly cruel forces. Even distinctions of religious affiliation have not precluded Ivoirian women's sense of their fundamental solidarity based on their primacy as guardians of the moral order. In an ode to the suffering nation, an Ivoirian blogger posted an impassioned "cry from the soul" in which one can hear reverberations of the ancient and ubiquitous reliance on the Mothers as the embodiment of the foundations of civilization and the bearers of an inviolable force:

> I therefore say NO to the slaughter of my people! / I say NO to the slaughter of women, whether they wear pants or boubous! . . . /Whether they are Christian or Muslim. / Whether you like them or not, we must respect them as MOTHER of HUMANITY, SYMBOL of UNITY! / If there is anything special in the eyes of God, woman and the mother are part of it. / Whether one agrees with their opinion or not, one must know how to see God in them! / One must know how to respect what God put in them, for the good of every nation, every family, every human being for Eternity . . . / These women are not your adversaries, nor your enemies, even if they are supporters of the opposing camp. Never more That! (Kouamé 2011)

The Mothers' righteous indignation and curse is an integral part of "the ideology of redemption—part religion, part morality—which characterizes much African politics . . . [and] the reflection of a fundamental existential demand which democracy will have to satisfy if it is to survive" (Bayart 1986, 123). Nevertheless, in today's world, where globalization and international marketization are the major forces driving change, international organizations with religious affiliation (like World Vision or outreach and support programs of the World Council of Churches) overshadow those efforts at the local level and certainly eclipse the intervention of actors, like the Adjanou dancers, who seem unmoored from any formal organization. Indigenous forms of civil engagement are easily overlooked, and its stakeholders risk losing even more ground on the social landscape if their presence goes unrecognized or is not deemed viable. Without the international scope of those cosmopolitan bodies, can the enactments of FGP have any effective reach *beyond the local*?

At this juncture anthropologist and global studies theorist Arjun Appadurai is a welcome conversation partner. He shifts the understanding of "locality" away from the association of the term with geographic circumscription or parochial spheres of engagement and identity that have no bearing on the wider world of historical interconnection and mutual definition. He urges that we need to "get away from the idea that group identities necessarily imply that 'cultures' need to be seen as spatially bounded, historically unselfconscious, or ethnically homogeneous forms" (Appadurai 1995, 208). Instead, he suggests that "the local" refers to a "property of social life" (207) that must be actively produced to create a sustained ethos. This requires "hard and regular work" and is achieved through "complex social techniques that inscribe and embody the local" (205–6). Ritual is the most obvious and effective of these complex social techniques. The rituals of FGP are among those "legible and reproducible patterns of action" regularly carried out to produce the "meaningful life-world" that *is* locality (209). The "hard and regular work" they do is to awaken the public conscience and recollect moral imperatives. The ritual rhetoric of FGP, regularly rehearsed in Africa, is a recognizable standard representing both the "local" (read "West African") moral values that the Mothers embody and the rallying cry against the evil of injustice, a demand that knows no border.

In 2011 the Ivoirian Association of Women Patriots in France gathered in the Place du Trocadero in Paris and brandished the "red kodjo," the traditional female undergarment, not only to manifest "their profound indignation and their revolt against the tragic situation in which their country is living" but *to curse* the politicians deemed responsible for the ongoing suffering (Zeka 2011). Thus, in today's globalizing world, the local values and techniques—so ubiquitous throughout West Africa—have not remained constrained to the continent. Such use of FGP in the European metropole demonstrates how it is deployed in the diaspora as a "technique for the production of locality" (Appadurai 1995, 207). It is a "return to knowledge" of a local kind—self-consciously asserting its worth even in the wider geopolitical sphere. The return to this ancient rhetorical form is an "insurrection of subjugated knowledges" through which "*criticism performs its work*" (Foucault and Gordon 1980, 81–82). And when the activism of the Mothers is broadcast on YouTube or given consideration within the wider phenomena of women's nudity in public protest, the effective reach of these manifestations is more visible than ever. In the postcolonial and globalizing world, where "the task of producing locality . . . is increasingly a struggle" (Appadurai 1995, 213), performances of FGP revivify foundational values, ensuring that they remain vital and insisting on their contemporary relevance.

An Ancient Subterfuge

Postcolonial theorist R. Radhakrishnan made the astute and ironic comment that the term *postcolonialism* is hardly ever used within the ex-colonized world (1993, 750). Platitudes about the new postcolonial order do not apply to the actual local situation.

The reiteration of FGP in politics in Côte d'Ivoire has been an emergency response to the terrible incursions of postcolonial forces on the local. They have appeared as a refusal of the brutal violations and demeaning effacement of women, as well as the subjugations masquerading as development politics. The Mothers' rehearsal of this ancient form of civil disobedience demonstrates that "tradition and modernity are not opposed but paired; 'tradition is a moving image of the past, it is opposed not to modernity but to *alienation*'" (Rabinow et al. 2008, 58, emphasis mine). The rite of FGP is a mirror that holds up to view an image of the factors that have brought about the alienation from home and the dislocation of the local—the imported apparatus of neocolonial power.

The fierce enactment of FGP is no mere *theoretical* critique, but a "*critique engagée*" (Bhabha 1994, 33). The Mothers' daring displays simultaneously embody lamentation, protest, and warning. When the Mothers crouch in the posture of childbirth they shame spectators with the reminder of the absolute primacy of woman as progenitor, the source of the primordial social bond, and the wellspring of moral obligation. When they expose their naked breasts and buttocks, slap their denuded bosoms, or bend over to display their bottoms with wanton defiance, there is no mistaking their intent to contest brute force with moral force. The spectacle is an expression of outrage that the centrality of women's place has been displaced in the hypermasculine forms of neocolonial conflict. It protests that fundamental African values have been overshadowed by the ideologies of nation and state, leaving the halls of power morally bankrupt. Adjanou and other manifestations of FGP in the contemporary political arena reject this unhoming disruption of their own more grounded epistemology and its grounding ethics.

The performers of Adjanou turn the tables on the players of the postcolonial game in yet another way. Their strategy does not rely on debate, negotiation, or jurisprudence but draws on a particular kind of power, the "ancient subterfuge" of ritual (Spivak 1988, 278). As a performative gesture, not articulated in word or text, the assertion of FGP escapes the problematic betrayal of language that typifies other forms of critique attempted by the subaltern and resists inscription into the postcolonial situation. The rite of FGP is an *extracolonial* discourse about the nature of power as a moral force. FGP embodies "a powerful repository of cultural knowledge that erases the rationalist and progressivist logics of the 'canonical' nation" (Bhabha 1994, 219).

Fighting Evil: Infrapolitical Rage and Moral Power

The portrait of the state as a bloodthirsty witch "sucking vital resources from an already debilitated society" (Fatton 1995, 76) is as common in scholarship on Africa as it is in the popular social imaginary. Using the cultural idiom of witchcraft as the source of evil, the Mothers fight fire with fire, countering the offense on the invisible, spiritual plane. Their threatening specter *recovers* the knowledge that has been repressed and obscured by the postcolonial state by bringing up the "unspeakable"—the evil inflicted on women and the whole suffering nation. The rite *displaces* the "regular" political discourse with a "supernatural" one that warns of the danger of neglecting moral authority in the wrangling for mere power. As a countermand of evil itself, their political rebuke in this form is a profound condemnation and profoundly damaging. Not only does FGP express "infrapolitical rage" (69), it is an actual weapon. For this reason the political regimes they condemn have every reason to fear it.

The image of a naked elderly woman standing before armed young men is, on one hand, a vivid commentary on power, showing that the battle for primacy is not a "struggle among equals" and that the "adversaries do not belong to a common space" (Foucault 1977, 150). On the other hand, while the Mothers appear naked and vulnerable, they present themselves as a *superior* force. Their emergence on the scene is always the occasion of contestation, and it is a battle that they clearly intend to win. They are not the kind of peacemakers who will accept a tepid détente. Those women enacting the ritual of FGP are warriors undertaking a combat that asserts the dominance of their own system of values and rules. That is, FGP is "by no means designed to temper violence but rather to satisfy it" (150). Their condemnation of political forces that fail to measure up is adamant and menacing, a "violently imposed interpretation" (151) in its own right that seeks to "force its participation in a different game" (Dreyfus and Rabinow 1982, 108).

In contemporary postcolonial politics, women have been largely excluded from statecraft and made "other," or at best made to serve the needs of the state in their projected image as mothers-of-the-nation. Their ritual reprimand rejects both. The activism of the Mothers refutes the dissembling forms of nationalism that replace moral foundations with the promises of modernity and rejects the forces of globalization that dismiss local values. The deployment of FGP announces that "the people will no longer be contained in that national discourse of the teleology of progress; ... the homogeneous time of social narratives. The liminality of the people ... demands a 'time' of narrative that is disavowed in the discourse of historicism," which the state represents (Bhabha 1994, 216–17). With their public manifestations they make a timely reappraisal of the trajectory of the nation and question its viability as home. The uncomfortable (unhomely) revelation of the state's betrayal of those values stands as a refusal of further encroachment of foreign ideology upon the values of that home.

When the Mothers rise up to reprimand the state, their purpose is not to overthrow the government, but to rectify its distorted course of action. The women's gathering and their ritual recollection of matrifocal morality therefore embodies a *critique* of power. Moreover, that critique retains a *local* character. The deployment of FGP in the public streets restores to the collective social imaginary the forgotten and overlooked moral imperatives of African tradition. While its purpose is to stir memory, it is not timeless but timely.

Timely Acts: Local Civil Society in a Time of Global Politics

The appearances of the Mothers are *timely*, both in the sense of *providing a necessary and appropriate response to the times* and in the sense of being charged with *urgency*. They are critical expressions of local knowledge that are especially relevant *now*. Like others caught up in the crisis of the times, the women who perform this public spectacle have "*little time* for the remembrance of *profound time*" (Richards 2007, 350, emphasis mine). The Mothers' acts are recollections of the repressed history of their status as bearers of moral authority. But they don't romanticize or fetishize tradition, nor do they stir nostalgia for the past.

Through FGP the submerged but still living traditions erupt into the present to interrogate and redirect the course of history.

The women's uprisings and appeal to FGP today are dedicated to "bringing back to life that which has been put to sleep" by the instigators of collective amnesia (Shipley et al. 2010, 661). But this longing for justice is not just a nostalgic lament over a lost "precolonial Eden." The deployment of FGP is a return to immortal mandates. It remains an abiding call to insurrection against their neglect. The Mothers invigorate a still vital yet subsumed ideal struggling to reassert itself—moral indignation and ethical righteousness. The performance of FGP draws on the "matri-archive" but has designs on the future.

With striking visual rhetoric, FGP challenges the apparatus of the neocolonial state with the living traditions that have precedence, both historical primacy and ethical preeminence. It recalls a fractured society back to the sustaining values of the matri-archive. It calls for accountability as a relevant reality now.

The Intimacy of a Postcolonial Rebuke

FGP makes plain that women are not just hapless corks bobbing on the violent and impersonal waves of history, but exercise agency, even "in tight corners"—that is, under conditions that are not of their own making (Lonsdale 2000, 6). African women have acted as determined and self-determining agents in circumstances that became increasingly tight, where their formal representation has all but disappeared and the social and economic constraints placed upon them have become increasingly repressive. The repeated organization and deployment of the ancient ritual of rebuke demonstrate an ongoing commitment to the dignity of women's personhood, the inviolable principles embodied by their sex, and the necessity to intercede when they are in jeopardy.

In *Feminism without Borders*, T. Mohanty argues that scholars could "[make] the case for the centrality of gender in processes of global restructuring" if they were to focus on "unexpected and unpredictable sites of resistance to the often devastating effects of global restructuring on women" (2003, 245). The women's own self-representation in the execution of FGP figures as just such a point of departure for a new assessment of the crisis women face in the globalizing world.

The history of FGP presents a new kind of history, "intelligible only within a cultural tradition but, potentially, standing some critical distance part from it . . . *a startling reinterpretation, an intimate rebuke*" (Lonsdale 2000, 14, emphasis mine). The enactment of FGP is an "intimate rebuke" not only because of its reference to the most sacred and most secreted parts of the anatomy, but because its expression of righteous indignation springs from the deepest values that define social affinity in African society and that define the local as home. In Côte d'Ivoire today, the women's rebuke is poignantly intimate in that their public condemnation is no longer aimed at the injustices, indignities, and violations of a foreign colonial imperialism, but rather at those of their own postcolonial state.

Women's bodies have been the site of the contest of power and the location where society's unhomely dislocation has been forcefully enacted (Grillo 2013). Resorting to female genital power, women make the female body the locus of public contest, but they also self-consciously make use of it for their own disruptive agenda. Using the naked female body as the unexpected and unpredictable site of resistance, the women of Côte d'Ivoire refuse to allow themselves to be mere victims. Forcing men, particularly statesmen and their armed troops, to gaze on their naked bodies in violation of taboo, the Mothers perpetrate an epistemic violence upon the aggressors. With their public spectacle they demand to be seen, not as objectified beings, but as the material emblem of that which is missing from the postcolonial state: authentic representation in the form of ethical reciprocity.

The ritual rhetoric of FGP reveals the degree to which the Ivoirian state's adoption of the terms of modernity alienates its people from a more authentic African identity and the civic virtues that traditionally define it. As a form of postcolonial *activism*, the appeal to FGP insists that the state ground itself in the long-standing ethical foundations of African society. "The state can never fully annihilate [this form of] civil society; civil society's murmurs and 'hidden transcripts' are always potentially explosive, they constitute the invisible zone of resistance to domination" (Fatton 1995, 68). When the murmurs of discontent with the state grow louder, "commitments and attachments (sometimes mislabeled 'primordial') that characterize local subjectivities are *more pressing, more continuous, and sometimes more distracting* than the nation-state can afford" (Appadurai 1995, 215). Women elders risk bullets to agitate for justice. The shocking juxtaposition of their moral stance with the moral bankruptcy of military might without conscience stirs public consciousness and evokes condemnation in international courts as well as local villages and neighborhoods. If the nation-state cannot afford to build on these values, neither can it afford to ignore them.

With their very bodies, the women throw down the gauntlet of judgment and challenge to spiritual combat those who would dare defy them. The women's public act of reprimand is an essential reminder of "*what it once was to be fully achieved men and women*," morally responsible and engaged (Lonsdale 2000, 15). Such a vividly embodied recollection may still be instructive, if it is recognized for what it is: a warning about the unthinkable cataclysm that befalls a society without moral anchor.

Notes

INTRODUCTION

1. I am coining this term, conscious that it stands as a counter to other, better-known but heinous ritual practices in Africa referring to women's genitals: FGM (female genital mutilation) and FGC (female genital cutting). Excision, now illegal in Côte d'Ivoire as elsewhere in West Africa, has no correlation with the rite that appeals to FGP. While neither the Abidji nor the Adioukrou people—who were the subjects of my fieldwork— traditionally practice genital cutting (or even any form of scarification), it is certain that other people whose traditions do include female excision simultaneously hold "the Mothers" in high regard and acknowledge their power, including their female genital power. A case in point is the Sande secret society, discussed in chapter 1.

2. "Baoulé" is variously spelled "Baoule," "Baulé," "Baule," "Bawule."

3. In 1910 Lucien Lévy-Bruhl forwarded the hypothesis that the traditions of non-Western peoples reflected the "prelogical mentality," characterized by an "undifferenti-ated consciousness" that did not distinguish between myth and history and that enabled "mystical participation" (*participation mystique*). Although Lévy-Bruhl later abandoned this hypothesis, it was obstinately maintained by other influential thinkers of the modern era, notably Carl Gustav Jung, who refused to abandon the discredited projection (Jung 1958, vol. 11, 817n28). Such ideas still circulate in the popular Western imagination.

4. This idea that societies without writing were without reflexivity was largely given currency by Karl Jaspers's lamentable theory of an Axial Age, an imagined period that supposedly signaled a metaphysical breakthrough and transcendence over the fixed ideologies of the past, "tradition." The Axial Age thesis elevated the Western values associated with modernity to the status of universal standards against which all cultural development can presumably be measured. It pits "higher" civilizations—those with writing—against societies that entrap its members in a "closed predicament": the "other" remains unaware of alternative worldviews or systems and unable to transcend a limiting and stagnant social definition. Robin Horton's influential essay "African Traditional Thought and Western Science" (Horton 1967), which relied on the thesis to compare African thought with Western natural science, failed to discredit the thesis but reinforced its applicability to the African case.

5. In referring to vestiges I do not mean to imply that I am making an appeal to an evolutionist view of the history of humanity or attempting to reinvigorate the anti-quated imperial theory that presumed Africa to be a fossilized remnant of the earliest cultures.

6. This is not to say that scholarship has no import in history. Certainly, we are far too aware of the devastating complicity of theory and politics. As Said put it, anthropology was "often [the] direct agent of political dominance" (Said 1989, 219–20).

7. As a domain, the moral extends beyond any particular ethical code. That is, I use the term *moral* to designate behavior that is sanctioned by conscience and values that are so deeply engrained as to become embodied, "second nature," and part of the cultural "habitus" (Bourdieu 1977, 72–95). Ethics, by contrast, refers to prescribed principles and the discipline of enforcing commonly held standards of right behavior. The two may overlap, but I attempt to maintain a distinction throughout, choosing the phrase *matrifocal morality* to signal the deeper and more affective nature of FGP and its distinction from particular "religious" mandates.

8. The proposition that matrifocal morality is an underlying principle common to West African society is quite distinct from the imagined ur-matriarchy that inspired Bachofen, Gimbutas, and proponents of a primordial goddess tradition. My thesis is not concerned with any universalizing theory about the origins of humanity. Instead, I maintain that this uniquely African phenomenon must be appreciated in its own terms and as an expression of a *particular* "ontological-cultural epistemology" that is not universally applicable (Long 2004, 90).

9. Even as I show that early female scholars' misguided application of feminist ideology to the interpretation of African women's mobilizations and ritual protests led to a distorted appraisal of their cause, I also warn against facile but misplaced comparison with political demonstrations using female nudity that have recently appeared on the sociopolitical landscape in the West, such as those of the women of the Ukranian political group Femen.

I. GENIES, WITCHES, AND WOMEN

1. *Adioukrou* is variously spelled in the literature as *Adjukru, Adyoukrou, Adyukru, Ajukru,* or according to the more authentic, phonetic version, *Odjukru.* I use the most common contemporary spelling except when quoting ethnographers such as Memel-Fotê, who prefers Odjukru.

2. In what follows, I will refer to the consonant festivals of Dipri and Kpol as "Dipri," unless quoting or referring to a practice that is unique to the Adioukrou (Kpol) tradition.

3. A fuller discussion of witchcraft will follow.

4. *Genie* is an adaptation of the Arabic word *djinn* [Arabic: الجني al-jinnī], referring to a spiritual being who inhabits a usually invisible realm, though able to interact physically with people in the visible world. Like human beings the genies are neither good nor evil, but exercise free will. Such beings are mentioned in the Qur'an as well as in Arabic folklore. The long history of Arabic and Islamic influence on sub-Saharan West Africa accounts for the adoption of the term. The English word *genie* is derived from Latin *genius,* originally referring to a guardian spirit that guided destiny. Africans speaking European languages regularly and unselfconsciously use *genie,* though their indigenous languages have their own precise terms. For the Abidji, the word is *Eikpa,* and the genies of the

water are *Dikpè-Eikpa*. West African water spirits are elsewhere referred to as divinities, and their cults are recognized to be a common feature of African indigenous religions. The adoration of the river genie in Dipri can be likened, for example, to the worship of the prominent river goddesses in the Yoruba pantheon. Therefore, the adoption of the term *genie* here is not intended to diminish the stature of the spirit being nor to distinguish the worship of that spirit from the practice of religion.

5. In Orbaff in 2010, I gave the Okpolu photos that I'd taken of Dipri thirty years earlier, and they delighted in identifying themselves and each other. The one who performed this feat was then identified as Owel Assra Antoine.

6. In the Adioukrou language, no word ends in a vowel. Therefore, *Egbiki* is pronounced with a nasal consonant at the end, *Egbikng*. For the sake of consistency, I will use *Egbiki* except when directly quoting from a transcription. Lafargue (1976) calls this same rite *sokroyibè*. The discrepancy is discussed later in the chapter.

7. This and all other translations from the original French to English that appear in this work are my own.

8. The Baoulé, one of the largest ethnicities in Côte d'Ivoire, are classified as Akan. The Abidji often use Baoulé as a ritual language. I consulted an aged Abidji diviner (*mrabapo*) in Sahuyé who conducted his reading by entering a trance and channeling his genies, who speak through him in Baoulé, although he himself did not understand the language. Lafargue confirmed that Baoulé "seems to be a type of secret language, as much among the Abidji as among certain Adjoukrou" (1976, 209).

9. From this point forward I will use the abbreviation FGP for "female genital power."

10. In Lafargue's account, the genie was not Kporu but the nameless genie of the forest who also taught the ancestor how to use agricultural tools. This becomes more significant when considering the second myth associated with the origin of Dipri.

11. The chef de terre is the head of the original clan (*boso*) and leader of all the clans that comprise Abidji society, each of which occupies a separate quarter of the village and maintains its own lineage head. This nonhierarchical social organization is typical of the stateless societies that predominated in West Africa, to be discussed in chapter 2. Upon this horizontal social arrangement the French colonials imposed a vertical structure by demanding that an administrative chief be named in each village. According to Lafargue, the village chief was chosen essentially for his knowledge of the French language and his loyalty to the enforcement of colonial governance (1976, 25). The office of chief is therefore a vestige of the colonial imposition of a doubled authority, religious and secular.

12. On May 7, 2009, in addition to Chief Tanau Langau, I met with Gnangra N'Guessan Bertin, chef de terre, and six sékèpuone: Djidja Anangba Marcel, Yao Tanoh Daniel, Lasme Tomah, Abo Brou André, Yede Okon Richard, and Kassi Aby Simeon. Also present were Victorine Akadee Dongo, François Binje, and Henry Pernet.

13. Referred to in French as "biche" and translated in English as "doe," the animal is actually a type of small antelope, or *duiker* (*Philantomba maxwellii*). The subject of human sacrifice, alluded to in Gnagra's remark, is beyond the purview of this discussion. However, it is noteworthy that it is known to have been practiced in West Africa little

more than a century ago and that kings and potentates could order mortuary slayings on the occasion of the death of important chiefs to accompany the deceased to the next world (Ellis and Ter Haar 2004, 90). Human sacrifice would therefore be both a means of accessing power and an accessory of power.

14. The occupation of the office by his younger relative was still the source of contestation for some villagers. According to some, the usurpation of N'Guessan's office would cause confusion over who would invoke Egbiki that year.

15. Here he named Bidjo as the sacrificed child, not the sacrificing ancestor. A youth sitting in on the interview intervened to protest that he was providing misinformation, and N'Guessan replied, "We must not tell all the secrets." This exchange in Abidji was recorded and later translated for me by François Binje. It is of special interest that the detail suppressed was the sex of the sacrificial victim.

16. The name changes slightly from one telling to the next, remaining phonetically similar.

17. N'Guessan's version also claimed that his great-grandfather Aiudibo was among those first elders in Sahuyé to receive the genie's gift. By his reckoning this dated the introduction of Dipri to c. 1850. The detail also asserted himself as rightful heir to the office of earth priest.

18. The double origin of Dipri is certain, but is of a different nature. The roots of the festival in both Adioukrou and Abidji sources, and specifically the "genii-ological" association of the two ethnic groups that celebrate the festival, will be fully explored in a subsequent chapter.

19. Niangoran-Bouah indicates that the New Year ceremony proper involves "chasing away death" to activate the renewal of the world and its fecundity ritually, but he makes no mention of Egbiki.

20. In her contemporary classic *Male Daughters, Female Husbands*, Ifi Amadiume (1987) presents the myth of origin of Nri, an Igbo state in Nigeria. Its details are remarkably consonant with the first of the founding myths of Dipri. It relates that the primordial ancestor Nri came to settle among the Igbo people, who at that time still had no agriculture. In a time of famine Nri sought God's help and, following God's directive, cut off the heads of his son and daughter and planted them. From the head of his daughter sprang cocoyam, a "subsidiary crop managed by women" (28) and from his son's head, the yam, which is prized in ritual and ceremony and monopolized by men.

21. As we shall see in chapter 4, the genies of Gomon and Sahuyé are linked in their own "genii-ological" alliance, considered goddess and consort respectively.

22. In 1979 I witnessed young men holding the same woven palm fronds during Lowe, the Adioukrou initiation into an age set, a class of successive generational groups that collectively organize the structure of village life. In the village of Mopoyem, initiates were led to the local stream. They held one end of the palm braid while a young woman from their maternal lineage held the other, and were thus united with this symbolic umbilical chord. In this way a man is born to the matrilineage.

23. Elsewhere the new yam harvest is the occasion for investing the chief or king with the spiritual authority that ensures his ability to foster fertility and abundance, the neces-

sary complement to military bloodshed. Among the Yoruba in the sacred city Ilé-Ifè, the king's New Yam Festival begins with a visit to the Òsàrà River, the abode of the goddess. There diviners and priests perform a ritual dramatizing the planting and harvest of the yam (Olupona 2011, 185). At the riverbank they also gather medicinal leaves, considered female and regarded as living entities engaged in a sacred pact with the king and community (187–88). Of special note in this parallel with Dipri is the fact that the yam not only inaugurates the New Year but is also ritually associated with the spiritual powers of the water goddess and her river abode.

24. As a society of initiates charged with the conservation and transmission of the deep knowledge of sékè, Dipri may be seen to function like the *Sigi* ceremony of the well-known Dogon people of Mali, through which "the power of deep knowledge and menstrual blood [is] domesticated and incorporated into the body politic, brought from the bush into the center of the village—in effect, cleansed and channeled into regeneration" (Apter 2007, 126).

25. Others present were Sangroh Esaïe, Essoh Nomel Salomon, son of the village chief who served as interpreter, Yedoh Edouard, Philippe Leite, and Henry Pernet.

26. Lafargue noted the existence of methods for the attenuation or ablation of power used in situations where its exercise is considered dangerous, such as the excessively strong manifestations of sékè among women at Dipri. For example, to remove a woman from trance, sacred plants were soaked in water and the juices squeezed into her eyes (cf. Lafargue 1976, 163–64).

27. The woman's sacrifice of fecundity is a perpetual one; her blood is diverted to aggrandize the genie's power, as Dipri assumes woman's power to aggrandize male prowess.

28. Here I relate an uncanny misadventure in the form of confession. In 1980, while my Adioukrou husband and I spent the night prior to Dipri in Sahuyé, we violated this taboo. When at first I'd resisted, in consideration of the taboo, he mocked my credulity. But within minutes great welt-like hives began to appear, first behind my knees and in the crux of my elbows, then on my neck and chest. Fearing anaphylactic shock, I wanted to seek medical attention, but he adamantly refused: "The village has been ritually sealed!" It was not until morning that the swellings began to subside.

29. Such a wound is also the notorious mark of a witch's spiritual attack and a sure sign of that kind of bewitchment. The symbolic association between the permanent wound and the female sex may further suggest the reason women are assumed to have an innate potential for witchcraft.

30. Because of such dangers, there had been some objection to Meledje becoming the "Dean" of Kpol, for although he was the rightful occupant of that office as the senior member of Yassap's original clan and renowned for his own strong powers, his wife was still of childbearing age: "If you have a young wife, they don't like that too much. If she forgets and approaches you on the day that she is in her period, it would be a provocation [for the genies] and that would bring misfortune."

31. In the 1960s, during Dipri in Gomon, "some kponpuone [masters of trance (Abidji: *kpon*)] took out their eyes from their sockets and let them hang on their cheeks, then put them back in place" (Lafargue 1976, 15). In 2010 I witnessed Sangroh's apprentice insert a knife into the eye socket and hold it there.

32. The sacrificial victim on which they "feast" is typically a member of an initiate's matrikin. So the object of the meal and this gesture together violate the core moral principles, for as Amadiume notes, in West Africa the matricentric unit was "also an eating unit; all the children of one woman ate out of their mother's pot. . . . This was the unit bound by the closest and strongest sentimental sibling tie" (1987, 36).

33. For further reflection on the consonance of diviners and witches and firsthand acknowledgments from diviners that they are indeed a kind of witch, see Grillo 2009.

34. Among the Yoruba, were your mother to call you into private quarters and kneel in the position of childbirth, it would instill terrible fear, for it is a signal of her condemnation (Jacob Olupona, private communication, March 2013). It is a threat so mighty that it calls for immediate repentance or doom. The gesture at once evokes her primacy as progenitor and her matching capacity to revoke the life she bore.

35. As we shall see later in other cases, women mobilize and evoke FGP to rebuke men who insult or injure women and defecate at the doorstep of the accursed.

36. Ifi Amadiume proposed that the primordial traditions subscribed to this belief, as the societies were also originally matriarchal: "The Earth is usually a goddess in African religion" (1997, 123).

37. In the 1970s Lafargue (1976) also witnessed this phenomenon, claiming they pounded raw plantains that miraculously produced cooked "fufu."

38. In this passage, Lafargue twice spells the word with a final acute accent on the final letter (é), but elsewhere in the passage and in most of the work including the glossary, the term is spelled with a "grave" accent on the final letter (è). I have adopted the most prevalent spelling.

39. The French version reads, "Un petit groupe composé principalement de vieilles femmes, celles qui ont la plus haute autorité dans le sokroyibé, se réunissent." Another intriguing clue to the possibility that the Mothers who perform Egbiki may originally have had their own secret society lies in the fact that among the Yoruba of Nigeria *egbe* is the name of the secret society of those powerful old women who are honored by the famous masked celebration, *Gelede.* The details of that performance suggest so great a consonance between the Yoruba conception of the Mothers' power and that of the women who enact Egbiki that one might conjecture that the origins of the principles and the rite itself may lie in the older societies to the east, from where many of the ethnicities that people the southeastern Côte d'Ivoire emigrated. These migrations and the way that FGP founded new settlements and ethnicities in this forest region are the subjects of chapter 4.

40. See chapter 3 on comparative cases of FGP in resistance efforts during colonialism.

2. MATRIFOCAL MORALITY

1. Adler noted that it was remarkable that even in the Christian West, the famous doctrine of "two bodies in one king" conceived of royalty as the embodiment of both sexes. "Thus, when one thinks of the relation between the body politic and the mystical body, of the king and his physical body according to the maxim *magis dignum trahit ad se minus dignum,* it refers . . . to the two sexes of a hermaphrodite" (2007, 86n3).

2. Mansa Musa's legendary passage through Cairo on his pilgrimage to Mecca has been dated with certainty to 1324 A.D. At that time the monarch was said to have brought so much gold from West Africa that it contributed to a fall in the price of gold there the following year (Bell 1972, 224).

3. Adler notes that a good number of myths of origin of the initiatory secret recount that "men robbed, or rather, tore it away from women," since its "original place is in the belly of woman" (Adler, 2007, 87). That men stole spiritual power from women is a widespread theme in the myths of Africa (cf. Pernet 1992, 138).

4. The ritual gestures involved in the Yoruba ceremonies that invest a king with spiritual power are also reminiscent of the Dipri performance. The deities (*orisha*) are "invoked in the bush, where their dangerous powers are enlisted and embodied by priestesses and are contained in calabashes and bottles that are . . . carried through the town to the palace and central shrines, where the powers are 'cooled' and 'delivered' on behalf of the king and his subjects" (Apter 2007, 25). As in Dipri, the spiritual entity is associated with the undomesticated terrain, the marshy waters. In both, the spirit is invoked "in the bush" and brought into the central domesticated space. In Dipri, calabashes and bottles containing water from the river, plants used in healing, kaolin clay, and other elements associated with the genie's powers are paraded through the village, carried by youths who follow the entranced initiates. While the Yoruba priestess is able to contain the dangerous powers of the *orisha* in her body and deliver them in an orderly fashion to the shrine, the young Abidji initiates can only embody the genie of the river in a state of frenzied possession trance, and their untamed, "hot" power builds to a violent crescendo. In Dipri, initiates' very bodies become the receptacles that deliver the power (through their "cooling" wound) to the central place of habitation, where it may then come under domesticating rule. For both the Yoruba and those celebrating Dipri, a ritual transfer and containment of power inaugurates the New Year.

5. The exploits of Queen Amina are related in the Kano Chronicles, a translation of precolonial documentation of Hausa tradition. For the original text, see H. R. Palmer, "The Kano Chronicle," *Journal of the Royal Anthropological Institute* 5, no. 38 (1908): 60, as noted by Djibo 2001, 38.

6. This applied both to clans, based on an early unnamed ancestress, and lineages, originating from a known ancestress in historical time.

7. As Stoeltje sagely noted, "The concept of motherhood slips and slides between the symbol (the queen mother) and its referent (both the social and biological role of mother)," at least for Western interpreters (1997, 57).

8. This source quotes Aidoo, suggesting that her courtiers were women, but Gilbert contradicts this, specifying that "members of her court are men," and therefore their force was more than symbolic (Gilbert 1993, 35n4).

9. The British colonial administration made the Omu subservient to the Obi, who received financial consideration to enforce "indirect rule" (Okonjo 1976, 55).

10. Sande is also known as *bundu*, *bundo*, and *bondo*, making reference to the name of the helmet mask that is worn at Sande initiation ceremonies and that represents the ideals of womanhood.

11. According to McGovern the esoteric "power associations" lend authority to "Gerontocratic Hierarchy" (2011, 57). However, closer examination of the actual dynamics

of power show features that are less visible than the structures of organizational authority and reveal that gerontocratic hierarchy is not as uniform, as stable, or as profound as it has often been made to appear.

12. Despite this homage to the seat of moral power, initiation into Sande includes female genital cutting (FGC), both clitoridectomy and excision, performed by the head of the society. FGC, also called female genital mutilation (FGM), is believed to eradicate the vestiges of the opposite sex to promote fertility and to instill morality. The study of FGC and FGM is beyond the scope of this study. But for a thorough discussion of Sande and FGM in Liberia, see "28 Too Many (2014) Country Profile: FGM in Liberia," www.28toomany.org/countries/liberia/.

13. In chapter 1, I suggested that the term *sokroyibé*, now known as "Egbiki" among the Abidji, by which Lafargue identified the rite of FGP, might be the name of the now-defunct female association responsible for conducting the rite.

14. The metaphor reflects the degree to which gender was a culturally inscribed role, not uniquely fixed to the physical body, and is an example of gender flexibility, so ably defended by Amadiume (1987).

15. These details are beyond the purview of our discussion here, but the commonalities between these rites of consecration at the spring during the Festival of Generations and the rites of consecration during Kpol (Yam Festival) and Dipri deserve further study.

16. As in the Adioukrou festival of *Angbandji* that precedes the "Festival of Generations" (*Ebeb*), the women who surround the male on parade are his matriclan. He is only the emblem of their power and wealth, and in essence servant to their cause (see chapter 4).

17. A fascinating detail in a study of precolonial Angola relates "an oral tradition of a woman pulverizing her own infant with a mortar and pestle. The resulting liquid was used ritually to bestow men with an invulnerability before engaging in war" (Hunt 1989, 372). This account suggests that the Angolan women would deploy magico-religious powers in times of war and links those powers in other ways that relate to Egbiki: the association of women's power with the sacrifice of maternity as opposed to fecundity; the use of the pestle to evoke that power; and enacting spiritual warfare.

18. In the department of Tanda in northeastern Côte d'Ivoire, and most notably among the Bron (also known as Brong, Abron, or Abrong), such a cleansing ritual is called *Mgbra*. It is executed not only to push back an enemy in time of war, but also to excise the danger to the community in cases of a prolonged drought and famine or when battling epidemics (chickenpox, measles, leprosy). "With the stalks and leaves of the Mgbra in hand, the elderly women make the rounds of the village in single file, dragging the Mgbra (a plant that grows along the banks of waterways). With the leafy branches of the palm tree wrapped on their heads, they sing in chorus while sprinkling kaolin here and there. . . . Only menopausal women have the right to participate in the ceremony. Men are formally prohibited. Women still of childbearing age are also excluded" (Ba Morou Ouattara, email communication, August 17 and 22, 2017, translation mine).

19. More recently, Oyèrónké Oyewùmí contends that early Western feminists, resisting the "essentialist" idea that biology is destiny, refused to give women's reproductive capacity its due or sufficiently value the role of motherhood. "That women bear children calls for a distinctive assessment" (2005a, 103). Yet here is exactly where many contemporary

interpreters go awry when interpreting African women's mobilization and FGP. They focus too much on maternity as the source of solidarity and as the motivating impulse for their fierce defense of justice.

20. Douglas attempted to reassess the prospects for the future survival of matrilineal descent. However, neglecting the *moral* dimension of matriliny (as well as the religious battle waged by the Christian missions against the indigenous religious systems), her analysis ends on what today reads as a sadly naïve note: "All [matriliny] needs for its full creative contribution to the twentieth century are *conditions for steady economic growth*" (1969, 133).

3. GENDER AND RESISTANCE

1. FGP is "essential" in nature because postmenopausal women are considered to bear that power innately. It is not the performance that evokes the special quality of their gender. The act only deploys that power.

2. This is one of many examples of comparable cases in other regions in Africa, both in precolonial and contemporary history. Our work limits the comparative frame to the more readily recognized culture area of the West African subregion.

3. Interestingly enough, the women who performed this were the wives of men who had been robbed of their property by their sister's sons, a matrilineal theft! Here again we see an ubiquitous mytho-ritual theme that attests to the preeminence of women's power despite the current appearance of female subservience.

4. One interesting exception is noted in the colonial court documents in Cameroon, which record charges being brought against a woman for revealing "women's secrets" (Ardener 1973).

5. The report of the commission was entitled "Report of the Commission of Inquiry appointed to look into the disturbances in the Calabar and Owerri Provinces, December 1929."

6. Sylvia Boone (1986) rejected W. L. Hommel's suggestion that the flared crest was sexually symbolic of the "vagina with the clitoris represented by the same forms as the phallus" that appear on other Sande masks, arguing that the allusion would not be in keeping with the Mende's strict codes of sexual conduct and propriety (223). However, her rejection is inconsistent with the depiction of other recognized sexual imagery, such as the cowrie shell, whose Mende name is a pun on the word for a woman's body where "the stone of life is embedded" (221).

7. Among the Yoruba, too, the "genitals become metaphors for the two kinds of power," generative and destructive (Drewal 1992, 178).

8. It is significant that this body was a colonial institution and not a traditional one. Where tradition provided for the defense of women's interests through self-rule, the colonial system had suppressed these self-governing bodies and their mode of enforcement. Therefore, "representation" in the Western style was women's only recourse at that point.

9. This last detail is particularly interesting, for the threat suggests a return to a sterile situation alluded to in many cosmogonic myths, one in which men and women live apart, often as enemies.

10. Since established male elders rejected the new faith, "young men" were trained to become catechists and priests. Once the advantages of a new cadre under the colonial administration were noticed, young men with allegiance to the Obi were sent for Western education in accounting; conversion was the unexpected consequence (Bastian 2000, 147–48).

11. In the literature "Takembeng" is alternatively spelled "Takumbeng," a version which I use only in direct quotes.

12. When I presented portions of this work at the 2017 MANSA conference in Grand-Bassam, Côte d'Ivoire, the respondent suggested that Muslim women would not be likely to engage in such behaviors. Many African colleagues there rejected this challenge and supplied validating examples of cases in Côte d'Ivoire as well as in Burkina Faso, Mali, and Niger that demonstrate that Muslim women indeed do participate. I am grateful to Bintou Koné for following up on her promise to provide her example in writing.

PART II. WORLDLINESS

1. The Ogbru clan is comprised of the three villages Gomon, Sahuyé, and Yaobou.

2. The classic definition of a lineage, according to the Ivoirian ethnographer Memel-Fotê, is "a community of relatives who claim the same ancestor and whose genealogy is clearly determined, who bear a name with which the members identify and by which they are identified, who follow the rules of exogamy" (Memel-Fotê and Brunet-Jailly 2007, 221).

4. FOUNDING KNOWLEDGE/BINDING POWER

1. We will return to this most egalitarian form of collective rule and its import; for now, suffice it to say that it is indicative of the degree to which age and sex are determinative factors for social organization and the exercise of power.

2. The words have a terribly ironic ring today after two civil wars and over a decade of violence fueled by contestation between "indigenous" Ivoirians and recent immigrants over rights of citizenship and land use. This is the subject of part III.

3. Memel-Fotê defines ethnicity in a way that attests to the complexity of the concept: "A relational notion, the ethnic group determines itself as much from within as from without according to the relations that link the society to its neighbors. The consciousness of belonging becomes explicit and reinforces itself by the opinion that the members of that society show towards other peoples" (1980, 86). This relational aspect is key for understanding the "profound similarities among the political cultures of far-flung African societies" (1987, 8).

4. On this basis Kopytoff questioned "whether 'lineages' have really existed in Africa" and proposes "corporate kin groups" as an alternative (Kopytoff 1987, 41).

5. Here we see operative a basic strategy of matriliny, which often resorts to creative means to allow for the expansion of its lineages.

6. According to both Memel-Fotê and Lafargue, sèkè was most likely of Adioukrou origin and brought to Gomon through Yassap, but "in order to erase any trace of depen-

dence [on the Adioukrou, the Abidji] have a tendency to affirm that [sékè] was given to them directly by a genie" (Lafargue 1976, 150).

7. In traditional society, the term *eb-ij* did not apply to foreigners, the uninitiated, or other persons not fully integrated into the ranks of society, such as slaves.

8. Among the Baoulé, the rite of FGP was performed at the funeral of a woman who died in childbirth, acknowledging her warrior spirit (Perrot 1982).

9. In using the compound expression "founding knowledge/binding power," I draw on Foucault's insight into the inextricable association of "knowledge" with "power" (Foucault and Gordon 1980). He expresses the connection between them with the composite term *power/knowledge* (*pouvoir/savoir*). Emphasizing its dynamic capacity, he proposes that power is not a thing with which either a person or a state is endowed, but a process. As strategic action, power is necessarily linked with knowledge and conveys a way of being in the world.

10. As we saw in chapter 2, the institution of the queen mother and the dynamics through which she selected her coregent demonstrate how matriliny was conceived not only in terms of bloodline—that is, descent from a common matriarch—but also as a means for including and engaging the support of patrilineal clans. The appointment of both rulers is based on female kinship, but patrilineal clans would compete to demonstrate their integration into the line of royal succession.

11. "In tributary societies, the communities preserve the means of production but they must give a tribute in kind to a leading class that masters the apparatus of the State" (Memel-Fotê 1980, 1n12).

12. Kopytoff challenges the idea that the stateless societies were more egalitarian: "It has often been remarked by ethnographers . . . that African cultures are suffused with a sense of hierarchy in social, political, and ritual relations. . . . This holds true even for those 'segmentary' or 'acephalous' or 'stateless' African societies that are sometimes labeled (or rather mislabeled) as 'egalitarian.' . . . [Within them] seniors stood over their juniors and patrons over their clients" (1987, 35–36). What cuts across every social rank, however, is the command of spiritual power. In this, elderly women always excelled and held ultimate authority.

13. While the stateless societies like those of the frontier, and the Akan groups in Côte d'Ivoire in particular, are generally assumed to be inferior to the "great" military empires, in fact "the basis of the state's power was more fragile" (Akyeampong and Obeng 2005, 34). This is borne out by the fact that the stateless societies were among the last to succumb to colonial domination.

14. Additional evidence that the origins of sékè were the *lagunaires* (the Adioukrou and other lagoon peoples) may be inferred from Visonà's research among the Akye. In the lagoon village of Memni, she was told that "the women had a power called *seke* that allows them to see invisible webs or poisonous substances left by evildoers" (Visonà 2010, 145). It is significant, too, that this power is ascribed especially to women.

15. "Bouboury" means "to gather together" (Lassm 1971, 43).

16. Significantly, according to the myth, Lodz's daughters founded the principal villages of the first Adioukrou confederation, Bouboury. Those striking out farther into the frontiers to found rival polities are sons.

17. An example is the rank one holds in the society of Sékèpone, as some are deemed to be born with sékè, or a greater power, and may consequently be granted authority over others, despite their younger age. This explains why the chef de terre of Sahuyé was not the eldest of them.

18. The Adioukrou held out against French colonialism, succumbing only in 1914, with the final battle of resistance being led by Debrimou. Colonialism imposed the reunification of Adioukrou governance, establishing artificial cantons and chiefs (Memel-Fotê 1980, 109).

19. Intra-ethnic division and war between villages was certainly a factor in precolonial Africa, made more volatile by the introduction of firearms and the destabilization of society through the slave trade. In the frontier, where egalitarian/acephalous polities determined the fates of their independent communities, skirmishes may not have been rare. Even as recently as 2010, during my visit to Orbaff, a "war" broke out with the youth of the neighboring village, Lopou, over land boundaries and the rights to exploit certain agricultural territories.

20. *Erng* signifies "water," and more specifically water into which one plunges, while *ok* means "to fall, in the collective sense, since this formulation is never applicable or applied to a fall or to an individual bath" (Memel-Fotê and Brunet-Jailly 2007, 715). The etymology therefore indicates a ritual immersion.

21. As we shall see in chapter 6, "Violation and Deployment," the Komye are, like the Mothers, endowed with the power to rid the community of evil and purify it from the bloodshed of war.

22. Such blood pacts were made at some point in the past between the Dida and Adioukrou as well as between the Dida and Abidji, and, as they were both inviolable and eternal, they remain in force to this day.

23. Atiéké is the staple food of the Adioukrou. The product resembles couscous but is made from cassava, through a laborious process of fermenting and pressing the cassava, sifting the resulting granules, drying, and finally steaming them.

24. An example comes from Nigeria at the turn of the last century, when, on the occasion of an influenza epidemic, Igbo women forced men to come to the central market to swear their innocence. "*The women dug a hole in the ground* . . . and poured into it water collected from the shrines of two of the most powerful Agbaja deities. . . . And they *killed a fowl and poured its blood into the hole.* . . . And the men came up one by one and had to dip their hands in the hole and wash their faces in the liquid" to make their oath (Amadiume 1997, 182).

25. The intimate pacts of marriage or broader social contracts, like military alliance, were both sealed with this ritual submission to metaphysical sanction. To this day, when referring to alliances, allusion is made to the ritual originally involved in their making, saying that the parties "have drunk" (Memel-Fotê and Brunet-Jailly 2007, 361).

5. WOMEN AT THE CHECKPOINT

1. The term *civil war* is formally ascribed to any internal armed conflict that meets the following two criteria: fighting is between rival claimants to the state who are from the same country, and the clash "produces enough deaths to cross the casualty threshold" of 2,000 people (Cramer 2006, 62).

2. At one time Europeans classified as "Krou" all the coastal populations between Monrovia and Grand Lahou. The Dida are therefore also included in the Krou cluster. But their territory borders the southwestern region; therefore, they are also culturally informed by alliances with the Abidji.

3. The blood pact described in chapter 4 was drawn among various subgroups self-identified as "Bété" and the Neyo peoples and dated to the nineteenth century.

4. The Ivoirian state maintained the first rights over coffee and cocoa harvests and guaranteed a fixed purchase price to farmers. In this way it assumed the risk, but also reaped the greatest share of the rewards as prices rose on the international market.

5. The coalition was composed of Guébié, Zabia, and Pacolo, as well as Bété, all belonging to the wider Krou ethnic group (Grah Mel 2010, 294).

6. McGovern appears indebted to Achille Mbembe (2001) for the idea of "pillaged territories" as well as ideas about the way that territorial disputes have "contributed to the crystallization of ethnic identities" and accentuated distinctions "between autochthonous peoples and foreigners" (31).

7. Regrettably, McGovern characterizes the infamous slave trader Samory Touré in particular in glowing terms as an "empire-builder" (McGovern 2011, 60) and "anti-colonial resistance hero" (61). While he acknowledges that the slave trade created social anarchy in the south, he fails to mention that Samory Touré was a significant player in this regional destabilization.

8. See chapter 6, "Violation and Deployment," which focuses on this issue.

9. McGovern ignores the fact that divination is at the heart of many traditional religious systems across the forest region along the Gulf of Guinea, from Benin to Côte d'Ivoire, including the formidable institution of Ifa. Elsewhere I have written extensively to show that divination is a means of negotiating destiny that sets the individual person as an independent and ethical agent in a position of responsiveness to the cosmos and spiritual world as well as responsibility with respect to the social world (cf. Grillo 2009, 2010).

10. McGovern uses the spelling *Jula*; I retain the more common spelling *Dyula* or, alternatively, *Dioula*, which appears in the literature in French.

11. Tokpè is not only a Dida tradition. The term is used throughout Côte d'Ivoire and employed as a rhetorical form not only in traditional society, but as a currency for breaking the ice in contemporary society. Even children are encouraged to practice the ritual exchange of insult as a means of solidifying relations among them (Cossette 2013, 87).

6. VIOLATION AND DEPLOYMENT

1. Postelection violence in 2011 claimed at least 3,000 civilian lives, and more than 150 women were raped. The casualties were so high during a five-month period of contested leadership and associated armed struggle that some refer to it now as "the second civil war." In 2015 HRW and the Paris-based International Federation for Human Rights (FIDH) jointly issued a call for the Ouattara government to realize its promises made in June 2011 to look into the postelection abuses and to execute impartial justice of these crimes against humanity (FIDH 2015).

2. *Dyula* is the term commonly applied to many of the ethnic groups from the north of Côte d'Ivoire or other countries in the subregion, particularly Burkina Faso and Mali. Under some circumstances it is used to describe any person with a Muslim name. It is alternatively spelled Dioula or Jula.

3. FESCI was once led by Charles Blé Goudé, who was sanctioned by the UN and later arrested for crimes against humanity.

4. The Forces Nouvelles was a politico-military alliance between the MPCI, Mouvement Patriotique de Côte d'Ivoire (Patriotic Movement of Côte d'Ivoire), and two western groups: the MJP and MPIGO, Mouvement Pour la Justice et la Paix (Movement for Justice and Peace) and Mouvement Populaire Ivoirien du Grand Ouest (Ivorian Popular Movement for the Far West).

5. It was at such a checkpoint that the vehicle in which anthropologist Mike McGovern was traveling stopped and where he witnessed the remarkable capitulation of armed forces to the threat of FGP made by elderly women (see chapter 5).

6. The Dozos are a "traditional hunter brotherhood that has existed in several West African countries for centuries. They recruit beyond ethnic and religious lines, although most are Malinke and Muslim" (Boisvert 2013). Some contend that their initiated membership is an ethical force committed to protecting the populace against wanton banditry. Claiming that their tradition forbids harassing, harming, or killing human beings, they patrol regions plagued by tensions ostensibly to defend civilians against criminality. However, in a report in 2013 the UNOCI found that "at least 228 people have been killed, 164 injured and 162 illegally arrested and detained by dozos in several regions of the country between March 2009 and May 2013 [and] that 274 confirmed cases of looting, fire and extortion have been committed by dozos" (Boisvert 2013).

7. Joseph Hellweg's *Hunting the Ethical State* (2011), an ethnography of Dozo hunters, argues that the ethics of Dozo ritual and hunting practices informed their emergence as political actors in Côte d'Ivoire. Ironically, the Dozo were perpetrators of the most reprehensible violence—including sexual violence—and involved in this, the worst massacre in the history of the Ivoirian civil war. Their partisan violence in an effort to seize control of the state is a far cry from the nonviolent rebuke of moral outrage enacted by the Mothers. Their moral grounding is far from comparable.

8. According to a report by Amnesty International, "Côte d'Ivoire: The Victors' Law," Bro-Grébé was herself a victim of the war, held in a prison in Katiola, in the north, for twenty-eight months. Along with other former ministers who served in Gbagbo's government, she was detained without recognizable criminal offense, access to legal representation or trial (Amnesty International 2013, 58–59).

9. Bro-Grébé's narrative about the rebels turning on each other implies that they did so because they were under the spell of the Mothers' curse.

10. French journalists Stéphane Haumant and Jérome Pin were present at the events as reporters for the French satellite TV channel Canal+. Their documentary film based on their footage as well as that obtained from Ivoirian journalists from Radio-télévision Ivoirienne (RTI), entitled "Black Tuesday of the French Army," witnesses to the violence and confirms that civilians were unarmed and that the French attacks on protestors on the

bridge and at the Hôtel Ivoire were unprovoked. The film was first shown at the Human Rights Film Festival in March of 2004 (cf. Aymard 2011).

11. It is worth noting that these women were largely from northern ethnic groups in which most identify as Muslim. That is, the phenomenon of FGP is not only a southern tradition, restricted to women belonging to matrilineal traditions.

7. MEMORY, MEMORIALIZATION, AND MORALITY

1. Gérard Mickel and Fatimata Mbaye headed the international commission investigating human rights abuses in Côte d'Ivoire in 2006 (Gneproust 2011).

2. Chérif Ousmane was the long-time commander of Forces Nouvelles in Bouaké and was implicated in extrajudicial killings of Liberian and Sierra Leonean mercenaries in 2004. He led Republican forces in the battle for Abidjan in 2011. That year, President Ouattara promoted Ousmane to second-in-command of the presidential security guard, Groupe de sécurité de la présidence de la République (HRW 2011b, 106).

3. Gbagbo's trial began on January 27, 2016.

4. The raid paralleled a brutal incident of postelection violence that preceded Ouattara's installation as president that took place in the town of Duékoué itself. On March 29, 2011, forces loyal to Ouattara captured Duékoué in western Côte d'Ivoire, considered a hub of pro-Gbagbo militia, and viciously retaliated against the populace. According to HRW, throughout their military offensive, the forces committed rape, executed civilians including women, children, and elderly, and razed villages. HRW as well as UN Operations in CI (UNOCI) identified Amandé Ouérémi as one of the commanders responsible for the massacre, fighting alongside Republican forces (Wells 2012). See reference to this incident and further comment on it in chapter 6 and in that chapter's endnote 7.

5. Côte d'Ivoire is a signatory of The Rome Statute of the International Criminal Court of 1998 that defines rape, sexual slavery, enforced prostitution, enforced sterilization, forced pregnancy, and any other form of sexual violence as war crimes, and when conducted as part of a systematic attack against a civilian population, as crimes against humanity (UNHCR 2007). In 1989 Côte d'Ivoire ratified *Article 4 of Additional Protocol II to the Geneva Conventions*, which prohibits violations of human rights, including acts of violence against women, namely "outrages upon personal dignity, in particular humiliating and degrading treatment, rape, enforced prostitution and any form of indecent assault; slavery and the slave trade in all its forms" (UNHCR 2007). It also has signed the *Protocol to the African Charter on Human and Peoples' Rights on the Rights of Women in Africa*, adopted by the African Union in 2003, obliging signatory states to prohibit all forms of violence against women and protect them in armed conflicts.

6. This "radical break with the past" is reminiscent of the style and call of Pentecostal Christian churches in Africa today that also foster a deliberate personal and cultural amnesia by calling for a rupture with any association with indigenous tradition, demonized as the cauldron of the diabolical works of witches and heathens. Such a narrative disavows Africa's cultural past as a literally "primitive" one in the classically denigrating sense of the term (cf. Meyer 1998).

7. The actual inscription reads, "'À nos vaillantes femmes qui par leur marche historique sur la prison de Grand-Bassam le 24 12 1949 ont arraché la liberté confisquée des hommes' le 06 02 1998 Maire F. Ablé."

8. Surprisingly, this reduction of FGP as a theatrical performance and representation of African cultural heritage was, in fact, organized recently in francophone Switzerland. An advertisement of the Association Vaudoise de danse contemporaine (AVDC) called for auditions for a spectacle to be entitled "Legacy," and reads, "Nadia Beugré invites 10 dancers of the greatest possible diversity of age and background to participate in the creation of a professional full-time and paid group, leading to the experience of a scenic presentation, at once singular and highly legitimate! Inspired by the march of Bassam (1949), during which Ivoirian compatriots were beaten, and the determination of the Ghanian queen Pokou (XVIII c) who sacrificed her son to enable the survival of her people, Nadia Beugré will work with the participants around the idea that the 'women are on the march' in the service of a cause, an ideology, a people . . . the participants will also be initiated to the 'Adjanou' dance, a sacred dance that African women practice in situations of grave conflict by stripping naked" (AVDC 2013).

9. Elsewhere I take up more extensively the theme of the logocentricity of the academy and the impossibility of representation of the subaltern through language (Grillo, 2013).

10. The Harrists are followers of a local prophet who foretold the arrival of Christian missionaries, and while they consider themselves Christian, their practice is a syncretic blend of indigenous traditions with Christianity.

11. The divided opinion is certainly related to the current discourse about gender and power that is shaping Christianity and Islam on the continent. Such matters are, however, beyond the scope of this discussion.

12. The term *ethnopornography* refers to "the synergy of sexuality and violence in the cultural process of colonialist observation and exploitation" (*Humanities and Social Sciences Online* 2013). In the past decade anthropological scholarship has increasingly come under scrutiny and has been critiqued for extending the legacy of the "ethnographic gaze" that objectified the other, and doing so by exposing the (colonized) bodies of others in voyeuristic and sexual manner in the guise of "purporting to know the intimate (or the 'authentic')" (*Humanities and Social Sciences Online* 2013).

CONCLUSION. AN INTIMATE REBUKE

The *kodjo* is the traditional female undergarment; the color refers to menstrual blood, which it is also intended to camouflage.

References

28TooMany.org. 2014. "28 Too Many (2014) Country Profile: FGM in Liberia." Accessed March 1, 2017. http://www.28toomany.org/countries/liberia/.

Adédé, Schadé. 2011. "Destruction de Monuments de la Ville d'Abidjan: Quand la Superstition Prend le Pouvoir en Côte d'Ivoire." *Le Blog de Aymard,* June 1. Accessed August 16, 2015. https://aymard.wordpress.com/2011/06/01/destruction-de-monuments -de-la-ville-d%e2%80%99abidjan-quand-la-superstition-prend-le-pouvoir-en-cote -d%e2%80%99ivoire/.

Adler, Alfred. 2007. "Initiation, Royauté et Fémininité en Afrique Noire: En Deça ou Au-Delà de la Difference des Sexes: Logique Politique ou Logique Initiatique?" *L'Homme* 183:77–115.

Adriel. 2012. "Côte d'Ivoire: Alassane Ouattara Dribble les Génies!" Koaci Infos, February 4. Accessed March 15, 2015. http://koaci.com/cote-divoire-alassane-ouattara -dribble-genies—72995.html.

AFP. 2015. *Côte d'Ivoire: Des Femmes Réunies en Soutien à Gbagbo.* Accessed August 6, 2015. http://video-streaming.orange.fr/actu-politique/cote-d-ivoire-des-femmes-reunies-en -soutien-a-gbagbo-VID0000000AHQO.html.

Aidoo, Agnes A. 1977. "Order and Conflict in the Asante Empire: A Study in Interest Group Relations." *African Studies Review* 20 (1): 1–36.

Akyeampong, Emmanuel, and Pashington Obeng. 2005. "Spirituality, Gender and Power in Asante History." In Oyewùmí, *African Gender Studies,* 23–48.

Al-Kassim, Dina. 2008. "Archiving Resistance: Women's Testimony at the Threshold of the State." *Cultural Dynamics* 20 (2): 167–92.

Amadiume, Ifi. 1987. *Male Daughters, Female Husbands: Gender and Sex in an African Society.* London: Zed, 1987.

Amadiume, Ifi. 1997. *Re-Inventing Africa: Matriarchy, Religion, and Culture.* Black Women Writers. London: Zed.

Amadiume, Ifi. 2002. "Bodies, Choices, Globalizing Neocolonial Enchantments: African Matriarchs and Mammy Water." *Meridians* 2 (2): 41–66.

Amadiume, Ifi. 2005. "Theorizing Matriarchy in Africa: Kinship Ideologies and Systems in Africa and Europe." In Oyewùmí, *African Gender Studies,* 83–98.

Amnesty International. 2006. "Côte d'Ivoire: Clashes between Peacekeeping Forces and Civilians: Lessons for the Future." Index number: AFR 31/005/2006. September 18. Accessed July 30, 2015. https://www.amnesty.org/en/documents/afr31/005/2006/en/.

Amnesty International. 2007. "Cote d'Ivoire—Targeting Women: The Forgotten Victims of the Conflict." March 15. Accessed July 5, 2013. http://www.refworld.org/docid /45ffa4dd2.html.

Amnesty International. 2013a. "Côte d'Ivoire: Revenge and Repression under the Pretense of Ensuring Security." February 26. Accessed July 19, 2015. https://www.amnesty .org/en/latest/news/2013/02/c-te-d-ivoire-revenge-and-repression-under-pretence -ensuring-security/.

Amnesty International. 2013b. "Côte d'Ivoire: The Victor's Law: The Human Rights Situation Two Years after the Post-Electoral Crisis." London, February. Accessed August 9, 2015. https://www.amnesty.org/en/documents/afr31/001/2013/en/.

Anctogo.com. 2013. "Les Femmes Togolaises Manifestent Leur Inquiétude et Leur Colère à Travers les Rues de Lomé." May 22. Accessed March 22, 2017. http://www.anctogo .com/les-femmes-togolaises-manifestent-leur-inquietude-et-leur-colere-a-travers-les -rues-de-lome-10376.

Anderson, Benedict. 1991. *Imagined Communities: Reflections on the Origin and Spread of Nationalism*. London: Verso.

Antze, Paul, and Paul Lambek, eds. 1996. *Tense Past: Cultural Essays in Trauma and Memory*. New York: Routledge.

Appadurai, Arjun. 1995. "The Production of Locality." In *Counterworks: Managing the Diversity of Knowledge*, edited by R. Fardon, 204–25. ASA Decennial Conference series "The Uses of Knowledge: Global and Local Relations." London: Routledge.

Appadurai, Arjun. 1999. "Dead Certainty: Ethnic Violence in the Era of Globalization." In *Globalization and Identity: Dialectics of Flow and Closure*, edited by Birgit Meyer and Peter Geschiere, 305–24. Oxford: Blackwell.

Apter, Andrew H. 2007. *Beyond Words: Discourse and Critical Agency in Africa*. Chicago: University of Chicago Press.

Apter, Andrew H. 2012. "Matrilineal Motives: Kinship, Witchcraft, and Repatriation among Congolese Refugees." *Journal of the Royal Anthropological Institute* 18 (1): 22–44.

Araoye, Lasisi Ademola. 2012. *Côte d'Ivoire: The Conundrum of a Still Wretched of the Earth*. Trenton, NJ: Africa World Press.

Ardener, Shirley G. 1973. "Sexual Insult and Female Militancy." *Man* 8 (3): 422–40.

Ardener, Shirley G. 1975. *Perceiving Women*. London: Malaby.

Arens, W., and Ivan Karp, eds. 1989. *Creativity of Power: Cosmology and Action in African Societies*. Washington, DC: Smithsonian Institution Press.

Assmann, Jan. 2006. *Religion and Cultural Memory: Ten Studies*. Stanford, CA: Stanford University Press.

Augé, Marc. 1976. "Savoir Voir et Savoir Vivre: Les Croyances à la Sorcellerie en Côte d'Ivoire." *Africa: Journal of the International African Institute* 46 (2): 128–36.

AVDC. 2013. "AVDC: Association Vaudoise de Danse Contemporaine: Auditions." August 30. Accessed August 2, 2015. http://www.avdc.ch/wq_pages/fr/agenda/auditions.php.

Awasom, Sussana Yene. 2005. "Anlu and Takubeng: The Adaptation of Traditional Female Political Institutions to Modern Politics in Cameroon." In *Tradition and Politics: Indigenous Political Structures in Africa*, edited by Olufemi Vaughan, 353–63. Trenton, NJ: Africa World Press.

Aymard. 2011. *L'armée Française ouvre les massacres en Côte d'Ivoire . . . partie 1.mp4*. January 4. Accessed August 2, 2015. https://www.youtube.com/watch?v=ylZgCoSsIh8.

Badmus, Isiaka Alani. 2009. "Even the Stones Are Burning: Explaining the Ethnic Dimensions of the Civil War in Côte d'Ivoire." *Journal of Social Science* 18 (1): 45–57.

Bal, Mieke. 1999. *Acts of Memory: Cultural Recall in the Present.* Hanover, NH: University Press of New England.

Bannister, Matthew. 2011. "Aya Virginie Touré Interviewed by BBC." *BBC World Service Outlook.* London and Abidjan, December 3. Accessed July 25, 2016. http://www.bbc.co.uk/programmes/pooffojq.

Barnes, Sandra T. 1997. "Gender and the Politics of Support and Protection in Precolonial West Africa." In Kaplan, *Queens, Queen Mothers, Priestesses, and Power*, 1–18.

Bass, Gary J. 2006. "What Really Causes Civil War?" *New York Times Magazine*, August 13. Accessed August 2, 2015. http://www.nytimes.com/2006/08/13/magazine/13wwln_idealab.html.

Bastian, Misty L. 2000. "Young Converts: Christian Missions, Gender and Youth in Onitsha, Nigeria 1880–1929." *Anthropological Quarterly* 73 (3): 145–58.

Bastian, Misty L. 2002. "'Vultures of the Marketplace': Southeastern Nigerian Women and Discourses of the Ogu Umanwaanyi (Woman's War) of 1929." In *Women in African Colonial Histories*, edited by Susan Geiger, Nakanyike Musisi, and Jean Marie Allman. Bloomington: Indiana University Press.

Bayart, Jean-François. 1986. "Civil Society in Africa." In Chabal, *Political Domination in Africa*, 109–25.

Bazin, Jean. 1988. "Princes Désarmés, Corps Dangereux: Les 'Rois-Femmes' de la Région de Segu (Disarmed Princes, Dangerous Bodies: 'Women-Kings' in the Segu Area)." *Cahiers d'Études Africaines* 28 (111–12): 375–441.

BBC. 2011. "23/03/2011, Outlook—BBC World Service." March 23. Accessed June 20, 2016. http://www.bbc.co.uk/programmes/pooffojq.

BBC News. 2007. "Ivoirian Women 'Forgotten Victims.'" March 15. Accessed July 4, 2013. http://news.bbc.co.uk/2/hi/africa/6453123.stm.

BBC News. 2011a. "Aya Virginie Touré Interviewed by BBC." *BBC World Service Outlook*, London, December 3. Accessed July 22, 2015. http://www.bbc.co.uk/programmes/pooffojq.

BBC News. 2011b. "Ivory Coast Eyewitness: Women 'Slaughtered by Soldiers.'" March 4. Accessed July 25, 2015. http://www.bbc.co.uk/news/world-africa-12646355.

BBC News. 2011c. "Ivory Coast: Anti-Gbagbo Protesters Killed in Abidjan." *BBC News Africa*, March 8. Accessed November 26, 2011. http://www.bbc.co.uk/news/world-africa-12682492.

BBC News. 2011d. "Ivory Coast: Women 'Shot during Pro-Ouattara March.'" *BBC*, March 3. Accessed July 25, 2015. http://www.bbc.co.uk/news/world-africa-12637088.

BBC News. 2015. "Togo's Faure Gnassingbe Wins Third Term as President." *BBC News*, April 29, sec. Africa. Accessed March 22, 2017. http://www.bbc.com/news/world-africa-32512615.

Bell, Nawal Morcos. 1972. "The Age of Mansa Musa of Mali: Problems in Succession and Chronology." *International Journal of African Historical Studies* 5 (2): 221–34.

Bellman, Beryl Larry. 1984. *The Language of Secrecy: Symbols and Metaphors in Poro Ritual.* New Brunswick, NJ: Rutgers University Press, 1984.

Benavides, Gustavo. 1998. "Modernity." In *Critical Terms for Religious Studies*, edited by Mark C. Taylor, 186–202. Chicago: University of Chicago Press.

Berger, Iris, and E. Frances White. 1999. *Women in Sub-Saharan Africa: Restoring Women to History*. Bloomington: Indiana University Press.

Bewes, Timothy. 2006. "Shame, Ventriloquy, and the Problem of the Cliché in Caryl Phillips." *Cultural Critique* 63:33–60.

Bhabha, Homi K. 1994. *The Location of Culture*. London: Routledge.

Biddick, Kathleen. 1993. "Genders, Bodies, Borders: Technologies of the Visible." *Speculum* 68 (2): 389–418.

Bindé, Jérôme. 2001. "Towards an Ethics of the Future." In *Globalization*, edited by Arjun Appadurai, 90–113. Durham, NC: Duke University Press.

Bledsoe, Caroline. 1980. *Women and Marriage in Kpelle Society*. Stanford, CA: Stanford University Press.

Blier, Suzanne Preston. 1995. *African Vodun: Art, Psychology, and Power*. Chicago: University of Chicago Press, 1995.

Boisvert, Marc-André. 2013. "Local Militias Hold Sway in Cote d'Ivoire's Lawless Duékoué/ Inter Press Service." December 22. Accessed July 23, 2015. http://www.ipsnews.net/2013 /12/local-militias-hold-sway-cote-divoire-lawless-duekoue/.

Bolougbeu, Elisée. 2011. "Une Manifestation de Femmes Dispersée par la Garde Républicaine (Gr)." February. Accessed June 5, 2011. http://www.afreekelection.com/crise/item /3713-article3198.html?tmpl=component&print=1.

Bonai, Cordélia. 2012. "Au Togo, une Grève du Sexe Très Politique." *Libération.fr*, August 28. Accessed March 22, 2017. http://www.liberation.fr/planete/2012/08/28/au -togo-une-greve-du-sexe-tres-politique_842391.

Boni, Stefano. 2008. "Female Cleansing of the Community: The Momome Ritual of the Akan World." *Cahiers D'études Africaines* 4:765–90.

Boone, Sylvia Ardyn. 1986. *Radiance from the Waters: Ideals of Feminine Beauty in Mende Art*. New Haven, CT: Yale University Press, 1986.

Bourdieu, Pierre. *Outline of a Theory of Practice*. Translated by Richard Nice. Cambridge: Cambridge University Press, 1977.

Bro-Grébé, Geneviève. 2004. *Mon Combat pour la Patrie: Mémoires d'une Guerre*. Abidjan-Riviera: PUCI, 2004.

Butler, Beverley. 2007. "'Taking on a Tradition': African Heritage and the Testimony of Memory.'" In *Reclaiming Heritage*, edited by Ferdinand De Jong and M. J. Rowlands, 31–69. Critical Perspectives on Cultural Heritage. Walnut Creek, CA: Left Coast.

Butler, Judith. 1999. *Gender Trouble: Feminism and the Subversion of Identity*. New York: Routledge.

Byaruhanga, Catherine. 2015. "The Ugandan Women Who Strip to Defend Their Land." *BBC News Africa*, June 1. Accessed July 18, 2015. http://www.bbc.com/news/world -africa-32938779.

Callimachi, Rukmini. 2011. "Ivory Coast Forces Kill 6 Women in Protest." *Huffington Post*, March 3. Accessed July 25, 2015. http://www.huffingtonpost.com/2011/03/03 /forces-kill-6-wome . . .

Canal+. 2004. "Côte d'Ivoire: Quatre Jours de Feu." November 30. Accessed July 29, 2015. http://www.telesatellite.com/actu/11744-cote-ivoire-quatre-jours-de-feu-un -reportage-de-canal-revient.html.

Chabal, Patrick, ed. 1986. *Political Domination in Africa: Reflections on the Limits of Power.* Cambridge: Cambridge University Press.

Chauveau, Jean-Pierre. 2001. "La Question Foncière en Côte d'Ivoire et le Coup d'Etat, ou: Comment Remettre à Zéro le Compteur de L'histoire." London: International Institute for Environment and Development.

Chauveau, Jean-Pierre, and Paul Richards. 2008. "West African Insurgencies in Agrarian Perspective: Côte d'Ivoire and Sierra Leone Compared." *Journal of Agrarian Change* 8 (4): 515–52.

Chidester, David. 2004. "'Classify and Conquer': Friedrich Max Müller, Indigenous Religious Traditions, and Imperial Comparative Religion." In *Beyond Primitivism: Indigenous Religious Traditions and Modernity*, edited by Jacob K. Olupona, 71–88. New York: Routledge.

Christaller, J. G. 1879. *Twi Mmebusem Mpensa-Ahansia Mmoano: A Collection of 3600 Tshi Proverbs in Use among the Negroes of the Gold Coast Speaking the Asante and Fante Language.* Basel: Missionsbuchhandlung.

Clifford, James. 1986. *Writing Culture: The Poetics and Politics of Ethnography.* Berkeley: University of California Press.

CNNIC [China Internet Network Information Center]. 2011. "Côte d'Ivoire: Manifestations Séparées des Femmes pro-Gbagbo et pro-Ouattara pour Réclamer la Paix dans le Pays Plongé dans la Violence (SYNTHESE)." March 8. Accessed August 6, 2016. http://french.news.cn/afrique/2011-03/09/c_13768297.htm.

CNN Wire Staff. 2011. "International Women's Day: Defiant Women March at Site of Grisly Killings.'" CNN World—Africa, March 9. Accessed November 26, 2011. http://articles.cnn.com/2011-03-09/world/ivory.coast.women_1_abidjan-ivory-coast-laurent -gbagbo?_s=PM:WORLD.

Cole, Catherine M., Takyiwaa Manuh, and Stephan F. Miescher, eds. 2007. *Africa after Gender?* Bloomington: Indiana University Press.

Comaroff, John L., and Jean Comaroff. 1999. *Civil Society and the Political Imagination in Africa: Critical Perspectives.* Chicago: University of Chicago Press.

Cossette, Ritha. 2013. *Éthique de la communication appliquée aux relations publiques.* Québec City, Canada: Presses de l'Université de Québec.

Cramer, Christopher. 2006. *Civil War Is Not a Stupid Thing: Accounting for Violence in Developing Countries.* London: Hurst.

Csordas, Thomas J. 2013. "Morality as a Cultural System?" *Current Antrhopology* 54 (5): 523–46.

Daily Independent. 2015. "Women Protest Naked in Ekiti." March. Accessed July 11, 2015. http://dailyindependentnig.com/2015/03/women-protest-naked-ekiti/.

Dankwa, Serena Owusua. 2005. "'Shameless Maidens': Women's Agency and the Mission Project in Akuapem." *Agenda* 63:104–16.

De Jong, Ferdinand, and M. J. Rowlands. 2007. *Reclaiming Heritage: Alternative Imaginaries of Memory in West Africa.* Walnut Creek, CA: Left Coast.

Delafosse, M. 1913. "Coutumes Observées par les Femmes en Temps de Guerre Chez les Agnis de Côte d'Ivoire." *Revue d'Ethnographie et de Sociologie* 4:266–68.

Delanne, Philippe, Viviane Froger-Fortaillier, Bernardine Biot Kouao, and Martin Aka Kouadio, eds. 2009. *Arts au Féminin en Côte d'Ivoire.* Paris: Le Cherche midi.

Devisch, René. 1995. "Frenzy, Violence, and Ethical Renewal in Kinshasa." *Public Culture* 7 (3): 593–629.

Diallo. 2011. "La Famille Boigny Indignée: 'La Résidence d'Houphouët est Devenue une Poudrière.'" *Abidjan.net Nord-Sud*, September 2. Accessed June 5, 2011. http://news .abidjan.net/article/imprimer.asp?n=390744.

Diduk, Susan. 1989. "Women's Agricultural Production and Political Action in the Cameroon Grassfields." *Africa: Journal of the International African Institute* 59 (3): 338–55.

Diduk, Susan. 2004. "The Civility of Incivility: Grassroots Political Activism, Female Farmers, and the Cameroon State." *African Studies Review* 47 (2): 27–54.

Dikeblé, Joséphine, and Madeleine Hiba. 1975. "La Femme dans la Vie Politique Traditionalle des Sociétés à Etat du Centre, de L'est et du Sud-Est de la Côte d'Ivoire." In *La Civilisation de la Femme dans la Tradition Africaine: Rencontre Organisée par la Société Africaine de Culture.* Paris: Présence Africaine.

Dindé, Fernand. 2011. "Femmes Danseuses D'adjanou de Sakassou." *Regards Croisés: Le Blog de Fernand Dindé*, March 5. Accessed June 5, 2011. http://regardscroises.ivoire -blog.com/tag/femmes+danseuses+d%27adjanou+de+sakassou.

Diop, Cheikh Anta. 1974. *The African Origin of Civilization: Myth or Reality.* New York: L. Hill.

Diop, Cheikh Anta. 1978. *The Cultural Unity of Black Africa: The Domains of Patriarchy and of Matriarchy in Classical Antiquity.* Chicago: Third World.

Djé, Abel. 2012. "Cérémonie de purification de la Cdvr: Banny Convoque les Morts, Désiré Tanoé s'Écroule." *Eburnienews.net*, March 18. Accessed December 10, 2012. http://www .eburnienews.net/index.php/2012/03/ceremonie-de-purification-de-la-cdvr-banny -convoque-les-morts-desire-tanoe-secroule/.

Djibo, Hadiza. 2001. *La Participation des Femmes Africaines à la Vie Politique: Les Exemples du Sénégal et du Niger.* Collection Sociétés Africaines et Diaspora. Paris: Harmattan.

Djinko, Nicole Bancouly. 2003. "'Un Génocide des Baoulé est Mis en oeuvre' Massacre des Danseuses d'adjanou l'unique Rescapée Témoigne." *L'Inter*, March 3. Accessed June 5, 2010. http://www.leconservateur.net/Roi_Baoules.htm.

Douglas, Mary. 1969. "Is Matriliny Doomed in Africa?" In *Man in Africa*, 121–35. London: Tavistock, 1969.

Douglas, Mary. 2004. "Traditional Culture—Let's Hear No More about It." In *Culture and Public Action*, edited by Vijayendra Rao and Michael Walton, 85–109. Stanford, CA: Stanford University Press.

Dozon, Jean-Pierre. 1979. "La Parenté Mise à Nu, ou Pandore Chez les Bete de Côte d'Ivoire (Kinship Laid Bare, or Pandora among the Bete [Ivory Coast])." *Cahiers d'Études Africaines* 19 (73/76): 101–10.

Dozon, Jean-Pierre. 2007. "Les Déchirures Ivoiriennes: Entre Excés et Manque de Transcendance. (French)." *Social Compass* 54 (4): 593–602.

Drewal, Henry. 1977. "Art and the Perception of Women in Yorùbá Culture (L'art et Le Concept de Féminité Dans La Culture Yoruba)." *Cahiers d'Études Africaines* 17 (68): 545–67.

Drewal, Henry John, and Margaret Thompson Drewal. 1983. *Gẹ̀lẹ̀dẹ́: Art and Female Power among the Yoruba.* Bloomington: Indiana University Press.

Drewal, Margaret Thompson. 1992. *Yoruba Ritual: Performers, Play, Agency.* Bloomington: Indiana University Press.

Dreyfus, Hubert L., and Paul Rabinow. 1982. "Interpretive Analytics." In *Michel Foucault: Beyond Structuralism and Hermeneutics*, 104–26. Chicago: University of Chicago Press.

Dubuisson, Daniel. 2003. *The Western Construction of Religion: Myths, Knowledge, and Ideology.* Translated by William Sayers. Baltimore: Johns Hopkins University Press.

Dupire, Marguerite, and J.-L. Boutillier. 1959. "Le Pays Adioukrou et Sa Palmeraie (Basse Côte-d'Ivoire)." *Population* 14 (1): 166–67.

Duval, Philippe. 2003. "Villepin Chahuté à Abidjan." *Le Parisien*, January 4. Accessed July 25, 2015. http://www.leparisien.fr/politique/villepin-chahute-a-abidjan-04-01 -2003-2003705563.php.

Elbadawi, E., and N. Sambanis. 2000. "Why Are There So Many Civil Wars in Africa? Understanding and Preventing Violent Conflict." *Journal of African Economies* 9 (3): 244–69.

Eliade, Mircea. 1968. "Masks: Mythical and Ritual Origins." *Encyclopaedia of World Art.* Vol. 8. New York: McGraw-Hill.

Ellis, Stephen. 2001. "Mystical Weapons: Some Evidence from the Liberian War." *Journal of Religion in Africa* 31 (2): 222.

Ellis, Stephen. 2007. "Witching-Times: A Theme in the Histories of Africa and Europe." In *Imagining Evil: Witchcraft Beliefs and Accusations in Contemporary Africa*, edited by Gerrie ter Haar, 31–53. Trenton, NJ: Africa World Press.

Ellis, Stephen, and Gerrie Ter Haar. 1998. "Religion and Politics in Sub-Saharan Africa." *Journal of Modern African Studies* 36 (2): 175–201.

Ellis, Stephen, and Gerrie Ter Haar. 2004. *Worlds of Power: Religious Thought and Political Practice in Africa.* New York: Oxford University Press, 2004.

Euronews. 2011. "Ivory Coast: Women, the 'Forgotten Victims.'" July 3. Accessed July 25, 2011. http://www.euronews.com/2011/03/07/ivory-coast-women-the-forgotten-victims/.

Evans-Pritchard, E. E. 1929. "Some Collective Expressions of Obscenity in Africa." *Journal of the Royal Anthropological Institute of Great Britain and Ireland* 59:311–31.

Fatton, Robert. 1995. "Africa in the Age of Democratization: The Civic Limitations of Civil Society." *African Studies Review* 38 (2): 67–99.

Fatton, Robert. 1999. "Civil Society Revisited: Africa in the New Millennium." *West Africa Review* 1 (1).

Fauré, Yves. 1993. "Democracy and Realism: Reflections on the Case of Cote d'Ivoire." *Africa: Journal of the International African Institute* 63 (3): 313–29.

FIDH-LIDHO-MIDH. 2013. "Ivory Coast: The Fight against Impunity at a Crossroad." October. Accessed July 19, 2015. https://www.fidh.org/IMG/pdf/cotedivoire617 uk2013basdef.pdf.

FIDH–Worldwide Human Rights Movement. 2013. "Ivory Coast: 43 Women Who Suffered Sexual Violence during the Post-Election Crisis Finally Access Justice." June 3. Accessed July 19, 2015. https://www.fidh.org/International-Federation-for-Human -Rights/Africa/cote-d-ivoire/ivory-coast-43-women-who-suffered-sexual-violence -during-the-post.

Fiéloux, Michèle. 1977. "'Femmes Invisibles' et 'Femmes Muettes': À Propos des Événements Ibo de 1929 ('Invisible' and 'Mute' Women: Concerning the Ibo Riots of 1929)." *Cahiers d'Études Africaines* 17 (65): 189–94.

Fonchingong, Charles C., and Pius T. Tanga. 2007. "Crossing Rural-Urban Spaces: The 'Takumbeng' and Activism in Cameroon's Democratic Crusade." *Cahiers d'Études Africaines* 47 (185): 117–43.

Foucault, Michel. 1977. "Nietzsche, Genealogy, History." In *Language, Counter-Memory, Practice: Selected Essays and Interviews*, edited by D. F. Bouchard, 139–64. Ithaca, NY: Cornell University Press, 1977.

Foucault, Michel, and Colin Gordon. 1980. *Power/Knowledge: Selected Interviews and Other Writings, 1972–1977*. New York: Pantheon.

Foucault, Michel, Paul Rabinow, and D. Rogers. Spotswood Collection. 1984. *The Foucault Reader*. New York: Pantheon.

Fred-Lille. 2011. *Côte d'Ivoire—7 Femmes Tuées lors d'une Manifestation 05-03-2011*. https://www.youtube.com/watch?v=E3HEX9qIpZ4.

Freud, Sigmund. 2003. *The Uncanny*. Translated by David McLintock. London: Penguin Classics.

Friesen, Steven J., ed. 2001. *Ancestors in Post-Contact Religion: Roots, Ruptures, and Modernity's Memory*. Cambridge, MA: Distributed by Harvard University Press for the Center for the Study of World Religions, Harvard Divinity School.

Frindéthié, K. Martial. 2012. "Dancers of Adjanou." March 15. Accessed March 15, 2015. https://frindethie.wordpress.com/tag/dancers-of-adjanou/.

Geertz, Clifford. 1995. *After the Fact: Two Countries, Four Decades, One Anthropologist*. Cambridge, Mass.: Harvard University Press, 1995.

Geschiere, Peter. 1997. *The Modernity of Witchcraft: Politics and the Occult in Postcolonial Africa*. Translated by Peter Geschiere and Janet L Roitman. Charlottesville: University Press of Virginia.

Geschiere, Peter. 2008. "Witchcraft and the State: Cameroon and South Africa; Ambiguities of 'Reality' and 'Superstition.'" *Past and Present*, August 3, 313–35.

Geschiere, Peter. 2013. *Witchcraft, Intimacy, and Trust: Africa in Comparison*. Chicago: University of Chicago Press.

Gibson, Fiona. 2010. "The Akan Queen Mothers in Ghana and the Implications of Covert Gynocracy." Thesis. University of Wales, Cardiff. http://repository.uwic.ac.uk /dspace/handle/10369/924.

Gilbert, Michelle. 1993. "The Cimmerian Darkness of Intrigue: Queen Mothers, Christianity and Truth in Akuapem History." *Journal of Religion in Africa* 23 (1): 2–43. http://dx.doi.org/10.2307/1581154.

Gluckman, Max. *Rituals of Rebellion in South-East Africa*. Manchester, UK: Manchester University Press, 1954.

Gneproust, Marcelline. 2011. "Les Victimes de Guerre de 2002 Veulent Être Prises en Compte." *Fraternité Matin*, July 8. Accessed July 8, 2015. http://www.eboutique .fratmat.info/e-download/Fraternite-Matin-13985-vendredi-08-juillet-2011.pdf.

Godson, K. 2013. "Togo: Une Marche de Femmes Nues du CST/FRAC en Perspective?/Actualité au Togo, Afrique et Monde." *27avril.com, Actualité Au Togo, Afrique et Monde*. April 24. Accessed March 22, 2017. http://www.27avril.com/blog/actualites /politiques/togo-une-marche-de-femmes-nues-du-cst-frac-en-perspective.

Gold Coast Nation. 1913. "Semi-Nude Women Parading." March 27.

Gouegnon, Tierry. 2011. "Côte d'Ivoire: Les Femmes en Première Ligne." *Paris Match*. Accessed August 6, 2015. http://www.parismatch.com/Actu/International/Gbagbo-vs -Ouattara-en-Cote-d-Ivoire-huit-femmes-tuees-trois-autres-morts-a-Abidjan-146681.

GOUV.CI. 2015. "Remise du Rapport Final de la CDVR: Charles Konan Banny Recommande des Journées Nationales de la Mémoire et du Pardon." December 12. Accessed August 9, 2016. http://www.gouv.ci/actualite_1.php?recordID=5153.

Grah Mel, Frédéric. 2010. *Félix Houphouët-Boigny: Biographie*. Vol. 2, *L'épreuve du Pouvoir*. Abidjan: Éd. du CERAP.

Griaule, Marcel, and Germaine Dieterlen. 1965. *Le Renard Pâle*. Paris: Institut d'ethnologie.

Grillo, Laura S. 1999. "African Religions." *Encyclopedia Britannica Online*. Chicago: Encyclopedia Britannica.

Grillo, Laura S. 2009. "Divination: Epistemology, Agency, and Identity in Contemporary Urban West Africa." *Religion Compass* 3:921–34.

Grillo, Laura S. 2010. "'When You Make Sacrifice, No One Is a Stranger': Divination, Sacrifice and Identity among Translocals in the West African Urban Diaspora." In *Religion Crossing Boundaries: Transnational Dynamics in African and the New African Diasporic Religions*, edited by A. Adogame and J. Spickard, 143–64. Religion and Social Order series. Leiden: E. J. Brill.

Grillo, Laura S. 2012. "Female Genital Power in Ritual and Politics: Violation and Deployment." *Cultural Anthropology, Hot Spot Forum*, July 9. http://culanth.org/?q =node/612.

Grillo, Laura S. 2013. "Catachresis in Côte d'Ivoire: Female Genital Power in Religious Ritual and Political Resistance." *Religion and Gender* 3 (2): 188–206.

Grillo, Laura S. 2014. "Ironic Reversals: Gender, Power and Sacrality in Ile-Ife." *Journal of Africana Religions* 2 (4): 465–77.

Gueye, J. B. 2004. "'Sourires de l'Hôtel Ivoire.'" *AbidjanDirect*. Accessed December 3, 2011. http://www.abidjandirect.net/index2.php?page=poli&id=2334.

Guyer, Jane. 1994. "The Spatial Dimensions of Civil Society in Africa: An Anthropologist Looks at Nigeria." In Harbeson, Rothchild, and Chazan, *Civil Society and the State in Africa*, 215–30.

Harbeson, John W., Donald S. Rothchild, and Naomi Chazan, eds. 1994. *Civil Society and the State in Africa*. Boulder, CO: Lynne Rienner.

Hauenstein, Alfred. 1984. "L'eau et les Cours D'eau dans Différents Rites et Coutumes en Afrique Occidentale." *Anthropos* 79 (4/6): 569–85.

Hellweg, Joseph. 2011. *Hunting the Ethical State: The Benkadi Movement of Côte d'Ivoire*. Chicago: University of Chicago Press.

Horton, Robin. 1967. "African Traditional Thought and Western Science." Part I, "From Tradition to Science." *Africa: Journal of the International African Institute* 37 (1): 50–71.

HRW [Human Rights Watch]. 2006. "'Because They Have the Guns . . . I'm Left with Nothing': The Price of Continuing Impunity in Côte d'Ivoire." May 25. Accessed July 6, 2013. http://www.hrw.org.

HRW [Human Rights Watch]. 2007. "'My Heart Is Cut': Sexual Violence by Rebels and Pro-Government Forces in Côte d'Ivoire." August 3. Accessed January 19, 2013. http://www.hrw.org/reports/2007/08/01/my-heart-cut.

HRW [Human Rights Watch]. 2010. "Côte d'Ivoire: Rampant Criminality, Sexual Violence in West." October 22. Accessed March 15, 2015. http://www.hrw.org/news/2010/10/22/c-te-d-ivoire-rampant-criminality-sexual-violence-west.

HRW [Human Rights Watch]. 2011a. "Côte d'Ivoire: Ouattara Forces Kill, Rape Civilians During Offensive." April 9. Accessed July 19, 2015. https://www.hrw.org/news/2011/04/09/cote-divoire-ouattara-forces-kill-rape-civilians-during-offensive.

HRW [Human Rights Watch]. 2011b. "'They Killed Them like It Was Nothing': The Need for Justice for Côte d'Ivoire's Post-Election Crimes." October 5. Accessed August 10, 2015. http://www.hrw.org/sites/default/files/reports/cdi1011webwcover_0.pdf.

HRW [Human Rights Watch]. 2013. "Côte d'Ivoire: 2 Years In, Uneven Progress—Root Causes of Politico-Military Violence Largely Unaddressed." May 21. Accessed July 7, 2013. http://www.hrw.org/news/2013/05/21/cote-d-ivoire-2-years-uneven-progress.

HRW [Human Rights Watch]. 2014. "Côte d'Ivoire: Nowhere to Turn for Protection." December 14. Accessed July 19, 2015. https://www.hrw.org/news/2014/12/15/cote-divoire-nowhere-turn-protection.

HRW [Human Rights Watch]. 2015. "Côte d'Ivoire: Don't Shut Down Investigations. Support Justice for Grave Post-Election Abuses." June 16. Accessed July 19, 2015. https://www.hrw.org/news/2015/06/26/cote-divoire-dont-shut-down-investigations.

Humanities and Social Sciences Online. 2013. "Ethnopornography: Sexuality, Colonialism and Anthropological Knowing." August 28. Accessed January 24, 2016. https://www.h-net.org/announce/show.cgi?ID=206187.

Hunt, Nancy Rose. 1989. "Placing African Women's History and Locating Gender." *Social History* 14 (3): 359–79.

Huyssen, Andreas. 2001. "Present Pasts: Media, Politics, Amnesia." In *Globalization*, edited by Arjun Appadurai, 57–77. Durham, NC: Duke University Press, 2001.

Ifeka-Moller, Caroline. 1973. "'Sitting on a Man: Colonialism and the Lost Political Institutions of Igbo Women': A Reply to Judith Van Allen." *Canadian Journal of African Studies/Revue Canadienne des Études Africaines* 7 (2): 317–18.

Ifeka-Moller, Caroline. 1975. "Female Militancy and Colonial Revolt: The Women's War of 1929, Eastern Nigeria." In *Perceiving Women*, edited by Shirley Ardener. London: Malaby.

Ikeji, Linda. 2009. "Welcome to Linda Ikeji's Blog: Half Naked Ekiti Women Protest." *Welcome to Linda Ikeji's Blog*, April 30. http://lindaikeji.blogspot.com/2009/04/half-naked-ekiti-women-protest.html.

Ina.fr. 2003. "Dominique de Villepin À Abidjan." January 3. Accessed August 6, 2015. http://www.ina.fr/video/2186833001037.

Jambo Jambo News Channel. 2014. *Les Mamans du Kananga Marchent Nues pour Soutenir Leur Gouverneur!* Accessed January 25, 2016. https://www.youtube.com/watch?v =BzgoVFLyiNI.

James, Wendy. 1978. "Matrifocus on African Women." In *Defining Females: The Nature of Women in Society*, edited by Shirley Ardener. New York: Wiley.

Jaspers, Karl. 1976. *The Origin and Goal of History*. Translated by Michael Bullock. Westport, CT: Greenwood Press.

Jeremy. 2009. "Naijablog: Scenes from Today's Naked Protest in Ekiti." April 29. Accessed January 24, 2016. http://www.naijablog.co.uk/2009/04/scenes-from-todays -naked-protest-in.html.

JeuneAfrique.com. 2013. "Togo: Des Femmes S'inspirent des Femen pour Dénoncer le Décès d'un Opposant." May 20. Accessed March 22, 2017. http://www.jeuneafrique .com/170716/politique/togo-des-femmes-s-inspirent-des-femen-pour-d-noncer-le-d-c -s-d-un-opposant/.

Jones, Adam. 1993. "'My Arse for Akou': A Wartime Ritual of Women on the Nineteenth-Century Gold Coast (Un Rituel de Guerre Féminin sur la Côte de l'Or au XIXe Siècle)." *Cahiers d'Études Africaines* 33 (132): 545–66.

Joy, Morny. "Feminist Scholarship: The Challenge to Ethics." In *Life Ethics in World Religions*, 139–56. Atlanta: Scholars Press, 1998.

Joy, Morny. 2001. "Postcolonial Reflections: Challenges for Religious Studies." *Method and Theory in the Study of Religion* 13 (2): 177–95.

Joy, Morny. 2006. "Gender and Religion: A Volatile Mixture." *Temenos* 42 (1): 7–30.

Joy, Morny. 2010. "The Impact of Gender on Religious Studies." *Part of Special Issue: Current Perspectives on Gender Studies* 57 (1): 93–102.

Jung, Carl Gustav. *The Collected Works of C. G. Jung, Volume 11: Psychology and Religion: West and East*. Translated by R. F. C. Hull. Bollingen Series XX. New York: Pantheon, 1958.

Kah, Henry Kam. 2011. "Women's Resistance in Cameroon's Western Grassfields: The Power of Symbols, Organization, and Leadership, 1957–1961." *African Studies Quarterly* 12 (3): 67–91.

Kaplan, Flora Edouwaye S. *Queens, Queen Mothers, Priestesses, and Power: Case Studies in African Gender*. New York: New York Academy of Sciences.

Keita, Outélé. 2015. "Massacre des Femmes d'Abobo: Le Procès des Tenants du Bissap." *Editions Le Pays*, August 6. http://lepays.bf/massacre-des-femmes-dabobo-le-proces -des-tenants-du-bissap/.

Koby Assa, Théophile. 1981. "Le Systeme Spatial de L'odjoukrou." *Annales de l'Université d'Abidjan*. Série G. Geographie, no. 10, 93–114.

Koffi, Daniel Messan. 2012. "Togo: Les Femmes Toujours Mobilisées." December 20. Accessed March 22, 2017. http://www.afrik.com/togo-les-femmes-du-cst-battent-le-pave.

Kopytoff, Igor. 1987. *The African Frontier: The Reproduction of Traditional African Societies*. Bloomington: Indiana University Press.

Kouamé, Rosalie. 2011. "Le Cri de Mon Âme: Yako Maman Côte d'Ivoire!" *Actualités Ivoirian*, May 4. Accessed June 5, 2011. http://actualites.ivorian.net/article/?p=739.

Kouano, Brussi. 2013. "Enfin la Vérité sur le Massacre des Danseuses d'adjanou." *Lebanco .net*, May 27. Accessed March 15, 2015. http://lebanco.net/banconet/bco18109.htm.

Kouevi, Louis. 2013. *Indignées et Furieuses les Femmes du CST, Torse Nu, Hurlent "Attention Faure, Libere Nos Enfants."* May 18. Accessed August 1, 2015. https://www.youtube.com/watch?v=X_W5xURdKZ4.

Label Ivoire. 2011. *La Marche des Femmes de Treichville-Abidjan 24 Fevrier 2011.* March 1. Accessed August 6, 2015. https://www.youtube.com/watch?v=QB1AN-MLrjo.

Lafargue, Fernand. 1970. "Notes sur la Fete de Dipri et le Culte Adressé au Genie de la Rivière á Gomon Village de la Tribu Abidi en Basse Côte d'Ivoire." *VIIme Congres International des Sciences Anthropologiques et Ethnologiques, Moscou* (3–10 Aout 1964) 8: 116–23.

Lafargue, Fernand. 1976. *Religion, Magie, Sorcellerie des Abidji en Côte d'Ivoire.* Paris: Nouvelles Editions Latines.

Lambek, Michael. 1996. "The Past Imperfect: Remembering as Moral Practice." In *Tense Past*, 235–55. New York: Routledge.

Laplantine, François. 2007. *Ethnopsychiatrie Psychanalytique.* Paris: Beauchesne.

La Rédaction. 2014. "Côte d'Ivoire—Les Faiblesses de La CDVR Commission Dialogue, Vérité et Réconciliation." *Connectionivoirienne*, January 15. Accessed August 8 2015. http://www.connectionivoirienne.net/95368/cote-divoire-les-faiblesses-de-la-cdvr-commission-dialogue-verite-reconciliation.

Lassm, L. 1971. "Croyances et Coutumes Adjoukrou." *Bulletin de Liaison—Centre Universitaire de Recherches de Developpement (Abidjan)*, 1: 43–53.

Launay, Robert. 1986. "Reviewed Work: La Société Bété: Côte d'Ivoire, by Jean-Pierre Dozon." *Canadian Journal of African Studies/Revue Canadienne des Études Africaines* 20 (2): 285–87.

Lawrance, Benjamin N. 2003. "La Révolte des Femmes: Economic Upheaval and the Gender of Political Authority in Lomé, Togo, 1931–33." *African Studies Review* 46 (1): 43–67.

Lawuyi, Olatunde Bayo, and Jacob Obafemi Kehinde Olupona. 1987. "Making Sense of the Aje Festival: Wealth, Politics and the Status of Women among the Ondo of Southwestern Nigeria." *Journal of Ritual Studies* 1 (2): 97–109.

Leach, Fiona. 2008. "African Girls, Nineteenth-Century Mission Education and the Patriarchal Imperative." *Gender and Education* 20 (4): 335–47.

Le Mandat. 2011. "Usurpation of Power: The Revolt of Women from the City and Villages." February 17. Accessed June 5, 2011. http://news.abidjan.net/h/391509.html.

Le Monde.fr. 2010. "Le Viol Comme Arme de Guerre: La Double Peine des Femmes." *Blog- Esprit de justice*, November 25. Accessed April 2, 2011. *http://justice-inter.blog.lemonde.fr/2010/11/25/le-viol-comme-arm . . . s/#xtor=EPR-32280229-%5BNL_Titresdujour%5D-20101126-%5Bderoule%5D.*

Le Monde.fr. 2015. "Côte d'Ivoire: Deux Anciens Chefs Rebelles pro-Ouattara Inculpés." July 8. http://www.lemonde.fr/afrique/article/2015/07/08/cote-d-ivoire-deux-anciens-chefs-rebelles-pro-ouattara-inculpes_4675895_3212.html. July 9, 2015.

Le Nouveau Reveil. 2010. "Didiévi: Les Femmes de L'adjanou Font Fuir le Préfet." February 17. Accessed August 13, 2013. http://news.abidjan.net/h/356982.html.

Le Nouveau Reveil. 2011. "Tous les Monuments d'Abidjan Bientôt Détruits/18 Corps Découverts sous le Monument de Siporex (Yopougon)—Actualités #CIV2010." April 20. Accessed August 20, 2015. http://news.abidjan.net/h/396972.html.

LeTogoVi. 2013a. "*Les Togolaises En Appellent aux Ancêtres et aux Divinités pour les Soute-nir [21/05/2013]*." May 21. Accessed January 27, 2016. https://www.youtube.com/watch?v=82iJMcEGFGw.

LeTogoVi. 2013b. "*Libérez Nos Enfants!!! C'est Eux (Les Policiers) qui Tuent nos Enfants à Dapaong*" [18/05/2013]. May 18. Accessed January 25, 2016. https://www.youtube.com/watch?v=RVhpP6aGAg4.

Lévy-Bruhl, Lucien, and Lilian A. Clare. 1926. *How Natives Think (Les Fonctions Mentales dans les Sociétés Inférieures)*. Authorized translation by Lilian A. Clare. London: G. Allen and Unwin.

Lewis, Desiree. 2005. "African Gender Research and Postcoloniality: Legacies and Challenges." In Oyewùmí, *African Gender Studies*.

Long, Charles. 2004. "A Postcolonial Meaning of Religion: Some Reflections from the Indigenous World." In *Beyond Primitivism: Indigenous Religious Traditions and Modernity*, edited by Jacob K. Olupona, 89–98. New York: Routledge.

Lonsdale, John. 1986. "Political Accountability in African History." In Chabal, *Political Domination in Africa*, 126–57.

Lonsdale, John. 2000. "Agency in Tight Corners: Narrative and Initiative in African History." *Journal of African Cultural Studies* 13 (1): 5–16.

Lousse, Franke. "Liste Nominative Des Femmes 'd'Adjanou' Mitraillees a Bout Portant." dialoguonns, July 2013. Accessed March 15, 2015. http://dialoguonns.over-blog.com/liste-nominative-des-femmes-%E2%80%98-d-adjanou-%E2%80%98-mitraillees-a-bout-portant.

MacCormack, Carol P. 1979. "Sande: The Public Face of a Secret Society." In *The New Religions of Africa*, edited by Bennetta Jules-Rosette, 27–37. Norwood, NJ: Ablex.

Marcus, George E. *Ethnography Through Thick and Thin*. Princeton, NJ: Princeton University Press, 1998.

Mbembe, Achille. 1992a. "The Banality of Power and the Aesthetics of Vulgarity in the Postcolony." *Public Culture* 42 (2): 1–30.

Mbembe, Achille. 1992b. "Provisional Notes on the Postcolony." *Africa* (Edinburgh University Press) 62 (1): 3–37.

Mbembe, Achille. 2001. "At the Edge of the World: Boundaries and Territorial Sovereignty in Africa." In *Globalization*, edited by Arjun Appadurai, translated by Steven Rendall, 22–51. Durham, NC: Duke University Press.

McGovern, Mike. 2011. *Making War in Côte d'Ivoire*. London: C. Hurst.

McGovern, Mike. 2012. "Turning the Clock Back or Breaking with the Past?: Charismatic Temporality and Elite Politics in Côte d'Ivoire and the United States." *Cultural Anthropology* 27 (2): 239–60.

Mel, César Djedje. 2015. "[VIDEO] Manifestation Devant la Conariv: Des Victimes de Guerre Battues et Gazées par la Police." *Linfodrome.ci*, October 6. Accessed March 5, 2016. http://www.linfodrome.com/societe-culture/23015-manifestation-devant-la-conariv-des-victimes-de-guerre-battues-et-gazees-par-la-police.

Memel-Fotê, Harris. 1980. *Le Système Politique de Lodjoukrou: Une Société Lignagère à Classes d'Âge (Côte-d'Ivoire)*. Paris: Présence africaine.

Memel-Fotê, Harris, and J. Brunet-Jailly. 2007. *L'esclavage dans les Sociétés Lignagères de la Forêt Ivoirienne, XVIIe-XXe Siècle.* Abidjan: CERAP.

Meyer, Birgit. 1998. "'Make a Complete Break with the Past': Memory and Post-Colonial Modernity in Ghanaian Pentecostalist Discourse." *Journal of Religion in Africa* 28 (3): 316–49.

Mielcarek, Romain. 2015. "Quand les Africaines Utilisent Leur Nudité comme Arme Politique." RFI, April 4. Accessed March 5, 2016. http://www.seneweb.com/news/Afrique /quand-les-africaines-utilisent-leur-nudi_n_151936.html.

"Minority Rights Group International: Côte d'Ivoire: Krou." 2015. *World Directory of Minorities and Indigenous Peoples.* Accessed February 20, 2015. http://www .minorityrights.org/5539/cte-divoire/krou.html.

Mintho, Jacqueline. 2011. "Pour Avoir Été Filmées dans Leur Nudité: Les Danseuses de 'l'Adjanou' Bloquent le Palais Présidentiel." *Abidjan.net*, September 2. Accessed July 25, 2015. http://news.abidjan.net/article/imprimer.asp?n=390724.

M05. 2012. "Manifestation du CST ce Mardi à Lomé: Des Jeunes Femmes Nues en Démonstration devant les Forces de L'ordre." August 28. Accessed March 22, 2017. http://www.icilome.com/nouvelles/news.asp?id=11&idnews=20508.

Mohanty, Chandra Talpade. 2003. *Feminism without Borders: Decolonizing Theory, Practicing Solidarity.* Durham, NC: Duke University Press.

Moore, Henrietta L., and Todd Sanders. 2004. "Magical Interpretations and Material Realities: An Introduction." In *Magical Interpretations, Material Realities: Modernity, Witchcraft and the Occult in Postcolonial Africa*, edited by Henrietta L. Moore and Todd Sanders, 1–27. London: Routledge.

Moran, Mary H. 1989. "Collective Action and the 'Representation' of African Women: A Liberian Case Study." *Feminist Studies* 15 (3): 443–60.

MyJoyOnline.Com. 2017. "Video: Togo Women Go Topless to Demand Resignation of Faure Gnassingbe—MyJoyOnline.Com." Accessed September 8, 2017. https://www .myjoyonline.com/politics/2017/September-6th/video-togo-women-go-topless-to -demand-resignation-of-faure-gnassingbe.php.

Nandy, Ashis. 1983. *The Intimate Enemy: Loss and Recovery of Self under Colonialism.* Delhi: Oxford.

N. B. D. 2003. "'Un Génocide des Baoulé est Mis en Oeuvre': Massacre des Danseuses D'adjanou L'unique Rescapée Témoigne.'" *L'Inter*, March 3. Accessed May 6, 2010. http://www.leconservateur.net/Guie_Roi_baoule.htm.

Neve, Alex, and Amnesty International. 2013. "Côte d'Ivoire: Even Nature Can't Disguise the Past." March 8. Accessed July 19, 2015. https://www.amnesty.org/en/latest /campaigns/2013/03/c%C3%B4te-d-ivoire-even-nature-can-t-disguise-the-past/.

N'Guessan, Issiaka. "Côte d'Ivoire: Trois Ans Après, Duékoué entre Ombre et Lumière." *JeuneAfrique.com.* Accessed July 25, 2015. http://www.jeuneafrique.com/133941 /politique/c-te-d-ivoire-trois-ans-apr-s-du-kou-entre-ombre-et-lumi-re/.

Ngoundoung, Julienne. 1999. "'Le Redoutable Sexe Opposé': Chez les Tikar de Nditam, Cameroun Central." In *Femmes Plurielles: Les Représentations des Femmes Discours, Norme et Conduites*, edited by Danielle Jonckers, Renée Carré, and Marie-Claude Dupré. Paris: Ed. de la Maison des Sciences de l'Homme.

Niangoran-Bouah, Georges. 1964. *La Division du Temps et le Calendrier Rituel des Peuples Lagunaires de Côte d'Ivoire*. Paris: Travaux et mémoires de l'Institut d'Ethnologie.

Niangoran-Bouah, Georges. 1973. "Symboles Institutionnels Chez Les Akan." *L'Homme* 13 (1/2): 207–32.

N'Zi, Serge Nicolas. 2010. "Voyage aux Sources du Patriotisme et du Nationalisme Ivoirien/ConnectionIvoirienne.net." February 7. Accessed July 25, 2015. http://www.connectionivoirienne.net/45410/cote-divoire-le-national-patriotisme-et-la-presidentielle.

O. A. M. 2011. "Justice: Les Tueurs des Danseuses d'Adjanou Récompensés." *Yako Cote d'Ivoire*, July. Accessed November 25, 2011. http://yakocotedivoire.over-blog.com/article-justice-les-tueurs-d . . . 1 of.

Ogbomo, Onaiwu W. 2005. "Women, Power and Society in Pre-Colonial Africa." *Lagos Historical Review: A Journal of the Department of History, University of Lagos* 5:49–74.

Ogwang, Tom. 2011. "The Root Causes of the Conflict in Ivory Coast." *Africa Portal*, April. Accessed February 8, 2015. www.africaportal.org/articles.

Okonjo, Kamene. 1976. "The Dual-Sex Political System in Operation: Igbo Women and Community Politics in Midwestern Nigeria." In *Women in Africa: Studies in Social and Economic Change*, edited by Nancy J. Hafkin and Edna G. Bay, 45–58. Stanford, CA: Stanford University Press, 1976.

Olupọna, Jacob Obafemi Kehinde. 1991. *Kingship, Religion and Rituals in a Nigerian Community*. Stockholm, Sweden: Almqvist and Wiksell International.

Olupọna, Jacob Obafemi Kehinde. 1997. "Women's Rituals, Kingship and Power among the Ondo-Yoruba of Nigeria." In Kaplan, *Queens, Queen Mothers, Priestesses, and Power*, 315–36.

Olupọna, Jacob Obafemi Kehinde. 2001. "To Praise and to Reprimand: Ancestors and Spirituality in African Society and Culture." In *Ancestors in Post-Contact Religion*, edited by Steven J. Friesen, 49–71. Cambridge, MA: Harvard University Press.

Olupọna, Jacob Obafemi Kehinde, ed. 2004. *Beyond Primitivism: Indigenous Religious Traditions and Modernity*. New York: Routledge.

Olupọna, Jacob Obafemi Kehinde. 2005. "Imagining the Goddess: Gender in Yorùbá Religious Traditions and Modernity." *Dialogue and Alliance* 18 (2): 71–86.

Olupọna, Jacob Obafemi Kehinde. 2011. *City of 201 Gods: Ilé-Ifè in Time, Space, and the Imagination*. Berkeley: University of California Press.

ONG—Action pour la Protection des Droits Humains [APDH]. 2015. "Côte d'Ivoire: Une Justice Transitionnelle . . . Piegée? Rapport Justice Transitionnelle Definitif." Accessed August 2, 2015. http://www.apdhci.org/images/documents_pdf/rapports/rapport%20justice%20transitionnelle%20definitif%20.pdf.

Oyewùmí, Oyèrónké. 1997a. *The Invention of Women: Making an African Sense of Western Gender Discourses*. Minneapolis: University of Minnesota Press.

Oyewùmí, Oyèrónké. 1997b. "Visualizing the Body: Western Theories and African Subjects." In *The Invention of Women: Making an African Sense of Western Gender Discourses*, 1–30. Minneapolis: University of Minnesota Press.

Oyewùmí, Oyèrónké, ed. 2005a. *African Gender Studies: A Reader*. New York: Palgrave Macmillan.

Oyewùmí, Oyèrónké. 2005b. "(Re) Constituting the Cosmology and Sociocultural Institutions of Oyo-Yoruba: Articulating the Yoruba World-Sense." In Oyewùmí, *African Gender Studies*, 99–119.

Pernet, Henry. 1992. *Ritual Masks: Deceptions and Revelations*. Translated by Laura S. Grillo. Columbia: University of South Carolina Press.

Perrot, Claude-Hélène. 1979. "Femmes et Pouvoir Politique dans L'ancienne Société Anyi-Ndenye (Côte d'Ivoire) [Women and Political Power in the Old Anyi-Ndenye Society)]." *Cahiers d'Études Africaines* 19 (73/76): 219–23.

Perrot, Claude-Hélène. 1982. "Formation d'États et Formation d'une Ethnie: Le Cas des Anyi-Ndenye [State Formation and Formation of an Ethnic Group: The Case of the Ndenye Anyi]." *Cahiers d'Études Africaines* 22 (87/88): 455–63.

Perrot, Claude-Hélène. 1987. "La Sensibilité des Sociétés Akan du Sud-Est de la Côte d'Ivoire aux Fluctuations Démographiques [The Influence of Demographic Fluctuations on the Akan Societies of South-Eastern Ivory Coast]." *Cahiers d'Études Africaines* 27 (105/106): 167–75.

Perrot, Claude-Hélène. 1996. "Genies and Humans in Anyi Country (Ivory Coast): Constraining Relations or Negotiable Exchanges?" *Social Compass* 43 (2): 171–78.

Perrot, Claude-Hélène. 2005. "L'importation du "Modèle" Akan par les Anyi au Ndenye et au Sanwi (Côte d'Ivoire)." *Journal des Africanistes* 75 (1): 139–62.

Piccolino, Giulia. 2012. "David against Goliath in Côte d'Ivoire? Laurent Gbagbo's War against Global Governance." *African Affairs* 111 (442): 1–23.

Piot, Charles. 1999. *Remotely Global: Village Modernity in West Africa*. Chicago: University of Chicago Press, 1999.

Pritchard, Annette, Eleri Jones, and Fiona Gibson. 2010. *The Akan Queen Mothers in Ghana and the Implications of Covert Gynocracy*. Cardiff: University of Wales Cardiff School of Management.

Prouteaux, Maurice. 1921. "Le Culte de Séké dans la Basse Côte d'Ivoire." *Revue D'ethnographie et des Traditions Populaires Annee* 2:166–87.

Rabinow, Paul, and George E. Marcus, with James D. Faubion and Tobias Rees. 2008. *Designs for an Anthropology of the Contemporary*. Durham, NC: Duke University Press, 2008.

Radhakrishnan, R. 1993. "Postcoloniality and Boundaries of Identity." *Callaloo* 16 (4): 750–71.

Radiosun. 2011. "Manifestations des Femmes Danseuses d'Adjanou Violemment Disperses." February 24. Accessed November 29, 2011. http://www.radiosun.fr/sun-news /5760-abidjan-manifestation-de.

Ramseyer, F., and J. Kühne. 1875. "Vier Jahre in Asante: Tagebucher der Missionare Ramseyer und Kuhne aus der Zeit ihrer Gefangenschaft." Edited by H. Gundert. Basel: Berlag des Missionskompoirs.

Rattray, R. S. [1923] 1969. *Ashanti*. Oxford: Clarendon.

re.ivoire-blog.com. 2015. "Pourquoi Nous Avons Détruit Tous les Monuments Bâtis sous Gbagbo." Accessed August 20, 2015. http://re.ivoire-blog.com/archive/2015/04/06 /pourquoi-nous-avons-detruit-tous-les-monuments-batis-sous-g-458921.html.

Reticker, Gini. 2008. *Pray the Devil Back to Hell*. DVD. http://www.forkfilms.net/pray -the-devil-back-to-hell/.

Rezo-Ivoire.net. 2005. "La Référence Culturelle de la Côte d'Ivoire." Accessed June 18, 2015. http://www.rezoivoire.net/cotedivoire/patrimoine/155/le-dipri-de-gomon.html#.V2WA007C14s.

RFI. 2011. "Côte d'Ivoire: Démolition de Statues et Monuments de L'ère Gbagbo." *RFI Afrique*, April 25. Accessed June 17, 2016. http://www.rfi.fr/afrique/20110425-cote -ivoire-demolition-statues-monuments-ere-gbagbo.

Richards, David. 2007. "Another Architecture." In *Classics in Post-Colonial Worlds*, edited by Lorna Harwick and Carol Gillespie, 349–409. Classical Presences. Oxford: Oxford University Press.

Ritzenthaler, Robert E. 1960. "Anlu: A Women's Uprising in the British Cameroons." *African Studies* 19 (3): 151–56.

Röschenthaler, Ute. 1993. *Die Kunst der Frauen: Zur Komplementarität von Nacktheit und Maskierung bei den Ejagham im Südwesten Kameruns*. Berlin: Verlag für Wissenschaft und Bildung.

Röschenthaler, Ute. 1998. "Honoring Ejagham Women." *African Arts* 31 (2): 38–49, 92–93.

Rosen, David M. 1983. "The Peasant Context of Feminist Revolt in West Africa." *Anthropological Quarterly* 56 (1): 35–43.

Rosenthal, John. 2005. "The Black Tuesday of the French Army." *TCS Daily*, November 8. Accessed July 30, 2015. http://www.ideasinactiontv.com/tcs_daily/2005/11/the-black -tuesday-of-the-french-army.html.

Rowlands, M. J., and Ferdinand De Jong. 2007. "Reconsidering Heritage and Memory." In *Reclaiming Heritage: Alternative Imaginaries of Memory in West Africa,* edited by Ferdinand De Jong and M. J. Rowlands, 13–27. Walnut Creek, CA: Left Coast.

Said, Edward W. 1989. "Representing the Colonized: Anthropology's Interlocutors." *Critical Inquiry* 15 (2): 205–25.

Scott, Joan Wallach. 1999. *Gender and the Politics of History*. Rev. Gender and Culture. New York: Columbia University Press.

Sembou, Evangelia. 2011. "Foucault's Genealogy." International Social Theory Consortium. University College, Cork, Ireland. Accessed July 15, 2014. http://www.academia .edu/679231/_Foucaults_Genealogy_.

Shipley, Jesse Weaver, Jean Comaroff, and Achille Mbembe. 2010. "Africa in Theory: A Conversation between Jean Comaroff and Achille Mbembe." *Anthropological Quarterly* 83 (3): 653–78.

Silué, Oumar. 2008. "Marche des Femmes Contre la Flambée des Prix en Côte d'Ivoire. Mourir de Faim ou d'une Balle dans la Tête?" *Les Billets de Silué*, April 3. Accessed April 24, 2010. http://silweyinfoblogspotcom.blogspot.com/2008/04/marche-des -femmes-contre-la-flambe-des_03.html.

Silva, Sónia. 2011. *Along an African Border: Angolan Refugees and Their Divination Baskets*. Contemporary Ethnography. Philadelphia: University of Pennsylvania Press.

Smith, David. 2011. "Ivory Coast Women Defiant after Being Targeted by Gbagbo's Guns." *Guardian*, March 11. Accessed June 5, 2011. https://www.theguardian.com /world/2011/mar/11/ivory-coast-women-defiant.

Sorokobi, Ives. 1999. "National Identity Politics Threaten to Destabilize the Ivory Coast." *New York Amsterdam News*, September 3.

Spivak, Gayatri. 1988. "Can the Subaltern Speak?" In *Marxism and the Interpretation of Culture*, edited by Cary Nelson, 271–316. Urbana: University of Illinois Press, 1988.

Spivak, Gayatri. 1990. "Poststructuralism, Marginality, Postcoloniality and Value." In *Literary Theory Today*. Ithaca, NY: Cornell University Press.

Steger, Manfred B. 2008. *The Rise of the Global Imaginary: Political Ideologies from the French Revolution to the Global War on Terror*. Oxford: Oxford University Press.

Stevens, Phillips, Jr. 2006. "Women's Aggressive Use of Genital Power in Africa." *Transcultural Psychiatry* 43 (4): 592–99.

Stoeltje, Beverly J. 1997. "Asante Queen Mothers: A Study in Female Authority." In Kaplan, *Queens, Queen Mothers, Priestesses, and Power*, 41–71.

Strobel, Margaret. 1982. "African Women's History." *History Teacher* 15 (4): 509–22.

Taky, F. 2014. "Hommage Aux Danseuses d'Adjanou: Assassinées Pour Avoir Dansé." Le blog de bouanzitaky.over-blog.com, May 22. Accessed July 11, 2015. http://bouanzitaky .over-blog.com/article-hommage-aux-danseuses-d-adjanou-assassinees-pour-avoir -danse-123699829.html.

Tanoh, Benoît. 2003. "Loi D'amnistie: Les Femmes, Victimes de Guerre, Prêtes à Marcher sur l'Assemblée Nationale." Politique. *Mediaf: Le Réseau des Médias Francophones*, August. Accessed July 5, 2015. http://mediaf.org/?p=184.

Ter Haar, Gerrie. 2007. *Imagining Evil: Witchcraft Beliefs and Accusations in Contemporary Africa*. Trenton, NJ: Africa World Press.

Terretta, Meredith. 2007. "A Miscarriage of Revolution: Cameroonian Women and Nationalism." *Stichproben: Wiener Zeitschrift für Kritische Afrikastudien* 12 (7): 61–96.

Thomann, Georges. 1903. *De La Côte d'Ivoire Au Soudan Français. Renseignements Coloniaux et Documents 1*. Paris: Bulletin du comité de l'Afrique Française.

Thompson, Robert Farris, and Frederick S. Wight Art Gallery. 1974. *African Art in Motion*. Los Angeles: University of California Press.

TogoVisions. 2013a. *Contre L'injustice et L'impunité au Togo, des Femmes Manifestent à Moitié Dénudées*. Accessed January 25, 2016. Togo: TogoVisions. https://www.youtube .com/watch?v=VDb5kPLJBgU.

TogoVisions. 2013b. *Les Femmes de Bè se Dénudent pour Exprimer Leur Colère Contre les Abus Policiers*. January 11. Accessed January 25, 2016. https://www.youtube.com/watch ?v=jhFxacUdLTw.

Toh, Nemlin François, N'guessan Donatien Yah, Fonon Fatogoma Yeo, and Ouagnon-fèhè Amara Yeo. 2013. "Les Premiers Habitants de la Côte d'Ivoire." Exposé Universitaire. Travaux dirigés Group 09 and 10. Abidjan: Université Alassane Ouattara.

Toungara, Jeanne Maddox. 2001. "Changing the Meaning of Marriage: Women and Family Law in Côte d'Ivoire." In *Gender Perspectives on Property and Inheritance: A Global Source Book*, edited by Sarah Cummings, 33–51. Amsterdam: KIT.

Tripp, Aili Mari, Isabel Casimiro, Joy Kwesiga, and Alice Mungwa. 2008. *African Women's Movements: Transforming Political Landscapes*. Cambridge: Cambridge University Press.

Turner, Victor W. 1969. *The Ritual Process: Structure and Anti-Structure*. Chicago: Aldine.

UNESCO. 2016. "Text of the Convention for the Safeguarding of the Intangible Cultural Heritage—Intangible Heritage—Culture Sector." Accessed January 19, 2016. http:// www.unesco.org/culture/ich/en/convention.

UNHCR. 2007. "Cote d'Ivoire—Targeting Women: The Forgotten Victims of the Conflict." *Refworld*. Accessed July 25, 2015. http://www.refworld.org/docid/45ffa4dd2 .html.

UNPF [United Nations Population Fund]. 2007. *Ivoiriennes aujourd'hui*. Edited by Moussa Touré, Anna Manouan, and Viviane Froger-Fortaillier. Saint-Maur-des-Fossés: Editions SEPIA, 2007.

Valliere, Paul. 2005. "Tradition." In *Encyclopedia of Religion*, 2nd ed., edited by Lindsay Jones, 9267–80. New York: Macmillan Reference USA, 2005.

van Allen, Judith. 1972. "'Sitting on a Man': Colonialism and the Lost Political Institutions of Igbo Women." *Canadian Journal of African Studies/Revue Canadienne des Études Africaines* 6 (2): 165–81.

van Binsbergen, Wim. 1999. "Globalization and Virtuality: Analytical Problems Posed by the Contemporary Transformation of African Societies." In *Globalization and Identity: Dialectics of Flow and Closure*, edited by Birgit Meyer and Peter Geschiere, 273–303. Oxford: Blackwell.

van Dijk, Rijk. 1998. "Pentecostalism, Cultural Memory and the State: Contested Representations of Time in Postcolonial Malawi." In *Memory and the Postcolony*, edited by Richard Werbner, 155–81. London: Zed.

Village de Grand-Alépé. 2012. "La Génération ou Foqué." Accessed June 17, 2016. http://www.village-de-grandalepe.com/culture/?vue=organisation.

Visonà, Monica Blackmun. 2010. *Constructing African Art Histories for the Lagoons of Côte d'Ivoire*. Farnham, UK: Ashgate.

Vogel, Susan Mullin, and Yale University Art Gallery. 1997. *Baule: African Art, Western Eyes*. New Haven, CT: Yale University Press.

WEF [World Economic Forum], in collaboration with KPMG International. 2013. "The Future Role of Civil Society." World Scenario Series. Accessed August 15, 2015. http://www3.weforum.org/docs/WEF_FutureRoleCivilSociety_Report_2013.pdf.

Wells, Matthew. 2012. "One Year On, Duékoué Massacre Belies Ouattara Government's Promises of Impartial Justice." *Human Rights Watch*, March 29. Accessed June 19, 2013. https://www.hrw.org/news/2012/03/29/one-year-duekoue-massacre-belies-ouattara -governments-promises-impartial-justice.

Wells, Matthew, Tirana Hassan, and HRW [Human Rights Watch]. 2010. *Afraid and Forgotten: Lawlessness, Rape, and Impunity in Western Côte d'Ivoire*. New York: Human Rights Watch. Accessed June 19, 2013. https://www.hrw.org/sites/default/files/reports /cotedivoire1010webwcover_0.pdf.

Werbner, Richard, ed. 1998. *Memory and the Postcolony: African Anthropology and the Critique of Power*. London: Zed.

Widener, Jennifer. 1994. "The Rise of Civic Associations among Farmers in Côte d'Ivoire." In Harbeson, Rothchld, and Chazan, *Civil Society and the State in Africa*, 191–211.

Wieviorka, Michel. 2003. "The New Paradigm of Violence." In *Globalization, the State, and Violence*, edited by Jonathan Friedman, 107–39. Walnut Creek, CA: AltaMira.

Witte, Hans. 1985–86. *The Invisible Mothers: Female Power in Yoruba Iconography*. Leiden: Visible Religion.

Zeka, Togui. 2011. "Manifestation des Femmes Patriotes à Paris: 'Les Kodjos Rouges en Action pour la Malediction Effective.'" *La Dépêche d'Abidjan*, July. Accessed August 6, 2015. http://www.ladepechedabidjan.info/MANIFESTATION-DES-FEMMES -PATRIOTES-A-PARIS-LES-KODJOS-ROUGES-EN-ACTION-POUR-LA -MALEDICTION-EFFECTIVE-_a3853.html.

Zobo, Paulin. 2004. "Cote d'Ivoire: Réconciliation Nationale: Les Femmes Victimes de Guerre Exigent Leur Réinsertion Sociale." Fr. *Allafrica.com—Fraternité Matin,* January 10.

Index

Ababio, Nanan Kossua Prao, Queen Mother of the Abron, 121

Abidji people, 1–2, 21, 54, 117–19; age set system of, 70; Akan culture of, 123, 129–30; alliance with Adioukrou of, 142–51, 250n18, 250nn22–25; alliance with Dida of, 165, 250n22, 251n2, 251n11; Earth Priest (chef de terre) of, 27–28, 241n11, 242nn14–16; geography and territory of, 129; governance of, 118, 248n2; intermarriage with Adioukrou of, 142; marriage customs of, 132–33, 142; matrifocal principles of, 131–33; Ogbru clan of, 248n1; origin myths of, 26–31, 57, 119, 124–25, 129–33, 241n10, 242nn15–18, 242nn20–21; origins of, 128–29; patrilineal organization of, 117, 122, 130–33. See also Dipri; Egbiki

Ablé, F., 207–8

Abubakar, Abdusalami, 108

Adioukrou people, 21, 117–19, 240n1, 241n6; age set system of, 122; Akan culture of, 123, 129, 133, 135–36; alliance with Abidji of, 143–51, 250n19, 250nn22–25; coming-of-age celebrations of, 137–38, 246n16; Festival of Yams of, 21, 36, 143–46, 242n23; geography and territory of, 129; governance of, 118; intermarriage with Abidji of, 142; legal and spiritual guidance of, 136–38; Lowe ceremony of, 242n22; matrilineal organization of, 117, 122, 133–38, 142, 249nn7–8; motherhood celebrations of, 137; oral tradition of, 163; origin myths of, 119, 124–25, 133–38, 143–45, 242n18; origins of, 128–29; origins of sékè among, 142–43, 146–48, 248n6, 249n14, 250nn20–21; rival confederations of, 143–45, 249–50nn15–18; spiritual source of power of, 134–35, 142–43. See also Dipri; Egbiki

Adjanou dancers, 74–75, 203, 204, 233; acknowledged power of, 187–88, 216–18, 220–21, 252n9; in anticolonial activism, 2–3, 188–89, 221; calls to performance of, 187; childbirth posture used by, 59, 224, 229, 234, 244n34; taboos against male observation of, 194–96, 217–18, 238; violent reprisals against, 175, 186–88, 193–97, 199, 252n10. See also contemporary uses of FGP; Egbiki

Adler, Alfred, 55–56, 244n1, 245n3

Adya (Abidji ancestress), 130–31

The African Frontier (Kopytoff), 122–23

"African Traditional Thought and Western Science" (Horton), 239n4

African Union, 253n5

age set system, 69–73, 75, 77–79, 122, 246nn14–16, 248n1

Agwa, 129. See also Adioukrou people

Aidoo, Agnes A., 245n8

AIDS, 182–83, 185, 198

Akan societies, 123, 129–30, 133, 135–36, 188; Festival of Yams of, 146; matrilineal traditions of, 157, 160, 178; slave trade and, 123, 251n7; statelessness of, 249n13. See also Baoulé people

Akpa Akpess, Paul, 51–52

Al-Kassim, Dina, 214–17

Amadiume, Ifi, 242n20; on conflated associations of female essentialism, 90; on essentialist feminist theory, 84; on neuter gender, 111; on stateless societies, 63–64; on West African matriarchal societies, 15, 65–66, 75–79, 127, 244n36, 246–47nn19–20; on West African women's essentialism, 84–85, 111; on women's spiritual power, 66–67, 75

Amina, Queen of Zaria, 59

amnesia. See post–civil war memory

Amnesty International (AI), 175–77, 179, 182, 191, 201

Anglican Church Missionary Society (CMS), 103

animal sacrifice, 28, 32–33, 41, 241n13

Anlu ritual, 96–97, 247n8

anticolonial activism, 81–82, 94–99, 105–6; Adjanou ritual in, 2–3, 188–89, 221; in Cameroon, 94–97, 247n4, 247n8; Grand-Bassam Women's March of 1949 in, 207–8, 211–12, 215, 221; in Nigeria, 87–90, 95, 247n4; sexual violence and, 17–18, 112–13

Antoine, Gnamien M'Bandama Kouakou, 194

Anyi spiritual mediums, 147

Appadurai, Arjun, 233

Ardener, Shirley, 85–86, 94–97

Article 4 of Additional Protocol II to the Geneva Conventions, 253n5

Association générale des élèves et étudiants de la Côte d'Ivoire (AGEE-CI), 180

Augé, Marc, 37

Axial Age thesis, 239n4

Bahida, Marthe, 113

Bakayoko, Anzata, 228–30

Bal, Mieke, 216

Bamako Black Friday, 113–14

Banny, Charles Konan, 202–3

Baoulé people, 24, 123; Adjanou ritual of, 2–3, 74–75, 186–88, 195; civil war and, 155–57; gender inversion performances of, 101–2; language of, 24, 51, 241n8; origin myths of, 130–31; as targets of sexual violence, 181. *See also* Akan societies

Bayart, Jean-François, 230–31

Bédié, Henri Konan, 158

Begré Koffi, 35, 44, 49–50

Bertin, Gnangra N'Guessan, 27–29, 34, 53, 241n12

Bété people, 74, 149, 155–57, 161–62, 181, 251n3, 251n5

Bhabha, Homi, 11, 19, 218, 226

Bidyo myth, 26–31, 57, 146, 241n10, 242nn15–18, 245n3

bilateral filiation, 136–38

Bindé, Jérôme, 171

blood pacts, 149–50, 165, 250nn22–25, 251n3

Boone, Sylvia, 247n6

Bro-Grébé, Geneviève, 72–73, 186–90, 252nn8–9

Burkina Faso, 157, 158–59

cannibalism, 182–83

castration, 56

Centre de Commandemente et de Sécurité (CECOS), 193

ceremonial nakedness, 1

Chauveau, Jean-Pierre, 145

Chia, Mr., 96–97

childbirth posture, 59, 224, 229, 234, 244n34

Chirac, Jacques, 191

Christianity, 16, 79, 209, 254n10; fundamentalist practices of, 3, 232; gender ideologies of, 52, 81, 103–6, 215–16, 232; on nakedness and sexuality, 104–5; official privileging of converts to, 106, 248n10; on witches and witchcraft, 38–39; women's resistance to, 66

civil society, 18, 230–31, 238

civil war, 10, 20, 26, 53, 151–69; amnesty and amnesia policies after, 198–208, 253n2; Black Tuesday at the Hôtel Ivoire of, 190–92, 252n10; Duékoué massacre of, 184, 201, 253n4; Eburnea rebellion of, 157; FGP and moral rebuke of, 3, 16–17, 53, 154–69, 205, 209–10; first eruption of, 159, 175, 198–99; foreign mercenaries in, 183; French role in, 159, 161, 188–92, 252n10; human rights abuses of, 175–77, 181, 190–92, 198–201, 253nn1–2; identity politics of, 11, 125, 159, 162–65, 168–69, 250n1; intergenerational tension in, 159–61, 168–69; intrawar period of, 161, 175, 181–83; land politics in, 154–61, 164; Ouattara's opposition forces in, 158–59, 171, 179–81; peace agreement (MLA) in, 159, 175; peacekeeping forces of, 175, 181, 183, 191, 201; political factions of, 155; postponed elections and, 159, 171–72, 175, 183–84; rhetoric of, 155; role of women elders in, 113, 160, 165–69; second (postelectoral) eruption of, 169, 171–72, 175, 183–85, 193–96, 231, 251n1; sexual violence of, 17–18, 161, 171–88, 208, 228–30. *See also* contemporary uses of FGP; post–civil war memory

civil wars (in general), 152–53, 260n1

Claverie, Danièle Boni, 197

clitoris, 93–94. *See also* genitalia

Collectif des Mouvements des Femmes
Patriotes, 186
collective memory, 210–15, 218; of Ivoirian
youth, 220–21, 254n11; official state versions
of, 210–15, 218, 254n8; remembering to
forget in, 204–7, 253n6. *See also* cultural
memory
Collective of Women Victims in Côte d'Ivoire
(CVCI), 228–30
colonial occupiers, 250n18; constructions of
ethnicity by, 155–56; economic policies
of, 88–89; on FGP rituals, 81–82; Grand-
Bassam Women's March against, 207–8,
211–12, 215, 221; invisibility of women's
agency to, 63–64, 79, 81, 88–89, 94–95, 154,
180, 247n8; reification of traditional culture
by, 211; sexual violence of, 112–13; uprisings
against, 2–3, 81–82, 87–90, 94–97. *See also*
strategic essentialism
Commission Dialogue, Vérité et Réconciliation (CDVR), 202–6, 214–16
Compagnie Républicaine de Sécurité (CRS), 193
contemporary uses of FGP, 98–99, 106–16,
151, 228–38; acknowledged power of,
187–88, 216–18, 220–21, 225–26, 231, 252n9;
cataclysmic circumstances causing, 172, 179,
186, 190, 206–7, 212–14; condemning the
civil war, 3, 16–17, 53, 154–69, 205, 209–10;
as demands for accountability, 228–38; in
Europe, 233–34; at Houphouët-Boigny's
funeral, 193–94; Internet postings of, 221–26,
228–30, 234; as memory-work, 218–19,
226–27; protesting French intervention,
188–92; protesting Gbagbo's Republican
Guard, 195–96; protesting rising food
prices, 192–93; protesting sexual violence,
112–16, 172–73, 178–79, 185–88, 216–18,
228–30; protesting state amnesia, 198–208,
253n2; protesting water and electricity
cuts, 193; strategic essentialism of women's
bodies in, 98–99, 106–12, 154, 179, 186–88,
193–96, 199; timeliness of, 10, 13–14, 17–18,
206–10, 216–20, 226–38; violent reprisals
against, 175, 186–88, 193, 195–97, 199,
252n10. *See also* post–civil war memory
cosmopolitans, 6, 219–21
Côte d'Ivoire, 10–18, 117–19, 121–51; age
set system of, 69–73, 75, 77–79, 122,

246nn14–16; civil society in, 18, 230–31,
238; cosmopolitan youth culture of, 219–21;
cultural and ethnic diversity of, 121–26, 138,
152–54, 161, 219, 220, 248nn2–3, 254n10;
ethnic alliances in, 16–17, 31, 117–19, 138–51,
154–58, 165–69; export crops of, 156, 251n4;
globalization and, 26; human rights
obligations of, 253n5; immigrant populations in, 157, 158–59, 161, 166, 181, 218; land
policies of, 156–61, 164; nationalism and
autochthonous privilege in, 152, 158–59,
168–69; nation-building and development
politics in, 203–8, 227, 234–35, 238, 253n6;
north/south and east/west axes of, 155, 181;
political elite of, 159–61; precolonial political organization of, 122–23; sexual violence
in, 17–18, 112–16, 171–88; unifying founding knowledge of, 126–38, 164–69. *See also*
civil war; colonial occupiers; contemporary
uses of FGP; post–civil war memory
Csordas, Thomas J., 40
cultural memory, 212–21; alternative heritage
discourse in, 212–14; postmodern disruptions of, 223–25; semiotic signs of, 219–20;
subjugated archives of, 225–27. *See also*
collective memory

Dan people, 155
Darwinism, 4
de Guise, Robert, 99
De Jong, Ferdinand, 210
Delafosse, Maurice, 2, 74–75
Democratic Union of Cameroonian Women
(UDEFEC), 113
Derrida, Jacques, 213
Désiré, Nanan Awoula Tanoé, 203
Dida people, 129, 165, 250n22, 251n2, 251n11
Diduk, Susan, 111
Dikeble, Joséphine, 130, 152
Diop, Cheikh Anta, 15
Dipri (definition), 31
Dipri (Kpol), 1–2, 14–17, 117–19, 142, 240n2;
Adioukrou Festival of Yams and, 21, 36,
143–46; animal sacrifice in, 28, 33, 41,
241n13; double mythic origin of, 26–31,
57, 124–25, 144–48, 241n10, 242nn15–18,
242nn20–21; Egbiki ritual of, 24–29, 31,
38, 40–53, 147–48, 242n19; initiate

Dipri (Kpol) (*continued*)
consecration in, 1–2, 21–24, 29, 31–32, 241n5,
243n24, 243n31; interethnic participants in,
31, 117–18, 145–51, 242n18; official oversight
of, 27–28, 36–37, 241nn11–12; preeminent
power of women in, 33–36, 243nn27–30;
protection of women in, 32–33, 243n26;
sékè (genie's power) in, 22–24, 33–38, 41,
49, 134, 146–48, 240n4, 248n6, 249n14;
spectators of, 21; symbolic elements of,
31–32. *See also* witches/witchcraft
Djedjero Nane Lili, 36, 43, 45, 47, 52
Djedjroh Edouard, 25, 33
Dogon society of Mali, 68–69
Douglas, Mary, 79, 246n20
Dozo hunters, 183–84, 200–201, 252nn6–7
Dozon, Jean-Pierre, 155
Drane, Sirah, 196
Duékoué massacre, 184, 201, 253n4
Dyanofwè relationships, 131–32
Dyula people, 153, 162–64, 179, 181, 251n10, 252n2

Eb, 136–37, 249n7. *See also* home
Ebeb festival, 33
Ebere society, 68
Eburnea rebellion, 157
Economic Community of West African States
(ECOWAS), 107–8, 175
Egbiki, 1–4, 14–17, 24–29, 40–53, 147–48;
evolving terminology for, 50–52; expulsion
of witches in, 24–25, 28–29, 31, 38–41,
135, 241n8, 242n19; magical potion in,
25; ritual components of, 47–53; taboos
against observation of, 1, 24, 25, 46–47,
95–96, 217–18; transformative potency of,
44–53, 244nn35–39; uncanny embodiment
of witchcraft in, 41–47, 244n32. *See also*
Abidji people; Adioukrou people; spiritual
warfare
eggs and eggshells, 1, 22–23, 30, 32, 34–35
Ejikpaf patriclan, 142, 147–48. *See also*
Adioukrou people
Ekpa-Atu society, 93, 109–10
Eliade, Mircea, 1
Emilienne, Low Agnime, 36–37
Erung Ok, 31. *See also* Dipri
essentialism, 82–83, 247n1. *See also* strategic
essentialism

ethics (as term), 240n7
ethnic identity, 152–53, 250n1; autochthonous
privilege and, 152, 158–59, 168–69; constructions of, 124–38; in Côte d'Ivoire's civil
war, 11, 125, 159, 162–65, 168–69, 250n1; in
stateless societies, 162–65. *See also* interethnic
alliances
ethnopornography, 222, 254n12
Evans-Pritchard, Edward, 85

Fafwê Women's Song, 175
Fearon, James D., 152
Fédération estudiantine et scolaire de Côte
d'Ivoire (FESCI), 180, 252n3
female genital mutilation/cutting (FGM/FGC),
239n1, 246n12
Female Genital Power (FGP), 1–14, 239n1; as
adaptive strategy, 9–10, 13–14, 16–18, 20, 52,
150–51, 154–69, 173, 228–38, 240n9; anticolonial work of, 2–3, 94–99, 105–6, 207–8;
founding knowledge of the Mothers and, 55,
126–38, 146–51, 164–69, 250n20; genealogical history of, 8–9, 15–16, 118–19, 138–51,
240n5; Internet postings of, 221–26, 228–30,
234; Muslim women's use of, 114, 248n12,
253n11; transformative potency of, 41–53,
244nn35–39; ubiquity in West Africa of, 7,
16–17, 62–63, 71–72, 232–34; wordless self-
representation of, 8, 235–38; youth awareness
of, 221, 254n11. *See also* Adjanou dancers;
civil war; contemporary uses of FGP; Egbiki;
matrifocal morality; strategic essentialism
Femen, 240n9
Feminism without Borders (Mohanty), 237
feminist theory, 84, 111–12
Festival of Yams, 21, 36, 143–46, 242n23
Festivals of Generations, 70–71, 138
el-Fettach, Tarickh, 59
Fofana, Loséni, 201
Fonchingong, Charles C., 108–10
Force Licorne, 191
Forces de défense et de sécurité (FDS), 194,
195–96
Forces Nouvelles, 181, 183, 191, 201, 252n4, 253n2
Foucault, Michel: on contested land, 172;
genealogical method of, 15, 26, 85, 128; on
knowledge and power, 249n9; on subju-
gated knowledge, 85, 206

founding knowledge, 126–51, 154, 164, 249n9; of Abidjis, 128–33; of Adioukrous, 133–38, 249nn7–8, 250n20; in interethnic alliances, 138–51, 165–69, 249n11; primacy of female power in, 146–51, 164–69, 250n20

François, Amany Goly, 186–87

Freedom House, 202

Freud, Sigmund, 12, 42–43

frontier model of mobility, 122–23, 127, 129, 138–40, 143

Front Populaire Ivoirien (FPI), 158, 202

Gbagbo, Laurent: blanket amnesty policy of, 198–201; Christian community support of, 209; contestation of 2010 election by, 183–84, 194–96; destruction of monuments representing, 208–10; opposition activism of, 157–58; presidency and civil war under, 155, 158–59, 161, 167, 171, 179–80, 190–93, 208–10; removal from office of, 184; war crimes trial of, 158, 200, 253n3; women's manifestations against, 195–97; women's support for, 186, 188–90

Gbagbo, Simone, 167–68

Gbowee, Leymah, 107–8

gender essentialism, 82–87, 247n1; conflated associations in, 90–94; maternity and, 43–45, 75–76, 86–87; postmenopausal status and, 2, 16, 69, 86–87, 92–94, 111, 132–33, 247n1; power of ritual exposure of genitals and, 15, 35, 62, 74, 85–86, 115–16, 229, 234–38, 247nn3–4; precolonial ideologies of, 111–12; supernatural power of genitalia in, 93–94, 189, 247n7. See also strategic essentialism

gender inversion, 101–2

gender troubles, 15–16

genealogical inquiry: into constructions of ethnic identities in, 124–38; into matrifocal morality, 8–9, 15–16, 128, 139–42, 240n5; into spiritual basis of interethnic alliances, 138–51, 249n9; uncovering of subjugated knowledge through, 26, 118–19, 206, 216–18

Geneva Convention, 253n5

genies, 146–47, 240n4. See also sékè

genitalia: curse of the childbirth posture and, 59, 224, 229, 234, 244n34; power of ritual

exposure of, 35, 62, 74, 85–86, 115–16, 229, 234–35, 247nn3–4; supernatural power of, 93–94, 189, 247n7; taboo against male looking at, 95–96, 194–96, 217–18, 238

gerontocratic hierarchies, 122, 144, 160–61, 168

Geschiere, Peter, 42

Gilbert, Michelle, 245n8

globalism, 5–7

globalization, 26, 79; alternative heritage discourse and, 213–14; cultural preservation and, 211–13

Gnassingbé, Eyadéma, 99, 114–15

Gnassingbé, Faure, 99, 114–15

Gomon, 29–31, 142–44, 242n21, 243n31, 248n1, 248n6. See also Abidji people

Goudé, Charles Blé, 191, 252n3

Grand-Bassam. See Women's March in Grand-Bassam

great talking drum, 35

Guéré people, 155, 181, 184, 200

Guro people, 155

Guyer, Jane, 232

Haumant, Stéphane, 252n10

Hellweg, Joseph, 252n6

hermaphrodism, 56, 244n1

Hiba, Madeleine, 130, 152

HIV/AIDS, 182–83, 185, 198–99

home, 6, 19–20, 41–43, 159; matrifocal morality of, 54–80; strategic essentialism of FGP and, 81–116. See also unhomeliness

Hommel, W. L., 247n6

Horton, Robin, 239n4

Houphouët-Boigny, Félix, 156–59, 187, 193–94, 209

Human Rights Watch (HRW), 176, 178, 180, 183–84, 200–201, 251n1

human sacrifice, 28, 241n13, 242n15

Hunt, Nancy, 86

Hunting the Ethical State (Hellwig), 252n6

identity. See ethnic identity

Ifeka-Moller, Caroline, 68, 89–92, 100

indigenous religion, 2, 232–34. See also matrifocal morality

"Initiation, Royalty and Femininity in Black Africa" (Adler), 55–56 interethnic alliances, 16–17, 117–19, 164–65; cash crop economics and, 154–58, 251n4; Dipri and, 31, 117–18, 145–48, 242n18; female power and, 147–51, 165–69; fundamental obligations of, 148; joking and insult rituals in, 164–65, 251n11; primacy of first settlers in, 145–46, 166; sacred blood pacts of, 149–50, 165, 250nn22–25, 251n3; spiritual grounding of, 31, 138–45, 164, 249n9, 249n11, 249–50nn15–18

International Committee of the Red Cross (ICRC), 184

International Criminal Court (ICC), 184

International Federation for Human Rights (FIDH), 201, 251n1

International Women's Day, 197

Internet postings of FGP, 221–26, 228–30, 234

The Intimate Enemy (Nandy), 223–24

Islam, 3, 248n4, 254n11; in Côte d'Ivoire's north, 162, 183, 252n2, 252n6; FGP practices and, 114, 248n12, 253n11; gender ideologies of, 232

Ivoirian Association of Women Patriots, 233–34

Ivoirian League for Human Rights (LIDHO), 201

Ivoirian Movement for Human Rights (MIDH), 201

Ivoirité, 125, 158–59, 168–69

James, Wendy, 76–77

Jaspers, Karl, 239n4

Jeunes Patriotes, 179–80, 191

Jones, Adam, 73, 101–2

Jung, Carl Gustav, 239n3

Kamenan, Adjoba, 45, 47, 49, 52

Kankurang masquerade, 211

Kano Chronicles, 245n5

kaolin clay, 31–32

Kobri, Monique, 198–99

kodjo, 189–90, 233–34, 254n1

Koffi, Akissi, 38

Koffi, N'goran, 187

Komian priestesses, 203

Koné, Bintou, 114

Kopytoff, Igor, 117, 121; on cultural coherence of southeastern Côte d'Ivoire, 126–27, 140, 141; frontier model of, 122–24, 127, 129, 138–39, 143; on kinship groups, 127, 248n4; on stateless societies, 249n12

Kouame, Affoue, 187

Kouamé, Yvonne, 194

Kpol. *See* Dipri

Kporu, 26, 28, 31–32, 142. *See also* genies

Kragbé, Didier, 193

Kru (Krou) people, 122, 181, 251n2, 251n5

Kuao Dungmbrou myth, 29–31, 242n18, 242nn20–21

Kwa people, 122

labia, 93–94. *See also* genitalia

Lafargue, Fernand, 30, 31; on Abidji marriage customs, 133; on Baoulé incantations, 241n8; on Bidyo and the genie, 241n10; on the origins of sékè, 142–43, 248n6; on ritual use of pestles, 244n37; on sékè and angrè, 37, 243n26; on sokoryibè, 50, 241n6, 244nn38–39, 246n13

Laitin, David D., 152

Laplantine, François, 51

Lawrance, Benjamin, 98–99

"Let's Save Togo" Collective (CST), 114–15

Lévy-Bruhl, Lucien, 239n3

Liberia United for Reconciliation and Democracy (LURD), 107–8

localism, 5–7

Lodz myth, 133–34, 144

logocentrism, 7–8

Longau, Julien, 27–28, 241n11

Lonsdale, John, 118, 166, 169, 228

Lossi, N'zue Jacqueline, 187

Maasai warrior performance, 211

Making War in Côte d'Ivoire (McGovern), 124, 154

Male Daughters, Female Husbands (Amadiume), 65–66, 242n20

Mandé people, 122, 153, 162–64

Mansa Musa, king of Mali, 56, 245n2

masking societies, 67–69. *See also* Sande society

maternity, 43–45, 75–76, 86–87

matriarchies, matriclans, and matrilineal organization, 18, 48, 54–66, 122, 127–28; Amadiume's conclusions on, 15, 65–66, 75–79, 127, 244n36, 246–47nn19–20; Christian missionary restructuring of, 52, 81, 103–6, 215–16, 232; dependence on fertility

of, 132, 137, 141, 248n5, 249n8; in dual-sexed
collective self-rule systems, 63–66, 92;
exogamous marriage in, 141–42; female rulers
and queen mothers in, 59–63, 178, 245nn5–8,
249n10; founding knowledge in, 133–38,
146–51, 164–69, 249nn7–8, 250n20; impact
of modernization on, 9, 55; invisibility to colonial occupiers of, 63–64, 79, 88–89, 94–95,
154, 180, 247n8; lineage of male rulers in,
55–59, 60, 244n1, 245n4; matricentric bonds
in, 65–66; ownership of land in, 160. *See also*
Adioukrou people; matrifocal morality
matrifocal morality, 8, 15–18, 20, 44, 54–80,
168, 240nn7–8; in Abidji founding knowledge of, 126–33; in Adioukrou founding
knowledge, 126–28, 133–38, 249nn7–9;
age set system and, 69–73, 75, 77–79,
246nn14–16; conceptual model of, 77–79;
demands for accountability in, 228–38; in
dual-sexed collective self-ruled systems,
63–66, 92; genealogical inquiry of, 8–9,
15–16, 128, 139–42, 240n5; origins in
traditional West African matriarchies of,
54–66; in patrilineal systems, 131–33; power
of ritual exposure of genitals and, 8–9, 35,
62, 66–67, 74, 85–86, 115–16, 229, 234–38,
247nn3–4; secret power associations of,
67–69, 245–46nn10–13; spiritual warfare
and, 73–75, 87–90, 96–97, 135, 150, 160,
246nn17–18; theory of matriarchy and, 15,
65–66, 75–80, 244n36, 246–47nn19–20
Mbaye, Fatimata, 253n1
Mbembe, Achille, 212, 251n6
McGovern, Mike, 245n11; on construction
of ethnic identity, 124–26, 155, 164–65,
168–69, 251n6; on the Côte d'Ivoire civil
war, 154–56, 159–69, 251nn6–7, 251n9,
252n5; on matrilineage, 131; on metacommunicative play, 119
Meledje Djedress, Philippe, 31, 33–35, 243n30
Memel-Fotê, Harris, 72–73, 152, 248n2; on
Adioukrou spiritual values, 136–37; on
Dipri, 142; on ethnicity, 248n3; on Ivoirian
unity, 126–27; on oral tradition, 124, 163;
on the origins of sékè, 248n6
memory. *See* post–civil war memory
memory crisis, 204, 214–16. *See also* post–civil
war memory

memory-work, 218–19, 226–27
menstrual blood, 32, 137; kodjo as symbol of,
189–90, 233–34, 254n1; as pollution, 34–35,
43, 74, 150; power in sacred oaths of, 149–50
Mickel, Gérard, 253n1
Mmobomme, 73–75, 90
modernity: eclipse of indigenous traditions by,
3–5, 239nn3–4; impact on women of, 9, 55;
orientalizing binarism of, 5; situating the
local in, 5–7
Mohanty, T., 237
moral (as term), 240n7
moral authority. *See* matrifocal morality
Moran, Mary H., 107
the Mothers. *See* Female Genital Power
Mouvement Patriotique de Côte d'Ivoire
(MPCI), 181, 183, 186–88, 252n4
Mouvement Populaire Ivoirien du Grand
Ouest (MPIGO), 181, 183, 252n4
Mouvement Pour la Justice et la Paix (MJP),
181, 183, 252n4
Muslim Brotherhood, 232
Muslim women, 114, 248n12, 253n11
myths: of the Abidji people, 26–31, 57, 119,
124–25, 129–33, 241n10, 242nn15–18,
242nn20–21; of the Adioukrou people,
119, 124–25, 133–38, 143–45, 242n18; of the
Baoulé people, 130–31; of Bidyo and the
origins of Dipri, 26–31, 57, 144–48, 241n10,
242nn15–18, 242nn20–21; of the Dogon
ancestress, 144; enmity between men and
women in, 247n9; genies in, 27–32, 57,
133–34, 144, 146, 241n10; "genii-ology"
and, 133, 142, 148; history (mytho-history)
and, 124, 130, 133, 143, 238n3; of Kuao
Dungmbrou and the origins of sékè, 29–31,
146, 242n18, 242nn20–21; of Nri and Igbo
origins, 242n20; role of yams in, 26–27,
30–32, 146, 242n20; of women's power,
245n3; of the Yoruba people, 57

Nahibly camp massacre, 200, 253n4
Nandy, Ashis, 223–24
National Commission for Reconciliation and
the Indemnification of Victims (CONARIV),
228–29
National Day of Remembrance and
Forgiveness, 203

neuter gender, 111
Neyo people, 251n3
N'Guessan Edouard, 28–29, 242nn14–15
Niangoran-Bouah, Georges, 30–31, 242n19
Nigerian Women's War, 87–90, 95
N'Zi, Serge-Nicolas, 189

Oduduwa, 57
Olupona, Jacob Obafemi Kehinde, 54, 58
Ondo-Yoruba. *See* Yoruba peoples
Orbaff, 241n5, 250n19; Egbiki in, 25, 47, 52;
    knowledge of FGP in, 221; Kpol in, 117,
    143–45; sékè in, 23, 32–33, 36. *See also*
    Adioukrou people
Ouattara, Alassane, 158, 171, 179–80, 183–84,
    195–97; Commission Dialogue, Vérité et
    Réconciliation (CDVR) of, 202–6, 214–16;
    compensation of victims under, 203; de-
    struction of Gbagbo-era monuments under,
    208–10; extra-judicial reprisals under,
    200–201, 253n4; prosecution of sexual
    crimes under, 180, 251n1; prosecution of
    war crimes under, 199–202
Ouérémi, Amadé, 201, 253n4
Ousmane, Chérif, 253n2
Oyewùmí, Oyèrónké, 11, 59, 246n19
Oyo-Yoruba. *See* Yoruba peoples

Parti Démocratique de Côte d'Ivoire (PDCI),
    157, 188
patriarchies, patriclans, and patrilineal organ-
    ization, 77–79, 122, 136–38; royal succession
    in, 249n10; titulary genies of, 142. *See also*
    Abidji people
Pechoux, Laurent, 188
Pentecostal Christian Church, 253n6
pestles, 1–2, 24–25; ritual use of, 46–49, 62,
    71, 244n37; spiritual power represented by,
    66, 74, 87, 147, 246n17
Pin, Jérome, 252n10
Piot, Charles, 5, 7
Pokou, queen of Akan, 130–31, 254n8
political uses of FGP. *See* contemporary uses
    of FGP
Poro society, 68–69
post–civil war memory, 18, 198–227; accounts
    of traumatized victims in, 214–18; alter-
    native heritage discourse in, 212–14;

Commission Dialogue, Vérité et
    Réconciliation (CDVR) and, 202–6,
    214–16; destruction of Gbagbo-era
    monuments in, 208–10; Internet postings
    of FGP in, 221–26, 228–30, 234; of Ivoirian
    youth, 219–20; monuments to women's
    power in, 207–8, 211–12, 215, 254n7; nation-
    building and omission of the Mothers,
    203–8, 227, 253n6; state-controlled collective
    memory of, 210–15, 218, 254n8; state policy
    of forgetting in, 198–201, 207–8; timeliness
    of FGP rebukes and, 206–10, 216–20,
    226–38; youth knowledge of FGP and,
    220–21, 254n11. *See also* cultural memory
postcolonial politics, 234–38. *See also* con-
    temporary uses of FGP; post–civil war memory
power associations, 66–69, 245–46nn10–13
primitivism, 4
*Protocol to the African Charter on Human and
    Peoples' Rights on the Rights of Women in
    Africa*, 253n5
Pupupu, 57

queen mothers, 59–63, 121, 178, 245nn5–8,
    249n10

Radhakrishnan, R., 234
rape and sexual violence, 17–18, 112–16, 161,
    171–88; by colonial occupiers, 17–18,
    112–13, 180; compensation of victims of,
    228–30; criminal prosecution of, 180, 201,
    251n1; FGP as response to, 172–73, 178–79,
    185–88, 216–18, 228–30; impact on survivors
    of, 185, 198–99, 214–18; international
    conventions prohibiting, 176, 201, 253n5;
    international documentation of, 175–83,
    191, 199, 251n1, 253n1; notions of shame and
    ruin in, 185; official amnesty and amnesia
    policies toward, 198–208; of the postelec-
    toral period, 171–72, 175–76, 184–85, 231,
    251n1, 252nn6–7; rates of, 176, 177, 181;
    ritual responses to, 178; victim accounts of,
    214–18; as a weapon of war, 172, 176–79.
    See also civil war; post–civil war memory
Rassemblement des Républicains (RDR),
    179–81, 202
Rattray, R. S., 60
Reinventing Africa (Amadiume), 75–76, 78

Remotely Global (Piot), 5
Republican Guard, 195–96, 199–200, 201
Republic Forces of Côte d'Ivoire (FRCI), 200–201
Réseau Ivoirien des Organisations Féminines
  (RIOF), 186
Richards, David, 14
Richards, Paul, 145
Rome Statute of the International Criminal
  Court of 1998, 253n5
Rowlands, M. J., 210

Sahuyé, 130, 242n21; Egbiki in, 1, 44, 49; FGP
  in, 35–36. *See also* Abidji people
Said, Edward, 10, 12–13, 198, 240n6
sanankuya, 164. *See also* Tokpè
Sande society, 68–69, 239n1, 245n10, 246n12;
  aggressive ritual appeals of, 100–103,
  247n9; Sowo-uwi mask of, 93, 248n6
Sangroh Esaïe, 36
Sarkozy, Nicolas, 189–90
Schelling, Friedrich, 42
séke̗, 22–24, 30–38, 41, 49, 240n4; origins
  of, 124–25, 134, 142–43, 146–48, 248n6,
  249n14, 250nn20–21; protection of women
  from, 33, 243n26; witchcraft compared to,
  36–38; women's possession of, 34–36
Séke̗puone, 23–24, 34, 41, 147, 241n12, 250n17
seniority systems. *See* gerontocratic hierarchies
sexual violence. *See* rape and sexual violence
Sikinsi, 130
"Sitting on a Man," 87–88
slavery and the slave trade, 123, 141, 160, 165, 251n7
sokoryibè, 50–52, 241n6, 244nn38–39, 246n13
Soro, Guillaume, 186
South African Truth and Reconciliation
  model, 202, 214–15
spiritual power, 8–9, 66–67, 118–19. *See also*
  Female Genital Power
spiritual warfare, 73–75, 135, 150, 160, 194–95,
  246nn17–18; of anticolonial uprisings,
  87–90, 96–97; contemporary uses of,
  160–69; female aggression in, 101–3,
  247n9; traditional forms of, 73–75; use of
  pestles in, 74, 87, 246n17. *See also* Egbiki
Spivak, Gayatri, 7, 14
stateless societies, 63–66, 122, 141, 249nn12–13;
  history and identity among, 162–65; warfare
  among, 160–61

Stoeltje, Beverly J., 245n5
strategic essentialism, 2, 12, 43–47, 81–116,
  244nn34–39; aggression and, 99–103,
  247n9; in anticolonial activism, 2–3, 81–82,
  87–90, 94–99, 105–6, 207–8, 247n8; in
  Bamako Black Friday, 113–14; conflated
  associations in, 90–94; in confronting missionary gender ideology, 81, 103–6; curse
  of the childbirth posture and, 59, 224, 229,
  234, 244n34; deployment in Cameroon of,
  94–97, 108–10, 112–13, 247n4, 247n8; deployment in Liberia of, 107–8; deployment
  in Togo of, 98–99, 114–15; dominant discourse of woman's bodies in, 81–87, 108–10,
  247n1; of Muslim women, 114, 248n12;
  Nigerian Women's War, 87–90, 95; in
  postcolonial and contemporary resistance,
  98–99, 106–16, 151, 154; of postmenopausal
  status, 2, 16, 69, 86–87, 92–94, 111, 132–33,
  247n1; precolonial gender ideologies and,
  111–12; ritual exposure of genitals and, 35, 62,
  74, 85–86, 115–16, 229, 234–38, 247nn3–4;
  self-understanding and self-definition in,
  84–85; supernatural power of genitalia in,
  93–94, 189, 247n7
Strobel, Margaret, 63
subjugated knowledge: genealogical inquiry
  into, 26, 85, 118–19, 206; reviving the archives
  of, 198–227. *See also* post–civil war memory

Takembeng society, 92–93, 108–12, 248n11
Taky, F., 175
Tanga, Pius T., 108–10
Tano, Nanan Kolia, 186
Tanoh, Marie-Claire, 49
Taylor, Charles, 107–8
Tchimu, 130–31
Thomann, G., 149
timeliness of FGP, 10, 13–14, 17–18, 226–38; of
  the Grand-Bassam Women's March, 207–8,
  211–12, 215, 221; impermanence of spontaneous ritual and, 212–14; in remembering
  subjugated archives of morality, 198–227;
  in responding to cataclysmic circumstances, 172, 179, 186, 190, 206–7, 212–14;
  in responding to sexual violence, 171–88,
  216–18, 228–30
Tokpè, 165, 251n11. *See also* sanankuya

Touré, Aya Virginie, 195–96
Touré, Samory, 251n7
tradition, 3–7; as a body of knowledge and
practices, 4–5; as fossilized imperialist
construct, 3–4, 239nn3–4; situating local
and global realities in, 5–7, 13–14
translocals, 6
Traoré, Moussa, 113–14
Traoré women-kings, 55–57
Truth and Reconciliation model, 202, 214–15
Turner, Victor, 76
Tutu, Desmond, 202

UNESCO World Heritage Convention, 210–14
UN High Commissioner for Human Rights, 176
UN Operation in Côte d'Ivoire (ONUCI), 175,
183, 201, 252n6
unhomeliness and the uncanny, 10–12, 14–16,
19–20; embodiment in intimate spheres of,
41–47; Freudian interpretation of, 42–43;
in postmodern disruptions of cultural
memory, 223–25; sexual violence and,
112–16; supernatural power of genitalia in,
93–94, 189, 247n7; in witchcraft and sékè,
11–12, 21–53, 235, 240n4, 244n32. See also
Dipri; home; witches/witchcraft
Union générale des victimes de guerre de
Côte d'Ivoire (UVGCI), 198–99
urine, 23, 25, 46–47, 96

vagina, 93–94. See also genitalia
van Allen, Judith, 87–89
Villepin, Dominique de, 188–90
Visonà, Monica Blackmun, 70–72, 249n14
Vodou, 98–99
vulva, 93. See also genitalia

Wawr, 137, 249n8. See also Adioukrou people
We people, 155
Werbner, Richard, 204
Wezza, Queen of Songhay, 59
witches/witchcraft, 11–12, 21–53, 150, 235;
African connotations of, 21–22; ambiguous power of, 36–41; Egbiki expulsion of,
24–29, 31, 38–53; political violence and,
26; of sékè (genie's power), 22–24, 33–38, 41,
49, 240n4; soul-eating power of, 39–40,

244n32; uncanny embodiment in the
Mothers of, 41–47, 244n32; Western
constructs of, 38–39. See also Dipri
womb, 93. See also genitalia
women. See Female Genital Power; matriarchies, matriclans, and matrilineal organization; matrifocal morality
women-kings, 55–59, 61, 244n1, 245n4
Women of Liberia Mass Action for Peace,
107–8
Women's Council of Nnobi, 67
Women's March in Grand-Bassam, 188–89,
193; deployment of Adjanou in, 2–3, 189,
221; official monument to, 207–8, 211–12,
215, 254n7; youth awareness of, 221, 254n11
Women's War, 87–90
World Heritage Convention, 210–14
worldliness of FGP, 10, 12–13, 16–17, 117–19;
in Côte d'Ivoire civil war contexts, 154–69,
205, 209–10; in interethnic alliances and
founding knowledge, 126–51, 165–69,
249n11; localized applications of, 150–51

Yaa Akyaa, Queen Mother of Asante Empire,
59
yams: Adioukrou Festival of, 21, 36, 143–46,
242n23; in origin myths, 26–27, 30–32, 146,
242n20. See also Dipri
Yao, Adjoua, 187
Yao, Amoin, 187
Yao, Flondoh, 187
Yao, Kouadio, 187
Yassap, 46. See also Adioukrou people
Yedoh, Edouard, 33
Yésone, Mme, 220
Yoko, chief of the Mende, 68
Yoruba peoples, 43–46, 244n34; on cooling
female domination, 100–101; Edì cele-
bration of Morèmi of, 45–46; Gelede
festival of, 43–44, 244n39; gender fluidity
in, 59; origin myths of, 57; political uses of
FGP among, 59, 222–25; on supernatural
power of female genitalia, 93, 247n7;
women-kings of, 57–59, 245n4
Youe, Yvonne, 35

Zeka, Togui, 228